MORE PRAISE FOR
A MOST IMPERFECT UNION

"True patriotism consists in wanting to make your country better, not in pretending that it is already perfect. In *A Most Imperfect Union*, Ilan Stavans and Lalo Alcaraz provide a warts-and-all take on US history—witty and pithy, creative and critical, subversive and constructive. By scanning the country's virtues and vices in a single sweep, they will make readers' love for America better informed; the book may also help to inspire young Americans to sustain the project of making the United States a model country in an increasingly plural hemisphere, an increasingly complex world, and an increasingly cynical age."

—Felipe Fernández-Armesto, author of *Our America:*
A Hispanic History of the United States

"Ilan Stavans and Lalo Alcaraz make a dynamic duo: spirited, energetic, sardonic, and irreverent. History is, after all, a *story*, and they are bravura storytellers, in words and pictures. They take issue, not only with the official story, but also with each other, demonstrating that the most essential element in the teaching of history—and the practice of democracy—is critical thought."

—Martín Espada, author of *The Trouble Ball*

"*Media mestizaje* at its finest. Alcaraz and Stavans present a tribute to America full of the binaries that make our country great: angry and loving, lyrical and scabrous, academic and street-smart. If you don't buy this book, you don't know modern-day America."

—Gustavo Arellano, ¡Ask a Mexican! syndicated columnist

"It's often said—half jokingly—that every country has an unpredictable past. Our histories are unique and the stories we tell about them are often contradictory. Lalo Alcaraz's dynamic, funny images and Ilan Stavans's clever commentaries offer a fresh, adventurous way of viewing the 'uncertain' past of this amazing American nation."

—Paquito D'Rivera, multiple Grammy Award—winning musician
and National Endowment for the Arts Jazz Master

"This dynamic duo has done it again. Wordsmith extraordinaire Stavans and virtuoso visual artist Alcaraz reveal the blind spots in our country's magisterial epic and open our eyes to the nation's real grand story, describing it less as a uniform and progressive history than as a 'symphony of creative destruction.' This merciless, witty, and deeply learned book will arm us and our children with the know-how to create a better tomorrow."

—Frederick Luis Aldama, Arts & Humanities Distinguished Professor
of English, Ohio State University, and author of
The Routledge Concise History of Latino/a Literature

A MOST IMPERFECT UNION

ALSO BY ILAN STAVANS

FICTION
The Disappearance • The One-Handed Pianist and Other Stories

NONFICTION
The Riddle of Cantinflas • Dictionary Days • On Borrowed Words • Spanglish •
The Hispanic Condition • Art and Anger • Resurrecting Hebrew • A Critic's Journey • The Inveterate Dreamer
• Octavio Paz: A Meditation • Imagining Columbus • Bandido • ¡Lotería! (with Teresa Villegas) •
José Vasconcelos: The Prophet of Race • Return to Centro Histórico • Singer's Typewriter and Mine
• The United States of Mestizo

CONVERSATIONS
Knowledge and Censorship (with Verónica Albin) • What Is La Hispanidad? (with Iván Jaksi) •
Ilan Stavans: Eight Conversations (with Neal Sokol) • With All Thine Heart (with Mordecai Drache)
• Conversations with Ilan Stavans • Love and Language (with Verónica Albin) •
¡Muy Pop! (with Frederick Luis Aldama) •
• Thirteen Ways of Looking at Latino Art (with Jorge J. E. Gracia)

ANTHOLOGIES
The Norton Anthology of Latino Literature • Tropical Synagogues • The Oxford Book of Latin American Essays •
The Schocken Book of Modern Sephardic Literature • Lengua Fresca (with Harold Augenbraum) • Wáchale!
• The Scroll and the Cross • The Oxford Book of Jewish Stories • Mutual Impressions •
Growing Up Latino (with Harold Augenbraum) •
The FSG Book of Twentieth-Century Latin American Poetry

CHILDREN'S BOOKS
Golemito (with Teresa Villegas)

GRAPHIC NOVELS
Mr. Spic Goes to Washington (with Roberto Weil) • Once@9:53 (with Marcelo Brodsky) •
El Iluminado (with Steve Sheinkin)
• Latino USA: A Cartoon History (with Lalo Alcaraz)

TRANSLATION
Sentimental Songs, by Felipe Alfau •
The Plain in Flames, by Juan Rulfo (with Harold Augenbraum) • The Underdogs (with Anna More)

EDITIONS
Spain, Take This Chalice from Me and Other Poems, by César Vallejo • The Poetry of Pablo Neruda
• Encyclopedia Latina (Four Volumes) • I Explain a Few Things, by Pablo Neruda •
Calvert Casey: The Collected Stories • Collected Stories, by Isaac Bashevis Singer (Three Volumes)
• An Organizer's Tale: Speeches, by Cesar Chavez • Selected Writings, by Rubén Darío •
Latin Music (Two Volumes) • All the Odes, by Pablo Neruda

GENERAL
The Essential Ilan Stavans

ALSO BY LALO ALCARAZ
Migra Mouse: Political Cartoons on Immigration •
La Cucaracha: The First Collection from the Daily Comic Strip

A MOST IMPERFECT UNION

A CONTRARIAN HISTORY OF THE UNITED STATES

BY ILAN STAVANS

ILLUSTRATED BY LALO ALCARAZ

BASIC BOOKS

New York

A Member of the Perseus Books Group

Published by Basic Books,
A Member of the Perseus Books Group

Books published by Basic Books are available at special discounts for bulk purchases in the United States by corporations, institutions, and other organizations. For more information, please contact the Special Markets Department at the Perseus Books Group, 2300 Chestnut Street, Suite 200, Philadelphia, PA 19103, or call (800) 810-4145, ext. 5000, or e-mail special.markets@perseusbooks.com.

LCCN: 2014931305

ISBN: 978-0-465-03669-1 (hardcover) — 978-0-465-08064-9 (e-book)

10 9 8 7 6 5 4 3 2 1

TO LUIS LOYA,
INVETERATE DREAMER.

I. S.

TO MI FAMILIA, AND ALL THE
IMMIGRANTS IN THE WORLD.

L. A.

Contents

FOREWORD: PLASTIC NATION, XI

INTRODUCTION, 1

CHAPTER 1: THE LAND IS OURS, 10
COLUMBUS SAILS THE OCEAN BLUE, 11
CABEZA DE VACA: OH, THE PLACES YOU'LL GO, 18
THE MAYFLOWER IS HERE! 19
PILGRIMS VS. INDIANS, 22
THE MAKING OF NEW YORK, 26
THE MIDDLE PASSAGE, 27
THOSE NASTY COLONISTS, 33
TEA BY THE BAY, 38

CHAPTER 2: THE FOUNDING FATHERS
HAVE A BABY! 40
THE ORIGINAL SUPERTEAM, 41
A STRONG CONSTITUTION, 48
JEFFERSON, THE PROPHET, 53
JOHN LOVES ABIGAIL, 58
LET'S HAVE A PARTY OR TWO, 60
WHERE THE BUFFALO ROAM, 75

CHAPTER 3: SLAVES Я US, 86
AMERICAN BOOK CLUB, 87
LINCOLN CONTINENTAL, 92
AN UNCIVIL WAR, 95
THE GETTYSBURG ADDRESS, 99
THE FALL OF A HERO, 101
COMMUNICATING WITH THE DEAD, 102
THE TASK OF RECONSTRUCTION, 103
PROGRESS FOR ALL! 104

CHAPTER 4: THE NEW COLOSSUS, 107
WRETCHED REFUSE, 108
SCHMENDRICKS AND SCHMUCKS, 110
DOWN WITH SPAIN! 114
THE NATIONAL PASTIME, 120
THE RHYTHMS OF JAZZ, 121
VÁMONOS CON PANCHO VILLA! 129
DOUGHBOYS ON THE MARCH, 132
BOTTOMS UP! 136

CHAPTER 5: THE PROGRESS MACHINE, 141
THE GREAT DEPRESSION, 142
THE GOOD NEIGHBOR POLICY, 147
OUR KAMPF: THE FIGHT AGAINST HITLER, 151
THE ENEMIES WITHIN, 154
CROSSING THE BORDER, 156
NUCLEAR NIGHTMARE, 159
ISRAEL IS REAL, 161
KOREA SPLITS UP, 165

CHAPTER 6: BEAT THE SOVIETS, 166
THE COLD WAR HEATS UP, 167
THE SEXUAL THERMOMETER, 173
HAPPY FAMILIES ARE ALIKE! 175
CIVIL RIGHTS AND WRONGS, 182
GOOD MORNING, VIETNAM, 186
THE WATERGATE FLUSH, 200
AFFIRMATIVE ACTION AND REACTION, 205

CHAPTER 7: NEW WORLD DISORDER, 207
THE IRAN HOSTAGE CRISIS, 208
COWBOY RON, 212
WHO WON THE ELECTION? 224
AL-QAEDA ATTACKS, 225
THE INFORMATION SUPERHIGHWAY, 230
OBAMA AIN'T BLACK, 237
PLAYING THE RACE CARD, 244

EPILOGUE, 247

ACKNOWLEDGMENTS, 253

INDEX, 257

Foreword

PLASTIC NATION

*PATRIOTISM IS CONSIDERED TO BE AN EMOTION
A PERSON OUGHT TO FEEL. BUT WHY?*

—WALLACE SHAWN

I am at once an unlikely American and an utterly typical one. I moved to the United States from Mexico in the mid-1980s. This was not an accident but an act of will: I wanted to live in freedom, to debate ideas openly, to test the limits of my talents. Since then, the country has been good to me, and I like to think that I have been good to the country.

Nonetheless, our relationship isn't idyllic. I often criticize the United States for those aspects of its culture and national character that make me uncomfortable: its insatiable appetite for pleasure, its plastic-surgery aesthetics, its love of consumption, its frequent ignorance of history, its xenophobic disposition, its condescending political correctness, its arrogant foreign policy. And I, in turn, usually find myself in the eye of the storm because of the critical stands I take.

This mutual censure, I have found over time, tends to change me for the better. And in response to my critical appraisal of the United States, I have frequently been described as a contrarian—an adjective that pleases me, to be frank, for I enjoy looking beyond embellishments and fabrications to the truth (or at least what I think is the truth) at the heart of things. One of my heroes is Ambrose Bierce, author of *The Devil's Dictionary*, who described history as "an account mostly false, of events mostly unimportant, which are brought about by rulers mostly knaves, and soldiers mostly fools." (It's often said that Bierce described war as God's way of teaching

Americans geography—but maybe the quote isn't his and one of his many rambunctious fans stuck him with it!)

Ask my students: I like to play devil's advocate. I often take conservative views when I'm among liberals, and liberal views when I'm among conservatives. I sometimes remind myself of the Rum Tum Tugger, the peculiar cat in *Old Possum's Book of Practical Cats* by T. S. Eliot:

> THE RUM TUM TUGGER IS A CURIOUS CAT:
> IF YOU OFFER HIM PHEASANT HE WOULD RATHER HAVE GROUSE.
> IF YOU PUT HIM IN A HOUSE HE WOULD MUCH PREFER A FLAT,
> IF YOU PUT HIM IN A FLAT THEN HE'D RATHER HAVE A HOUSE.
> IF YOU SET HIM ON A MOUSE THEN HE ONLY WANTS A RAT,
> IF YOU SET HIM ON A RAT THEN HE'D RATHER CHASE A MOUSE.

I share Rum Tum Tugger's contrarian streak—although, to be sure, mine stems from different roots: an inquisitive, restless disposition.

My contrarianism is intimately linked to my experience as an immigrant. Immigrants, you see, know a lot about flightiness. After all, they are Americans by choice. Many lacked basic freedoms in their country of origin, and were ready to delve into the unknown in order to obtain them. Immigrants know what it means to be displaced, in transition, continually perplexed. They know what it means *not* to have something they cherish.

And, just as significantly, many immigrants know what life is like in an uncritical milieu—a place where ideas are fixed and unchanging, rather than existing in a marketplace, as they do in the United States. That, to me, is this country's most precious quality: its readiness to question, to innovate, to experiment. Winston Churchill supposedly said that you can always count on Americans to do the right thing—after they've tried everything else.

Immigrants also know the value of the word *home*. Not *house*, but *home*: a place where you feel secure and appreciated, a place where you're confident enough to take a stand. Maybe that's why so many immigrants are enthusiastic supporters of the United States: because America is the first real home they've ever had.

The history of the United States is the history of the generations of entrepreneurial people who built their homes here. As these homes grew in number and diversity, they formed cities, colonies, and eventually the American nation itself. This American home, broadly defined, is never static. It's always in a state of flux, as new tenants arrive and old ones leave, as its premises expand, and as its landscape changes over time. These transformations are driven by the people who live in America, and by their continual asking of questions: What do I have that my parents didn't have? How can we balance tradition and progress? How can I make my children want more?

Viewed from a distance, the path these countless trailblazing Americans have taken through the centuries may appear uniform. But, in fact, it is made up of many millions of *individual* paths wending their way from the past to the present. I stress the word *individual* because although we are a nation—that is, the sum of our many parts—we are also a collection of separate and singular people. Indeed, nowhere else on the planet is the concept of individualism as deeply rooted as it is in the United States.

We Americans are cutthroat egoists looking to advance our own personal agendas. Because these agendas often coincide with those of our fellow citizens, we have the right to call ourselves a society. But of course our dreams and goals are not always the same.

I believe it was Walter Benjamin who said that the word *civilization* shines bright because it knows how to hide its shameless record of barbarism. Individualism necessarily results in inequality—in the abuse and subjugation of some people by others. American history is full of examples of this sad truth. Settlers against Indians, masters against slaves, millionaires against slum-dwellers—oppression has taken many forms on the North American continent. Ours is a microcosm of the entire world, the good as well as the bad.

When vastly different people interact in the United States, as elsewhere in the world, violence often results. And Americans often justify the use of violence by invoking the concept of progress, as will be seen in the following pages. Connecting the different stories of *A Most Imperfect Union* is a single, controlling leitmotif: the idea of *creative destruction*. In order to rise up, we Americans feel that we must push others down. This is an attitude that, despite its moral indefensibility, we have nevertheless adopted as our mantra. It isn't enough to emerge victorious from our struggles; we must also see others defeated.

I didn't learn any of these things in the classroom. In Mexico, where I attended school through the twelfth grade, lessons about the United States only offered an outsider's perspective. My teachers viewed America with a mix of awe and repulsion: so mighty a nation, yet one so nearsighted in its judgment. That perception, I now know, resulted from the clash between American individualism and Mexican collectivism. Mexicans don't put themselves first; they think of others as equals, not as inferiors in need of improvement. These fundamental differences in people's outlooks in the two countries meant that I entered the US with preconceived notions that were quickly swept aside by my own experiences. What I know about the United States, I learned in its Darwinian jungle.

Perhaps the hardest thing for me to wrap my head around has been Americans' sense of time. The only verbal conjugation that matters in the United States is the present tense. We study the past mostly to justify our actions in the here and now, and the future is nothing but an improvement on this eternal present. "Live now," we Americans seem to be telling each other, "and the rest will take care of itself."

This view of time has but one objective: to make us feel like we're always at the top. It's also an unabashedly anachronistic attitude: the past is elastic; the past is fictional; the past is a myth, a means, a mirage. The past, in short, is what we choose to make of it. Each new generation decides how to interpret the lives of its ancestors, and often these interpretations are not the same as those that came before.

The book that you're holding, then, is one such interpretation—but it's also a celebration of the American marketplace of ideas. My first collaboration with Lalo Alcaraz, the creator of the celebrated comic strip *La Cucaracha*, was a modest undertaking called *Latino USA: A Cartoon History*, released in 2000. I've always been drawn to graphic novels as a vehicle for storytelling. I grew up reading the works of Mexican artist Eduardo del Río, who published under the name Rius. He was the creator of *Marx for Beginners*, the first in a series of popular guides to high-brow subjects for lay readers. Despite his occasional anti-Semitism, I loved Rius's fast, self-deprecating style and admired his nihilistic views. When I met Lalo, I felt I was in the presence of an American version of Rius. I quickly proposed a collaboration.

Neither of us expected our first book to be a runaway success. We simply wanted to mock certain misconceptions about Hispanic history that prevailed north of the Rio Grande, and, in doing so, to make the reader less complacent, more critical. But the book found an eager, appreciative audience. Since then, Lalo and I talked several times about collaborating on another project, but didn't land on an idea that suited us both until Lalo sent me an e-mail asking why no Latino had ever told the entire history of *Gringolandia*. It seemed like an inspiring thought, and the two of us were comfortable enough in our discomfort as happy Americans to give it a try.

A Most Imperfect Union isn't a sequel to *Latino USA*, but rather a prequel. Our first book's focus was Hispanic history in the United States, with forays south of the border and into the Caribbean, and even a few quick stops in Spain: *la madre patria* (the motherland)—or better, *la patria desmadreadora* (the reckless motherland). The focus of this new book is much broader. Its subjects are dispossessed and minority groups of all stripes, as well as individuals known and unknown to most students of American history. While the earlier volume might be said to be about a particular tree, meandering in its structure, this one is about a thick, thorny forest.

Latino USA could even be considered a chapter in *A Most Imperfect Union*. What the two books have in common, of course, is sarcasm.

Although *A Most Imperfect Union* is organized in chronological fashion, it borrows the style of a movie, with inflated characters, unlikely plot twists, and occasional cheap thrills. It pays homage to Rius by presenting front-and-center the collective genius of this safe haven for immigrants, as well as its appetite for competition, its use and abuse of the notion of progress, and its tendency toward vitriol and disagreement.

Where else in the world does one have the freedom to contradict oneself? Famously celebrated by Walt Whitman, this discordant, sometimes unruly quality of the United States has inspired this book from the start. Lalo and I, after all, are both "hyphenated Americans": Mexican-American, and (in my case) Jewish-Mexican-American. We are a part of this country, yet separate from it; we're a part of the collective American *we*, but also proud owners of the fragmented American *I*. Our heritage is complex and sometimes confusing, but then so is the history of this nation we've come to call home.

The United States, to me, is a nation where freedom is sometimes wasted on its citizens. We are a pompous bunch with an abundance of talent, and we exist as if the rest of the world was but a speck of dust. Eugene Burdick and William J. Lederer once wrote a book called *The Ugly American*, and America does indeed have an ugly side: when abundance becomes opulence, morality often falls by the wayside.

Perhaps this is indeed the best country in the world—but does that make it immune from criticism? Shouldn't we make good on the invitation we've offered ourselves to be free? I don't see the point of treating America with muted reverence. To help our country live up to its full potential, we must sometimes call our love of that country into question.

—ILAN STAVANS,
AMHERST, MASSACHUSETTS,
JUNE 2014

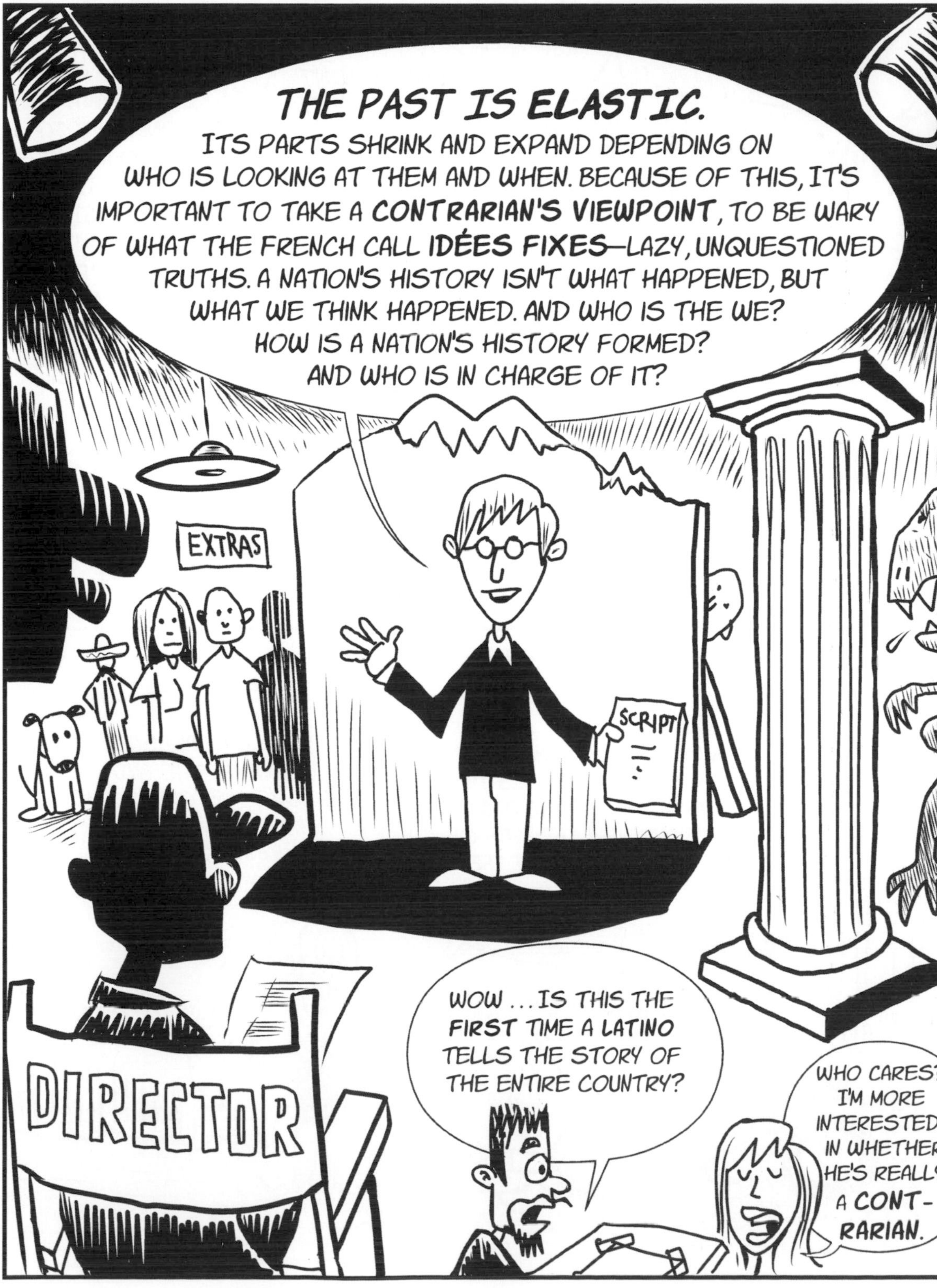
THE PAST IS ELASTIC.
ITS PARTS SHRINK AND EXPAND DEPENDING ON WHO IS LOOKING AT THEM AND WHEN. BECAUSE OF THIS, IT'S IMPORTANT TO TAKE A **CONTRARIAN'S VIEWPOINT**, TO BE WARY OF WHAT THE FRENCH CALL **IDÉES FIXES**—LAZY, UNQUESTIONED TRUTHS. A NATION'S HISTORY ISN'T WHAT HAPPENED, BUT WHAT WE THINK HAPPENED. AND WHO IS THE WE? HOW IS A NATION'S HISTORY FORMED? AND WHO IS IN CHARGE OF IT?
EXTRAS
SCRIPT
DIRECTOR
WOW ... IS THIS THE **FIRST** TIME A **LATINO** TELLS THE STORY OF THE ENTIRE COUNTRY?
WHO CARES? I'M MORE INTERESTED IN WHETHER HE'S REALLY A **CONTRARIAN**.

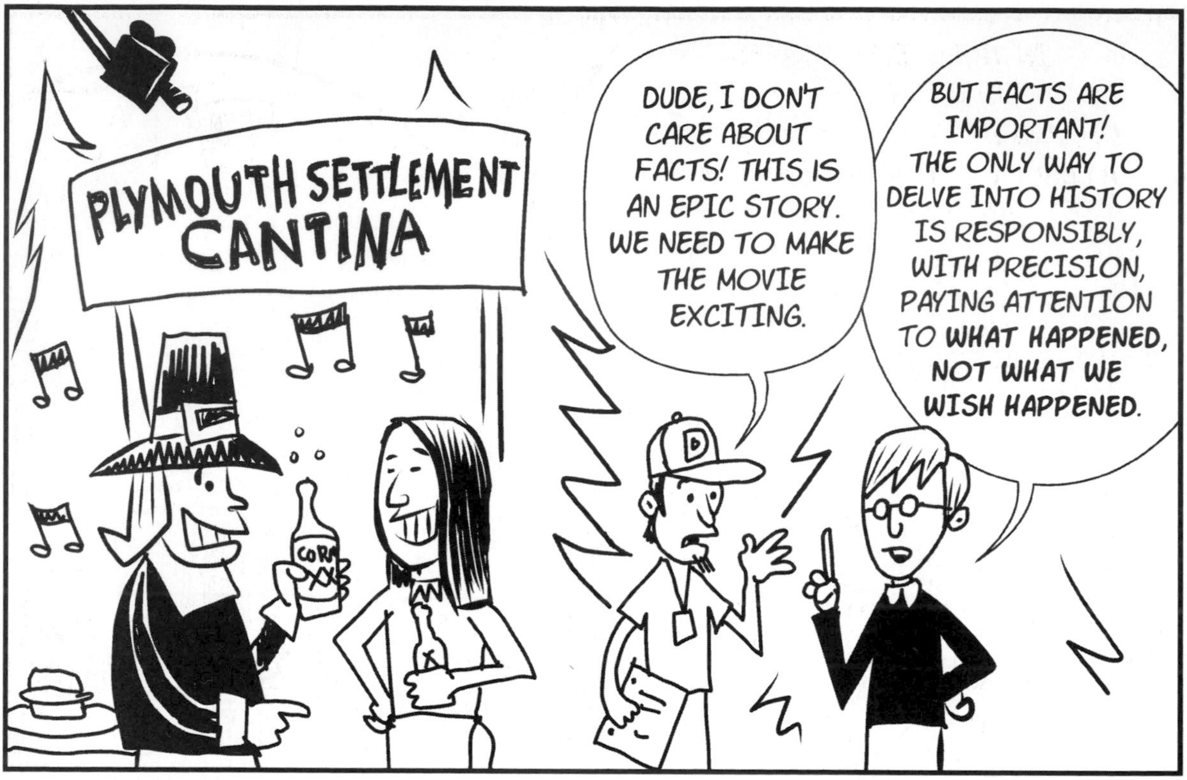
PLYMOUTH SETTLEMENT CANTINA
DUDE, I DON'T CARE ABOUT FACTS! THIS IS AN EPIC STORY. WE NEED TO MAKE THE MOVIE EXCITING.
BUT FACTS ARE IMPORTANT! THE ONLY WAY TO DELVE INTO HISTORY IS RESPONSIBLY, WITH PRECISION, PAYING ATTENTION TO WHAT HAPPENED, NOT WHAT WE WISH HAPPENED.

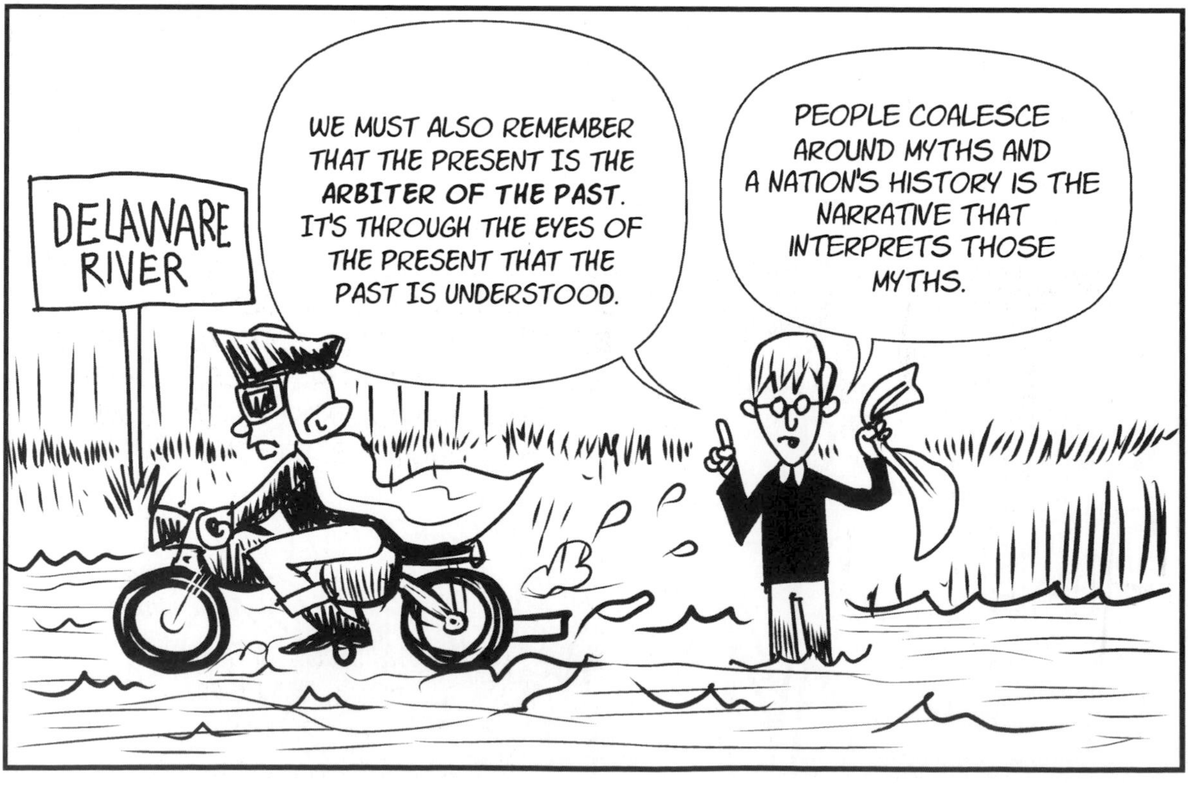
DELAWARE RIVER
WE MUST ALSO REMEMBER THAT THE PRESENT IS THE ARBITER OF THE PAST. IT'S THROUGH THE EYES OF THE PRESENT THAT THE PAST IS UNDERSTOOD.
PEOPLE COALESCE AROUND MYTHS AND A NATION'S HISTORY IS THE NARRATIVE THAT INTERPRETS THOSE MYTHS.

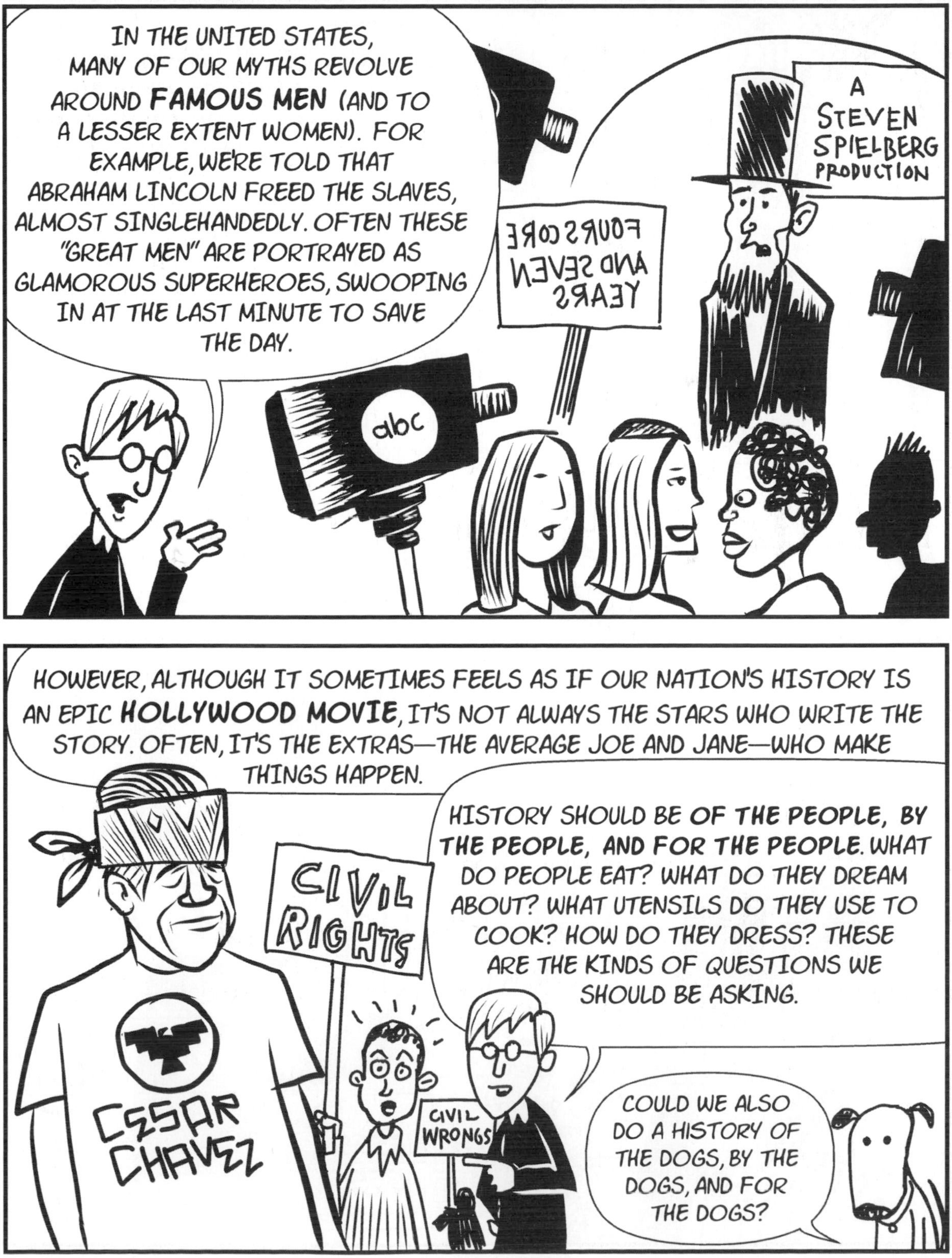

IN THE UNITED STATES, MANY OF OUR MYTHS REVOLVE AROUND **FAMOUS MEN** (AND TO A LESSER EXTENT WOMEN). FOR EXAMPLE, WE'RE TOLD THAT ABRAHAM LINCOLN FREED THE SLAVES, ALMOST SINGLEHANDEDLY. OFTEN THESE "GREAT MEN" ARE PORTRAYED AS GLAMOROUS SUPERHEROES, SWOOPING IN AT THE LAST MINUTE TO SAVE THE DAY.
FOURSCORE AND SEVEN YEARS
A STEVEN SPIELBERG PRODUCTION
abc
HOWEVER, ALTHOUGH IT SOMETIMES FEELS AS IF OUR NATION'S HISTORY IS AN EPIC **HOLLYWOOD MOVIE**, IT'S NOT ALWAYS THE STARS WHO WRITE THE STORY. OFTEN, IT'S THE EXTRAS—THE AVERAGE JOE AND JANE—WHO MAKE THINGS HAPPEN.
HISTORY SHOULD BE **OF THE PEOPLE, BY THE PEOPLE, AND FOR THE PEOPLE**. WHAT DO PEOPLE EAT? WHAT DO THEY DREAM ABOUT? WHAT UTENSILS DO THEY USE TO COOK? HOW DO THEY DRESS? THESE ARE THE KINDS OF QUESTIONS WE SHOULD BE ASKING.
CIVIL RIGHTS
CESAR CHAVEZ
CIVIL WRONGS
COULD WE ALSO DO A HISTORY OF THE DOGS, BY THE DOGS, AND FOR THE DOGS?

ONE MOTIF THAT HAS SHAPED THE UNITED STATES SINCE ITS ORIGIN IS THE TENSION BETWEEN DESTRUCTION AND REBUILDING, THE FORCES OF ORDER INFRINGING ON THE FORCES OF CHAOS, AND VICE VERSA. THINGS OFTEN GET DESTROYED SO THEY CAN BE REBUILT WITH A DIFFERENT SHAPE. IN OTHER WORDS, BIRTH AND DEATH GO HAND IN HAND—THE MOVEMENT FORWARD CAN ONLY PROCEED BY LEAVING THE PAST IN RUINS. IN AMERICA, THIS SYMPHONY OF **CREATIVE DESTRUCTION** IS CALLED **PROGRESS**. THE PURSUIT OF PROGRESS STOPS AT NOTHING, ESPECIALLY WITH REGARD TO THE **SPILLING OF BLOOD.**

PROGRESS, SHMOGRESS!

POET PEDRO PIETRI!

THE MASSES ARE ASSES!

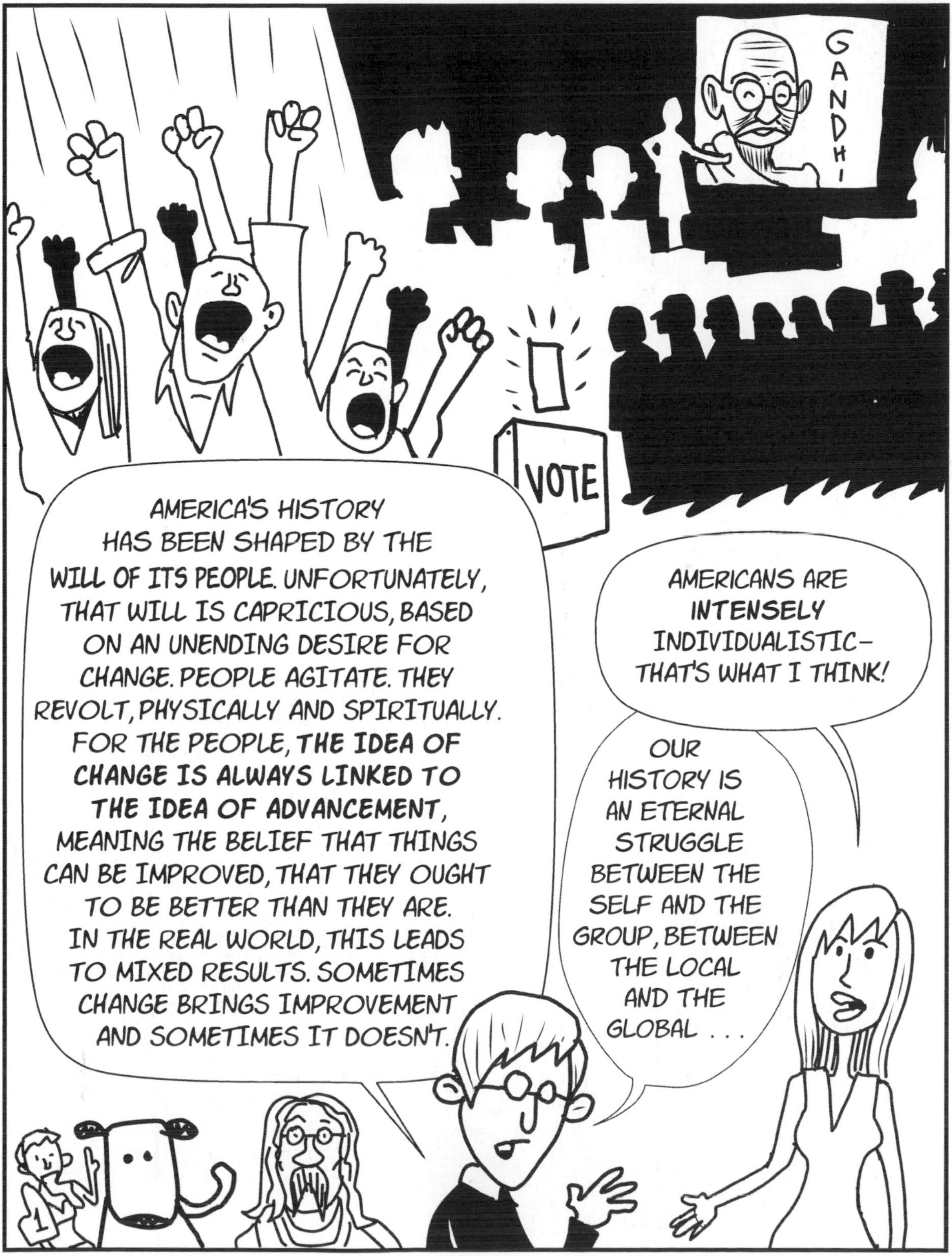
GANDHI
VOTE
AMERICA'S HISTORY HAS BEEN SHAPED BY THE WILL OF ITS PEOPLE. UNFORTUNATELY, THAT WILL IS CAPRICIOUS, BASED ON AN UNENDING DESIRE FOR CHANGE. PEOPLE AGITATE. THEY REVOLT, PHYSICALLY AND SPIRITUALLY. FOR THE PEOPLE, THE IDEA OF CHANGE IS ALWAYS LINKED TO THE IDEA OF ADVANCEMENT, MEANING THE BELIEF THAT THINGS CAN BE IMPROVED, THAT THEY OUGHT TO BE BETTER THAN THEY ARE. IN THE REAL WORLD, THIS LEADS TO MIXED RESULTS. SOMETIMES CHANGE BRINGS IMPROVEMENT AND SOMETIMES IT DOESN'T.
AMERICANS ARE INTENSELY INDIVIDUALISTIC— THAT'S WHAT I THINK!
OUR HISTORY IS AN ETERNAL STRUGGLE BETWEEN THE SELF AND THE GROUP, BETWEEN THE LOCAL AND THE GLOBAL . . .
1

HOBBES VS LOCKE

THERE IS TENSION BETWEEN THE PRIVATE AND THE PUBLIC, BETWEEN THE NATURAL AND THE SOCIAL STATE OF PEOPLE. ONE OF THE TWO BRITISH THINKERS WHOSE VIEWS SHAPED THE AMERICAN UNDERSTANDING OF NATURAL AND SOCIAL RIGHTS WAS **THOMAS HOBBES**. HE BELIEVED THAT IN A NATURAL STATE WE ALL HAVE THE RIGHT TO HAVE EVERYTHING. YET WE AGREE TO LIVE IN A SOCIETY, AND FOR THAT REASON WE ESTABLISH A SOCIAL CONTRACT.

JOHN LOCKE, MEANWHILE, ESTABLISHED THE FOUNDATIONS OF CLASSICAL REPUBLICANISM. HE BELIEVED THAT GOVERNMENT DEPENDS ON THE WILL OF THE PEOPLE, BUT THAT THIS WILL CAN BE VESTED IN INDIVIDUALS SUCH AS THE PRESIDENT, SUPREME COURT JUSTICES, SENATORS, ETC. THERE ARE MANY DIFFERENCES BETWEEN THE TWO MEN'S IDEAS, BUT ULTIMATELY THEIR PHILOSOPHIES ARE COMPATIBLE.

DUDE! THIS MOVIE IS ALREADY GETTING TOO PHILOSOPHICAL! THE AUDIENCE WANTS ACTION.

AMERICANS CAN BE INDIVIDUALISTIC AND **SELFISH**, BUT WE'RE EQUALLY CAPABLE OF BEING **SELFLESS**. THE UNITED STATES IS BUILT ON THE IDEA OF A COLLECTIVE GOOD THAT RESULTS FROM ACTS OF KINDNESS AND COMPASSION!

JFK

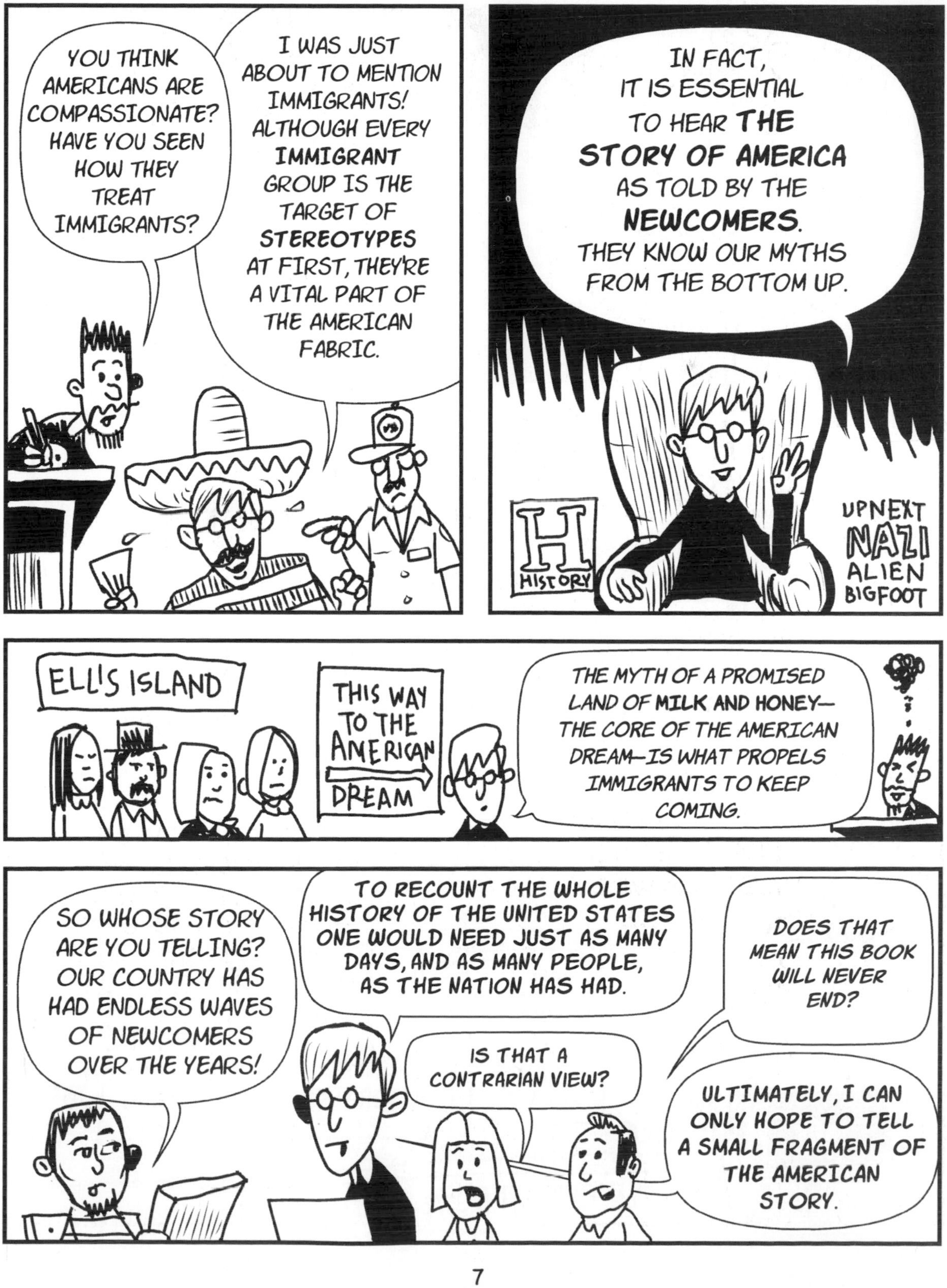
YOU THINK AMERICANS ARE COMPASSIONATE? HAVE YOU SEEN HOW THEY TREAT IMMIGRANTS?
I WAS JUST ABOUT TO MENTION IMMIGRANTS! ALTHOUGH EVERY IMMIGRANT GROUP IS THE TARGET OF STEREOTYPES AT FIRST, THEY'RE A VITAL PART OF THE AMERICAN FABRIC.
IN FACT, IT IS ESSENTIAL TO HEAR THE STORY OF AMERICA AS TOLD BY THE NEWCOMERS. THEY KNOW OUR MYTHS FROM THE BOTTOM UP.
H
HISTORY
UPNEXT
NAZI
ALIEN
BIGFOOT
ELLIS ISLAND
THIS WAY TO THE AMERICAN DREAM
THE MYTH OF A PROMISED LAND OF MILK AND HONEY—THE CORE OF THE AMERICAN DREAM—IS WHAT PROPELS IMMIGRANTS TO KEEP COMING.
SO WHOSE STORY ARE YOU TELLING? OUR COUNTRY HAS HAD ENDLESS WAVES OF NEWCOMERS OVER THE YEARS!
TO RECOUNT THE WHOLE HISTORY OF THE UNITED STATES ONE WOULD NEED JUST AS MANY DAYS, AND AS MANY PEOPLE, AS THE NATION HAS HAD.
IS THAT A CONTRARIAN VIEW?
DOES THAT MEAN THIS BOOK WILL NEVER END?
ULTIMATELY, I CAN ONLY HOPE TO TELL A SMALL FRAGMENT OF THE AMERICAN STORY.

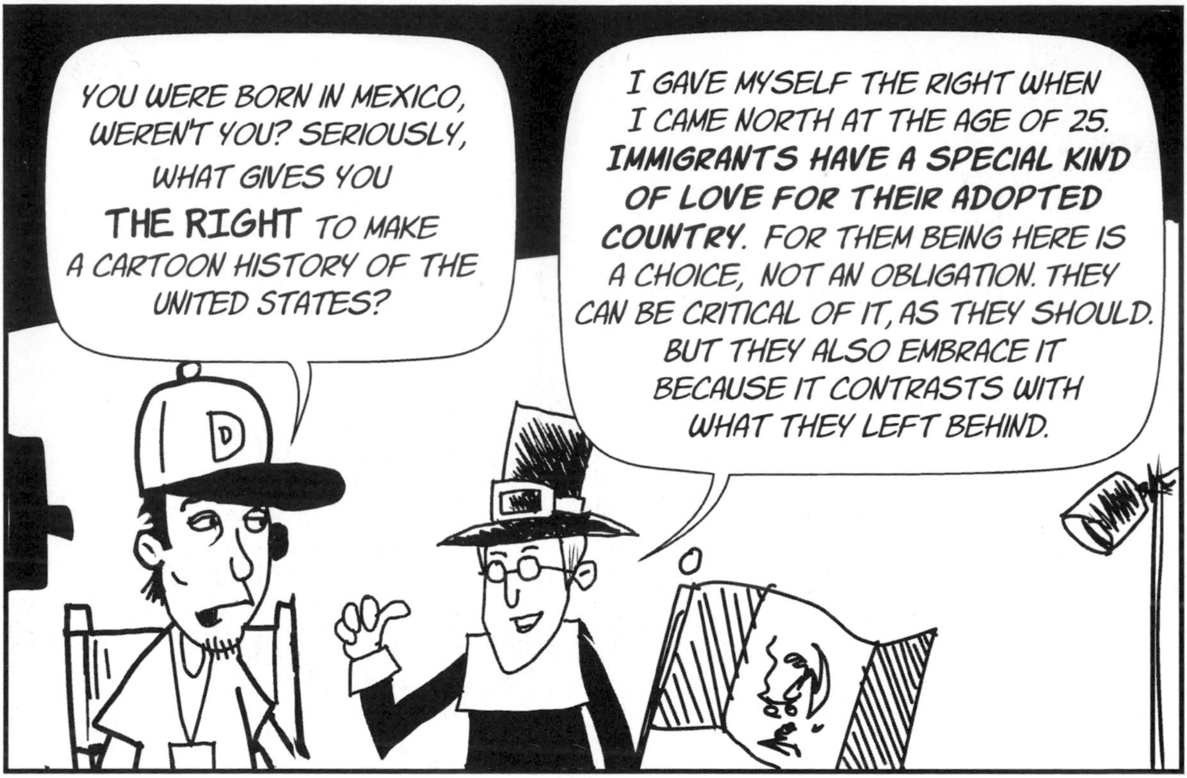
YOU WERE BORN IN MEXICO, WEREN'T YOU? SERIOUSLY, WHAT GIVES YOU THE RIGHT TO MAKE A CARTOON HISTORY OF THE UNITED STATES?
I GAVE MYSELF THE RIGHT WHEN I CAME NORTH AT THE AGE OF 25. IMMIGRANTS HAVE A SPECIAL KIND OF LOVE FOR THEIR ADOPTED COUNTRY. FOR THEM BEING HERE IS A CHOICE, NOT AN OBLIGATION. THEY CAN BE CRITICAL OF IT, AS THEY SHOULD. BUT THEY ALSO EMBRACE IT BECAUSE IT CONTRASTS WITH WHAT THEY LEFT BEHIND.
D

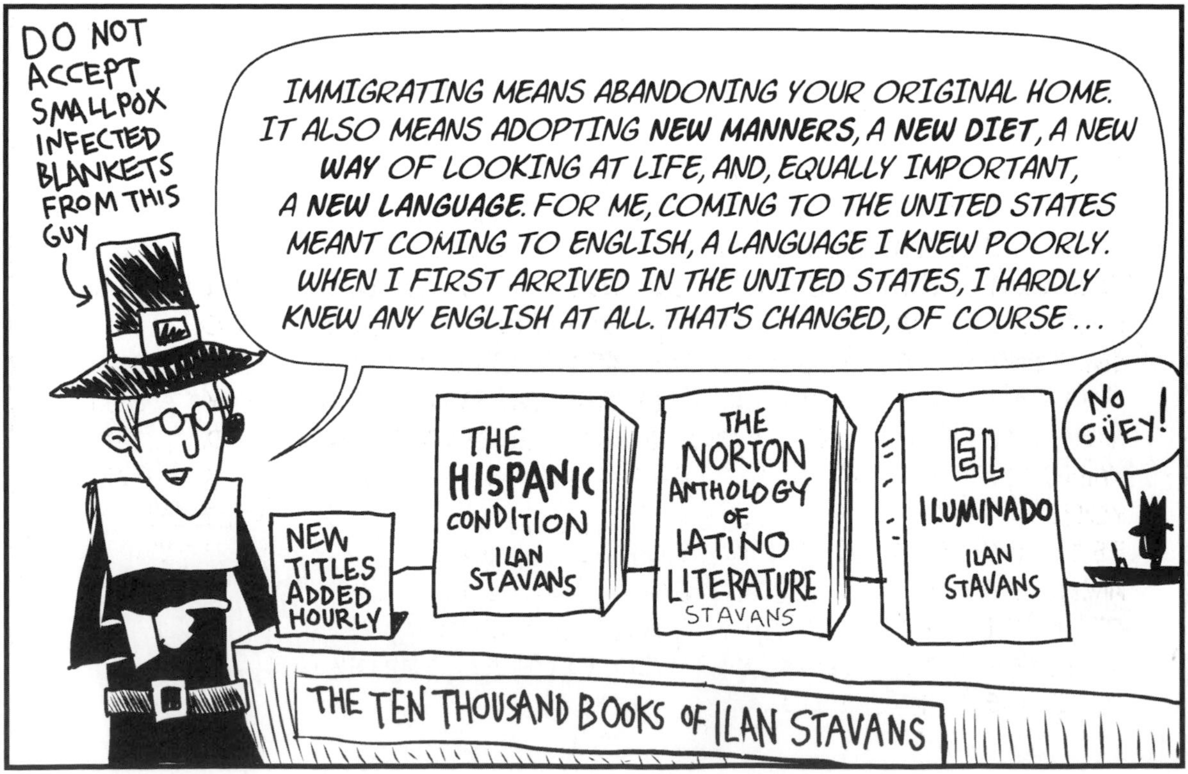
DO NOT ACCEPT SMALLPOX INFECTED BLANKETS FROM THIS GUY
IMMIGRATING MEANS ABANDONING YOUR ORIGINAL HOME. IT ALSO MEANS ADOPTING NEW MANNERS, A NEW DIET, A NEW WAY OF LOOKING AT LIFE, AND, EQUALLY IMPORTANT, A NEW LANGUAGE. FOR ME, COMING TO THE UNITED STATES MEANT COMING TO ENGLISH, A LANGUAGE I KNEW POORLY. WHEN I FIRST ARRIVED IN THE UNITED STATES, I HARDLY KNEW ANY ENGLISH AT ALL. THAT'S CHANGED, OF COURSE . . .
NO GÜEY!
NEW TITLES ADDED HOURLY
THE HISPANIC CONDITION ILAN STAVANS
THE NORTON ANTHOLOGY OF LATINO LITERATURE STAVANS
EL ILUMINADO ILAN STAVANS
THE TEN THOUSAND BOOKS OF ILAN STAVANS

ANOTHER THING I HAD TO ADJUST TO AFTER COMING TO THE UNITED STATES WAS THE AMERICAN ATTITUDE TOWARD **MONEY**. OFTENTIMES, AMERICANS FIND THEIR INDIVIDUAL IDENTITY THROUGH THE OWNERSHIP OF PRIVATE PROPERTY AND THROUGH THE PRODUCTION OF **SELLABLE MERCHANDISE** THAT HAS PUBLIC VALUE. THEY WORK, WORK, WORK. AS THE DECLARATION OF INDEPENDENCE TELLS US, EVERYONE HAS THE RIGHT TO LIFE, LIBERTY, AND THE **PURSUIT OF HAPPINESS**. UNFORTUNATELY, HOWEVER, THIS VERY PURSUIT HAS ENDED UP CREATING A FAIRLY UNEQUAL SOCIETY. IN THE EYES OF MOST AMERICANS, THE METHODS YOU USE TO **ACHIEVE HAPPINESS**—AND THE PEOPLE YOU STEP ON TRYING TO GET IT—ARE YOUR OWN BUSINESS. AND BUSINESS IS THE WORD FOR IT: THE ACCUMULATION OF CAPITAL—MATERIAL, SOCIAL, AND EMOTIONAL—IS THE ENGINE THAT KEEPS EVERYTHING MOVING. TO BE **RICH**, TO BE **POWERFUL**, TO BE **FAMOUS**, TO BE THE **FIRST**.... THAT'S WHAT AMERICA—AND ITS HISTORY—IS ALL ABOUT! IN FACT, IT'S BEEN THAT WAY SINCE THE VERY BEGINNING ...

CHAPTER 1

THE LAND IS OURS

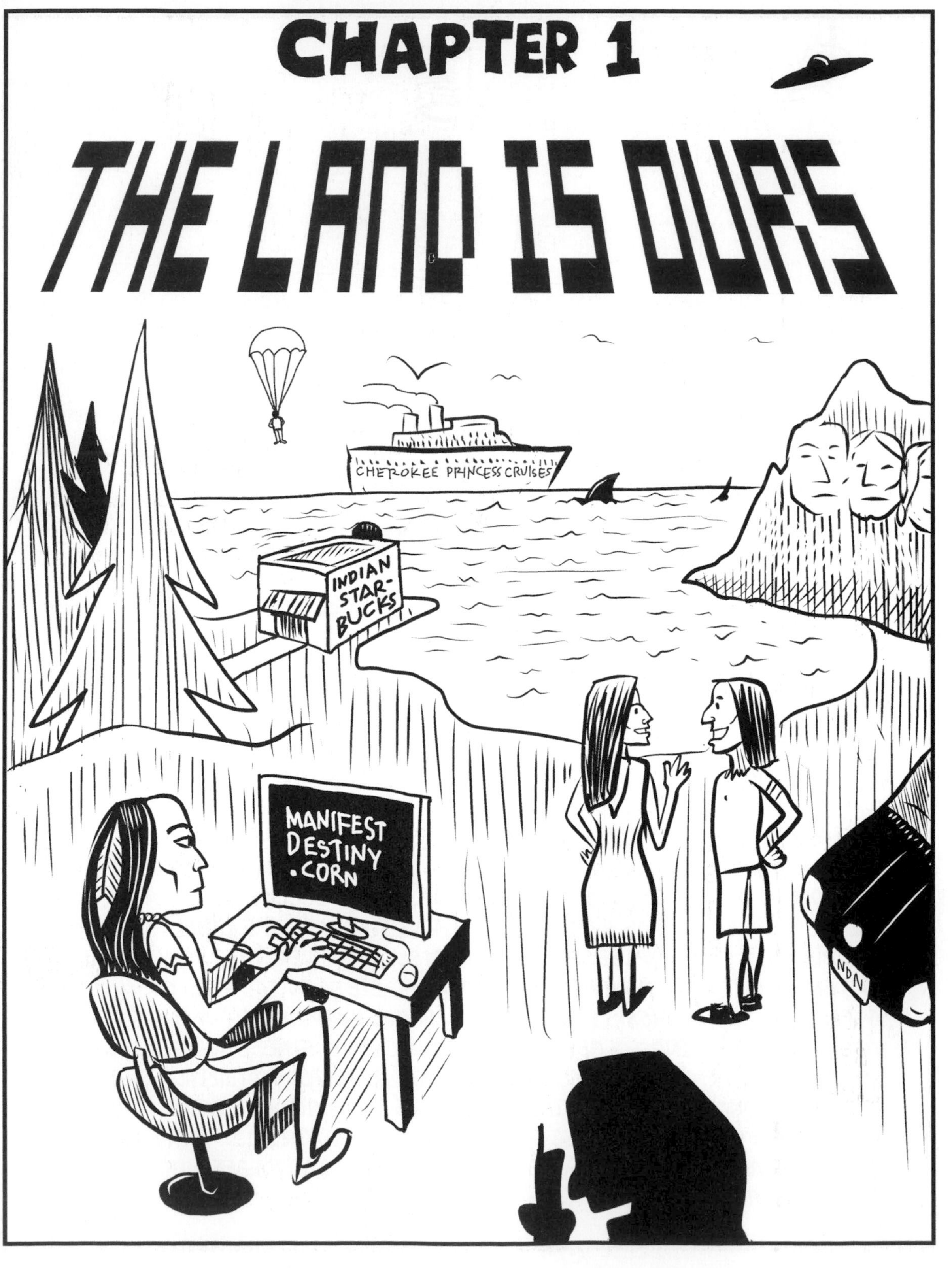

CHEROKEE PRINCESS CRUISES
INDIAN STAR-BUCKS
MANIFEST DESTINY .CORN
NDN

MEET **CHRISTOPHER COLUMBUS**, THE MAN CREDITED (WRONGLY) WITH DISCOVERING AMERICA AND ONE OF OUR HISTORY'S GREATEST SCOUNDRELS. (MAKE HIM LOOK HANDSOME, OK? AFTER ALL, HE'S A HERO. HEROES ARE SUPPOSED TO BE PERFECT.)

BUT COLUMBUS IS FAR FROM PERFECT!

ACTUALLY, WE DON'T KNOW MUCH ABOUT HIM OTHER THAN WHAT HE WROTE IN HIS DIARIES. HE WAS PROBABLY A **CONVERSO JEW**, CONVINCED THERE WAS AN ALTERNATIVE TRADE ROUTE TO THE FAR EAST—TO INDIA IN PARTICULAR. THAT'S WHERE THE MISNOMER INDIANS COMES FROM!

COLUMBUS TRIED TO CONVINCE VARIOUS GOVERNMENTS TO SPONSOR HIS TRAVELS AROUND THE GLOBE BEFORE FINALLY SUCCEEDING WITH SPAIN. THE THREE CARAVELS HE USED HAD SEEN BETTER DAYS. HE ASSEMBLED A CREW OF **ADVENTURE-SEEKERS**, **OCEAN NAVIGATORS**, **MARINE MERCHANTS**, AND **SOCIAL REJECTS**.

COLUMBUS'S CREW

ADVENTURE-SEEKERS

NAVIGATORS

MARINE MERCHANTS

SOCIAL REJECTS

COLUMBUS'S ENTERPRISE

IN JUST FOUR TRIPS, COLUMBUS RESHAPED THE WORLD. SUDDENLY, SPAIN—AN EMPIRE IN POLITICAL TURMOIL AND FINANCIAL DECLINE—WAS IN POSSESSION OF A VAST COLONIAL TERRITORY, RICH IN NATURAL RESOURCES. THAT TERRITORY WAS SOON THE SITE OF A FEEDING FRENZY! AN ONSLAUGHT OF CONQUISTADORS, EXPLORERS, AND MISSIONARIES SOUGHT THEIR FUTURE IN THE NEW WORLD. THEY WANTED TO PLEASE THE MONARCHY, EXPAND THE REACH OF THE CATHOLIC CHURCH, ACHIEVE FAME, WEALTH, AND GLORY ...

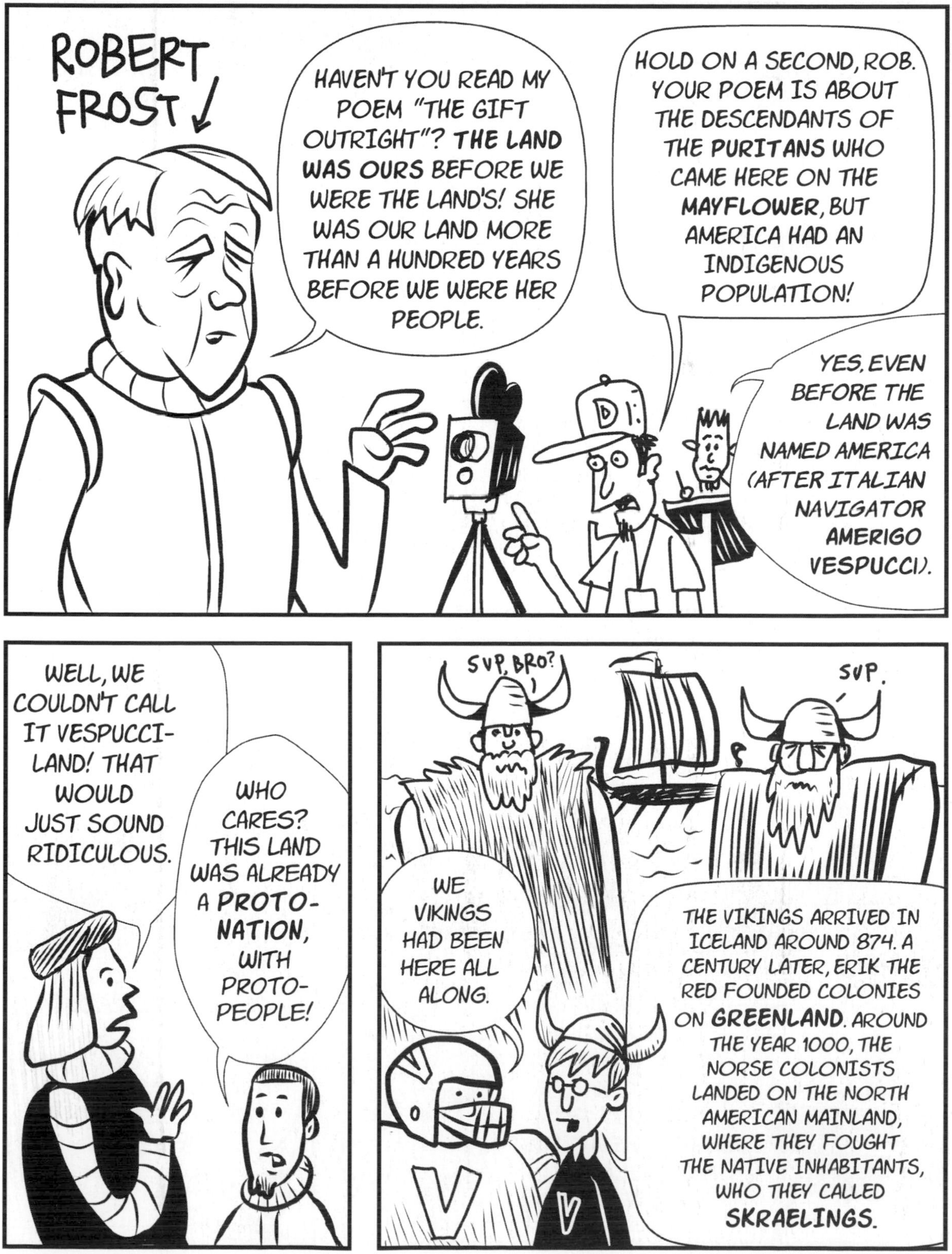
ROBERT FROST
HAVEN'T YOU READ MY POEM "THE GIFT OUTRIGHT"? **THE LAND WAS OURS** BEFORE WE WERE THE LAND'S! SHE WAS OUR LAND MORE THAN A HUNDRED YEARS BEFORE WE WERE HER PEOPLE.
HOLD ON A SECOND, ROB. YOUR POEM IS ABOUT THE DESCENDANTS OF THE **PURITANS** WHO CAME HERE ON THE **MAYFLOWER**, BUT AMERICA HAD AN INDIGENOUS POPULATION!
DI
YES, EVEN BEFORE THE LAND WAS NAMED AMERICA (AFTER ITALIAN NAVIGATOR **AMERIGO VESPUCCI**).
WELL, WE COULDN'T CALL IT VESPUCCI-LAND! THAT WOULD JUST SOUND RIDICULOUS.
WHO CARES? THIS LAND WAS ALREADY A **PROTO-NATION**, WITH PROTO-PEOPLE!
SUP, BRO?
SUP.
WE VIKINGS HAD BEEN HERE ALL ALONG.
THE VIKINGS ARRIVED IN ICELAND AROUND 874. A CENTURY LATER, ERIK THE RED FOUNDED COLONIES ON **GREENLAND**. AROUND THE YEAR 1000, THE NORSE COLONISTS LANDED ON THE NORTH AMERICAN MAINLAND, WHERE THEY FOUGHT THE NATIVE INHABITANTS, WHO THEY CALLED **SKRAELINGS**.
V
V

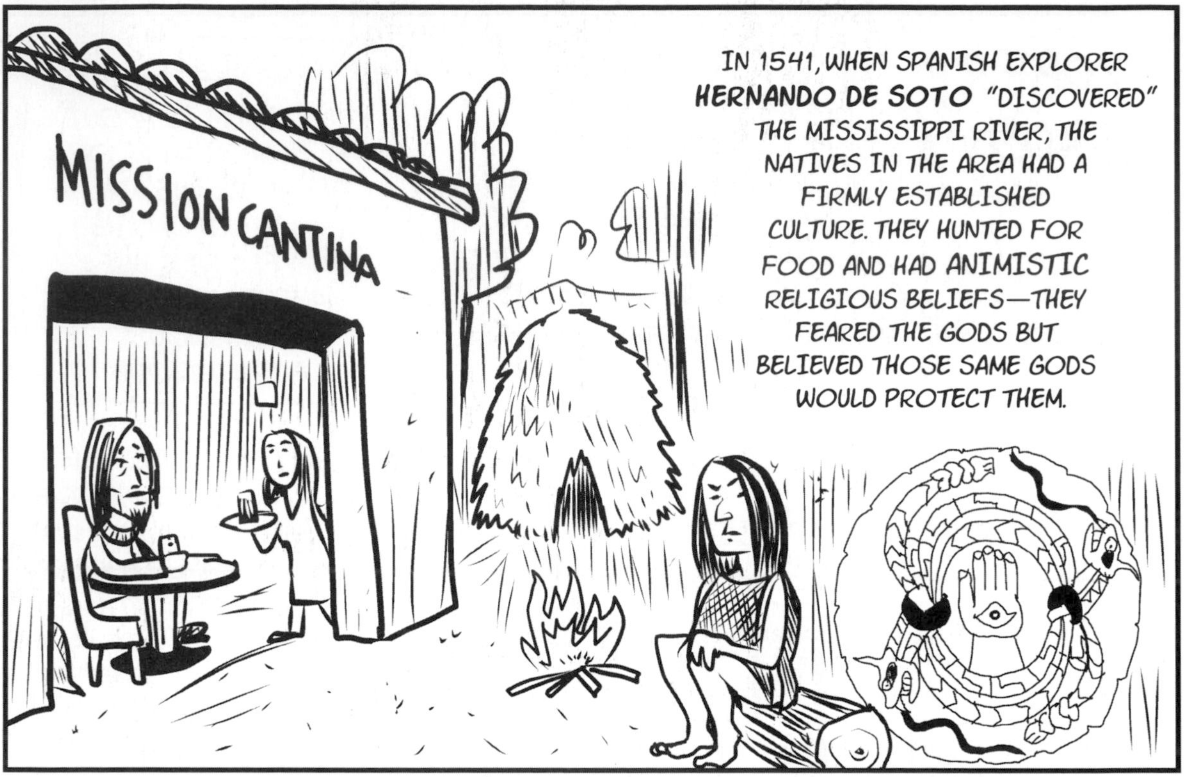
IN 1541, WHEN SPANISH EXPLORER **HERNANDO DE SOTO** "DISCOVERED" THE MISSISSIPPI RIVER, THE NATIVES IN THE AREA HAD A FIRMLY ESTABLISHED CULTURE. THEY HUNTED FOR FOOD AND HAD ANIMISTIC RELIGIOUS BELIEFS—THEY FEARED THE GODS BUT BELIEVED THOSE SAME GODS WOULD PROTECT THEM.
MISSION CANTINA

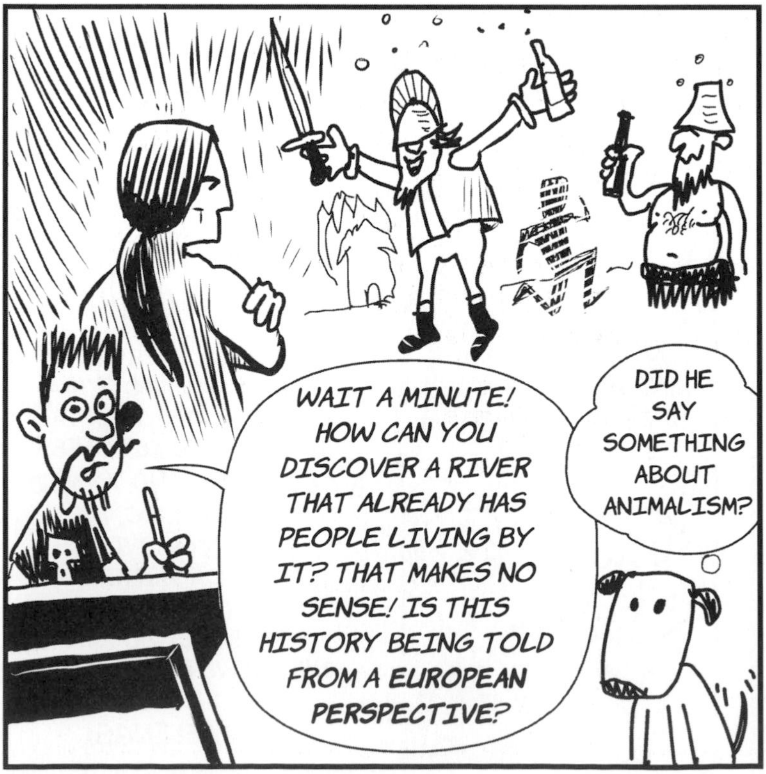
WAIT A MINUTE! HOW CAN YOU DISCOVER A RIVER THAT ALREADY HAS PEOPLE LIVING BY IT? THAT MAKES NO SENSE! IS THIS HISTORY BEING TOLD FROM A **EUROPEAN** PERSPECTIVE?
DID HE SAY SOMETHING ABOUT ANIMALISM?

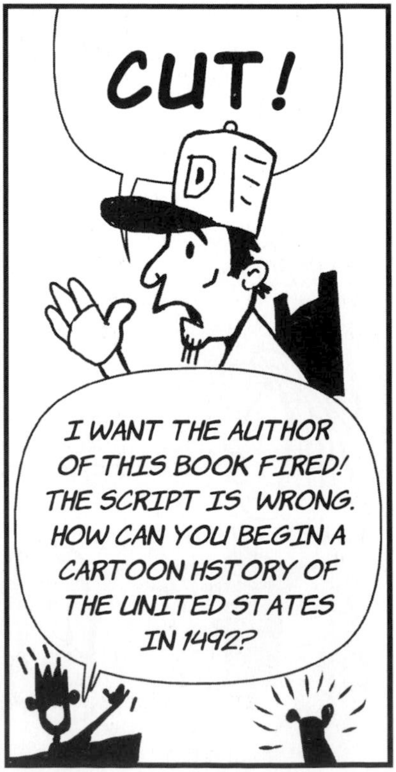
CUT!
D
I WANT THE AUTHOR OF THIS BOOK FIRED! THE SCRIPT IS WRONG. HOW CAN YOU BEGIN A CARTOON HSTORY OF THE UNITED STATES IN 1492?

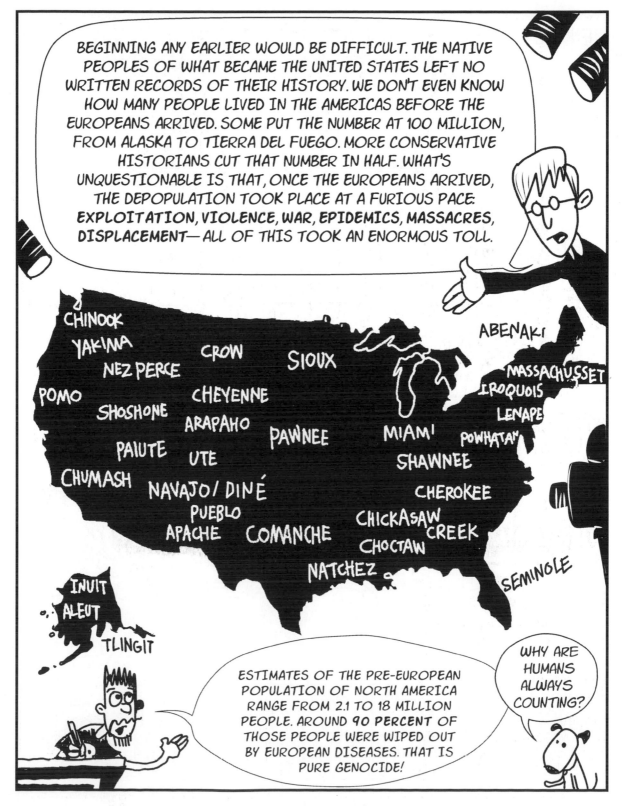

BEGINNING ANY EARLIER WOULD BE DIFFICULT. THE NATIVE PEOPLES OF WHAT BECAME THE UNITED STATES LEFT NO WRITTEN RECORDS OF THEIR HISTORY. WE DON'T EVEN KNOW HOW MANY PEOPLE LIVED IN THE AMERICAS BEFORE THE EUROPEANS ARRIVED. SOME PUT THE NUMBER AT 100 MILLION, FROM ALASKA TO TIERRA DEL FUEGO. MORE CONSERVATIVE HISTORIANS CUT THAT NUMBER IN HALF. WHAT'S UNQUESTIONABLE IS THAT, ONCE THE EUROPEANS ARRIVED, THE DEPOPULATION TOOK PLACE AT A FURIOUS PACE: **EXPLOITATION, VIOLENCE, WAR, EPIDEMICS, MASSACRES, DISPLACEMENT**— ALL OF THIS TOOK AN ENORMOUS TOLL.

CHINOOK
YAKIMA
NEZ PERCE
CROW
SIOUX
ABENAKI
MASSACHUSSET
IROQUOIS
LENAPE
POMO
CHEYENNE
SHOSHONE
ARAPAHO
PAWNEE
MIAMI
POWHATAN
PAIUTE
UTE
SHAWNEE
CHUMASH
NAVAJO/DINÉ
CHEROKEE
PUEBLO
APACHE
COMANCHE
CHICKASAW
CREEK
CHOCTAW
NATCHEZ
SEMINOLE
INUIT
ALEUT
TLINGIT

ESTIMATES OF THE PRE-EUROPEAN POPULATION OF NORTH AMERICA RANGE FROM 2.1 TO 18 MILLION PEOPLE. AROUND **90 PERCENT** OF THOSE PEOPLE WERE WIPED OUT BY EUROPEAN DISEASES. THAT IS PURE GENOCIDE!

WHY ARE HUMANS ALWAYS COUNTING?

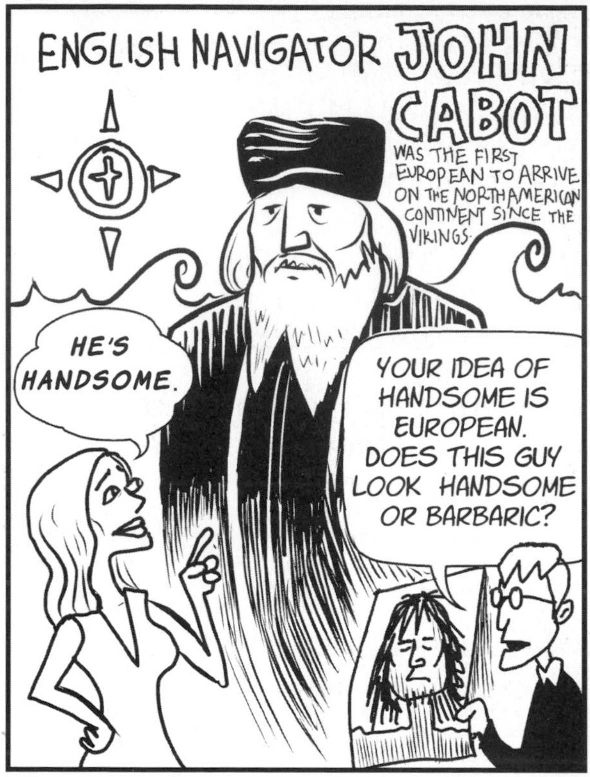
ENGLISH NAVIGATOR JOHN CABOT
WAS THE FIRST EUROPEAN TO ARRIVE ON THE NORTH AMERICAN CONTINENT SINCE THE VIKINGS.
HE'S HANDSOME.
YOUR IDEA OF HANDSOME IS EUROPEAN. DOES THIS GUY LOOK HANDSOME OR BARBARIC?

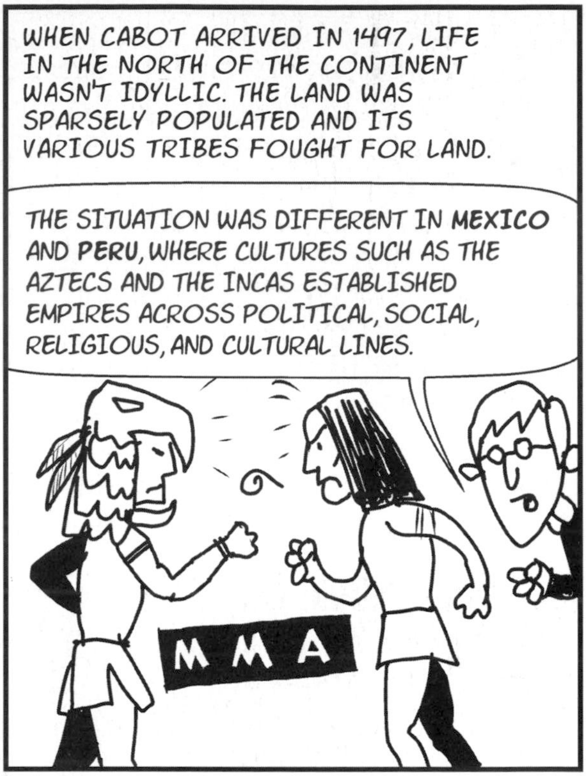
WHEN CABOT ARRIVED IN 1497, LIFE IN THE NORTH OF THE CONTINENT WASN'T IDYLLIC. THE LAND WAS SPARSELY POPULATED AND ITS VARIOUS TRIBES FOUGHT FOR LAND.
THE SITUATION WAS DIFFERENT IN MEXICO AND PERU, WHERE CULTURES SUCH AS THE AZTECS AND THE INCAS ESTABLISHED EMPIRES ACROSS POLITICAL, SOCIAL, RELIGIOUS, AND CULTURAL LINES.
MMA

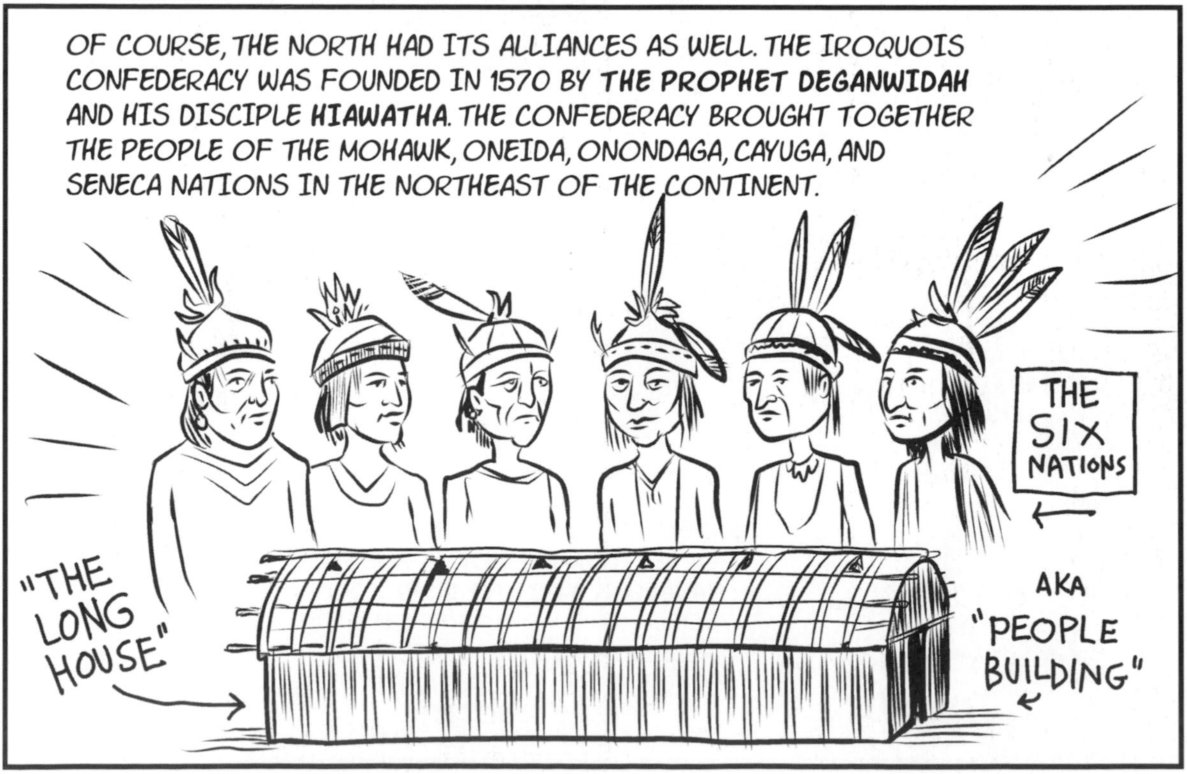
OF COURSE, THE NORTH HAD ITS ALLIANCES AS WELL. THE IROQUOIS CONFEDERACY WAS FOUNDED IN 1570 BY THE PROPHET DEGANWIDAH AND HIS DISCIPLE HIAWATHA. THE CONFEDERACY BROUGHT TOGETHER THE PEOPLE OF THE MOHAWK, ONEIDA, ONONDAGA, CAYUGA, AND SENECA NATIONS IN THE NORTHEAST OF THE CONTINENT.
THE SIX NATIONS
"THE LONG HOUSE"
AKA "PEOPLE BUILDING"

THIS CONFEDERACY (WHICH LATER INCLUDED ANOTHER NATION, THE TOSCARORA) LIVED IN WHAT WE KNOW NOW AS NEW YORK STATE, FROM THE HUDSON RIVER IN THE EAST TO THE ST. LAWRENCE AND GENESEE RIVERS IN THE WEST.

WHO WERE THE MOHAWKS? ORIGINALLY, THEIR TRIBE NAME WAS "KANIENKEH." THE MEN HUNTED DEER AND THE WOMEN RAISED TOBACCO AND CORN. TOBACCO, IN PARTICULAR, WAS A VERY IMPORTANT CROP—THE MOHAWKS SNIFFED IT, CHEWED IT, DIPPED IT, AND SMOKED IT IN SHAMANIC CEREMONIES. THE EUROPEANS SOON PICKED UP THE HABIT AND BROUGHT TOBACCO HOME WITH THEM. THAT'S ANOTHER THING THAT HISTORY IS ALL ABOUT: THE BACK-AND-FORTH MOVEMENT OF MATERIAL GOODS.

LATER, THEY REPACKAGED IT AND SOLD IT BACK TO THE NATIVES AT A HIGHER PRICE.

TOBACCO WASN'T THE ONLY AMERICAN EXPORT TO MAKE A SPLASH IN EUROPE—OTHERS INCLUDE TOMATOES, CHOCOLATE, MAIZE ...

17

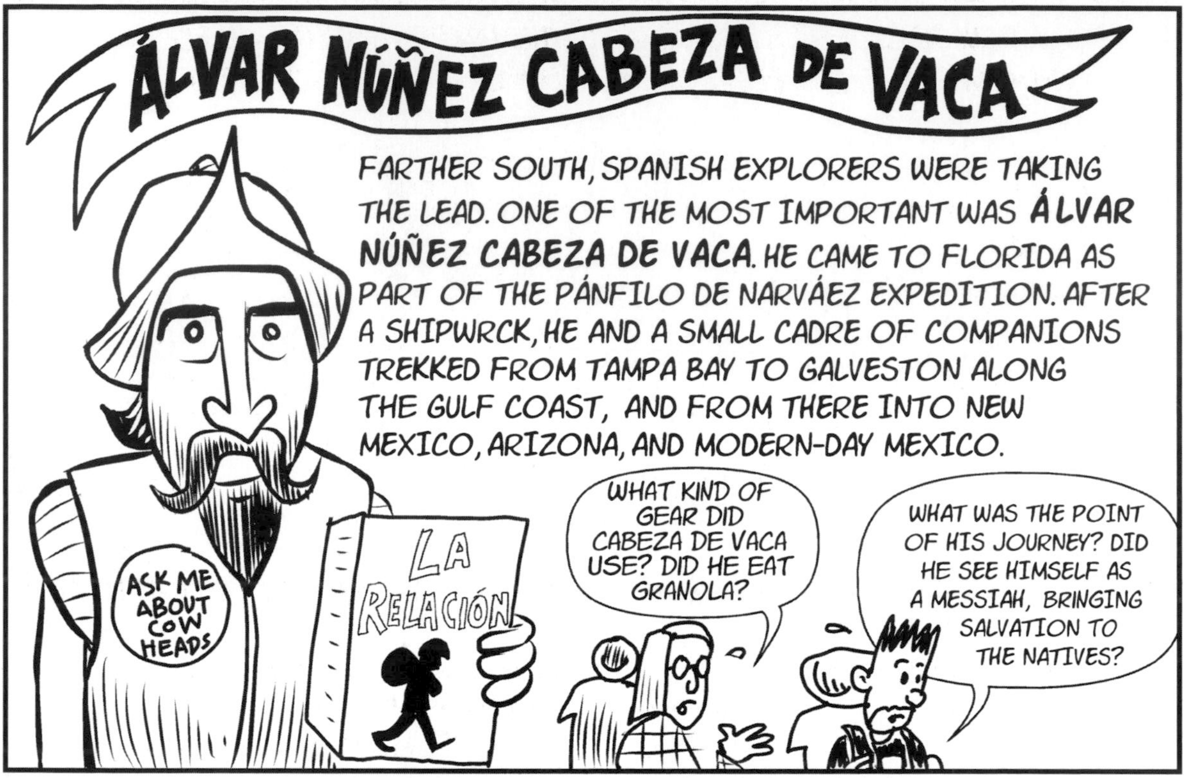
ÁLVAR NÚÑEZ CABEZA DE VACA
FARTHER SOUTH, SPANISH EXPLORERS WERE TAKING THE LEAD. ONE OF THE MOST IMPORTANT WAS **ÁLVAR NÚÑEZ CABEZA DE VACA**. HE CAME TO FLORIDA AS PART OF THE PÁNFILO DE NARVÁEZ EXPEDITION. AFTER A SHIPWRCK, HE AND A SMALL CADRE OF COMPANIONS TREKKED FROM TAMPA BAY TO GALVESTON ALONG THE GULF COAST, AND FROM THERE INTO NEW MEXICO, ARIZONA, AND MODERN-DAY MEXICO.
ASK ME ABOUT COW HEADS
LA RELACIÓN
WHAT KIND OF GEAR DID CABEZA DE VACA USE? DID HE EAT GRANOLA?
WHAT WAS THE POINT OF HIS JOURNEY? DID HE SEE HIMSELF AS A MESSIAH, BRINGING SALVATION TO THE NATIVES?

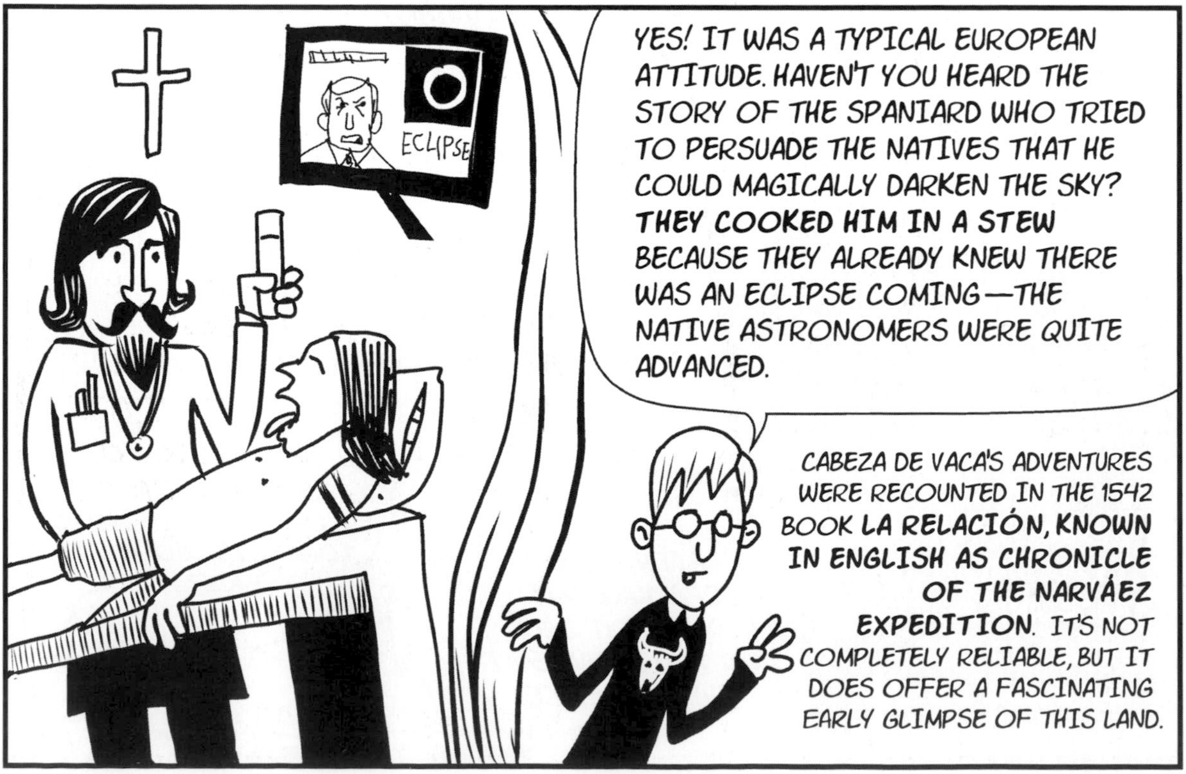
ECLIPSE
YES! IT WAS A TYPICAL EUROPEAN ATTITUDE. HAVEN'T YOU HEARD THE STORY OF THE SPANIARD WHO TRIED TO PERSUADE THE NATIVES THAT HE COULD MAGICALLY DARKEN THE SKY? **THEY COOKED HIM IN A STEW** BECAUSE THEY ALREADY KNEW THERE WAS AN ECLIPSE COMING—THE NATIVE ASTRONOMERS WERE QUITE ADVANCED.
CABEZA DE VACA'S ADVENTURES WERE RECOUNTED IN THE 1542 BOOK **LA RELACIÓN, KNOWN IN ENGLISH AS CHRONICLE OF THE NARVÁEZ EXPEDITION**. IT'S NOT COMPLETELY RELIABLE, BUT IT DOES OFFER A FASCINATING EARLY GLIMPSE OF THIS LAND.

A FEW DECADES LATER, IN 1620, THE **MAYFLOWER** SAILED FROM PLYMOUTH, ENGLAND, TO PLYMOUTH, MASSACHUSETTS.

WE ROCK!

ON BOARD THERE WERE 120 PASSENGERS, ALONG WITH TWENTY TO THIRTY CREW MEMBERS. THE PASSENGERS—KNOWN AS PURITANS OR PILGRIMS— WERE PERSECUTED PEOPLE, FLEEING RELIGIOUS INTOLERANCE. THEY WERE MOSTLY ENGLISH AND DUTCH SEPARATISTS, THOUGH SOME WERE FRENCH HUGUENOTS. THEY SAW HISTORY THROUGH A **BIBLICAL LENS**: THEIR GOAL WAS TO FIND—TO CREATE—A NEW CANAAN, A PROMISED LAND WHERE THEY COULD BEGIN ANEW.

YE MAYFLOWER PASSENGERS:

JOHN ALLERTON

DESIRE MINTER

ROBERT CARTER

ILAN STAVANS (RUNNING AWAY FROM HIS MOM)

PERSECUTION—THAT'S OUR ORIGIN MYTH! THE SETTLERS WERE SEARCHING FOR A PLACE WHERE THEIR CULTURE WOULDN'T BE UNDER ATTACK. THEY WANTED TO START OVER, TO CREATE A **FREE NATION**. YET THE PLACE WHERE THEY CHOSE TO ESTABLISH THAT NATION ALREADY HAD ITS OWN CULTURE, WHICH THE SETTLERS CONVENIENTLY IGNORED. THAT'S THE ONLY WAY TO START ANEW AFTER ALL—BY **NEGATING THE PAST.**

IN 1614, THE DUTCH CLAIMED THE TERRITORY OF **NEW NETHERLAND**.

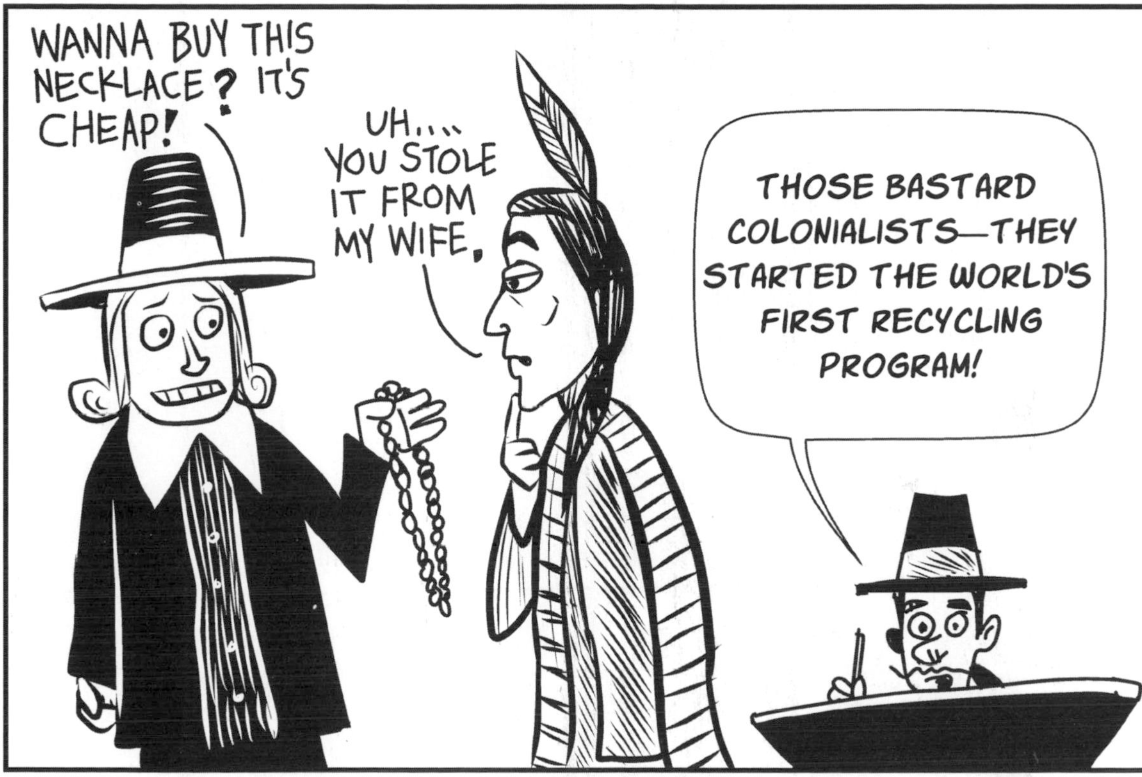
WANNA BUY THIS NECKLACE? IT'S CHEAP!
UH.... YOU STOLE IT FROM MY WIFE.
THOSE BASTARD COLONIALISTS—THEY STARTED THE WORLD'S FIRST RECYCLING PROGRAM!

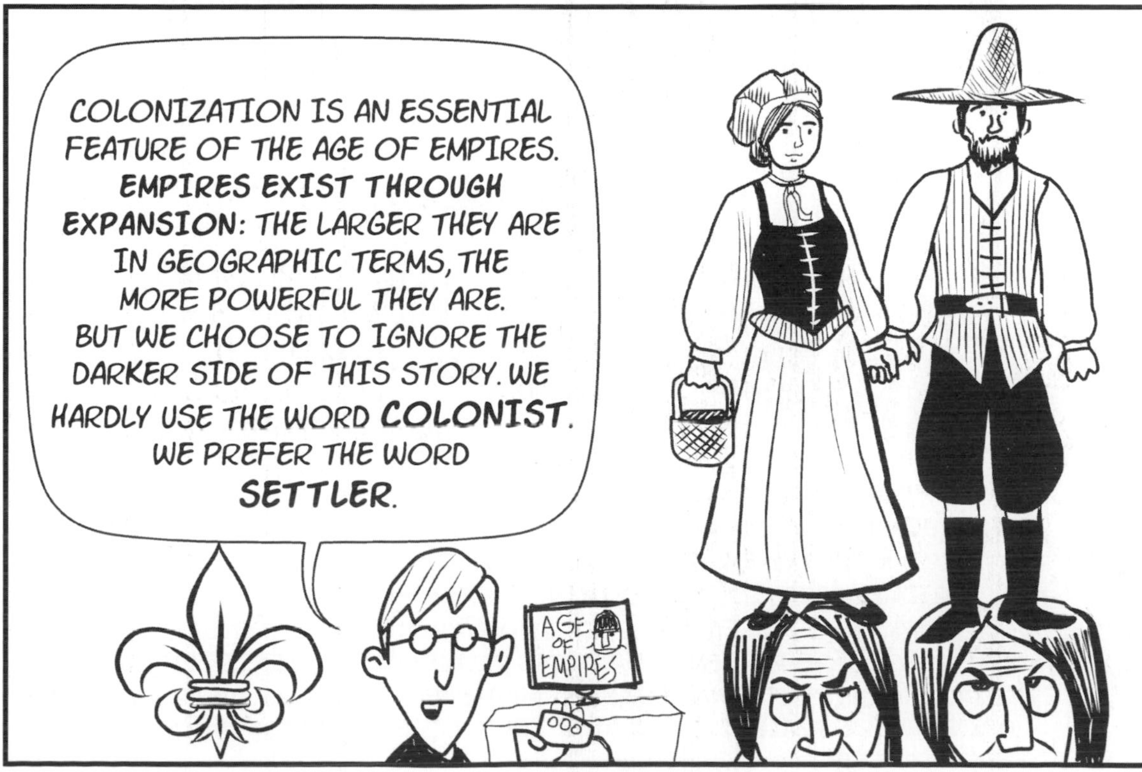
COLONIZATION IS AN ESSENTIAL FEATURE OF THE AGE OF EMPIRES. **EMPIRES EXIST THROUGH EXPANSION**: THE LARGER THEY ARE IN GEOGRAPHIC TERMS, THE MORE POWERFUL THEY ARE. BUT WE CHOOSE TO IGNORE THE DARKER SIDE OF THIS STORY. WE HARDLY USE THE WORD **COLONIST**. WE PREFER THE WORD **SETTLER**.
AGE OF EMPIRES

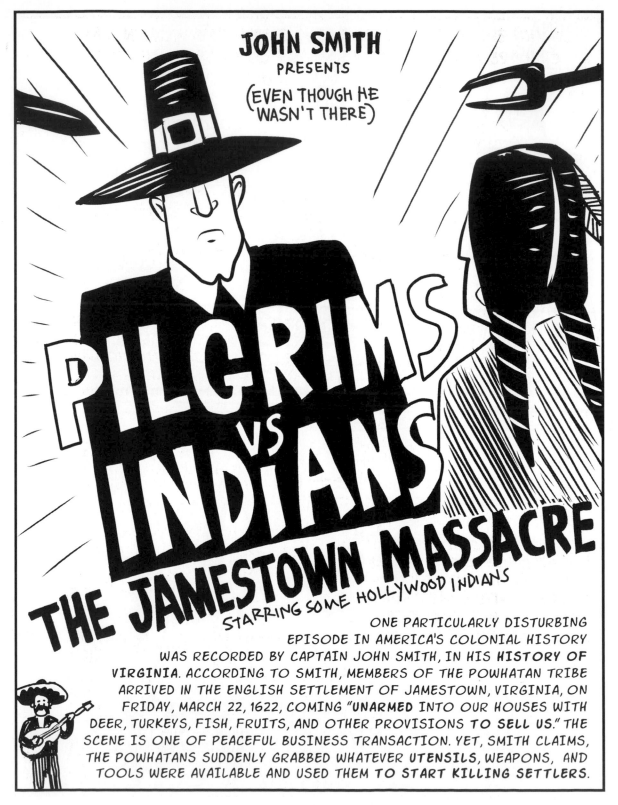

ONE PARTICULARLY DISTURBING EPISODE IN AMERICA'S COLONIAL HISTORY WAS RECORDED BY CAPTAIN JOHN SMITH, IN HIS **HISTORY OF VIRGINIA**. ACCORDING TO SMITH, MEMBERS OF THE POWHATAN TRIBE ARRIVED IN THE ENGLISH SETTLEMENT OF JAMESTOWN, VIRGINIA, ON FRIDAY, MARCH 22, 1622, COMING "**UNARMED** INTO OUR HOUSES WITH DEER, TURKEYS, FISH, FRUITS, AND OTHER PROVISIONS **TO SELL US**." THE SCENE IS ONE OF PEACEFUL BUSINESS TRANSACTION. YET, SMITH CLAIMS, THE POWHATANS SUDDENLY GRABBED WHATEVER **UTENSILS**, WEAPONS, AND TOOLS WERE AVAILABLE AND USED THEM **TO START KILLING SETTLERS**.

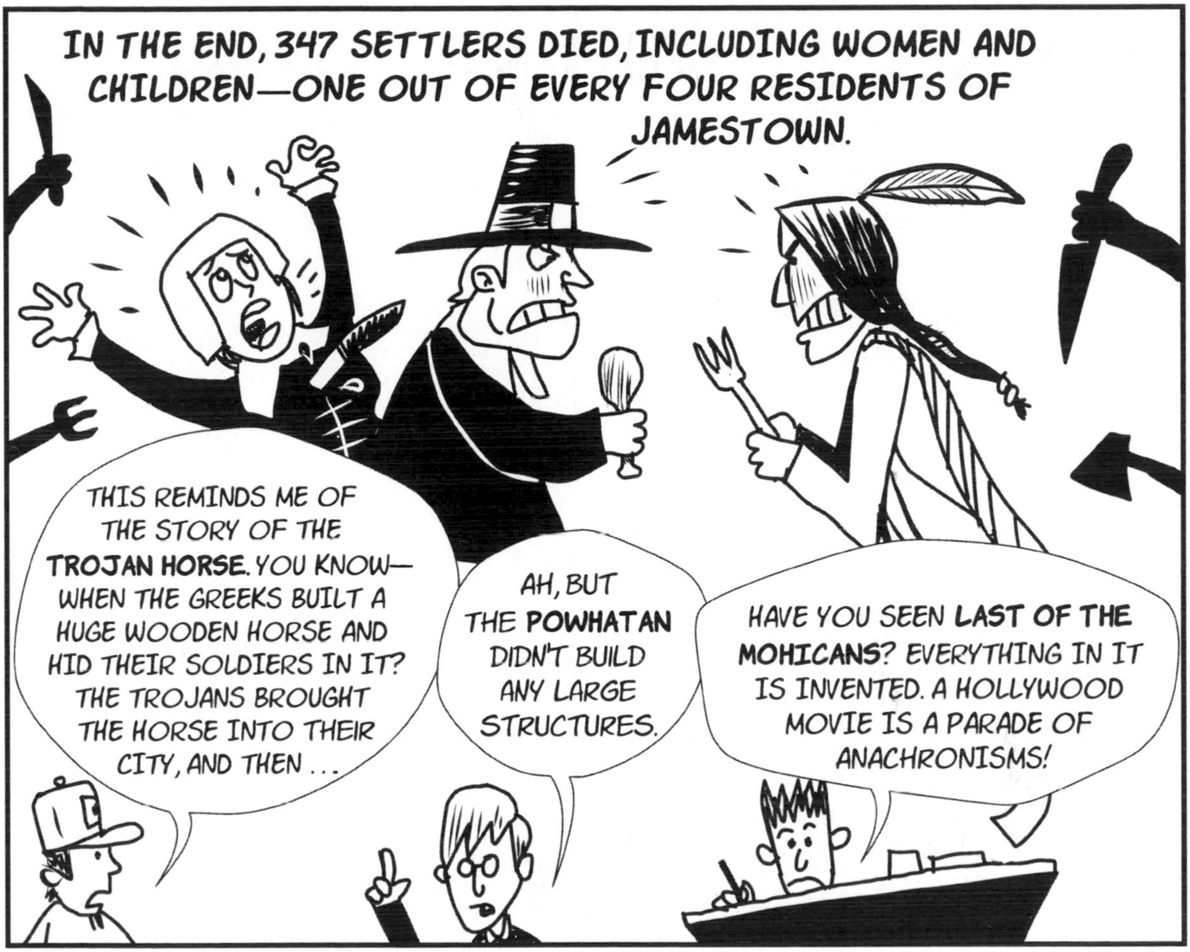
IN THE END, 347 SETTLERS DIED, INCLUDING WOMEN AND CHILDREN—ONE OUT OF EVERY FOUR RESIDENTS OF JAMESTOWN.
THIS REMINDS ME OF THE STORY OF THE TROJAN HORSE. YOU KNOW—WHEN THE GREEKS BUILT A HUGE WOODEN HORSE AND HID THEIR SOLDIERS IN IT? THE TROJANS BROUGHT THE HORSE INTO THEIR CITY, AND THEN . . .
AH, BUT THE POWHATAN DIDN'T BUILD ANY LARGE STRUCTURES.
HAVE YOU SEEN LAST OF THE MOHICANS? EVERYTHING IN IT IS INVENTED. A HOLLYWOOD MOVIE IS A PARADE OF ANACHRONISMS!

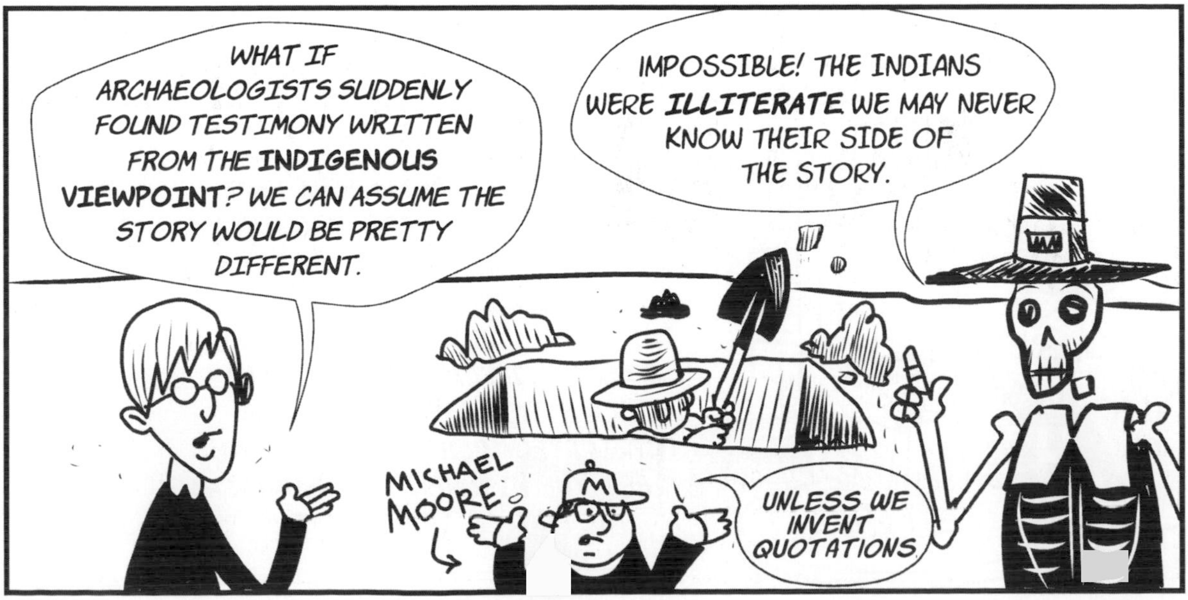
WHAT IF ARCHAEOLOGISTS SUDDENLY FOUND TESTIMONY WRITTEN FROM THE INDIGENOUS VIEWPOINT? WE CAN ASSUME THE STORY WOULD BE PRETTY DIFFERENT.
IMPOSSIBLE! THE INDIANS WERE ILLITERATE. WE MAY NEVER KNOW THEIR SIDE OF THE STORY.
MICHAEL MOORE
UNLESS WE INVENT QUOTATIONS.

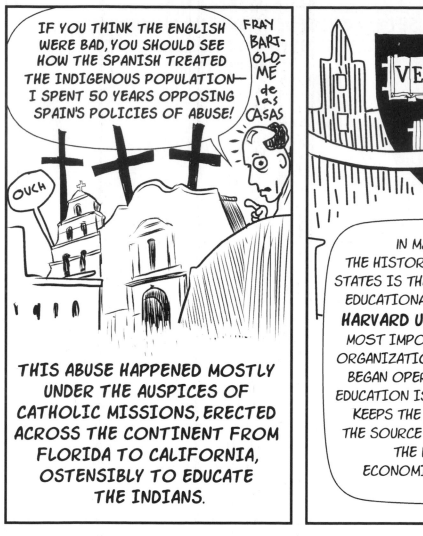

IF YOU THINK THE ENGLISH WERE BAD, YOU SHOULD SEE HOW THE SPANISH TREATED THE INDIGENOUS POPULATION—I SPENT 50 YEARS OPPOSING SPAIN'S POLICIES OF ABUSE!

FRAY BARTOLOME de las CASAS

OUCH

THIS ABUSE HAPPENED MOSTLY UNDER THE AUSPICES OF CATHOLIC MISSIONS, ERECTED ACROSS THE CONTINENT FROM FLORIDA TO CALIFORNIA, OSTENSIBLY TO EDUCATE THE INDIANS.

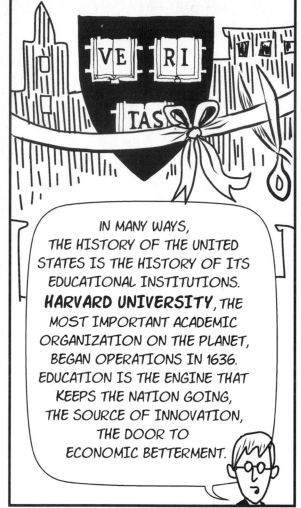

VE RI TAS

IN MANY WAYS, THE HISTORY OF THE UNITED STATES IS THE HISTORY OF ITS EDUCATIONAL INSTITUTIONS. **HARVARD UNIVERSITY**, THE MOST IMPORTANT ACADEMIC ORGANIZATION ON THE PLANET, BEGAN OPERATIONS IN 1636. EDUCATION IS THE ENGINE THAT KEEPS THE NATION GOING, THE SOURCE OF INNOVATION, THE DOOR TO ECONOMIC BETTERMENT.

Ye firste protest

IT IS IN THE CLASSROOM THAT HISTORIANS ARE MADE. AFTER ALL, WHAT IS A CLASSROOM? A **COLLECTIVE BRAIN** MADE OF MULTIPLE INTERDEPENDENT PARTS. BUT THE CLASSROOM CANNOT EXIST IN ISOLATION. IT NEEDS TO BE INTRICATELY CONNECTED TO THE STREET, THE KITCHEN, THE BEDROOM, THE CHURCH, THE SENATE ...

COLONISTS USING INDIAN IDEAS

SPEAKING OF EDUCATION, LET'S GET BACK TO OUR HISTORY LESSON.... WHAT KIND OF **ROUTINE** DID THE SETTLERS HAVE DURING THE **COLONIAL PERIOD**? IT WAS CERTAINLY A DEMANDING ONE. KEEPING THEMSELVES AND THEIR LOVED ONES ALIVE WAS HARD WORK, BUT IT PAID OFF. IN 1610, THERE WERE 3,800 SETTLERS IN THE NORTH AMERICAN COLONIES. FORTY YEARS LATER, THERE WERE 50,400.

WE TEND TO REGARD THESE EARLY AMERICANS AS WAX FIGURES IN A MUSEUM. BUT THAT'S THE WRONG APPROACH! THE COLONISTS DIDN'T HAVE SIMPLER LIVES THAN WE DO. THAT'S A **ROMANTIC VIEW!** ANY LIFE CAN BE SIMPLE OR COMPLICATED, DEPENDING ON ONE'S ATTITUDE TOWARD LIVING.

LOVE, SEX, AND CRIME EXHIBIT

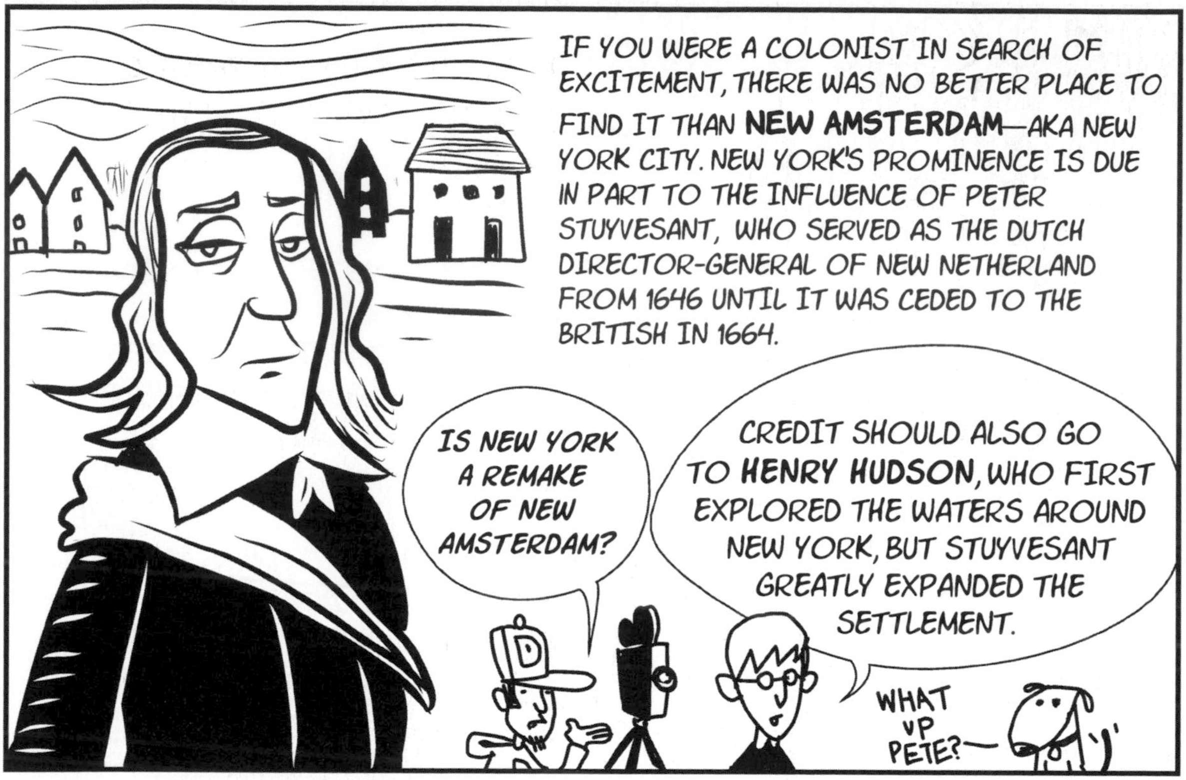
IF YOU WERE A COLONIST IN SEARCH OF EXCITEMENT, THERE WAS NO BETTER PLACE TO FIND IT THAN **NEW AMSTERDAM**—AKA NEW YORK CITY. NEW YORK'S PROMINENCE IS DUE IN PART TO THE INFLUENCE OF PETER STUYVESANT, WHO SERVED AS THE DUTCH DIRECTOR-GENERAL OF NEW NETHERLAND FROM 1646 UNTIL IT WAS CEDED TO THE BRITISH IN 1664.
IS NEW YORK A REMAKE OF NEW AMSTERDAM?
CREDIT SHOULD ALSO GO TO **HENRY HUDSON**, WHO FIRST EXPLORED THE WATERS AROUND NEW YORK, BUT STUYVESANT GREATLY EXPANDED THE SETTLEMENT.
D
WHAT UP PETE?

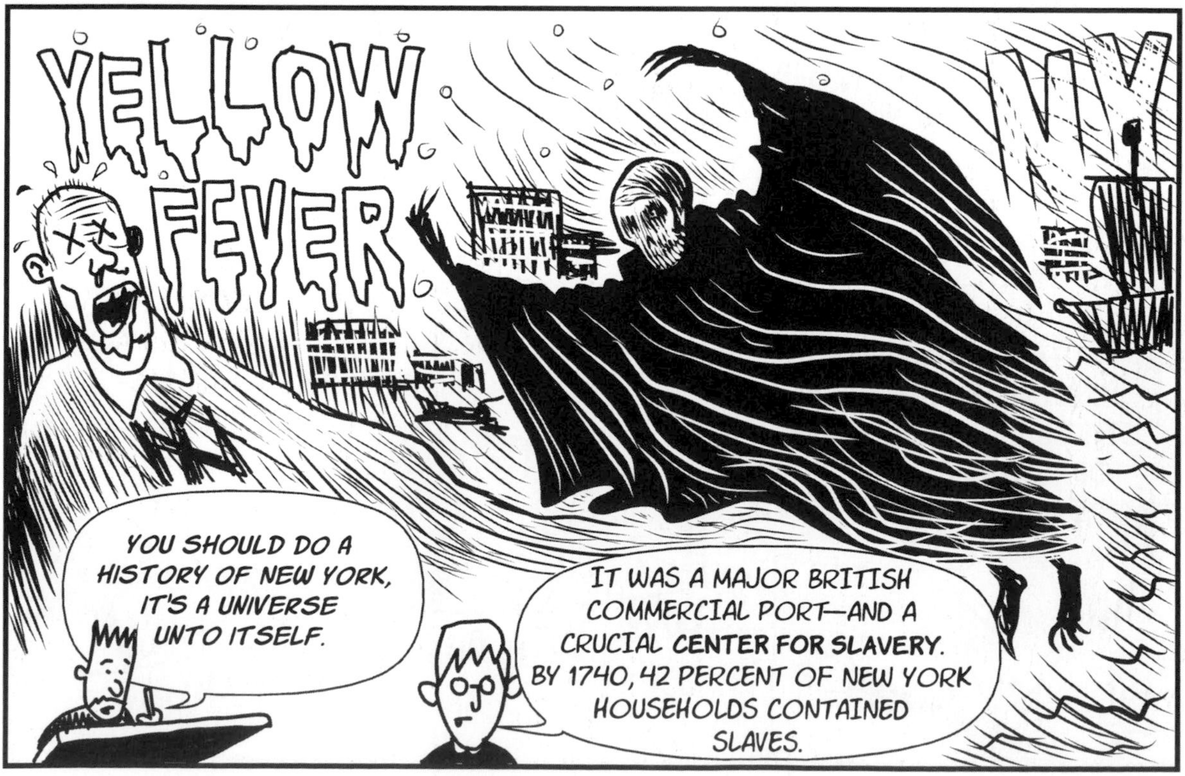
YELLOW FEVER
NY
YOU SHOULD DO A HISTORY OF NEW YORK, IT'S A UNIVERSE UNTO ITSELF.
IT WAS A MAJOR BRITISH COMMERCIAL PORT—AND A CRUCIAL **CENTER FOR SLAVERY**. BY 1740, 42 PERCENT OF NEW YORK HOUSEHOLDS CONTAINED SLAVES.

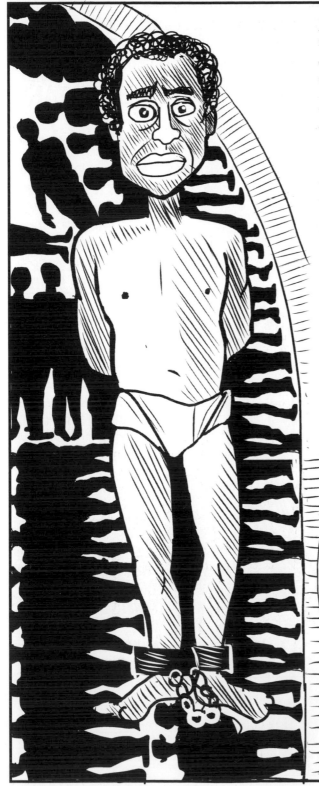

IN 1619, THE FIRST SHIPMENT OF AFRICAN SLAVES ARRIVED IN VIRGINIA. IN THE EIGHTEENTH CENTURY, THROUGH A SLAVE TRADING ROUTE CALLED **THE MIDDLE PASSAGE**, 6 MILLION AFRICANS WERE TRANSPORTED TO THE NEW WORLD. IT WAS A MASS RELOCATION OF EPIC PROPORTIONS. WHILE THE UNITED STATES WAS STILL BEING CONCEIVED, SLAVERY WAS CORRODING ITS INFRASTRUCTURE. A NATION FOUNDED ON PRINCIPLES OF JUSTICE AND FREEDOM WOULD SPEND ITS EARLY DECADES SUPPORTING **THE MORALLY BANKRUPT DOMINATION OF ONE RACE OVER ANOTHER.**

SLAVERY GOES BACK TO ANCIENT TIMES—IT'S FREQUENTLY MENTIONED IN THE BIBLE. AMERICANS ONLY TOOK SMALL STEPS TOWARD ABOLISHING IT UNTIL ABRAHAM LINCOLN SHOWED UP AND SAID, "FINITA LA COMMEDIA!"

RONNIE REAGAN

FREEDOM IS NEVER MORE THAN ONE GENERATION AWAY FROM EXTINCTION.

AYUBA SULEIMAN DIALLO

(AKA JOB BEN SOLOMON) WAS BORN IN GAMBIA, WEST AFRICA, IN 1701. HE CAME FROM A FAMILY OF MUSLIM RELIGIOUS LEADERS. CAPTURED BY HIS FELLOW AFRICANS, HE WAS BROUGHT TO THE **NEW WORLD** IN THE 1730S AS PART OF THE ATLANTIC SLAVE TRADE. AFTER ARRIVING IN ANNAPOLIS, HE WAS SOLD TO A PROPERTY OWNER AND PUT TO WORK ON A FARM ON KENT ISLAND, MARYLAND. UNABLE TO PHYSICALLY PERFORM HIS DUTIES, DIALLO RAN AWAY. HE WAS CAPTURED AND IMPRISONED AT THE KENT COUNTY COURTHOUSE, WHERE LAWYER THOMAS BLUETT DEFENDED HIM.

FREEDOM ISN'T FREE!

BLUETT RECOGNIZED THAT DIALLO WROTE ARTICULATELY IN ARABIC, AND ARRANGED TO PURCHASE HIM FROM HIS OWNER. IN 1733, HE TOOK DIALLO TO ENGLAND, WHERE THE FORMER SLAVE LEARNED ENGLISH AND WAS INTRODUCED TO PROMINENT FIGURES OF BRITISH SOCIETY. EVENTUALLY, DIALLO RETURNED TO HIS NATIVE GAMBIA. HE DIED IN 1773.

BASED ON CONVERSATIONS WITH DIALLO, BLUETT WROTE AN ACCOUNT OF THE FORMER SLAVE'S EXPERIENCES ENTITLED **SOME MEMOIRS OF THE LIFE OF JOB, THE SON OF SOLOMON THE HIGH PRIEST OF BOONDA IN AFRICA; WHO WAS A SLAVE ABOUT TWO YEARS IN MARYLAND; AND AFTERWARDS BEING BROUGHT TO ENGLAND, WAS SET FREE, AND SENT TO HIS NATIVE LAND IN THE YEAR 1734.** THE BOOK WAS ORIGINALLY PUBLISHED IN ENGLISH AND FRENCH. IN IT, BLUETT EMPHASIZES DETERMINISM—OR PROVIDENCE—AS THE DRIVING FORCE BEHIND DIALLO'S ORDEAL: "IT IS VERY HAPPY FOR US THAT THE DIRECTION OF **ALL EVENTS BELONGS TO GOD;** SO WE OUGHT TO TAKE ALL OPPORTUNITIES TO EXCITE AND STRENGTHEN IN OUR SELVES, AND OTHERS, A DUE SENSE OF HIS GOVERNMENT..."

BLUETT'S BOOK WAS AN EARLY EXAMPLE OF THE SLAVE NARRATIVE GENRE, IN WHICH THE LIFE STORIES OF INDIVIDUAL SLAVES WERE RECOUNTED AS A WAY OF EXPOSING THE EVILS OF THE SLAVE TRADE.

OFTEN CALLED AMERICA'S FIRST BLACK POET, **PHILLIS WHEATLEY** WAS BORN AROUND 1753, IN THE SAME REGION OF WEST AFRICA AS AYUBA SULEIMAN DIALLO. SHE CAME TO BOSTON AS A SLAVE WHEN SHE WAS A CHILD. IN 1761, SHE WAS PURCHASED BY JOHN WHEATLEY, A WEALTHY MERCHANT AND TAILOR WHO ALLOWED HER TO BE TUTORED BY HIS FAMILY.

A PIONEER OF AFRICAN AMERICAN LITERATURE, WHEATLEY PUBLISHED A BOOK OF POETRY IN 1773. CALLED **POEMS ON VARIOUS SUBJECTS, RELIGIOUS AND MORAL**, THE BOOK BECAME A GREAT SUCCESS, PRAISED BY CRITICS AND EVEN PUBLIC FIGURES SUCH AS GEORGE WASHINGTON. DUE TO HER REPUTATION AS A POET, WHEATLEY WAS SOON EMANCIPATED, BUT SHE CHOSE TO REMAIN WITH THE WHEATLEY FAMILY. SHE DIED IN 1784.

ON BEING BROUGHT FROM AFRICA TO AMERICA
BY PHILLIS WHEATLEY

'TWAS MERCY BROUGHT ME
FROM MY PAGAN LAND.
TAUGHT MY BENIGHTED SOUL
TO UNDERSTAND
THAT THERE'S A GOD,
THAT THERE'S A SAVIOUR TOO:
ONCE I REDEMPTION NEITHER
SOUGHT NOR KNEW.
SOME VIEW OUR SABLE RACE
WITH SCORNFUL EYE,
"THEIR COLOUR IS A DIABOLIC DIE."
REMEMBER, CHRISTIANS,
NEGROS, BLACK AS CAIN,
MAY BE REFIN'D, AND
JOIN TH'ANGELIC TRAIN.

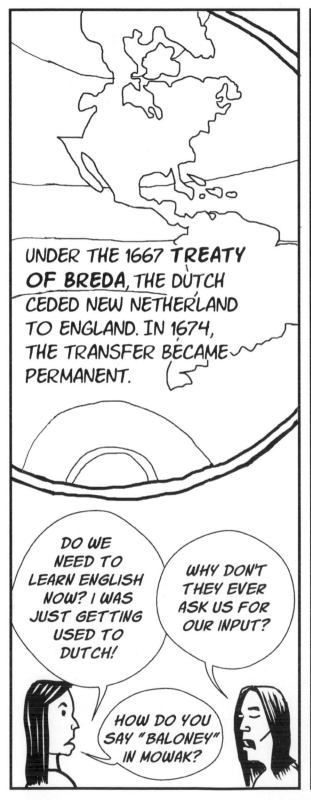

UNDER THE 1667 **TREATY OF BREDA**, THE DUTCH CEDED NEW NETHERLAND TO ENGLAND. IN 1674, THE TRANSFER BECAME PERMANENT.

DO WE NEED TO LEARN ENGLISH NOW? I WAS JUST GETTING USED TO DUTCH!

WHY DON'T THEY EVER ASK US FOR OUR INPUT?

HOW DO YOU SAY "BALONEY" IN MOWAK?

WE NEED A "DJANGO,"

VIRGINIA IS FOR SLAVERS

IN 1671, THERE WERE ABOUT 2,000 SLAVES IN VIRGINIA (POPULATION: 40,000).

MEANWHILE IN WHAT IS KNOWN TODAY AS THE SOUTHWEST...

WHILE SLAVES WERE SUFFERING ALL ALONG THE ATLANTIC COAST DURING THE COLONIAL ERA, SPANISH SETTLERS AND EXPLORERS WERE EXPANDING THEIR INFLUENCE ELSEWHERE ON THE NORTH AMERICAN CONTINENT. THE REGION KNOWN TODAY AS NEW MEXICO WAS SETTLED BY SPANISH EXPLORER **JUAN DE OÑATE**. IT BECAME A BASTION OF CATHOLICISM, THOUGH IT ALSO ATTRACTED A CONSTITUENCY OF SECRET JEWS, WHO NEEDED TO HIDE THEIR RELIGIOUS IDENTITY TO AVOID BEING CAUGHT AND TORTURED BY THE INQUISITION.

THIS SECRET JEWISH POPULATION IS THE SUBJECT OF THE GRAPHIC NOVEL **EL ILUMINADO**.

IN 1680, THE **PUEBLO INDIANS** AROUND SANTA FE REVOLTED AGAINST SPANISH RULE. IT WAS A VIOLENT REJECTION OF THE SPANISH RULERS AND THEIR INHUMANE TREATMENT OF THE NATIVES. IN THE END, THE REBELS KILLED FOUR HUNDRED SPANIARDS AND DROVE THE REST OUT OF THE REGION, THOUGH THE SPANISH WOULD COME BACK TO CONQUER IT TWELVE YEARS LATER.

CLASHES LIKE THIS ARE HOW THE NATION TOOK SHAPE. BY 1686, THE BRITISH HAD ESTABLISHED THE **DOMINION OF NEW ENGLAND**—A STRIP OF BRITISH LAND ON WHAT HAD PREVIOUSLY BEEN THE HOME OF MANY DIVERSE PEOPLES.

NEW YORK
NEW HAMPSHIRE
MASSACHUSETTS
RHODE ISLAND
CONNECTICUT
PENNSYLVANIA
NEW JERSEY
DELAWARE
MARYLAND
VIRGINIA
NORTH CAROLINA
SOUTH CAROLINA
GEORGIA
FUTURE TROUBLE SPOT ↓

EVENTUALLY, BRITISH POSSESSIONS IN NORTH AMERICA WERE DIVIDED INTO THIRTEEN COLONIES. NONE OF THE COLONIES COULD SURVIVE ON ITS OWN—THE POPULATION WAS SCATTERED, AND THERE WAS NO SENSE OF UNITY. CALL IT THE AGE OF DEPENDENCY.

LIFE IN THE BRITISH COLONIES WAS DOMINATED BY AN ETHOS OF **INTENSE LABOR**. IN A NATURAL ENVIRONMENT PERCEIVED AS SAVAGE, RELIGION HELPED ESTABLISH A REGIME OF STRICT MORALITY. THE EARLY COLONISTS FELT THAT EVERYTHING AROUND THEM WAS NEW —A NEW LAND, A NEW SELF, A NEW COMMUNITY.

COLONIAL TOWNS WERE CENTERED AROUND AN OPEN SPACE KNOWN AS THE **VILLAGE GREEN**. THE COLONISTS LIVED ON FARMS IN THE SURROUNDING AREAS—THE ONLY PLACE THEY MET REGULARLY WAS THE VILLAGE CHURCH. CHILDREN WERE OFTEN EDUCATED AT HOME, BY TEACHERS WHO MADE HOUSE CALLS, THOUGH PUBLIC SCHOOLS ALSO EXISTED. FAMILIES GREW CROPS SUCH AS CORN AND TOBACCO, WHICH THEY SOLD FOR MONEY OR CREDIT AT THE LOCAL MARKETPLACE. TYPICALLY, FAMILIES LIVED IN ONE- OR TWO-BEDROOM WOODEN HOUSES NO LARGER THAN SIXTEEN BY TWENTY FEET. THE KITCHEN, BARN, AND STORAGE BUILDINGS WERE SEPARATE FROM THE HOUSE. SLAVES LIVED IN THESE OUTBUILDINGS OR IN CABINS OF THEIR OWN.

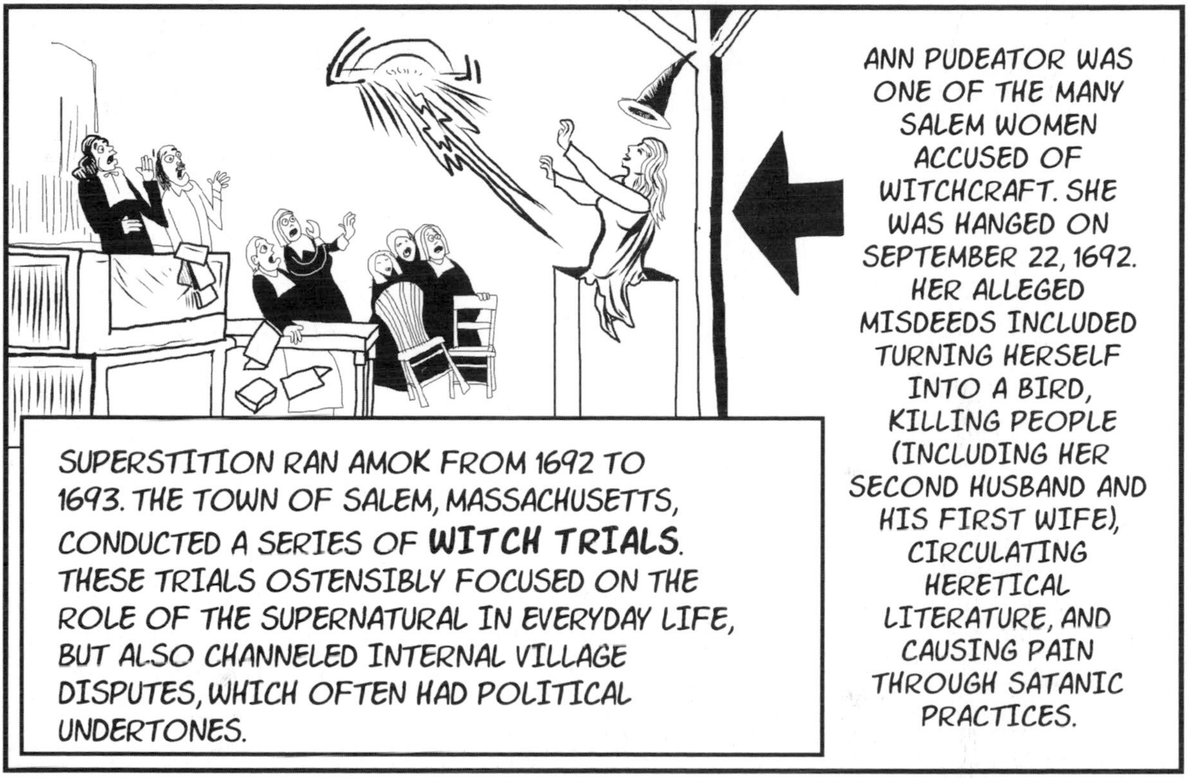
ANN PUDEATOR WAS ONE OF THE MANY SALEM WOMEN ACCUSED OF WITCHCRAFT. SHE WAS HANGED ON SEPTEMBER 22, 1692. HER ALLEGED MISDEEDS INCLUDED TURNING HERSELF INTO A BIRD, KILLING PEOPLE (INCLUDING HER SECOND HUSBAND AND HIS FIRST WIFE), CIRCULATING HERETICAL LITERATURE, AND CAUSING PAIN THROUGH SATANIC PRACTICES.
SUPERSTITION RAN AMOK FROM 1692 TO 1693. THE TOWN OF SALEM, MASSACHUSETTS, CONDUCTED A SERIES OF **WITCH TRIALS**. THESE TRIALS OSTENSIBLY FOCUSED ON THE ROLE OF THE SUPERNATURAL IN EVERYDAY LIFE, BUT ALSO CHANNELED INTERNAL VILLAGE DISPUTES, WHICH OFTEN HAD POLITICAL UNDERTONES.

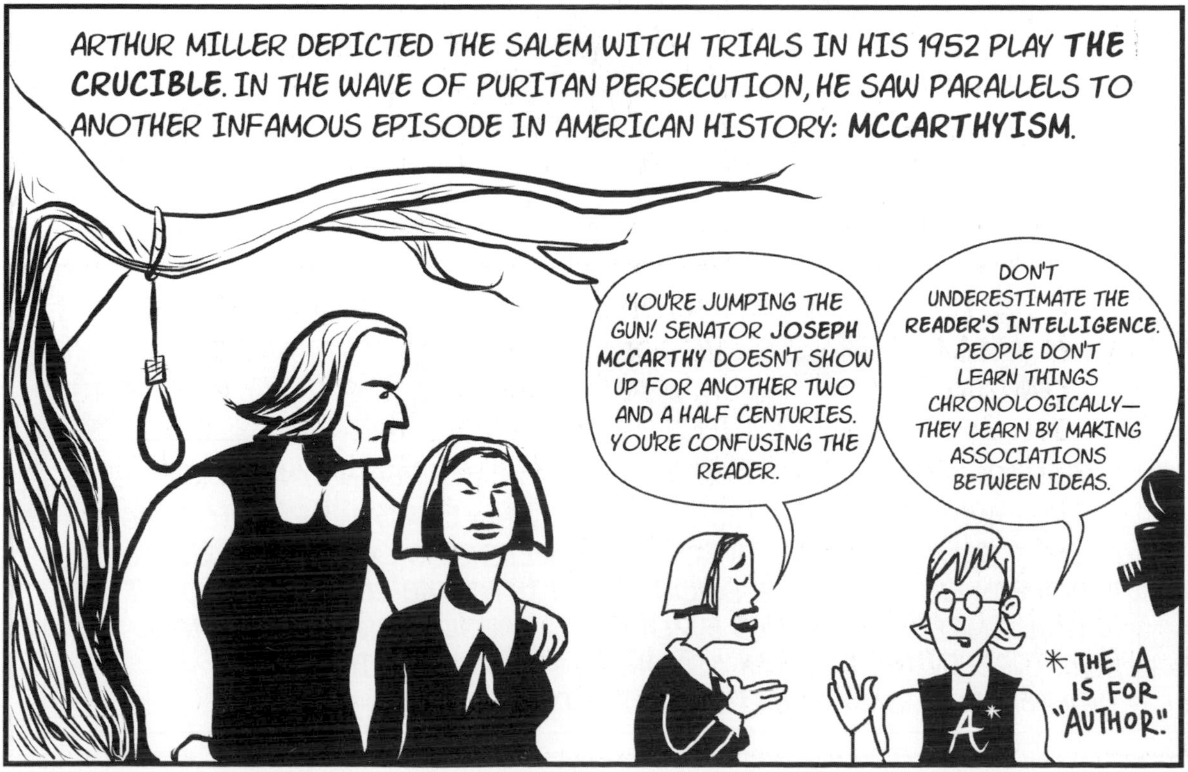
ARTHUR MILLER DEPICTED THE SALEM WITCH TRIALS IN HIS 1952 PLAY **THE CRUCIBLE**. IN THE WAVE OF PURITAN PERSECUTION, HE SAW PARALLELS TO ANOTHER INFAMOUS EPISODE IN AMERICAN HISTORY: **MCCARTHYISM**.
YOU'RE JUMPING THE GUN! SENATOR **JOSEPH MCCARTHY** DOESN'T SHOW UP FOR ANOTHER TWO AND A HALF CENTURIES. YOU'RE CONFUSING THE READER.
DON'T UNDERESTIMATE THE **READER'S INTELLIGENCE**. PEOPLE DON'T LEARN THINGS CHRONOLOGICALLY— THEY LEARN BY MAKING ASSOCIATIONS BETWEEN IDEAS.
A*
* THE A IS FOR "AUTHOR."

A DISPUTE BETWEEN GREAT BRITAIN AND THE BOURBON DYNASTY OF FRANCE AND SPAIN RESULTED IN THE **SEVEN YEARS' WAR**, WHICH RAGED FROM 1756 TO 1763. THE OVERSEAS TERRITORIES OF THESE MAJOR EUROPEAN EMPIRES WERE SOON DRAWN INTO THE CONFLICT, AND THE WAR ULTIMATELY WEAKENED EUROPE'S CONTROL OVER ITS COLONIAL HOLDINGS. IN THE BRITISH COLONIES, THOSE STRIVING FOR INDEPENDENCE SAW AN OPPORTUNITY TO SECEDE.

No. 265430
ONE THIRD OF A DOLLAR,
According to a Resolution of Congress passed at Philadelphia February 17. 1776.
MIND YOUR BUSINESS
ONE THIRD.

One Third of a DOLLAR.
Printed by Hall in Philadelphia

YEAH, UH, THANKS FOR THE HUNDRED BUT I THINK MY OLD BILLS ROCK.

FEDERAL
H84627985O1 82
100
BEN FRANKLIN

THE COLONIES STARTED TO PUSH FOR **SELF-DETERMINATION**, CAUSING GREAT BRITAIN TO TIGHTEN ITS GRIP. IN 1764, THE BRITISH PARLIAMENT FORBADE THE COLONIES FROM ISSUING THEIR **OWN CURRENCY**. A FEW MONTHS LATER IT ISSUED A TAX ON PRINTED MATERIAL. THEN IT WANTED THE COLONIES TO PROVIDE HOUSING AND FOOD TO BRITISH TROOPS.

WE ARE LIKE SOOO BETTER OFF WITHOUT YOU GUYS.

THINGS SOON GOT EVEN WORSE FOR THE COLONISTS. IN *1766*, THE BRITISH PARLIAMENT DECREED THAT IT HAD FULL POWER TO MAKE LAWS AND STATUTES TO BIND THE PEOPLE IN THE COLONIES.

IN 1773, COLONISTS PROTESTED AGAINST INCREASED TAXES—AND THEIR LACK OF REPRESENTATION IN THE BRITISH GOVERNMENT—BY THROWING TEA INTO BOSTON HARBOR. THE EVENT CAME TO BE KNOWN AS THE **BOSTON TEA PARTY.**

CIVIL DISOBEDIENCE IS A LEITMOTIF IN AMERICAN LIFE. AS THE SAYING GOES, IF YOU AREN'T APPALLED BY CURRENT EVENTS, IT'S BECAUSE YOU AREN'T PAYING ATTENTION. BEING APPALLED MEANS YOU DISSENT, AND DISSENT IS ESSENTIAL TO PROGRESS—TURNING THAT DISSENT INTO ACTION IS THE FIRST STEP TOWARD CHANGE. OF COURSE, WE SHOULD ALWAYS MAKE SURE THAT SUCH ACTION IS **NONVIOLENT** IN NATURE.

ARE THERE OCCASIONS WHEN VIOLENCE IS JUSTIFIED?

IN MY OPINION, NO, NEVER—ALTHOUGH VIOLENCE OFTEN OCCURS AS A RESULT OF OPEN DISSENT.

THE BOSTON TEA PARTY WAS THE CLIMAX OF A RESISTANCE MOVEMENT. ITS ECHOES WOULD PROVE TO BE LONG LASTING, FOR IT WAS THE BEGINNING OF THE AMERICAN REVOLUTION.

IT WOULD TAKE DECADES FOR SLAVERY TO BE ERADICATED ON THE CONTINENT, BUT **ABOLITIONIST** DREAMS WERE VERY MUCH ALIVE, EVEN IN THE LATE COLONIAL ERA. MASSACHUSETTS AND PENNSYLVANIA, FOR EXAMPLE, BOTH HAD MANY RESIDENTS WHO SUPPORTED THE EMANCIPATION OF SLAVES. NEVERTHELESS, SLAVERY PROVED DIFFICULT TO GET RID OF, CHIEFLY FOR ECONOMIC REASONS—SLAVERY, AFTER ALL, WAS AN ENGINE OF CAPITAL.

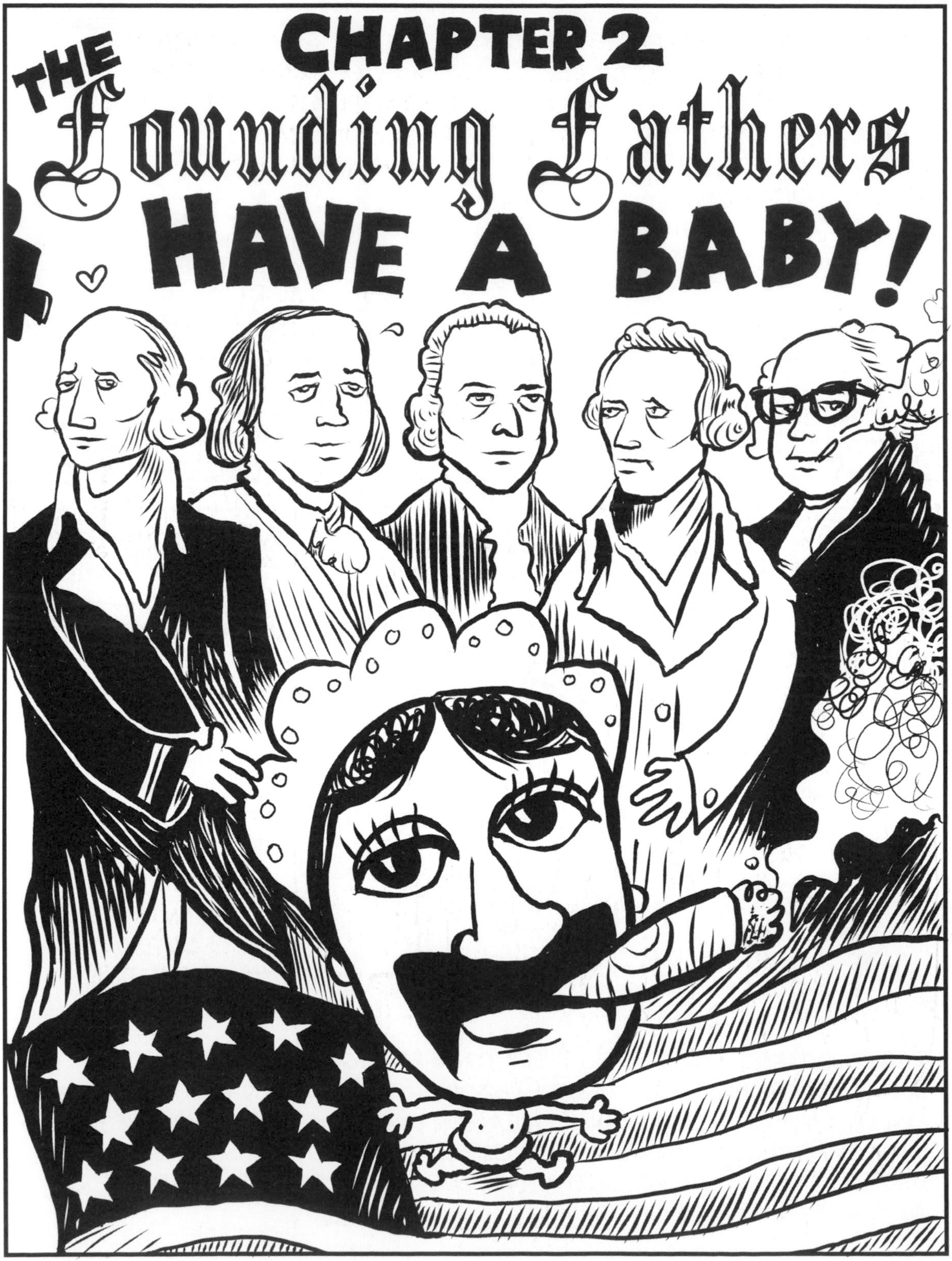
CHAPTER 2
THE Founding Fathers
HAVE A BABY!

EVERY SO OFTEN, THE CHANCE ENCOUNTER OF A GROUP OF INDIVIDUALS ALTERS HISTORY. IN THE SECOND HALF OF THE EIGHTEENTH CENTURY, THE GATHERING OF THE MEN WHO CAME TO BE KNOWN AS THE **FOUNDING FATHERS**, MEN OF POLITICAL SAVVY AND PHILOSOPHICAL INSIGHT, PLAYED A CRUCIAL ROLE IN ESTABLISHING THE PRINCIPLES ON WHICH THE NEW COUNTRY WOULD BE BASED.

THEY WERE A DIVERSE BUNCH. **BENJAMIN FRANKLIN**, IN PARTICULAR, WORE MANY HATS: POLITICIAN, PRINTER, POSTMASTER, INVENTOR, MUSICIAN, DIPLOMAT, AND SATIRIST. IN SHORT, HE WAS A POLYMATH.

41

GEORGE WASHINGTON WAS A FEARLESS COMMANDER IN CHIEF, AS SHREWD IN BATTLE AS HE WAS WISE IN POLITICS. **JOHN ADAMS** WAS THE CONSCIENCE OF THE REVOLUTION. **THOMAS JEFFERSON** WAS A FIRST-RATE WRITER. **JOHN JAY** WAS A PROPONENT OF CENTRALIZED GOVERNMENT. **JAMES MADISON** AUTHORED THE BILL OF RIGHTS AND WAS INSTRUMENTAL IN THE CREATION OF THE CONSTITUTION. **ALEXANDER HAMILTON** WAS AN ECONOMIST AND POLITICAL PHILOSOPHER—A CHAMPION OF THE NATIONAL BANK AND THE FIRST SECRETARY OF THE TREASURY.

OF COURSE THEY WEREN'T PERFECT—FAR FROM IT. JEFFERSON CHAMPIONED JUSTICE AND EQUALITY, YET WAS AN ACTIVE SLAVEHOLDER AND EVEN FATHERED A CHILD WITH HIS SLAVE MISTRESS, SALLY HEMINGS. HAMILTON RESIGNED FROM OFFICE AFTER AN EXTRAMARITAL AFFAIR BECAME PUBLIC, AND MANY OF THE FOUNDING FATHERS ENGAGED IN BACKSTABBING.

ON APRIL 19, 1775, THE TENSIONS BETWEEN BRITAIN AND THE COLONIES REACHED A BOILING POINT. FIGHTING BROKE OUT, SOON EXPANDING INTO ALL-OUT WAR. THE **REVOLUTIONARY WAR** WOULD ULTIMATELY LAST EIGHT YEARS, AND WOULD INVOLVE NOT ONLY THE UNITED STATES AND BRITAIN, BUT ALSO SPAIN, FRANCE, THE DUTCH REPUBLIC, THE VERMONT REPUBLIC, GERMAN AUXILIARIES, AND INDIAN TRIBES SUCH AS THE MOHAWK, SENECA, AND CHEROKEE.

AT THE WAR'S HEIGHT, 35,000 CONTINENTAL SOLDIERS FOUGHT AGAINST 56,000 BRITISH SOLDIERS. **AMERICAN CASUALTIES** TOTALED AROUND 50,000 DEAD AND WOUNDED VERSUS ALMOST 40,000 ON THE BRITISH SIDE.

AT FIRST, **BOSTON** WAS AT THE **CENTER OF THE WAR.** BUT THE FIGHTING SOON MOVED SOUTH AND WEST TO NEW YORK, NEW JERSEY, PENNSYLVANIA—AND EVENTUALLY NORTH CAROLINA, GEORGIA, VIRGINIA, OHIO, AND ILLINOIS. THE WAR ALSO BECAME AN INTERNATIONAL CONFLICT, AS AMERICA GARNERED THE SUPPORT OF THE FRENCH, SPANISH, AND DUTCH.

WHEN IN THE COURSE OF HUMAN EVENTS, IT BECOMES **NECESSARY** FOR ONE PEOPLE TO DISSOLVE THE POLITICAL BANDS WHICH HAVE CONNECTED THEM WITH ANOTHER, AND TO ASSUME AMONG THE POWERS OF THE EARTH, THE **SEPARATE AND EQUAL STATION** TO WHICH THE **LAWS OF NATURE** AND OF **NATURE'S GOD** ENTITLE THEM, A DECENT RESPECT TO THE OPINIONS OF MANKIND REQUIRES THAT THEY SHOULD DECLARE THE CAUSES WHICH IMPEL THEM TO THE SEPARATION ...

CAN I RECITE THE DECLARATION OF INDEPENDENCE IN SPANGLISH?

THIS IS THE IMAGE THAT ALWAYS POPS UP IN MY MIND WHEN I THINK OF THE REVOLUTION: **WASHINGTON CROSSING THE DELAWARE**, ON THE NIGHT OF DECEMBER 25, 1776. THE IMAGE COMES FROM THE 1851 PAINTING BY GERMAN AMERICAN ARTIST EMANUEL GOTTLIEB LEUTZE.

BLIND FAITH IN YOUR LEADERS WILL GET YOU KILLED...

BRUCE SPRINGSTEEN ← THE BOSS

THE BOSSY →

BUT MEDIA INFORMATION IS OFTEN **ERRONEOUS**. FOR INSTANCE, IN THE PAINTING WASHINGTON CARRIES THE ORIGINAL AMERICAN FLAG, BUT THIS FLAG WOULDN'T BE CREATED UNTIL 1777.

WHY WAS WASHINGTON CROSSING THE DELAWARE ANYWAY?

TO GET TO THE OTHER SIDE.

FOR THE MOST PART, NORTH AMERICA'S **INDIAN NATIONS**—INCLUDING THE IROQUOIS, THE SHAWNEE, AND THE CHICKAMAUGA—SIDED WITH THE BRITISH AGAINST THE AMERICAN COLONISTS, WHO THEY SAW AS RAPACIOUS INVADERS.

THE WAR ENDED ON SEPTEMBER 3, 1783, WITH THE FORMAL SIGNING OF THE **TREATY OF PARIS**. THE BRITISH AGREED TO WITHDRAW FROM A LARGE SECTION OF NORTH AMERICA, GIVING VAST TRACTS OF NATIVE LAND TO THE UNITED STATES WITHOUT CONSULTING THE INDIAN TRIBES THAT HAD SUPPORTED THEM.

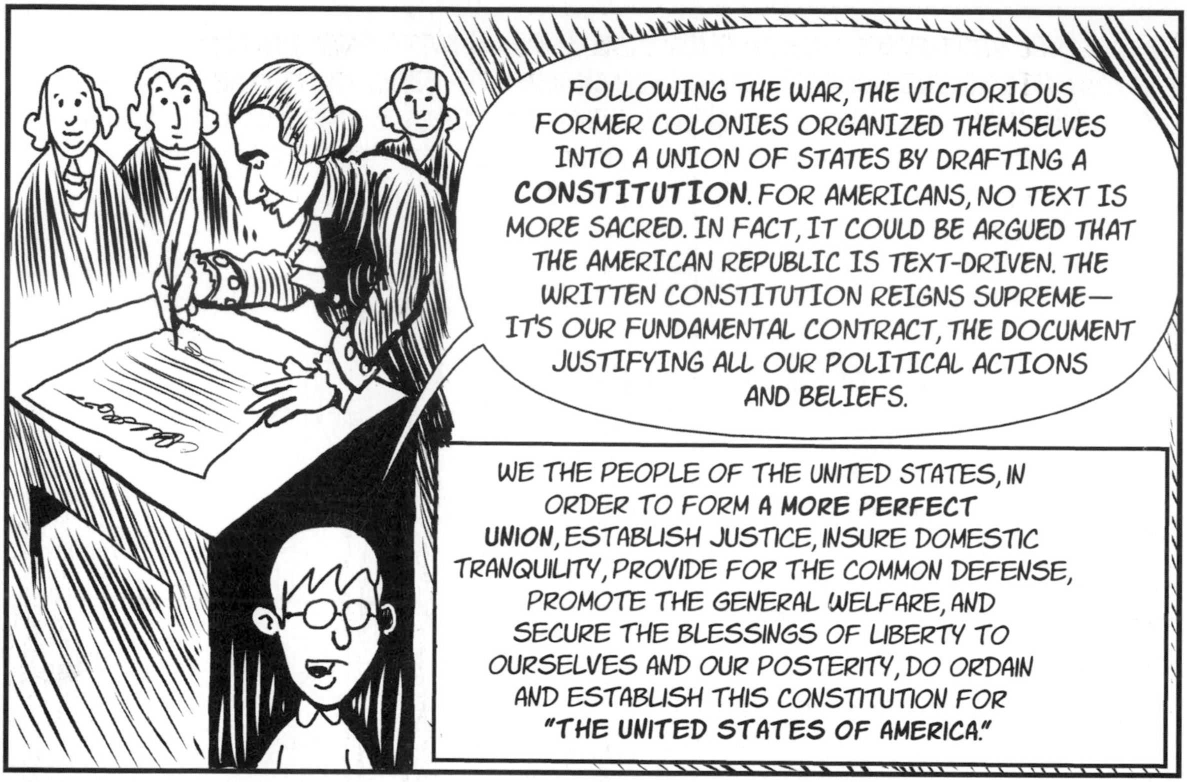
FOLLOWING THE WAR, THE VICTORIOUS FORMER COLONIES ORGANIZED THEMSELVES INTO A UNION OF STATES BY DRAFTING A **CONSTITUTION**. FOR AMERICANS, NO TEXT IS MORE SACRED. IN FACT, IT COULD BE ARGUED THAT THE AMERICAN REPUBLIC IS TEXT-DRIVEN. THE WRITTEN CONSTITUTION REIGNS SUPREME— IT'S OUR FUNDAMENTAL CONTRACT, THE DOCUMENT JUSTIFYING ALL OUR POLITICAL ACTIONS AND BELIEFS.
WE THE PEOPLE OF THE UNITED STATES, IN ORDER TO FORM **A MORE PERFECT UNION**, ESTABLISH JUSTICE, INSURE DOMESTIC TRANQUILITY, PROVIDE FOR THE COMMON DEFENSE, PROMOTE THE GENERAL WELFARE, AND SECURE THE BLESSINGS OF LIBERTY TO OURSELVES AND OUR POSTERITY, DO ORDAIN AND ESTABLISH THIS CONSTITUTION FOR **"THE UNITED STATES OF AMERICA."**

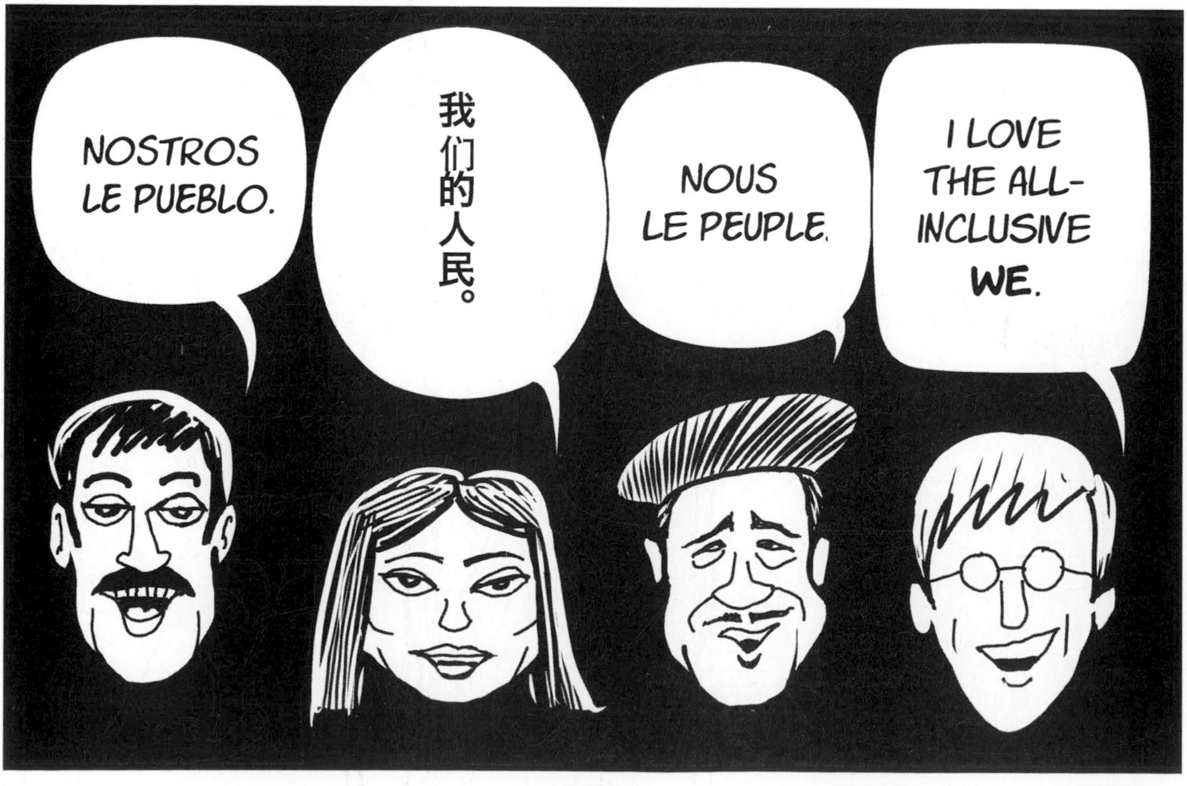
NOSTROS LE PUEBLO.
我们的人民。
NOUS LE PEUPLE.
I LOVE THE ALL-INCLUSIVE **WE**.

STILL, NOT EVERYONE WAS ON BOARD WITH THE CONSTITUTION AT FIRST. THEY NEEDED TO BE CONVINCED. BETWEEN OCTOBER 1787 AND AUGUST 1788, **ALEXANDER HAMILTON**, JAMES MADISON, AND **JOHN JAY** WROTE 85 ARTICLES—KNOWN AS THE **FEDERALIST PAPERS**—PROMOTING THE RATIFICATION OF THE CONSTITUTION.

THE

FEDERALIST:

A COLLECTION OF

ESSAYS,

WRITTEN IN FAVOUR OF THE

NEW CONSTITUTION,

AS AGREED UPON BY THE

FEDERAL CONVENTION,

SEPTEMBER 17, 1787.

DID ANYBODY GET SNACKS?

I HOPE NO ONE EVER MIS-INTERPRETS THIS.

JOKES! THE AUTHOR SAYS WE NEED MORE JOKES!

LIKE THE FRENCH REVOLUTION OF 1789, THE AMERICAN REVOLUTION WAS A HIGHLIGHT OF THE ANTIMONARCHIC AGE, WHEN ORDINARY PEOPLE SEIZED POLITICAL POWER FROM KINGS AND QUEENS. THE IDEAS OF THE ENLIGHTENMENT NURTURED THESE MOVEMENTS, CREATING AN ATMOSPHERE IN WHICH **PERSONAL FREEDOM** AND THE RIGHTS OF THE INDIVIDUAL TOOK CENTER STAGE. FOR PERHAPS THE FIRST TIME IN HISTORY, HUMANS AND THEIR INTELLECTUAL POWERS WERE AT THE CENTER OF CREATION.

ONE EXTRAORDINARY CHARACTER FROM THIS TIME WAS **HECTOR ST. JOHN DE CRÈVECOEUR**, BORN IN NORMANDY, FRANCE, IN 1735. DURING THE FRENCH AND INDIAN WAR, HE USED HIS CARTOGRAPHY SKILLS TO SURVEY AND MAP FRENCH LANDS IN CANADA. AFTER THE WAR WOUND DOWN IN 1759, HE MOVED TO ULSTER COUNTY, NEW YORK, WHERE HE BECAME A NATURALIZED CITIZEN.

A LOYALIST DURING THE AMERICAN REVOLUTION, CRÈVECOEUR LEFT THE COUNTRY IN 1780, TAKING WITH HIM A MANUSCRIPT WRITTEN IN ENGLISH ABOUT HIS EXPERIENCES IN THE UNITED STATES. TWO YEARS LATER, THE MANUSCRIPT WAS PUBLISHED AS **LETTERS FROM AN AMERICAN FARMER**. IN HIS BOOK, HE ASKED, PROPHETICALLY, "WHAT THEN IS THE AMERICAN, THIS NEW MAN?" CRÈVECOEUR RETURNED TO THE UNITED STATES IN 1783 AS A FRENCH CONSUL, REMAINING IN THE COUNTRY FOR SEVEN YEARS. HE DIED IN SARCELLES, NEAR PARIS, IN 1813.

"WHENCE CAME ALL THESE PEOPLE? THEY ARE A MIXTURE OF ENGLISH, SCOTCH, IRISH, FRENCH, DUTCH, GERMANS, AND SWEDES. ... WHAT THEN IS THE AMERICAN, THIS NEW MAN? HE IS EITHER A EUROPEAN, OR THE DESCENDANT OF A EUROPEAN. ... HE IS AN AMERICAN, WHO LEAVING BEHIND HIM ALL HIS ANCIENT PREJUDICES AND MANNERS, RECEIVES NEW ONES FROM THE NEW MODE OF LIFE HE HAS EMBRACED, THE NEW GOVERNMENT HE OBEYS, AND THE NEW RANK HE HOLDS."
   —HECTOR ST. JOHN DE CRÈVECOEUR,
   LETTERS FROM AN AMERICAN FARMER

ARGUABLY THE MOST INFLUENTIAL PERSON IN THE EARLY REPUBLIC, IF ALSO ONE OF THE MOST FLAWED, WAS **THOMAS JEFFERSON**. AT DIFFERENT TIMES, HE SERVED AS A DELEGATE TO THE CONTINENTAL CONGRESS, THE GOVERNOR OF VIRGINIA, THE U.S. MINISTER TO FRANCE, AND EVEN THE FIRST SECRETARY OF STATE. HE WAS ALSO THE PRINCIPAL AUTHOR OF THE DECLARATION OF INDEPENDENCE AND BECAME THE COUNTRY'S THIRD PRESIDENT.

GEORGE WASHINGTON DIED ON DECEMBER 14, 1799. IN HIS WILL, HE ORDERED THAT ALL 124 OF HIS SLAVES BE FREED THE MOMENT HIS WIFE, MARTHA, DIED. AS IT TURNED OUT, SHE FREED THEM EARLY— IN 1801, EIGHTEEN MONTHS BEFORE HER DEATH.

LET MY SLAVES GO WHEN MARTHA DIES . . .

MY STARS! HE SOUNDS DELIRIOUS. BETTER KEEP SLAVERY GOING FOR A WHILE.

A GESTURE OF EMPATHY! ACCORDING TO THE U.S. CENSUS, THERE WERE 893,602 SLAVES IN THE UNITED STATES IN 1800.

WHAT A MELODRAMA! YOU SHOULD ADD MUSIC IN THE BACKGROUND.

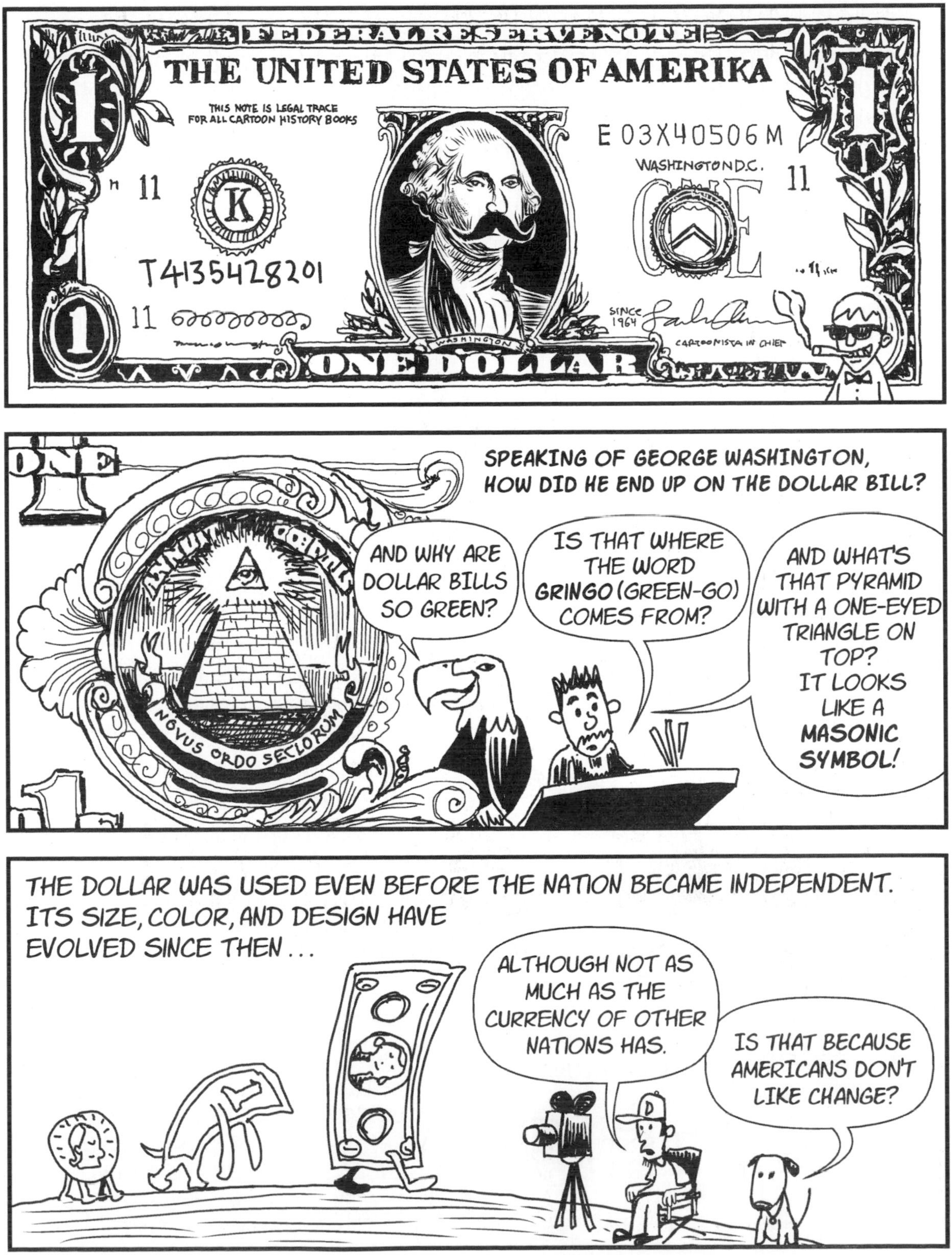

FEDERAL RESERVE NOTE
THE UNITED STATES OF AMERIKA
THIS NOTE IS LEGAL TRACE FOR ALL CARTOON HISTORY BOOKS
E 03X40506 M
WASHINGTON D.C.
K
T4135428201
SINCE 1964
CARTOONISTA IN CHIEF
WASHINGTON
ONE DOLLAR
SPEAKING OF GEORGE WASHINGTON, HOW DID HE END UP ON THE DOLLAR BILL?
AND WHY ARE DOLLAR BILLS SO GREEN?
IS THAT WHERE THE WORD **GRINGO** (GREEN-GO) COMES FROM?
AND WHAT'S THAT PYRAMID WITH A ONE-EYED TRIANGLE ON TOP? IT LOOKS LIKE A **MASONIC SYMBOL!**
NOVUS ORDO SECLORUM
THE DOLLAR WAS USED EVEN BEFORE THE NATION BECAME INDEPENDENT. ITS SIZE, COLOR, AND DESIGN HAVE EVOLVED SINCE THEN . . .
ALTHOUGH NOT AS MUCH AS THE CURRENCY OF OTHER NATIONS HAS.
IS THAT BECAUSE AMERICANS DON'T LIKE CHANGE?

JEFFERSON WAS CONCERNED LESS WITH DOLLAR BILLS THAN WITH BANKS, WHICH HE SAW AS A **THREAT TO DEMOCRACY**. IN HIS VIEW, BANKS WERE BLOODSUCKERS THAT UNDERMINED INDIVIDUAL FREEDOM. HE BELIEVED THAT THE INCURRING OF DEBT WAS A SERIOUS HINDRANCE TO PROGRESS BECAUSE IT GAVE PEOPLE A FICTITIOUS IDEA OF HOW MUCH CAPITAL THEY ACTUALLY POSSESSED.

"I CONTEMPLATE [BANKING] AS A BLOT LEFT IN ALL OUR CONSTITUTIONS, WHICH, IF NOT COVERED, WILL END IN THEIR DESTRUCTION."

JEFFERSON COULD BE MERCILESS WHEN IT CAME TO PRESERVING THE COUNTRY HE HAD HELPED TO CREATE. HE ARGUED THAT SACRIFICING A HANDFUL OF PEOPLE FOR THE GREATER GOOD WAS JUSTIFIED AND THAT GOVERNMENTS SHOULD BE AFRAID OF THEIR PEOPLE. IN A LETTER TO **JAMES MADISON**, DATED JANUARY 30, 1787, HE WROTE:

I TOLD YOU: AMERICA RUNS ON VIOLENCE.

"**A LITTLE REBELLION**, NOW AND THEN, IS A GOOD THING, AND AS NECESSARY IN THE POLITICAL WORLD AS STORMS IN THE PHYSICAL.... IT IS A MEDICINE NECESSARY FOR THE SOUND HEALTH OF GOVERNMENT."

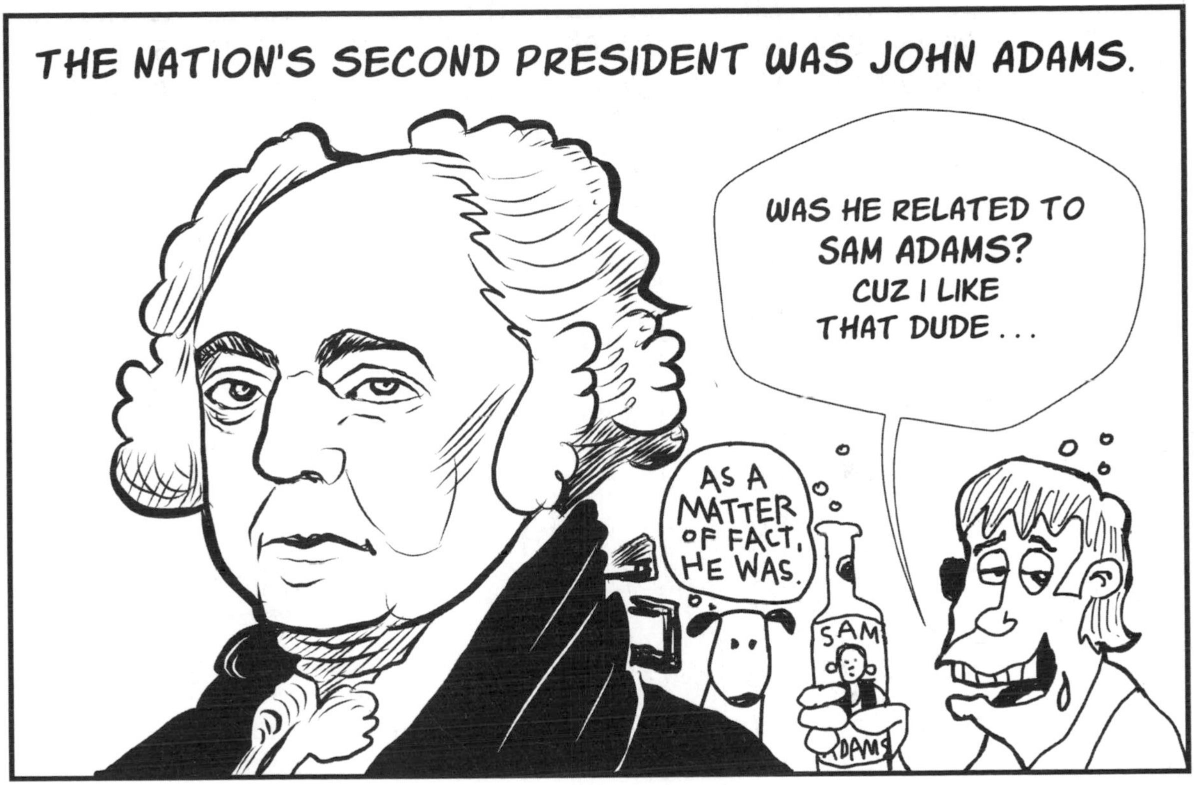
THE NATION'S SECOND PRESIDENT WAS JOHN ADAMS.
WAS HE RELATED TO SAM ADAMS? CUZ I LIKE THAT DUDE . . .
AS A MATTER OF FACT, HE WAS.
SAM ADAMS

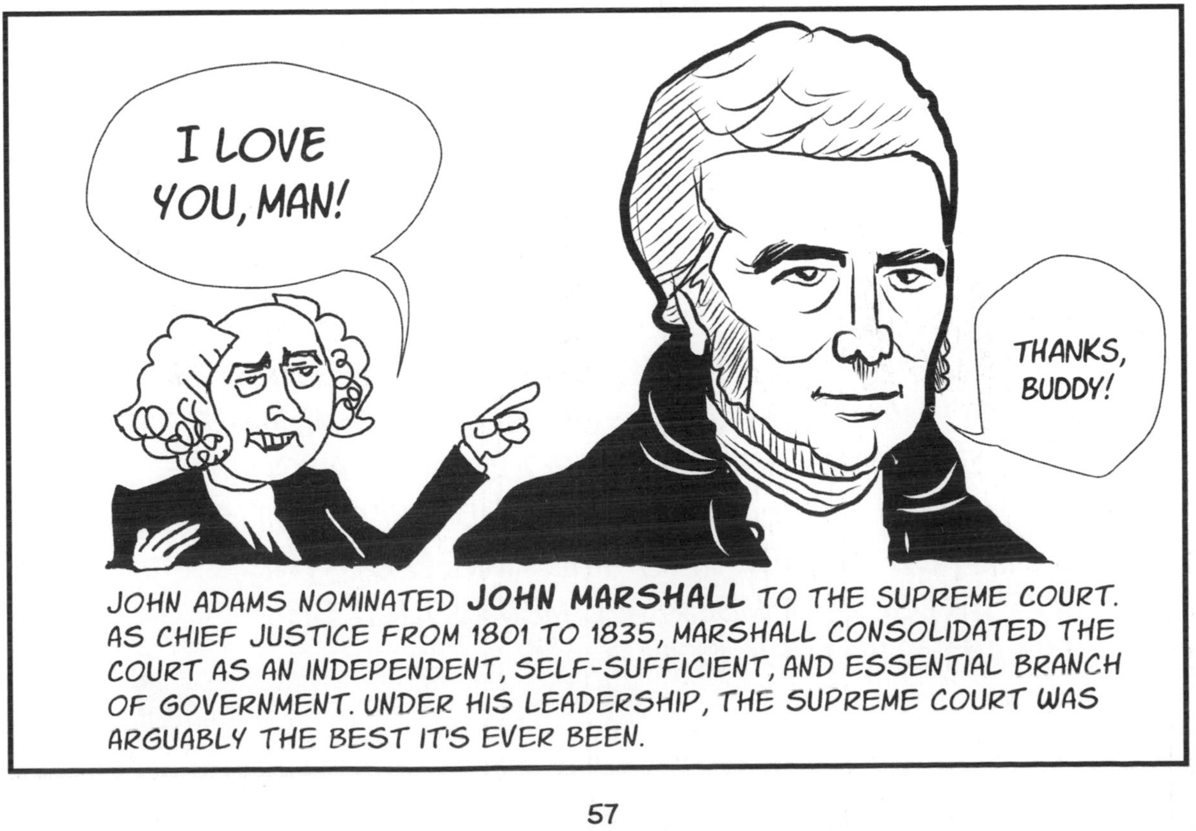
I LOVE YOU, MAN!
THANKS, BUDDY!

JOHN ADAMS NOMINATED **JOHN MARSHALL** TO THE SUPREME COURT. AS CHIEF JUSTICE FROM 1801 TO 1835, MARSHALL CONSOLIDATED THE COURT AS AN INDEPENDENT, SELF-SUFFICIENT, AND ESSENTIAL BRANCH OF GOVERNMENT. UNDER HIS LEADERSHIP, THE SUPREME COURT WAS ARGUABLY THE BEST IT'S EVER BEEN.

ONE OF THE MOST CAPTIVATING STORIES OF THE REVOLUTIONARY PERIOD IS THAT OF THE LOVE BETWEEN **JOHN ADAMS** AND HIS WIFE, **ABIGAIL**. SHE WROTE EXCELLENT LETTERS, AND WAS ALSO THE MOTHER OF JOHN QUINCY ADAMS, WHO BECAME THE SIXTH PRESIDENT. JOHN SOUGHT HER ADVICE WHILE HE WAS IN PHILADELPHIA DURING THE CONTINENTAL CONGRESS —AND HER VIEWS ON THE POLITICAL ROLE OF WOMEN WERE FAR AHEAD OF THEIR TIME.

ABIGAIL TO JOHN, MARCH 13, 1776:
"I LONG TO HEAR THAT YOU HAVE DECLARED AN INDEPENDENCY. AND, BY THE WAY, IN THE NEW CODE OF LAWS WHICH I SUPPOSE IT WILL BE NECESSARY FOR YOU TO MAKE, I **DESIRE** YOU WOULD REMEMBER THE LADIES AND BE MORE GENEROUS AND FAVORABLE TO THEM THAN YOUR **ANCESTORS**. DO NOT PUT SUCH **UNLIMITED POWER** INTO THE HANDS OF THE HUSBANDS. REMEMBER, ALL MEN WOULD BE **TYRANTS** IF THEY COULD..."

JOHN TO ABIGAIL, APRIL 14, 1776:
"AS TO YOUR EXTRAORDINARY CODE OF LAWS, I CANNOT BUT LAUGH. WE HAVE BEEN TOLD THAT OUR STRUGGLE HAS LOOSENED THE BONDS OF GOVERNMENT EVERYWHERE; THAT **CHILDREN** AND APPRENTICES WERE **DISOBEDIENT**; THAT SCHOOLS AND COLLEGES WERE GROWN TURBULENT; THAT INDIANS SLIGHTED THEIR GUARDIANS, AND NEGROES GREW INSOLENT TO THEIR MASTERS. BUT YOUR LETTER WAS THE FIRST INTIMATION THAT ANOTHER TRIBE, MORE NUMEROUS AND POWERFUL THAN ALL THE REST, WERE GROWN DISCONTENTED. . . . DEPEND UPON IT, WE KNOW BETTER THAN TO REPEAL OUR MASCULINE SYSTEMS. ALTHOUGH THEY ARE IN FULL FORCE, YOU KNOW THEY ARE LITTLE MORE THAN THEORY . . ."

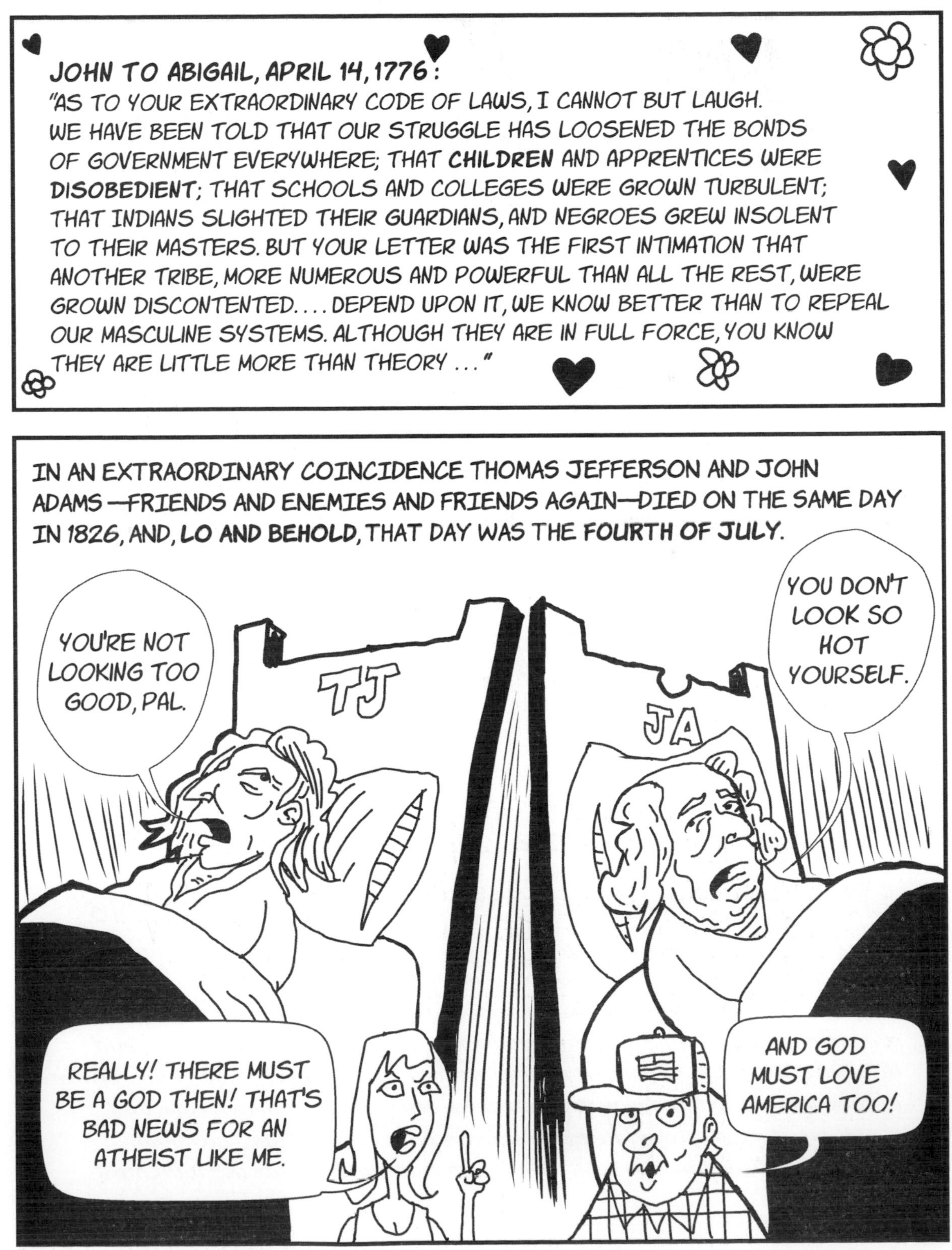
IN AN EXTRAORDINARY COINCIDENCE THOMAS JEFFERSON AND JOHN ADAMS—FRIENDS AND ENEMIES AND FRIENDS AGAIN—DIED ON THE SAME DAY IN 1826, AND, LO AND BEHOLD, THAT DAY WAS THE FOURTH OF JULY.
YOU'RE NOT LOOKING TOO GOOD, PAL.
YOU DON'T LOOK SO HOT YOURSELF.
TJ
JA
REALLY! THERE MUST BE A GOD THEN! THAT'S BAD NEWS FOR AN ATHEIST LIKE ME.
AND GOD MUST LOVE AMERICA TOO!

IMMEDIATELY AFTER THE CREATION OF THE REPUBLIC, **THE FIRST PARTY SYSTEM** WAS ESTABLISHED. IT WAS REPRESENTED BY TWO OPPOSING POLITICAL PARTIES—THE FEDERALIST PARTY, CREATED PRINCIPALLY BY ALEXANDER HAMILTON, AND THE DEMOCRATIC-REPUBLICAN PARTY, CREATED BY THOMAS JEFFERSON AND JAMES MADISON. IT LASTED FROM 1792 TO 1824.

JEFFERSON WROTE IN A LETTER DATED FEBRUARY 12, 1798:

Two political Sects have arisen within the U.S., the one believing that the executive branch is the branch of our government which the most needs support; the other that, like the analogous branch in the English Government, it is already too strong for the republican parts of the Constitution; and therefore in equivocal cases they incline to the legislative powers: the former of these are called federalists, sometimes aristocrats or monocrats, and sometimes tories ... the latter are stiled republicans, whigs, jacobins, anarchists, disorganizers, etc. These terms are in familiar use with most persons.

WHILE AMERICA'S POLITICAL SYSTEM WAS TAKING SHAPE, THE COUNTRY WAS ALSO INDULGING ITS **SWEET TOOTH**. THE FOUNDING FATHERS ARE KNOWN TO HAVE EATEN SWEETS AVIDLY. DOLLY MADISON, WIFE OF JAMES MADISON, APPARENTLY SERVED ICE CREAM DURING MADISON'S INAUGURAL BALL IN 1813.

Coca-Cola

SPEAKING OF ICE-CREAM FLOATS, THE SECOND INGREDIENT IS **COCA-COLA**. ALTHOUGH IT WAS BASED ON A EUROPEAN DRINK CALLED COCA WINE, THIS DRINK IS AS CONNECTED TO AMERICAN CULTURE AS ... WELL, APPLE PIE.

CHEWING COCA LEAVES WAS A RELIGIOUS ACTIVITY AMONG THE INCAS OF PERU. IN THE SIXTEENTH CENTURY, COCA TRAVELED TO EUROPE, WHERE IT WAS SEEN AS A **STIMULANT, ENHANCING COGNITION.** IT WAS THE AMERICANS, HOWEVER, WHO TURNED IT INTO A THIRST-CRUSHING, MONEYMAKING ENTERPRISE—THOUGH **THE EXACT FORMULA** FOR COKE HAS ALWAYS BEEN **KEPT SECRET.** THE FIRST BOTTLING TOOK PLACE IN VICKSBURG, MISSISSIPPI, IN 1891.

ANOTHER TIMELESS AMERICAN INDULGENCE, **CHEWING GUM**, IS AT LEAST FIVE THOUSAND YEARS OLD. IT WAS USED BY THE ANCIENT GREEKS AS WELL AS BY THE AZTECS, AMONG OTHER CIVILIZATIONS. AMERICAN INDIANS CHEWED A TYPE OF RESIN FROM THE SAP OF SPRUCE TREES, AND NEW ENGLANDERS WERE ALSO HABITUAL GUM CHEWERS. THE FIRST COMMERCIAL CHEWING GUM WAS SOLD IN THE UNITED STATES IN 1848.

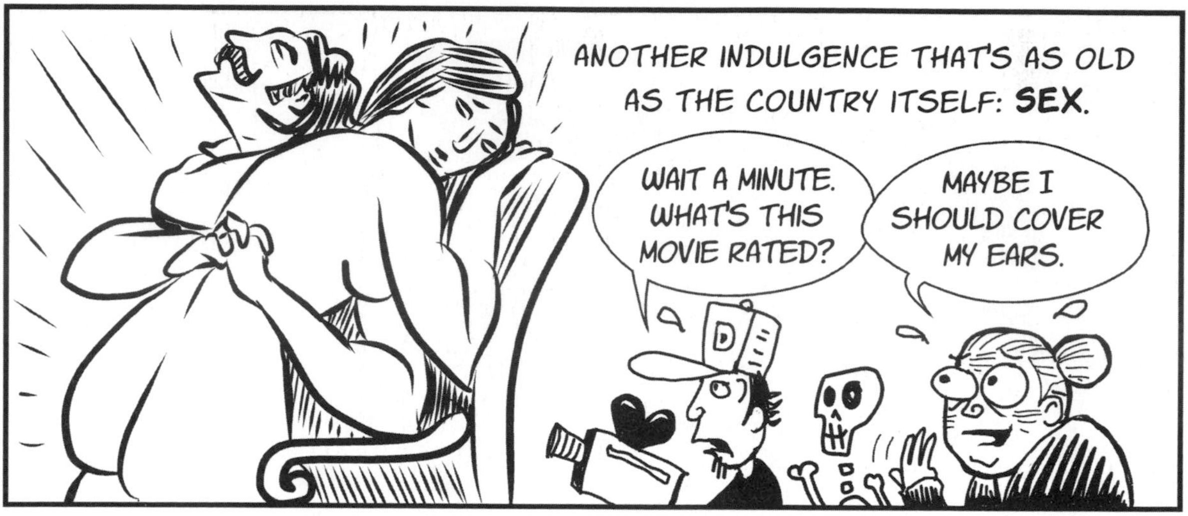
ANOTHER INDULGENCE THAT'S AS OLD AS THE COUNTRY ITSELF: **SEX.**
WAIT A MINUTE. WHAT'S THIS MOVIE RATED?
MAYBE I SHOULD COVER MY EARS.

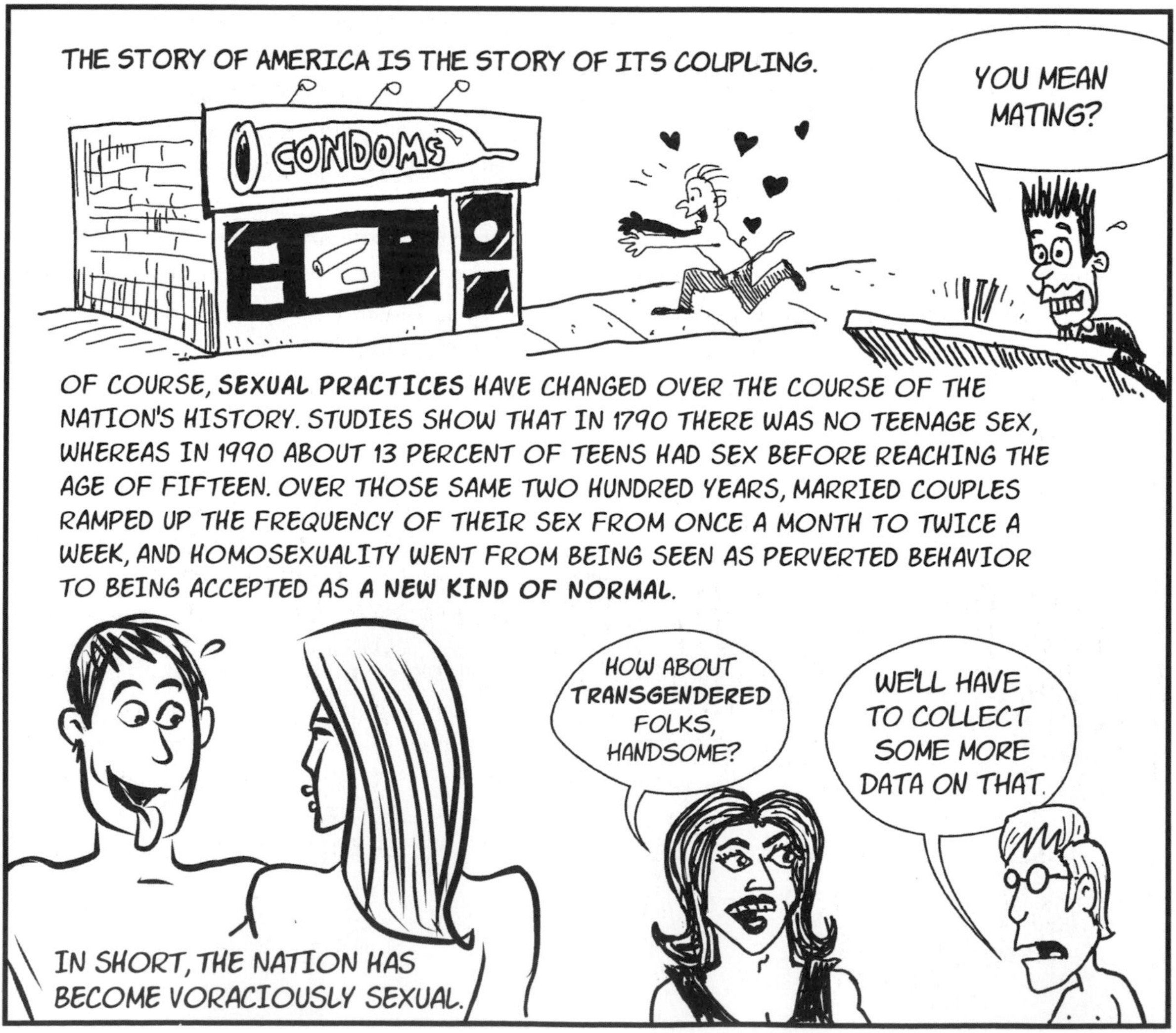
THE STORY OF AMERICA IS THE STORY OF ITS COUPLING.
CONDOMS
YOU MEAN MATING?
OF COURSE, **SEXUAL PRACTICES** HAVE CHANGED OVER THE COURSE OF THE NATION'S HISTORY. STUDIES SHOW THAT IN 1790 THERE WAS NO TEENAGE SEX, WHEREAS IN 1990 ABOUT 13 PERCENT OF TEENS HAD SEX BEFORE REACHING THE AGE OF FIFTEEN. OVER THOSE SAME TWO HUNDRED YEARS, MARRIED COUPLES RAMPED UP THE FREQUENCY OF THEIR SEX FROM ONCE A MONTH TO TWICE A WEEK, AND HOMOSEXUALITY WENT FROM BEING SEEN AS PERVERTED BEHAVIOR TO BEING ACCEPTED AS **A NEW KIND OF NORMAL.**
HOW ABOUT **TRANSGENDERED** FOLKS, HANDSOME?
WE'LL HAVE TO COLLECT SOME MORE DATA ON THAT.
IN SHORT, THE NATION HAS BECOME VORACIOUSLY SEXUAL.

STILL, THE EARLY REPUBLIC WAS HARDLY A BED OF ROSES. ONE OF THE EARLIEST SIGNS OF PUBLIC HOSTILITY TOWARD THE NEW GOVERNMENT TOOK SHAPE IN 1791, WHEN PEOPLE BEGAN **REFUSING TO PAY A TAX** ON THE GRAIN USED TO MAKE WHISKEY. THE UPHEAVAL CULMINATED IN 1794, WHEN MORE THAN 500 CITIZENS OF WESTERN PENNSYLVANIA ATTACKED THE HOUSE OF TAX INSPECTOR JOHN NEVILLE.

PRESIDENT WASHINGTON SENT IN A MILITIA TO DEAL WITH THE SITUATION. FORTUNATELY, THE REBELS DISPERSED BEFORE A CONFRONTATION COULD TAKE PLACE.

THERE WERE SOME ARRESTS, BUT WHAT REALLY MATTERS IS THAT THE **NEW FEDERAL GOVERNMENT** HAD MADE CLEAR THAT IT WOULD NOT TOLERATE VIOLENT RESISTANCE TO ITS AUTHORITY. STILL, THE WHISKEY TAX REMAINED DIVISIVE, AND IT WAS ULTIMATELY REPEALED WHEN THE DEMOCRATIC-REPUBLICAN PARTY CAME TO POWER IN 1801.

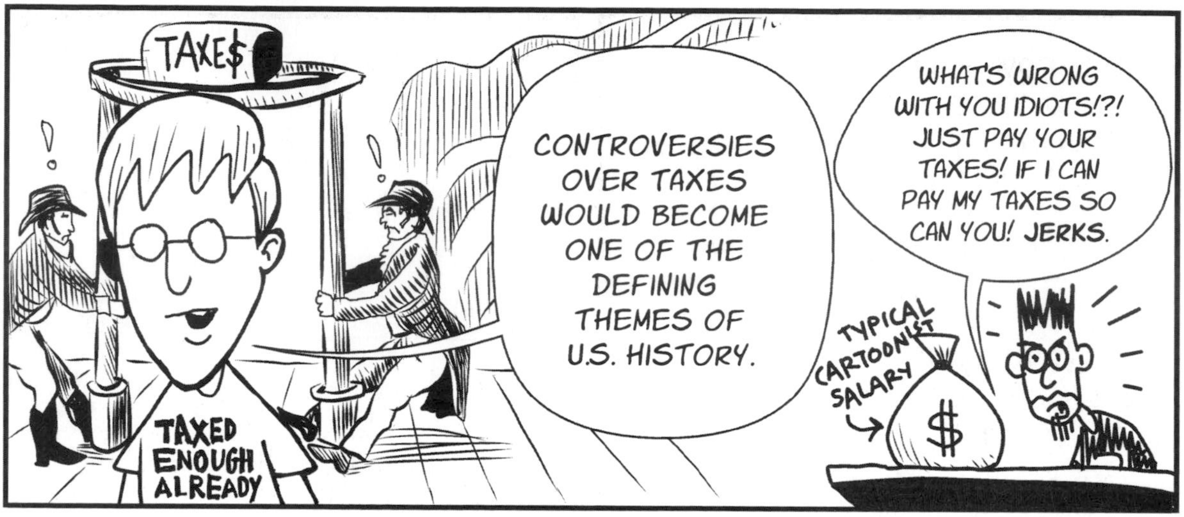
TAXE$
CONTROVERSIES OVER TAXES WOULD BECOME ONE OF THE DEFINING THEMES OF U.S. HISTORY.
WHAT'S WRONG WITH YOU IDIOTS!?! JUST PAY YOUR TAXES! IF I CAN PAY MY TAXES SO CAN YOU! **JERKS**.
TYPICAL CARTOONIST SALARY
TAXED ENOUGH ALREADY

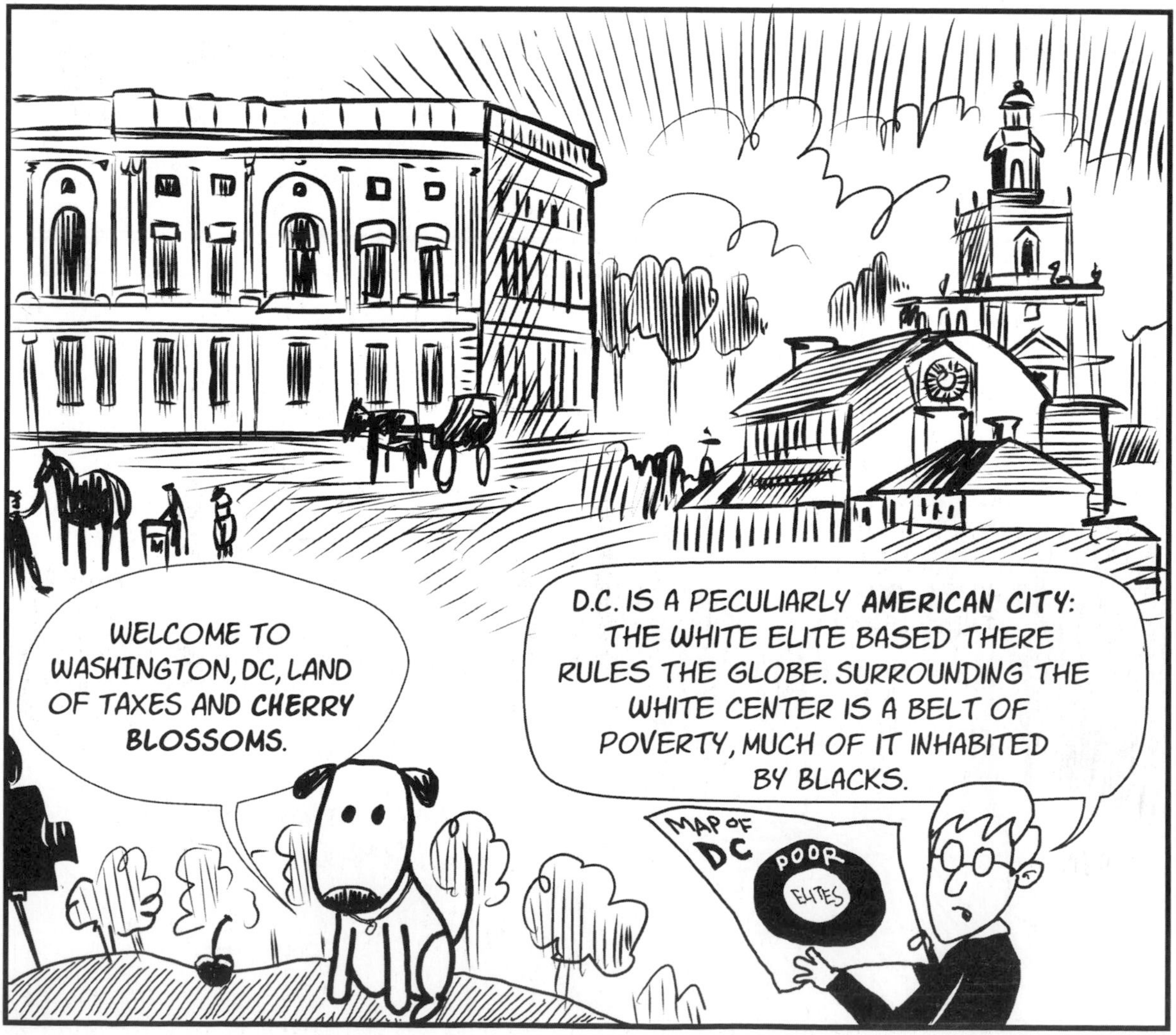
WELCOME TO WASHINGTON, DC, LAND OF TAXES AND **CHERRY** BLOSSOMS.
D.C. IS A PECULIARLY **AMERICAN CITY**: THE WHITE ELITE BASED THERE RULES THE GLOBE. SURROUNDING THE WHITE CENTER IS A BELT OF POVERTY, MUCH OF IT INHABITED BY BLACKS.
MAP OF DC
POOR
ELITES

ABOLITIONISM GREW IN THE UNITED STATES FOLLOWING THE REVOLUTIONARY WAR. PARTS OF THOMAS JEFFERSON'S ORIGINAL DRAFT OF THE DECLARATION OF INDEPENDENCE EXPRESS STRONG **ABOLITIONIST VIEWS,** BUT OTHER FOUNDERS TOOK OUT THESE PASSAGES. BEGINNING IN 1780, NORTHERN STATES LIKE PENNSYLVANIA PASSED LEGIS-LATION ABOLISHING SLAVERY. HOWEVER, THE PRACTICE OF OWNING AND SELLING SLAVES CONTINUED ELSEWHERE IN THE COUNTRY, PARTICULARLY IN THE SOUTH.

ABOLITION FREEDOM SLAVERY NOT GOOD

THE MONTICELLO FOLKS SAY THIS QUOTE IS SPURIOUS.

WHEN THE GOVERNMENT **FEARS** THE PEOPLE, THERE IS LIBERTY. WHEN THE PEOPLE FEAR THE GOVERNMENT, THERE IS TYRANNY.

THOMAS JEFFERSON

ABOLITIONISTS

JOHN GREENLEAF WHITTIER

HARRIET BEECHER STOWE

FREDERICK DOUGLAS

AS THE NATION EXPANDED, SLAVERY EXPANDED WITH IT. SINCE 1699, FRANCE AND SPAIN HAD BEEN TRADING THE **LOUISIANA TERRITORY** BACK AND FORTH. THEN, IN 1803, THE UNITED STATES—ORIGINALLY PLANNING TO ONLY BUY NEW ORLEANS— ENDED UP ACQUIRING THE ENTIRE TERRITORY FOR $15 MILLION.

IN 1793, ELI WHITNEY HAD INVENTED THE COTTON GIN, WHICH INCREASED THE DEMAND ON LABOR IN THE SOUTHERN STATES. THAT DEMAND WAS SATISFIED THROUGH AN **INCREASE IN SLAVES.**

IN 1804, **MERIWETHER LEWIS** AND **WILLIAM CLARK** SET OFF ON A WESTBOUND EXPEDITION TOWARD THE PACIFIC, COMMISSIONED BY PRESIDENT THOMAS JEFFERSON. LASTING OVER TWO YEARS, THE JOURNEY WAS FULL OF BOTH HARDSHIPS AND DISCOVERIES. ITS PURPOSE WAS SCIENTIFIC AS WELL AS ECONOMIC: LEWIS AND CLARK WERE TASKED WITH CATALOGING THE FLORA AND FAUNA THEY FOUND DURING THEIR TRAVELS, AND TO ASSESS POSSIBLE INVESTMENTS THE NEWLY FORMED NATION MIGHT MAKE ON ITS WESTERN FRONTIER. THE EXPEDITION PRODUCED MAPS, DOCUMENTED NATURAL RESOURCES (INCLUDING TWO HUNDRED PREVIOUSLY UNRECORDED PLANTS), AND PROFILED THE HUMAN RESIDENTS OF THE REGION, IDENTIFYING SEVENTY-TWO DISTINCT TRIBES. MUCH OF THE LORE SURROUNDING THE EXPEDITION INVOLVES **SACAGAWEA**, AN INDIAN WOMAN WHO IS REMEMBERED AS A GUIDE AND INTERPRETER BUT WHO IN FACT APPEARS TO HAVE PLAYED ONLY A SMALL ROLE ON THE TRIP.

As Americans were exploring the continent, they were also delineating the boundaries of their **own language**. The first attempt at codifying American English was made by Noah Webster, a lexicographer and Federalist spokesman. The very title of his 1828 **American Dictionary of the English Language** reveals the contradiction at the heart of the national project: to be autonomous, self-sufficient, and independent, while also being a continuation of England. Webster was a **pragmatist**. He didn't have the blockbuster talents of Samuel Johnson—the English essayist, poet, literary critic, and all-around polymath whose 1755 dictionary served as Webster's inspiration (and from which he occasionally plagiarized). Instead, Webster hoped to infuse his new dictionary with a **realistic American spirit**.

THE **ENGLISH LANGUAGE** WILL GO TO THE DOGS IF WE DON'T PROTECT IT FROM THE ABUSE OF THE UNEDUCATED. I PROPOSE ESTABLISHING AN **ACADEMY** WHOSE MISSION WILL BE TO SAFEGUARD AND PROTECT IT.

JOHN ADAMS

NO! THIS IS OUR COUNTRY, AND THIS IS OUR LANGUAGE! WE'LL BE ITS KEEPERS, FOR BETTER OR FOR WORSE!

H. L. MENCKEN, JOURNALIST AND EDITOR OF THE **AMERICAN MERCURY**, IS A CRUCIAL FIGURE IN THE HISTORY OF AMERICAN ENGLISH. KNOWN AS THE "SAGE OF BALTIMORE," MENCKEN PUBLISHED AN IDIOSYNCRATIC BOOK CALLED **THE AMERICAN LANGUAGE** IN 1919. ALTHOUGH CUMBERSOME IN ITS STRUCTURE, MENCKEN'S WORK IS A PERCEPTIVE EXPLORATION OF THE VICISSITUDES OF AMERICAN ENGLISH, AS USED BY IMMIGRANTS AS WELL AS NATIVE SPEAKERS.

AMERICAN EXPANSION TRANSFORMED THE NATION'S POLITICS. THE SECOND PARTY SYSTEM LASTED FROM 1828 UNTIL 1854. LIKE ITS PREDECESSOR, IT INVOLVED TWO PARTIES: THE **WHIG PARTY**, LED BY HENRY CLAY, AND THE **DEMOCRATIC PARTY**, LED BY ANDREW JACKSON, WHO BECAME THE NATION'S SEVENTH PRESIDENT. ALTHOUGH HE WAS A SLAVEHOLDER AND A STRONG SUPPORTER OF SLAVERY, JACKSON BELIEVED DEMOCRACY SHOULD BE OPENED UP TO EVERYONE, NOT JUST ELITES. HE LOOKED UNFAVORABLY ON MONOPOLIES AND VIGOROUSLY OPPOSED THE NATIONAL BANK, BELIEVING THAT IT UNFAIRLY BENEFITED FINANCIAL ELITES. **JACKSONIAN DEMOCRACY** LAY THE GROUNDWORK FOR THE MODERN DEMOCRATIC PARTY.

AND NOW HE'S ON THE TWENTY DOLLAR BILL!

NICE HAIR, DUDE.

I SHALL KILL YOU, GOOD SIR!

JACKSON WAS THE FIRST PRESIDENT TO BE THE TARGET OF AN **ASSASSINATION ATTEMPT!**

THE HELL YOU WILL, YOUNG VILE NE'ER-DO-WELL!

NINETEENTH-CENTURY AMERICA BECAME CONVINCED OF ITS EXCEPTIONAL ROLE IN THE WORLD AND ITS **MANIFEST DESTINY** TO EXPAND ACROSS THE CONTINENT, FROM THE EAST COAST TO THE WEST. NOTHING BLOCKED THIS AMBITION, WHICH WAS OCCASIONALLY REALIZED THROUGH WAR AND INVASION.

IN 1811, **JOHN QUINCY ADAMS** (WHO WOULD LATER BECOME THE NATION'S SIXTH PRESIDENT) WROTE:

"THE WHOLE CONTINENT OF NORTH AMERICA APPEARS TO BE DESTINED BY DIVINE PROVIDENCE TO BE PEOPLED BY ONE NATION. SPEAKING ONE LANGUAGE, PROFESSING ONE GENERAL SYSTEM OF RELIGIOUS AND POLITICAL PRINCIPLES, AND ACCUSTOMED TO ONE GENERAL TENOR OF SOCIAL USAGES AND CUSTOMS."

DIVINE PROVIDENCE? ¡JODER! AND YOU GRINGOS WONDER WHY EVERYONE HATES YOU ...

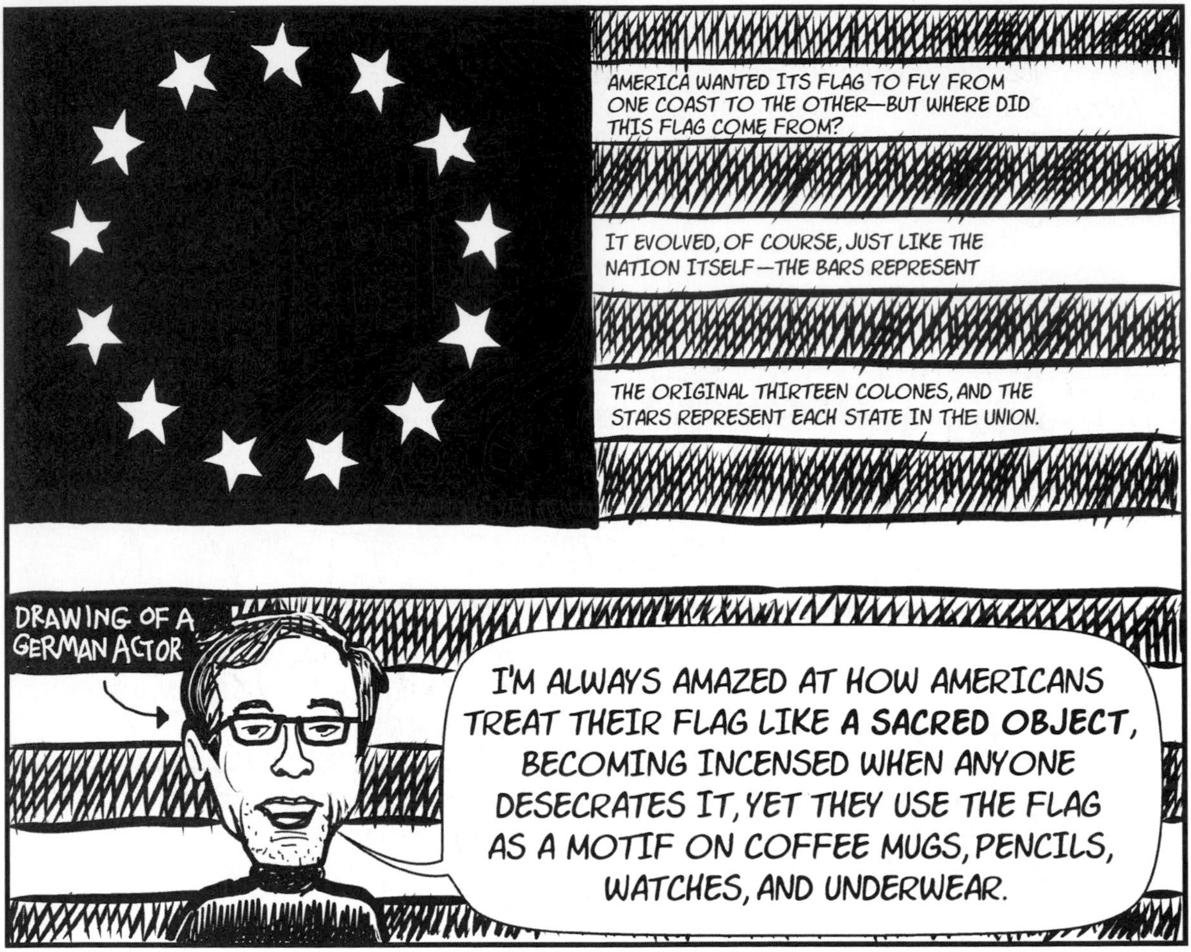
AMERICA WANTED ITS FLAG TO FLY FROM ONE COAST TO THE OTHER—BUT WHERE DID THIS FLAG COME FROM?
IT EVOLVED, OF COURSE, JUST LIKE THE NATION ITSELF—THE BARS REPRESENT
THE ORIGINAL THIRTEEN COLONES, AND THE STARS REPRESENT EACH STATE IN THE UNION.
DRAWING OF A GERMAN ACTOR
I'M ALWAYS AMAZED AT HOW AMERICANS TREAT THEIR FLAG LIKE **A SACRED OBJECT**, BECOMING INCENSED WHEN ANYONE DESECRATES IT, YET THEY USE THE FLAG AS A MOTIF ON COFFEE MUGS, PENCILS, WATCHES, AND UNDERWEAR.

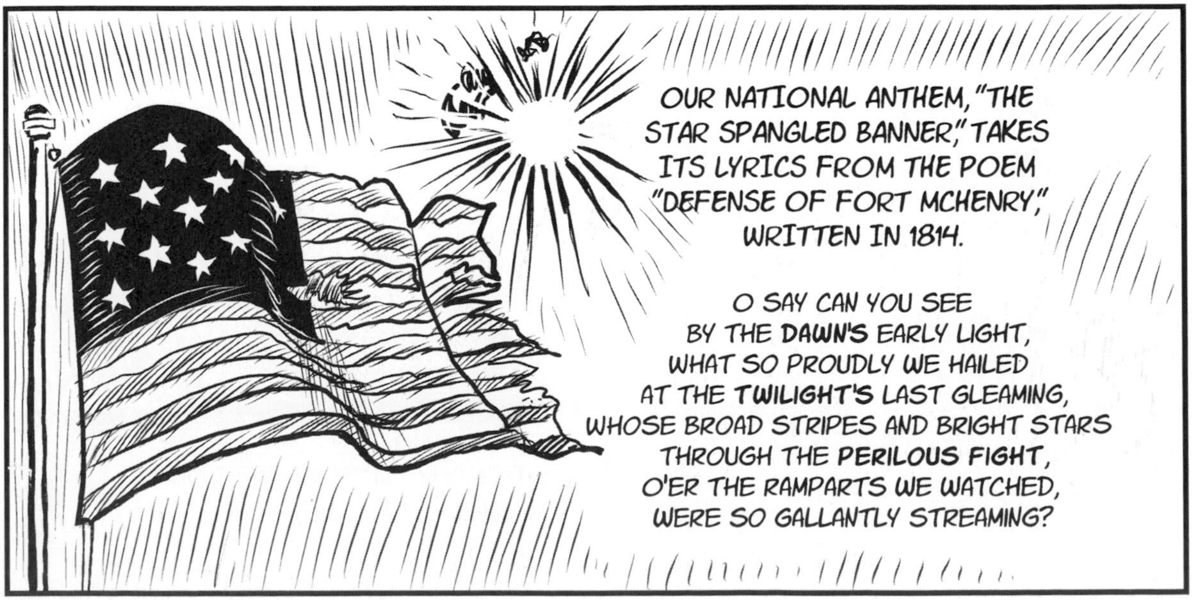
OUR NATIONAL ANTHEM, "THE STAR SPANGLED BANNER," TAKES ITS LYRICS FROM THE POEM "DEFENSE OF FORT MCHENRY," WRITTEN IN 1814.
O SAY CAN YOU SEE
BY THE **DAWN'S** EARLY LIGHT,
WHAT SO PROUDLY WE HAILED
AT THE **TWILIGHT'S** LAST GLEAMING,
WHOSE BROAD STRIPES AND BRIGHT STARS
THROUGH THE **PERILOUS FIGHT**,
O'ER THE RAMPARTS WE WATCHED,
WERE SO GALLANTLY STREAMING?

I LEARNED THE LYRICS WHEN I BECAME A U.S. CITIZEN, AFTER EMIGRATING FROM MEXICO. I STILL STUMBLE IN SEVERAL PARTS — IT'S NOT AN EASY SONG TO MEMORIZE WHEN YOU'RE AN ADULT. HONESTLY, I PREFER "HOME ON THE RANGE." IT'S **KITSCHY**, BUT THE MUSIC MAKES ME THINK OF THE OLD WEST. PLUS, I LIKE BUFFALO.

MY CHILDREN, ON THE OTHER HAND, KNOW "THE STAR-SPANGLED BANNER" BY HEART! PROOF OF SUCCESSFUL ASSIMILATION?

BUFFALO, OR BISON, ARE A SYMBOL OF THE **AMERICAN WILDERNESS.** IRONICALLY, THE UNITED STATES — A COUNTRY OBSESSED WITH PROGRESS — HAS A DEEPLY INGRAINED NOSTALGIA FOR THAT WILDERNESS.

IN THE NINETEENTH CENTURY, THE MOST VISIBLE SYMBOL OF PROGRESS WAS THE RAILROAD.

THE FIRST AMERICAN RAILROADS WERE ESTABLISHED IN THE 1830S, WITH LOCOMOTIVES TRANSPORTING MOVING TRAIN CARS ON RAIL TRACKS. BY 1860, THERE WERE 30,600 MILES OF RAILROADS IN THE COUNTRY. THE CONSEQUENCES WERE SIGNIFICANT: TRAIN TRAVEL REDUCED DISTANCE, CONNECTED ONCE-ISOLATED REGIONS TO THE REST OF THE COUNTRY, AND FACILITATED INDUSTRIAL DEVELOPMENT. THE EXPANSION REACHED A SYMBOLIC PEAK WITH THE COMPLETION OF THE **FIRST TRANSCONTINENTAL RAILROAD** IN 1869.

THE COUNTRY'S RAPID GROWTH WAS A SOURCE OF PRIDE FOR AMERICANS, AND FASCINATED OBSERVERS BACK IN THE OLD WORLD. IN 1831, FRENCH HISTORIAN AND SOCIAL OBSERVER **ALEXIS DE TOCQUEVILLE** WAS SENT TO THE UNITED STATES ALONG WITH A COLLEAGUE TO STUDY THE AMERICAN PRISON SYSTEM. HE ENDED UP EXPLORING A MUCH LARGER TOPIC, PRODUCING A BOOK NOW CONSIDERED A CLASSIC OF POLITICAL THOUGHT: **DEMOCRACY IN AMERICA**, PUBLISHED IN TWO VOLUMES IN 1835 AND 1840. TOCQUEVILLE WAS AN ADMIRER OF THE UNITED STATES, BUT HE WAS ALSO CRITICAL OF ITS SHORTCOMINGS.

DEMOCRACY **IN** AMERICA

"AN AMERICAN CANNOT CONVERSE, BUT HE CAN DISCUSS, AND HIS TALK FALLS INTO A DISSERTATION. HE SPEAKS TO YOU AS IF HE WAS ADDRESSING A MEETING AND IF HE SHOULD CHANCE TO BECOME **WARM IN THE DISCUSSION**, HE WILL SAY 'GENTLEMEN' TO THE PERSON WITH WHOM HE IS CONVERSING."

"IN NO OTHER COUNTRY IN THE WORLD IS THE LOVE OF PROPERTY **KEENER** OR **MORE ALERT** THAN IN THE UNITED STATES, AND NOWHERE ELSE DOES THE MAJORITY DISPLAY LESS INCLINATION TOWARD DOCTRINES WHICH IN ANY WAY THREATEN THE WAY PROPERTY IS OWNED."

"THE GREATNESS OF AMERICA LIES NOT IN BEING MORE ENLIGHTENED THAN ANY OTHER NATION, BUT RATHER IN HER ABILITY TO **REPAIR HER FAULTS**."

ONE QUINTESSENTIALLY AMERICAN STATE IS **TEXAS**, WHICH BEGAN EDGING TOWARD THE UNION AROUND THIS TIME. TEXAS HAS ALWAYS REPRESENTED AN INDEPENDENCE OF SPIRIT WITHIN THE COUNTRY. ITS PEOPLE LIKE TO DO THINGS THEIR OWN WAY.

BEFORE JOINING THE UNITED STATES, TEXAS HAD TO FIGHT FOR ITS INDEPENDENCE FROM MEXICO. ONE OF THE CRUCIAL EVENTS OF THE CONFLICT WAS THE **BATTLE OF THE ALAMO**, WHICH LASTED FROM FEBRUARY 23 TO MARCH 6, 1836. IN THIS FAMOUS BATTLE, THE ALAMO—A FORMER MISSION, NOW USED AS A FORT BY TEXAN SOLDIERS—WAS ATTACKED BY MEXICAN TROOPS LED BY GENERAL ANTONIO LÓPEZ DE SANTA ANNA, WHO WAS HOPING TO KEEP TEXAS UNDER MEXICAN CONTROL.

MEXICAN AND TEXAN ACCOUNTS OF THE BATTLE DIFFER SHARPLY. ALTHOUGH BOTH SEE IT AS A MOMENT OF BETRAYAL AND TRIUMPH, EACH DESCRIBES IT IN DIFFERENT TERMS. WHAT'S UNDISPUTED IS THAT THE MEXICAN TROOPS UTTERLY DEFEATED THE TEXAN DEFENDERS. ACCORDING TO ESTIMATES, BETWEEN 182 AND 257 TEXANS DIED, EITHER IN THE BATTLE OR IN THE EXECUTIONS THAT FOLLOWED, AND BETWEEN 400 AND 600 MEXICAN SOLDIERS PERISHED. THE DEFEAT AT THE ALAMO WAS PAINFUL FOR THE TEXANS, BUT IT GAVE THEM THE COURAGE TO FIGHT ON. EVEN TODAY, THE PHRASE **"REMEMBER THE ALAMO!"** IS UTTERED BY TEXANS AND MEXICANS IN DIFFERENT TONES. ULTIMATELY, THE TEXANS SURGED BACK TO VICTORY AND SUCCEEDED IN WINNING THEIR INDEPENDENCE.

BETWEEN MARCH 2, 1836, WHEN IT GAINED INDEPENDENCE FROM MEXICO, AND DECEMBER 29, 1845, WHEN IT WAS ANNEXED BY THE UNITED STATES, **TEXAS** WAS ITS OWN REPUBLIC. IN LARGE PART, ITS **INDEPENDENCE** CAME ABOUT BECAUSE OF THE TURMOIL IN MEXICAN POLITICS ...

I CAIN'T BELIEVE THIS, Y'ALL!!

IN FACT, BEFORE ATTACKING THE ALAMO, GENERAL SANTA ANNA HAD ABOLISHED MEXICO'S CONSTITUTION AND DELCARED HIMSELF **EL JEFE MAXIMO.**

LIKE A BOSS!

THIS WOULD MAKE A GREAT MOVIE SOMEDAY!

IT'S NOT TOTALLY CLEAR HOW SANTA ANNA'S ELEVATION OF HIMSELF TO DICTATOR STATUS WAS HELPFUL FOR TEXAN INDEPENDENCE, GIVEN THAT HE LATER PERSONALLY LED THE MEXICAN ARMY AGAINST THE TEXANS ...

WHEN TEXAS FIRST BECAME A REPUBLIC, THE GOVERNMENT WAS HEADED BY AN INTERIM PRESIDENT, **DAVID G. BURNET**, WHO WAS ORIGINALLY FROM NEWARK, NEW JERSEY. THE REPUBLIC'S FIRST ELECTED PRESIDENT WAS **SAM HOUSTON**, A SOLDIER AND FORMER GOVERNOR OF TENNESSEE. AFTER RELOCATING TO TEXAS FROM THE ARKANSAS TERRITORY, HOUSTON BECAME A LEADER OF THE TEXAS REVOLUTION, SEEKING TO HELP THE REGION GAIN ITS AUTONOMY FROM MEXICO. DESPITE SERVING AS PRESIDENT, HOUSTON SUPPORTED THE PLAN FOR TEXAS TO BE ANNEXED BY THE UNITED STATES.

WHEN THE U.S. ANNEXED TEXAS IN 1845, IT SPARKED **THE MEXICAN-AMERICAN WAR**, WHICH LASTED FROM 1846 TO 1848. IT WAS ANOTHER EXPRESSION OF AMERICA'S DOCTRINE OF **MANIFEST DESTINY**.

AFTER THIS, TACOS AND CERVEZAS ON ME!

IN 1848, THE TREATY OF GUADALUPE HILDALGO,

ALSO KNOWN AS **THE TREATY OF PEACE, FRIENDSHIP, LIMITS, AND SETTLEMENT BETWEEN THE UNITED STATES OF AMERICA AND THE MEXICAN REPUBLIC**, WAS SIGNED. AS A RESULT, A LARGE PORTION OF MEXICO—WHAT IS NOW KNOWN AS THE **SOUTHWEST**—BECAME PART OF THE UNITED STATES. TODAY THE CEDED AREA SPANS ALL OR PART OF EIGHT STATES: CALIFORNIA, NEVADA, UTAH, ARIZONA, NEW MEXICO, TEXAS, COLORADO, AND WYOMING.

YET ANOTHER TREATY THAT'S NEVER BEEN HONORED!

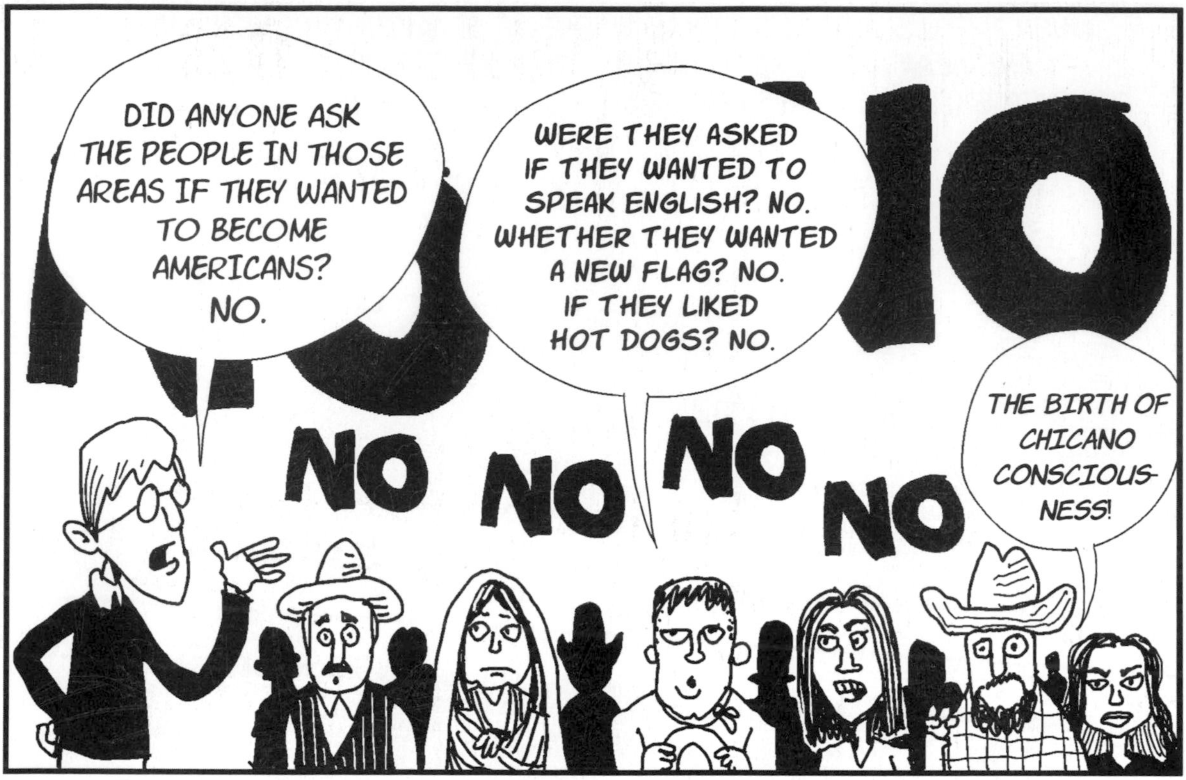
DID ANYONE ASK THE PEOPLE IN THOSE AREAS IF THEY WANTED TO BECOME AMERICANS? NO.
WERE THEY ASKED IF THEY WANTED TO SPEAK ENGLISH? NO. WHETHER THEY WANTED A NEW FLAG? NO. IF THEY LIKED HOT DOGS? NO.
NO NO NO NO
THE BIRTH OF CHICANO CONSCIOUSNESS!

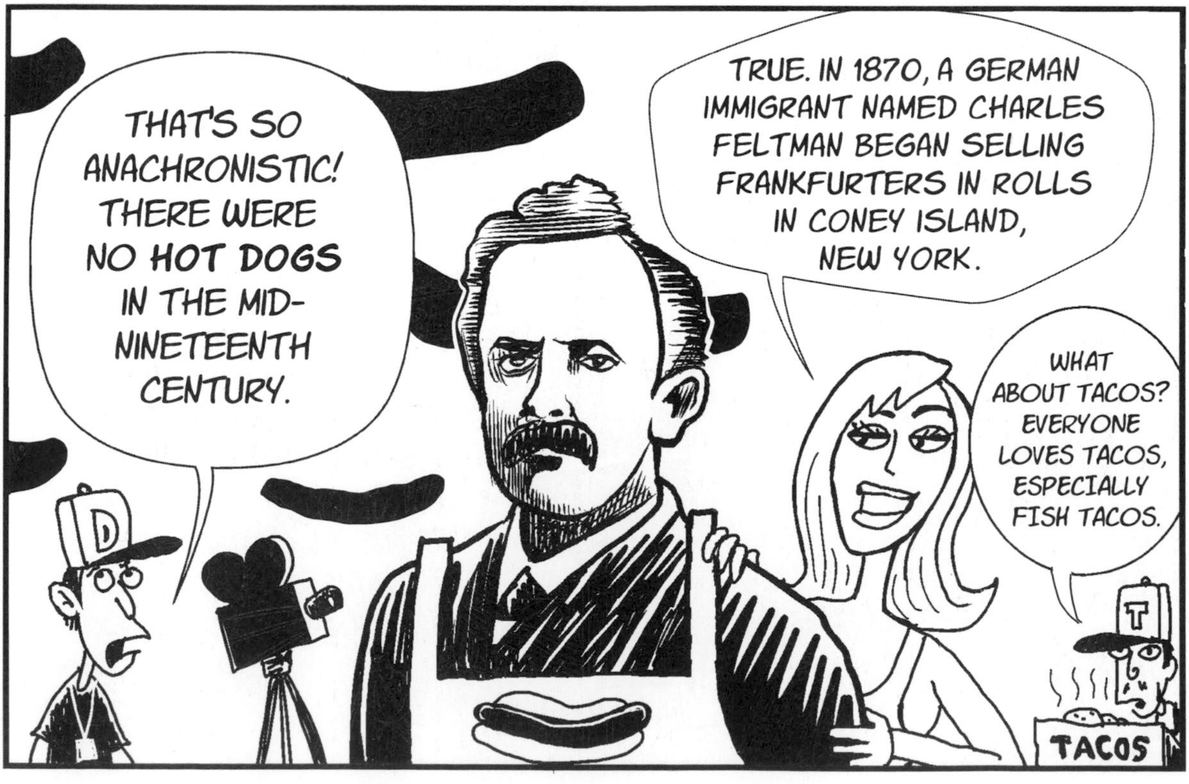
THAT'S SO ANACHRONISTIC! THERE WERE NO HOT DOGS IN THE MID-NINETEENTH CENTURY.
TRUE. IN 1870, A GERMAN IMMIGRANT NAMED CHARLES FELTMAN BEGAN SELLING FRANKFURTERS IN ROLLS IN CONEY ISLAND, NEW YORK.
WHAT ABOUT TACOS? EVERYONE LOVES TACOS, ESPECIALLY FISH TACOS.
D
T
TACOS

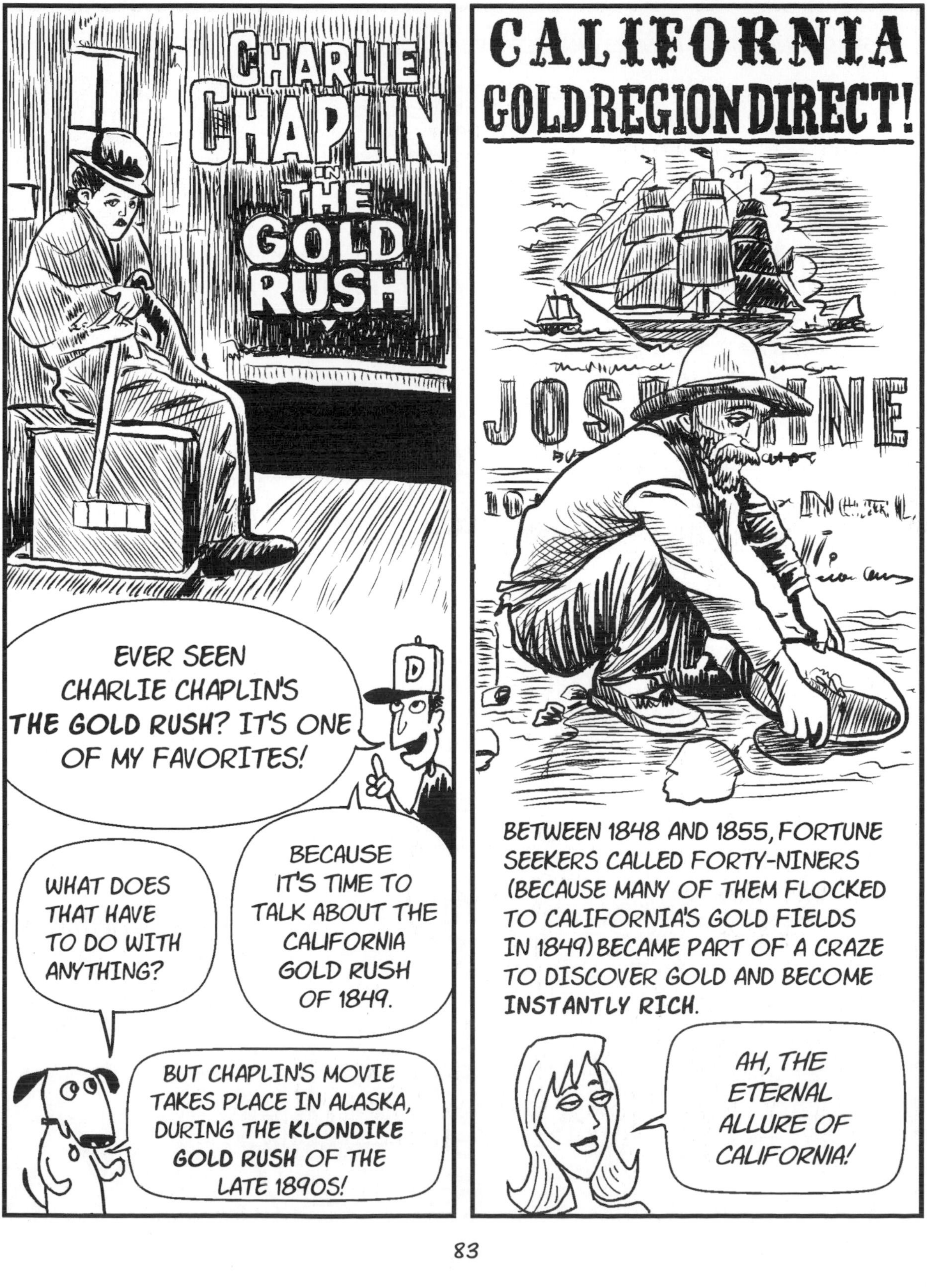
CHARLIE CHAPLIN IN THE GOLD RUSH
EVER SEEN CHARLIE CHAPLIN'S **THE GOLD RUSH**? IT'S ONE OF MY FAVORITES!
WHAT DOES THAT HAVE TO DO WITH ANYTHING?
BECAUSE IT'S TIME TO TALK ABOUT THE CALIFORNIA GOLD RUSH OF 1849.
BUT CHAPLIN'S MOVIE TAKES PLACE IN ALASKA, DURING THE **KLONDIKE GOLD RUSH** OF THE LATE 1890S!
CALIFORNIA
GOLD REGION DIRECT!
BETWEEN 1848 AND 1855, FORTUNE SEEKERS CALLED FORTY-NINERS (BECAUSE MANY OF THEM FLOCKED TO CALIFORNIA'S GOLD FIELDS IN 1849) BECAME PART OF A CRAZE TO DISCOVER GOLD AND BECOME **INSTANTLY RICH**.
AH, THE ETERNAL ALLURE OF CALIFORNIA!

A SMALL NUMBER OF MINERS AMASSED GREAT FORTUNES DURING THE GOLD RUSH...

BUT THERE WERE OTHER CONSEQUENCES, TOO. SCHOOLS, TRADING POSTS, AND ROADS WERE BUILT IN THE REGIONS WHERE THE MINERS CONGREGATED. RANCHING AND AGRICULTURE EXPANDED SIGNIFICANTLY. **SAN FRANCISCO**, FOR EXAMPLE, GREW FROM A SMALL SETTLEMENT INTO A BOOMTOWN OF ALMOST 40,000 PEOPLE.

THE POSSIBILITIES SEEMED LIMITLESS FOR MANY AMERICANS—BUT SOME WERE EXCLUDED FROM THE DREAM. EARLY ATTEMPTS TO GIVE AMERICAN WOMEN THE SAME VOTING RIGHTS AS MEN STARTED IN THE MID-1700S, BUT IT WASN'T UNTIL THE NINETEENTH CENTURY THAT REAL PROGRESS WAS MADE ON THE ISSUE. IN 1850, LUCY STONE ORGANIZED THE **NATIONAL WOMEN'S RIGHTS CONVENTION** IN WORCESTER, MASSACHUSETTS. AROUND THIS SAME TIME, SUSAN B. ANTHONY, EDITOR OF A PROGRESSIVE JOURNAL CALLED **THE REVOLUTION**, DELIVERED NUMEROUS SPEECHES AT HOME AND ABROAD, PUSHING FOR WOMEN'S SUFFRAGE. ON AUGUST 18, 1920, AFTER MANY MARCHES, ARRESTS, PUBLISHED TRACTS, AND HUNGER STRIKES, THE NINETEENTH AMENDMENT WAS RATIFIED, GRANTING AMERICAN WOMEN THE RIGHT TO VOTE.

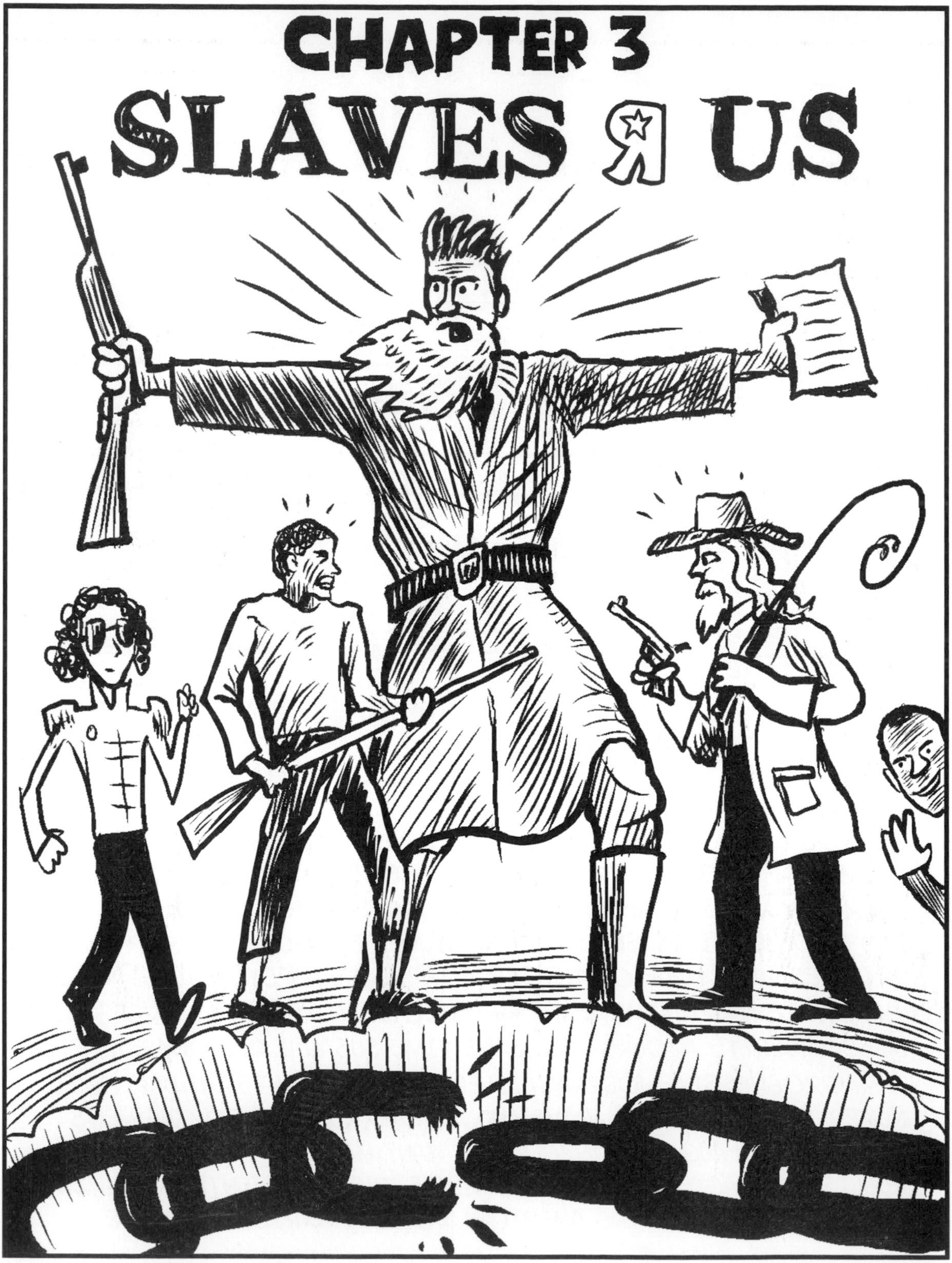
CHAPTER 3
SLAVES Я US

BY THE MIDDLE OF THE NINETEENTH CENTURY, A UNIQUE AMERICAN CULTURE WAS EMERGING, GIVING EXPRESSION TO SOME OF THE NATION'S DEFINING CHARACTERISTICS AND CONFLICTS. **AMERICAN IDENTITY**, AS WE RECOGNIZE IT TODAY, TRULY BEGAN TO TAKE SHAPE DURING THIS ERA.

A HOST OF DIFFERENT VOICES—FROM WRITERS, STATESMEN, ACTIVISTS, AND INSURGENTS—WOULD IMPEL THE NATION FORWARD IN THE DECADES THAT FOLLOWED, TAKING IT TO THE BRINK OF DESTRUCTION IN THE QUEST TO DEFINE THE SPIRIT OF THE **EVER-EXPANDING COUNTRY** AND ITS PEOPLE.

UNCLE TOM'S CABIN

By Harriet Beecher Stowe

IN 1852, HARRIET BEECHER STOWE PUBLISHED THE ABOLITIONIST NOVEL **UNCLE TOM'S CABIN**, ONE OF THE MOST INFLUENTIAL BOOKS IN AMERICAN HISTORY. SOME CREDIT IT WITH PRECIPITATING THE CIVIL WAR.

THE SOCIAL CONCERNS OF NINETEENTH-CENTURY AMERICA CAN OFTEN BE SEEN IN LITERATURE FROM THIS ERA: CONCERNS OVER SLAVERY, WHICH WOULD TEAR THE NATION APART; AN APPRECIATION FOR THE **NATURAL LANDSCAPE** AS AN EXPRESSION OF A DIVINE ORDER; THE DESIRE TO COMPETE, TO BE BETTER THAN EUROPE IN THE ECONOMIC, **TECHNOLOGICAL**, AND **ARTISTIC SPHERES**. PERHAPS THE MOST INFLUENTIAL AND REVOLUTIONARY WRITER FROM THIS PERIOD WAS THE POET **WALT WHITMAN**. HE FIRST RELEASED HIS CLASSIC **LEAVES OF GRASS** IN 1855. AS THE YEARS WENT BY, HE KEPT CHANGING ITS CONTENT. WHITMAN WAS FAT AND WAS ALSO PRONE TO ALLEGORY. "I AM LARGE," HE WROTE. "I CONTAIN MULTITUDES."

WHITMAN WAS THE POET OF DEMOCRACY. HE WAS ALSO THE POET OF PLURALISM. IF A BOOK CAN DEFINE A NATION, THEN **LEAVES OF GRASS** MIGHT BE SAID TO BE THE GLUE THAT BINDS US ALL TOGETHER.

Leaves of Grass

YEP, WE'RE ALL AMERICANS THANKS TO WHITMAN!

THE TRANSCENDENTALISTS: RALPH WALDO EMERSON, HENRY THOREAU, MARGARET FULLER, AND LOUISA MAY ALCOTT.

IN THE 1830S, AN AESTHETIC —AND PERHAPS EVEN RELIGIOUS— MOVEMENT WAS GAINING FORCE IN NEW ENGLAND. **TRANSCENDENTALISM** WAS INTIMATELY CONNECTED WITH THE ROMANTIC SPIRIT. ITS ADHERENTS BELIEVED IN COSMIC HARMONY, THE CONNECTION BETWEEN MAN AND NATURE, AND *THE GOODNESS OF THE HUMAN HEART.*

WAS NATHANIEL HAWTHORNE A TRANSCENDENTALIST? SOME SAY HE WAS, BUT I DOUBT IT. HE WAS TOO DARK, TOO FATALISTIC. NEVERTHELESS, HIS NOTEBOOKS ARE ARGUABLY THE BEST WINDOW INTO THE **NEW ENGLAND SOUL.**

OF COURSE, MY FAVORITE AMERICAN BOOK OF ALL TIME IS **MOBY-DICK** BY HERMAN MELVILLE. IN THE TRADITION OF SHAKESPEARE, IT'S FULL OF SOLILOQUIES, AND IT OFFERS A BREATHTAKING, ROMANTIC VIEW OF NATURE. ACTUALLY, MANY WORDS USED TO DESCRIBE **MOBY-DICK** ALSO APPLY TO LATIN AMERICAN FICTION: **EPIC, RESTLESS, ENCYCLOPEDIC** ...

HAS ANYONE STOPPED TO THINK ABOUT ABOUT HOW MEAN CAPTIAN AHAB IS TO WHALES?

HERMAN MELVILLE

MELVILLE'S NOVEL WAS A FLOP WHEN IT CAME OUT IN 1851, BUT BECAME HUGELY POPULAR AFTER HIS DEATH. THE BOOK IS AN EXPRESSION OF THE AGE OF **OCEANIC ENTREPRENEURSHIP.** IT STARTS OFF IN NANTUCKET, OFF THE COAST OF **CAPE COD,** AS SAILORS ARE PREPARING TO TRAVERSE THE WORLD'S SEAS IN SEARCH OF **WHALES,** WHOSE **BLUBBER** WAS ESSENTIAL FOR LAMPS, SOAP, WAX, AND COUNTLESS OTHER PRODUCTS AT THE HEART OF THE INDUSTRIAL REVOLUTION. IN OTHER WORDS, MOBY-DICK IS ABOUT HOW THE UNITED STATES BECAME MODERN.

SO MOBY-DICK FLOPPED LIKE A FISH, HUH?

ANOTHER AUTHOR WHO WAS IGNORED DURING HER LIFETIME, BUT WHO IS CELEBRATED TODAY, WAS **EMILY DICKINSON**—A FAMOUSLY RECLUSIVE WOMAN WHO LIVED IN AMHERST, MASSACHUSETTS.

HER HOUSE IS A FEW BLOCKS FROM MINE!

I'M NOBODY! WHO ARE YOU? ARE YOU -NOBODY- TOO?

A MOST IMPERFECT UNION

DICKINSON RIVALS WHITMAN FOR THE TITLE OF BEST AMERICAN POET. HER STYLE, HER SYNTAX, HER WORLD BECOME MORE AND MORE PERPLEXING AS TIME GOES BY.

SHE'S BEYOND INTERPRETATION!

IN TRUTH, HER ANONYMITY SPEAKS TO AN AMERICAN NEED TO HAVE—AND HIDE—AN **INDIVIDUAL IDENTITY**.

FAMOUS LITERARY CRITIC

FAMOUS CARTOON PROFESSOR

IN 1858, A SERIES OF POLITICAL DEBATES TOOK PLACE BETWEEN REPUBLICAN **ABRAHAM LINCOLN** AND DEMOCRAT **STEPHEN A. DOUGLAS**, BOTH RUNNING FOR A SPOT IN THE U.S. SENATE. THE CORE ISSUE WAS SLAVERY, A TOPIC THAT WOULD LATER DEFINE LINCOLN'S PRESIDENCY.

THESE ARE OFTEN DESCRIBED AS THE MOST INSPIRING AND LITERATE POLITICAL DEBATES IN AMERICAN HISTORY.

A HOUSE DIVIDED AGAINST ITSELF CANNOT STAND. I BELIEVE THIS GOVERNMENT CANNOT ENDURE PERMANENTLY HALF SLAVE AND HALF FREE.

I HOLD THAT NEW YORK HAD AS MUCH RIGHT TO ABOLISH SLAVERY AS VIRGINIA HAS TO CONTINUE IT, AND THAT EACH AND EVERY STATE OF THIS UNION IS A SOVEREIGN POWER, WITH THE RIGHT TO DO AS IT PLEASES UPON THIS QUESTION OF SLAVERY, AND UPON ALL ITS DOMESTIC INSTITUTIONS.... AND WHY CAN WE NOT ADHERE TO THE GREAT PRINCIPLE OF **SELF-GOVERNMENT**, UPON WHICH OUR INSTITUTIONS WERE ORIGINALLY BASED?

THIS DECLARED INDIFFERENCE, BUT, AS I MUST THINK, COVERT REAL ZEAL FOR THE SPREAD OF SLAVERY, I CANNOT BUT HATE. I HATE IT BECAUSE OF THE **MONSTROUS INJUSTICE OF SLAVERY** ITSELF. I HATE IT BECAUSE IT DEPRIVES OUR REPUBLICAN EXAMPLE OF ITS JUST INFLUENCE IN THE WORLD— ENABLES THE ENEMIES OF FREE INSTITUTIONS, WITH PLAUSIBILITY, TO TAUNT US AS HYPOCRITES ...

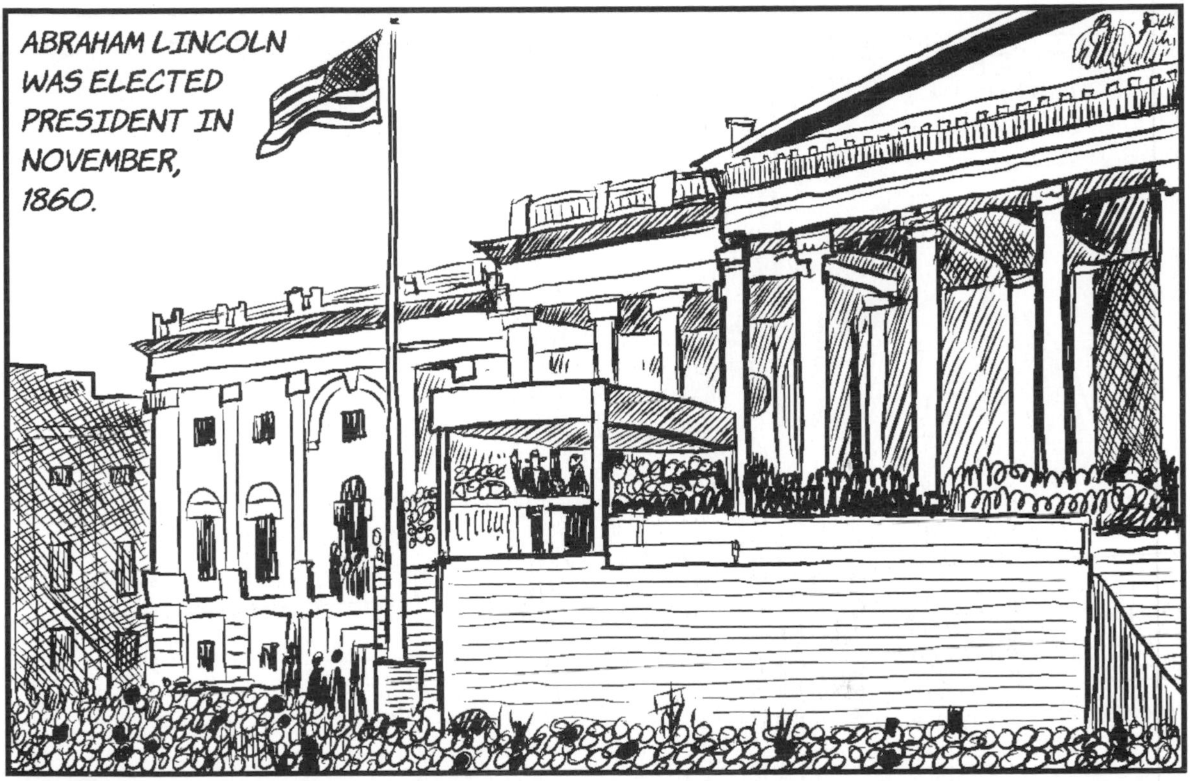
ABRAHAM LINCOLN WAS ELECTED PRESIDENT IN NOVEMBER, 1860.

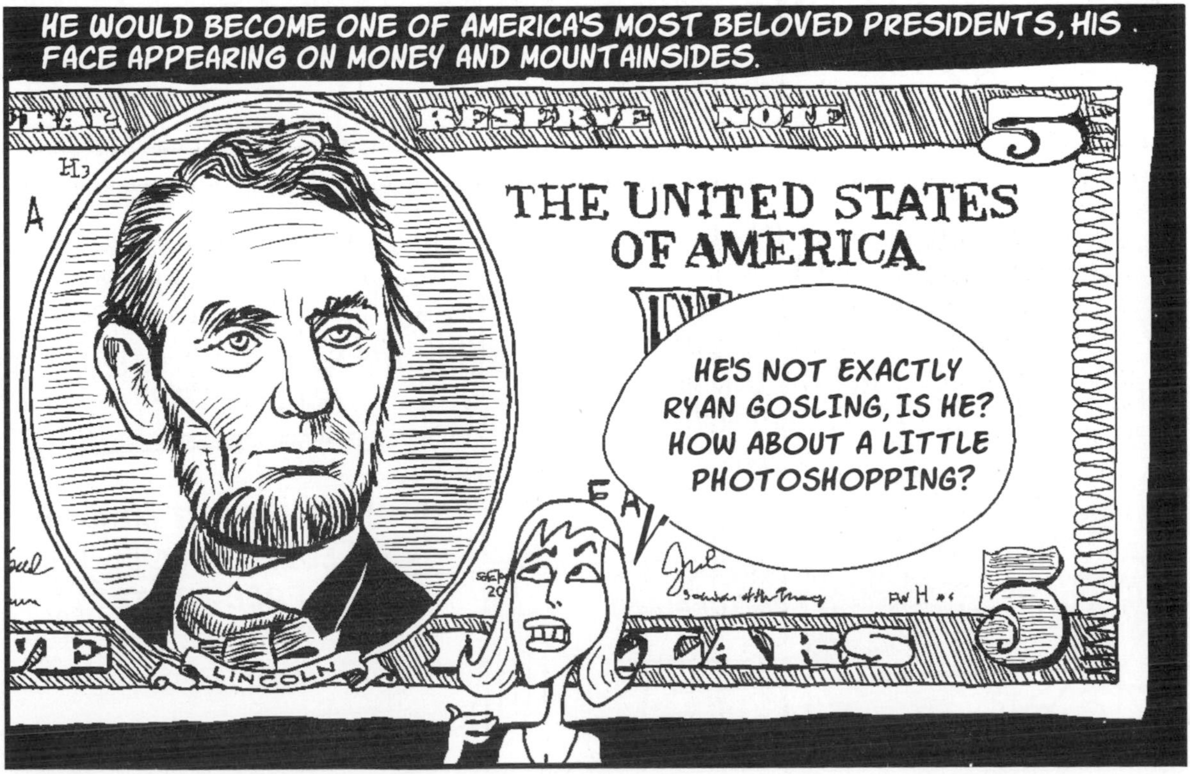
HE WOULD BECOME ONE OF AMERICA'S MOST BELOVED PRESIDENTS, HIS FACE APPEARING ON MONEY AND MOUNTAINSIDES.
RESERVE NOTE
THE UNITED STATES OF AMERICA
LINCOLN
HE'S NOT EXACTLY RYAN GOSLING, IS HE? HOW ABOUT A LITTLE PHOTOSHOPPING?

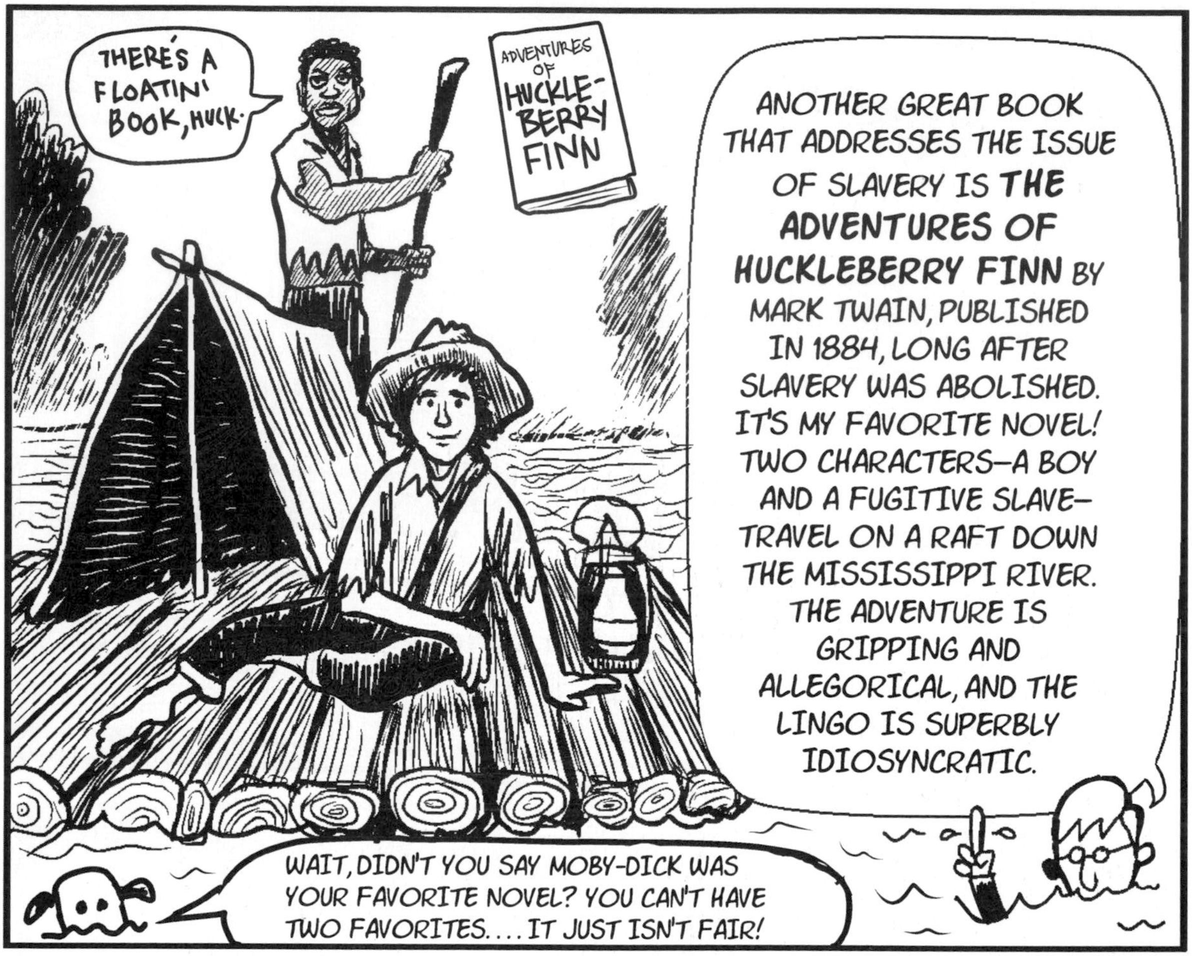
THERE'S A FLOATIN' BOOK, HUCK.
ADVENTURES OF HUCKLE-BERRY FINN
ANOTHER GREAT BOOK THAT ADDRESSES THE ISSUE OF SLAVERY IS **THE ADVENTURES OF HUCKLEBERRY FINN** BY MARK TWAIN, PUBLISHED IN 1884, LONG AFTER SLAVERY WAS ABOLISHED. IT'S MY FAVORITE NOVEL! TWO CHARACTERS—A BOY AND A FUGITIVE SLAVE—TRAVEL ON A RAFT DOWN THE MISSISSIPPI RIVER. THE ADVENTURE IS GRIPPING AND ALLEGORICAL, AND THE LINGO IS SUPERBLY IDIOSYNCRATIC.
WAIT, DIDN'T YOU SAY MOBY-DICK WAS YOUR FAVORITE NOVEL? YOU CAN'T HAVE TWO FAVORITES.... IT JUST ISN'T FAIR!

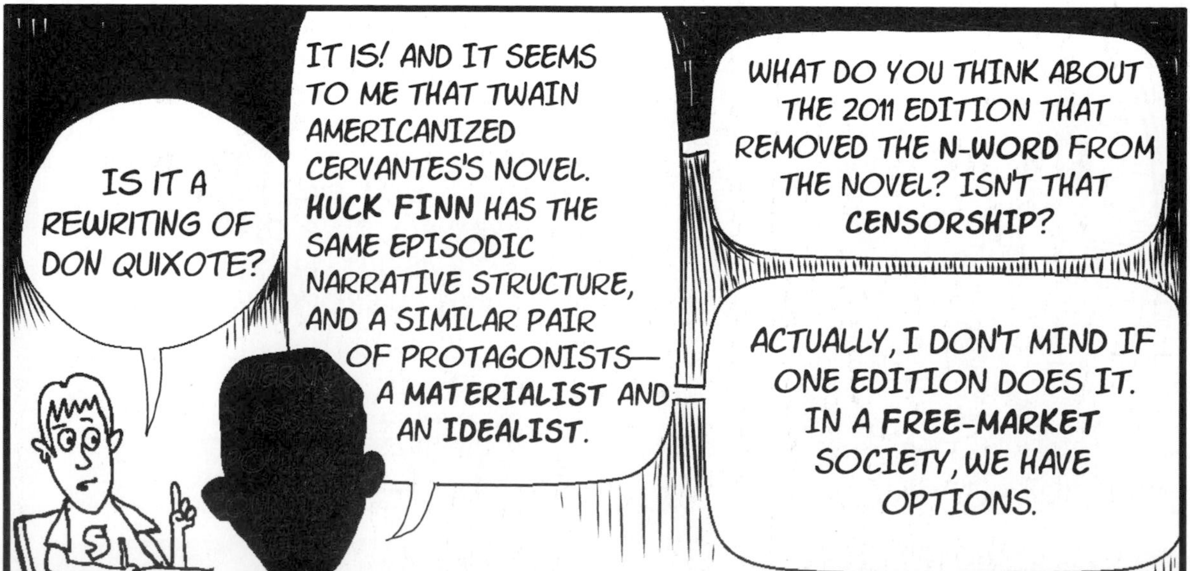
IS IT A REWRITING OF DON QUIXOTE?
IT IS! AND IT SEEMS TO ME THAT TWAIN AMERICANIZED CERVANTES'S NOVEL. **HUCK FINN** HAS THE SAME EPISODIC NARRATIVE STRUCTURE, AND A SIMILAR PAIR OF PROTAGONISTS—A **MATERIALIST** AND AN **IDEALIST**.
WHAT DO YOU THINK ABOUT THE 2011 EDITION THAT REMOVED THE **N-WORD** FROM THE NOVEL? ISN'T THAT **CENSORSHIP**?
ACTUALLY, I DON'T MIND IF ONE EDITION DOES IT. IN A **FREE-MARKET** SOCIETY, WE HAVE OPTIONS.

TENSIONS OVER SLAVERY GREW STEADILY OVER THE FIRST HALF OF THE NINETEENTH CENTURY. THE SOUTHERN STATES WERE COMMITTED TO THE INSTITUTION, WHILE THE **NORTHERN STATES** THOUGHT IT WAS TIME TO END IT. THE ELECTION OF LINCOLN, WHO MADE NO SECRET OF HIS OPPOSITION TO SLAVERY, PUSHED THE **SOUTHERN STATES** TO SECEDE.

A BLOODY WAR ENSUED, LASTING FROM 1861 TO 1865.

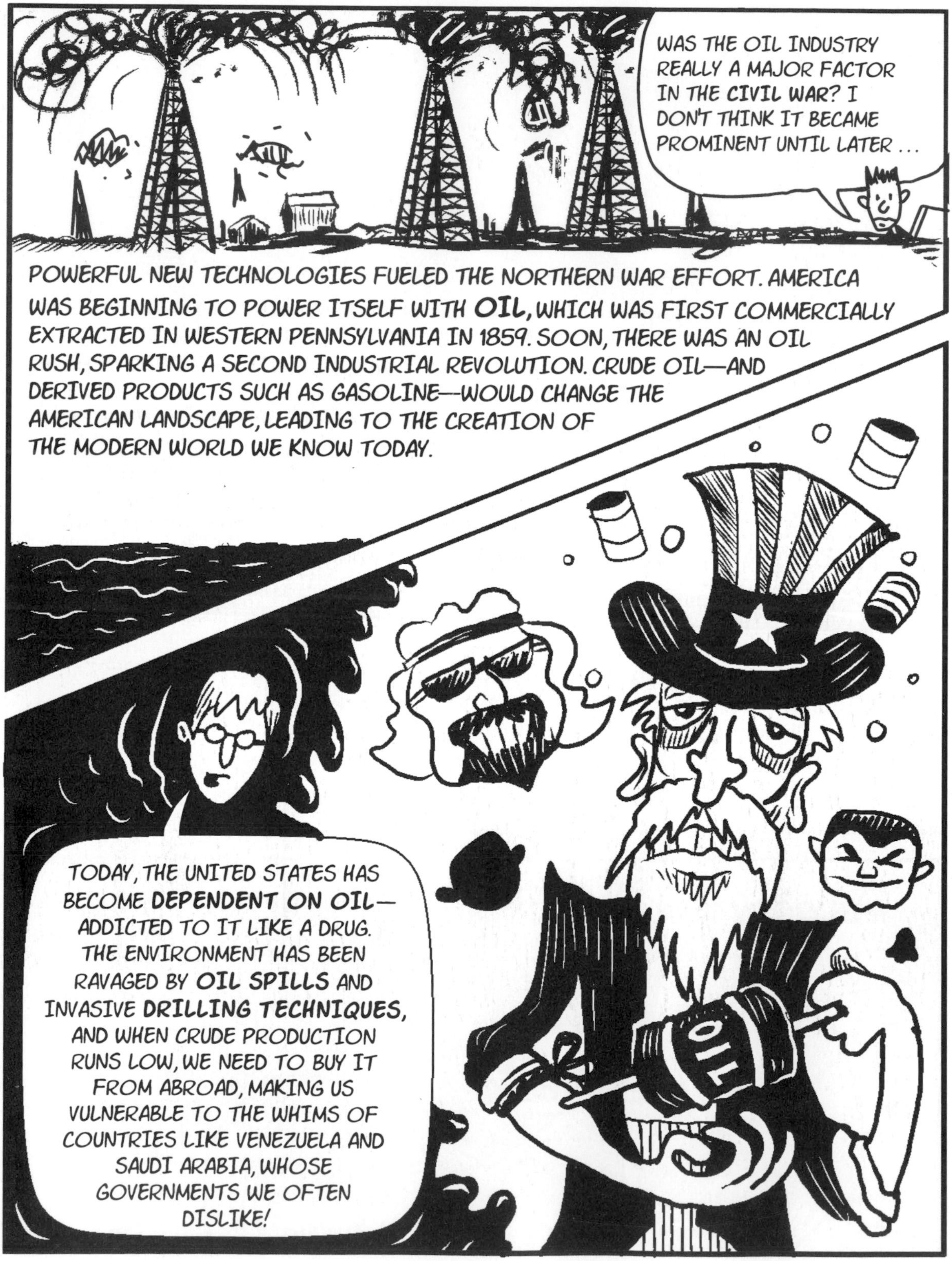
WAS THE OIL INDUSTRY REALLY A MAJOR FACTOR IN THE CIVIL WAR? I DON'T THINK IT BECAME PROMINENT UNTIL LATER ...
POWERFUL NEW TECHNOLOGIES FUELED THE NORTHERN WAR EFFORT. AMERICA WAS BEGINNING TO POWER ITSELF WITH OIL, WHICH WAS FIRST COMMERCIALLY EXTRACTED IN WESTERN PENNSYLVANIA IN 1859. SOON, THERE WAS AN OIL RUSH, SPARKING A SECOND INDUSTRIAL REVOLUTION. CRUDE OIL—AND DERIVED PRODUCTS SUCH AS GASOLINE—WOULD CHANGE THE AMERICAN LANDSCAPE, LEADING TO THE CREATION OF THE MODERN WORLD WE KNOW TODAY.
TODAY, THE UNITED STATES HAS BECOME DEPENDENT ON OIL—ADDICTED TO IT LIKE A DRUG. THE ENVIRONMENT HAS BEEN RAVAGED BY OIL SPILLS AND INVASIVE DRILLING TECHNIQUES, AND WHEN CRUDE PRODUCTION RUNS LOW, WE NEED TO BUY IT FROM ABROAD, MAKING US VULNERABLE TO THE WHIMS OF COUNTRIES LIKE VENEZUELA AND SAUDI ARABIA, WHOSE GOVERNMENTS WE OFTEN DISLIKE!
OIL

ON JANUARY 1, 1863, ABRAHAM LINCOLN ISSUED THE EXECUTIVE ORDER KNOWN AS THE **EMANCIPATION PROCLAMATION,** WHICH GRANTED FREEDOM TO ALL SLAVES IN THE STATES THAT WERE OPENLY REBELLING. THIS OCCURRED IN THE MIDDLE OF THE CIVIL WAR, AND THE DECLARATION MADE SLAVERY THE UNCONTESTED CENTRAL THEME OF THAT WAR, AND FOREVER REDEFINED THE AMERICAN SOCIAL TAPESTRY. AT THE TIME, THERE WERE ABOUT FOUR MILLION SLAVES IN AMERICA, AND THE DECLARATION APPLIED TO MORE THAN TWO-THIRDS OF THEM.

OTHER NATIONS HAD ALREADY ABOLISHED SLAVERY. IN 1833, BRITAIN ELIMINATED SLAVERY THROUGHOUT MOST OF ITS EMPIRE WITH THE PASSAGE OF THE **SLAVE ABOLITION ACT.** FRANCE FOLLOWED SUIT IN 1848, MAKING GOOD ON ITS REVOLUTIONARY PRINCIPLES OF **LIBERTÉ, EGALITÉ, FRATERNITÉ.** FINALLY, IN 1865, THE THIRTEENTH AMENDMENT TO THE CONSTITUTION WOULD GO INTO EFFECT, MAKING SLAVERY ILLEGAL IN THE UNITED STATES.

THE CIVIL WAR BATTLE WITH THE GREATEST NUMBER OF CASUALTIES TOOK PLACE IN **GETTYSBURG, PENNSYLVANIA**, ON JULY 1–3, 1863. SOME 46,000 TO 51,000 SOLDIERS WERE KILLED OR INJURED.

THE CIVIL WAR **DIVIDED AMERICANS**—AND THE FAULT LINES WEREN'T ALWAYS BETWEEN NORTH AND SOUTH. FOR FOUR DAYS IN 1863, A SERIES OF **RIOTS** TOOK PLACE IN NEW YORK CITY, MAINLY PERPETRATED BY WORKING-CLASS WHITES WHO RESENTED THE DRAFT AND TOOK THEIR **ANGER** OUT ON LOCAL BLACK RESIDENTS. IN THE END, LINCOLN HAD TO SEND IN THE ARMY.

ON NOVEMBER 19, 1863,
LINCOLN DELIVERED HIS
FAMOUS **GETTYSBURG ADDRESS:**

Four score and seven years ago

our fathers brought forth on this continent a new nation, conceived in liberty, and dedicated to the proposition that all men are created equal. Now we are engaged in a great civil war, **testing** whether that nation, or any nation, so conceived and so dedicated, can long endure.

We are met on a great battle-field of that war. We have come to dedicate a portion of that field, as a **final resting** place for those who here gave their lives that that nation might live. It is altogether fitting and proper that we should do this. But, in a larger sense, we can not dedicate, we can not consecrate, we can not hallow this ground. The brave men, living and dead, who struggled here, have **consecrated** it, far above our poor power to add or detract. The world will little note, nor long remember what we say here, but it can **never forget** what they did here. It is for us the living, rather, to be dedicated here to the unfinished work which they who **fought here** have thus far so nobly advanced. It is rather for us to be here dedicated to the great task remaining before us—that from these honored dead we take increased devotion to that cause for which they gave the last full measure of devotion—that we here highly resolve that these dead shall not have died in vain—that this nation, **under God**, shall have a new birth of freedom—and that government of the people, **by the people, for the people,** shall not perish from the earth.

JUST 217 WORDS IN NINE SENTENCES BROKEN INTO THREE PARAGRAPHS. BUT WHAT PERFECT WORDS! WHAT POLITICAL SAVVY! WHAT PROPHETIC WISDOM! LINCOLN CONSECRATES THE SOLDIERS' NATIONAL CEMETERY, IN GETTYSBURG, BUT IN DOING SO FORCES A SENSE OF MISSION UPON THE LIVING. THE DEAD HAVE NOT DIED IN VAIN, HE ANNOUNCES. FOR THE SURVIVORS WILL HONOR THEM BY FULFILLING THEIR TASK: FORGING A UNIFIED NATION.

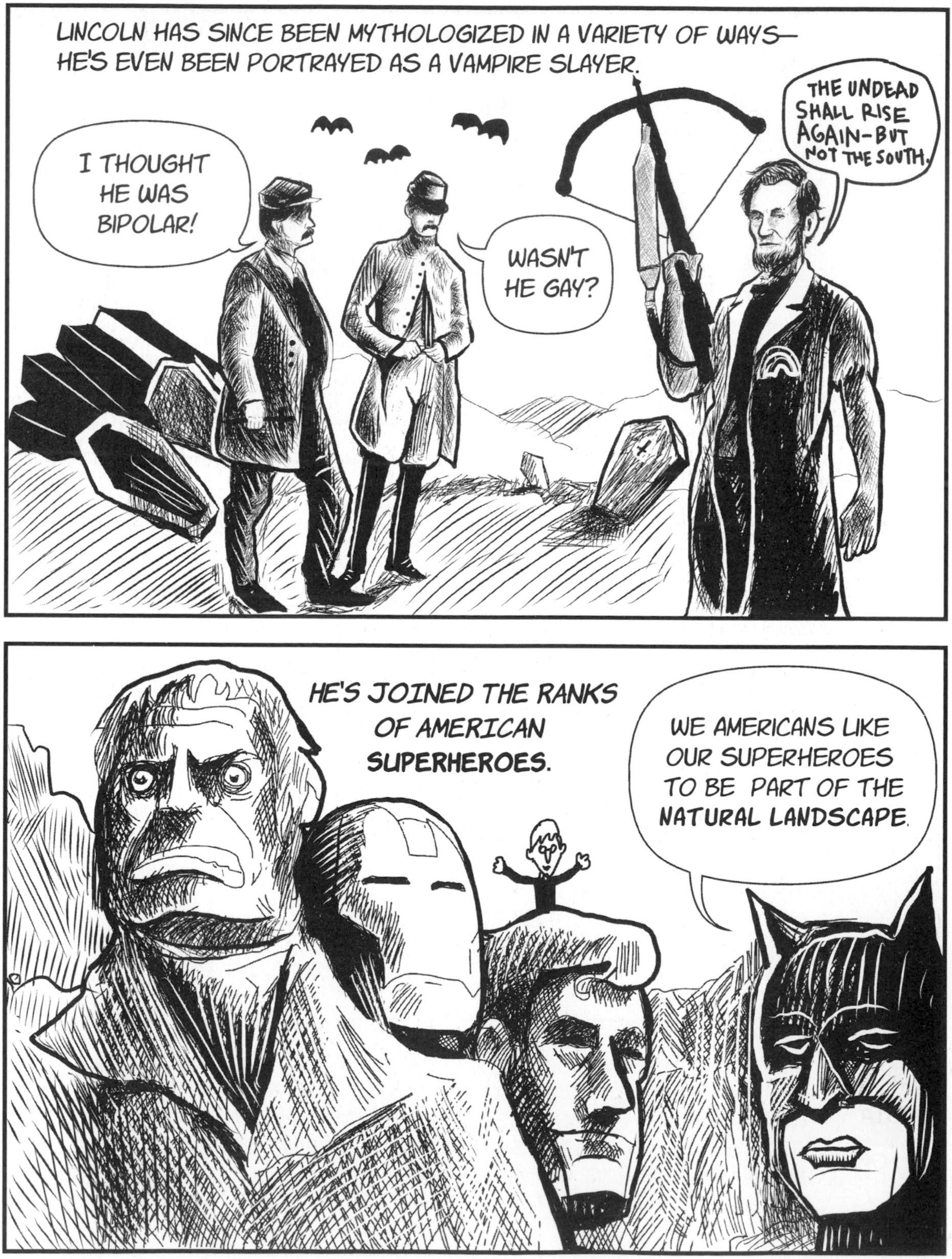
LINCOLN HAS SINCE BEEN MYTHOLOGIZED IN A VARIETY OF WAYS—HE'S EVEN BEEN PORTRAYED AS A VAMPIRE SLAYER.
I THOUGHT HE WAS BIPOLAR!
WASN'T HE GAY?
THE UNDEAD SHALL RISE AGAIN—BUT NOT THE SOUTH.
HE'S JOINED THE RANKS OF AMERICAN SUPERHEROES.
WE AMERICANS LIKE OUR SUPERHEROES TO BE PART OF THE NATURAL LANDSCAPE.

LINCOLN'S DEATH WAS THE LAST, AND MOST WIDELY MOURNED, TRAUMA OF THE WAR. GIVEN THE ANIMOSITY OF THE **CONFLICT** AND THE **UPROAR** CAUSED BY LINCOLN'S PUSH TO ABOLISH SLAVERY, IT IS PERHAPS UNSURPRISING THAT HE WAS **ASSASSINATED.**

JOHN WILKES BOOTH, A WELL-KNOWN ACTOR, WAS PART OF A CONSPIRACY TO REENERGIZE THE CONFEDERACY BY KILLING LINCOLN, VICE PRESIDENT ANDREW JOHNSON, AND SECRETARY OF STATE WILLIAM H. SEWARD. BOOTH SHOT LINCOLN IN THE BACK OF THE HEAD WITH A PHILADELPHIA DERRINGER PISTOL, WHILE LINCOLN WAS WATCHING THE PLAY **OUR AMERICAN COUSIN** AT FORD'S THEATRE IN WASHINGTON, DC, IN THE COMPANY OF HIS WIFE AND OTHER GUESTS. AFTER FIRING THE GUN, BOOTH JUMPED ONTO THE STAGE, LANDING AWKWARDLY AND BREAKING HIS TIBIA. HE THEN SCREAMED "SIC SEMPER TYRANNIS" (THUS ALWAYS TO TYRANTS), A PHRASE ALLEGEDLY UTTERED BY BRUTUS WHEN KILLING JULIUS CAESER. PEOPLE IN THE AUDIENCE THOUGHT BOOTH WAS PART OF THE PLAY. LINCOLN DIED THE FOLLOWING MORNING.

SO MANY LIVES WERE LOST DURING THE CIVIL WAR THAT AMERICANS BEGAN SEEKING WAYS TO **COMMUNICATE WITH THE DEAD**. SÉANCE SESSIONS WERE COMMON, AND SELF-PROFESSED MEDIUMS CLAIMED TO BE ABLE TO TAKE DICTATION FROM THE SPIRITS OF SOLDIERS WHO HAD BEEN KILLED ON THE BATTLEFIELD.

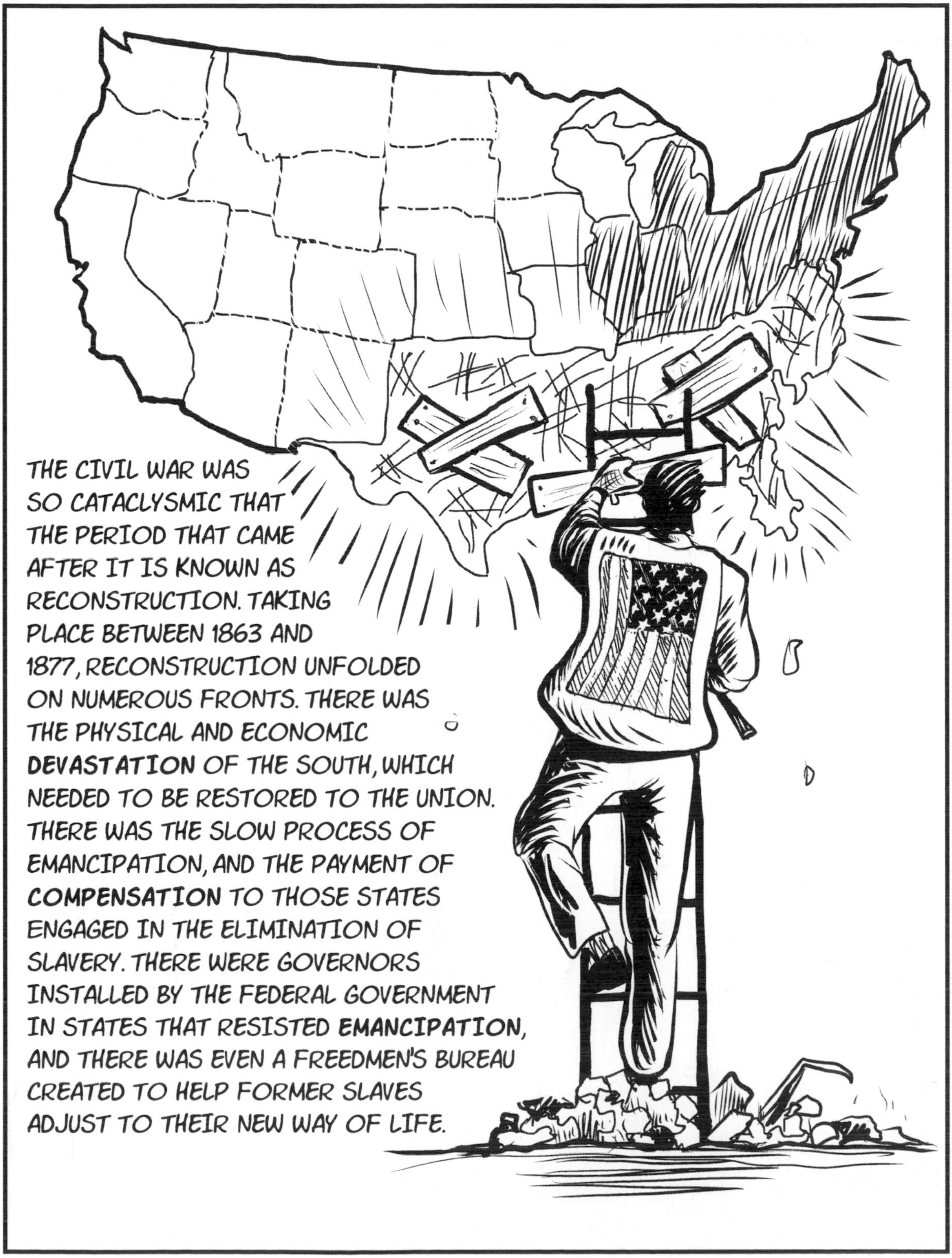
THE CIVIL WAR WAS SO CATACLYSMIC THAT THE PERIOD THAT CAME AFTER IT IS KNOWN AS RECONSTRUCTION. TAKING PLACE BETWEEN 1863 AND 1877, RECONSTRUCTION UNFOLDED ON NUMEROUS FRONTS. THERE WAS THE PHYSICAL AND ECONOMIC **DEVASTATION** OF THE SOUTH, WHICH NEEDED TO BE RESTORED TO THE UNION. THERE WAS THE SLOW PROCESS OF EMANCIPATION, AND THE PAYMENT OF **COMPENSATION** TO THOSE STATES ENGAGED IN THE ELIMINATION OF SLAVERY. THERE WERE GOVERNORS INSTALLED BY THE FEDERAL GOVERNMENT IN STATES THAT RESISTED **EMANCIPATION**, AND THERE WAS EVEN A FREEDMEN'S BUREAU CREATED TO HELP FORMER SLAVES ADJUST TO THEIR NEW WAY OF LIFE.

LIFE WAS CHANGING RAPIDLY IN THE FOMER CONFEDERATE STATES—AND IN THE REST OF THE NATION, TOO. IN MANY CASES, THIS RAPID CHANGE WAS ENABLED BY POWERFUL **NEW TOOLS.**

WHAT KIND OF TOOLS?

THE TELEPHONE, FOR INSTANCE. IN JUNE 1875, **ALEXANDER GRAHAM BELL,** ALONG WITH ELECTRICAL DESIGNER THOMAS A. WATSON, INVENTED THE SOUND-POWERED TELEPHONE, WHICH WAS ABLE TO TRANSMIT SOUND BUT NO CLEAR VOICES. THIS WAS THE START OF A MURKY PERIOD IN WHICH VARIOUS **INVENTORS** CLAIMED TO BE THE FIRST TO DEVELOP THE NEW TECHNOLOGY.

HE INVENTED THE METAL DETECTOR, WORKED ON **HYDROFOILS** AND **AERONAUTICS,** AND ALSO CREATED DEVICES TO HELP THE DEAF.

IT WAS A PERIOD OF REMARKABLE TRANSFORMATION, AND IT'S NO COINCIDENCE THAT IT HAPPENED AFTER SUCH **A TERRIBLE WAR.** HOW ELSE DOES ONE CREATE IF NOT BY DESTROYING?

AT THE HEART OF THE NINETEENTH CENTURY WAS A CENTRAL CONCEPT: **PROGRESS.** THIS CONCEPT COULD BE TRACED BACK TO THE ENLIGHTENMENT IDEAS OF THE SEVENTEENTH AND EIGHTEENTH CENTURY, WHEN SOCIETY BEGAN TO DISENTANGLE ITSELF FROM RELIGION. NOT GOD BUT THE HUMAN MIND WAS NOW AT THE CENTER OF THE UNIVERSE. THE INVENTORS AND LEADERS OF THIS AGE WERE IN **A FORWARD-LOOKING RACE** TO IMPROVE LIFE THROUGH ADVANCES IN **SCIENCE, TECHNOLOGY, EDUCATION,** AND **MEDICINE.**

THE FABRIC OF THE NATION WOULD ALSO BE AFFECTED BY EVENTS OVERSEAS. BETWEEN 1845 AND 1852, IRELAND WAS HIT BY AN ATROCIOUS **FAMINE**, CAUSED BY A DISEASE THAT INFECTED POTATO PLANTS. POTATOES WERE A STAPLE FOOD FOR BOTH THE IRISH AND THEIR LIVESTOCK, AND THE DEATH COUNT WAS ENORMOUS. APPROXIMATELY **ONE MILLION PEOPLE DIED**, AND THE SAME NUMBER EMIGRATED, MOSTLY TO THE UNITED STATES. ALTOGETHER, IRELAND LOST ABOUT ONE-QUARTER OF ITS POPULATION.

THE IRISH WHO ARRIVED IN THE UNITED STATES DURING THE FAMINE WERE MOSTLY POOR. MANY TRAVELERS DIED EN ROUTE, IN WHAT CAME TO BE KNOWN AS **COFFIN SHIPS**. THE SURVIVORS SETTLED IN BIG CITIES, SUCH AS BOSTON, PHILADELPHIA, AND NEW YORK. FOR THE MOST PART, THE IRISH QUICKLY CLIMBED AMERICA'S ECONOMIC, SOCIAL, AND POLITICAL LADDERS. MANY EXCELLED IN THE FIELDS OF EDUCATION, RELIGION, POLITICS, AND LAW ENFORCEMENT. A NUMBER OF PRESIDENTS HAVE HAD **IRISH LINEAGE** IN THEIR BACKGROUNDS, INCLUDING ANDREW JACKSON, JOHN F. KENNEDY, RONALD REAGAN, AND BARACK OBAMA.

CHAPTER 4
The New Colossus

NOT LIKE THE BRAZEN GIANT OF GREEK FAME,
WITH CONQUERING LIMBS ASTRIDE **FROM LAND TO LAND;**
HERE AT OUR SEA-WASHED, SUNSET GATES SHALL STAND
A MIGHTY WOMAN WITH A TORCH, WHOSE FLAME
IS THE IMPRISONED LIGHTNING, AND HER NAME
MOTHER OF EXILES. FROM HER BEACON-HAND
GLOWS WORLD-WIDE WELCOME; HER MILD EYES COMMAND
THE AIR-BRIDGED HARBOR THAT TWIN CITIES FRAME.
"KEEP ANCIENT LANDS, YOUR STORIED POMP!" CRIES SHE
WITH SILENT LIPS. "**GIVE ME YOUR TIRED, YOUR POOR,**
YOUR HUDDLED MASSES YEARNING TO BREATHE FREE,
THE WRETCHED REFUSE OF YOUR TEEMING SHORE.
SEND THESE, THE HOMELESS, TEMPEST-TOST TO ME,
I LIFT MY LAMP BESIDE **THE GOLDEN DOOR!**"

THE STATUE OF LIBERTY IS ARGUABLY THE MOST IMPORTANT MONUMENT IN THE COUNTRY. IN YEARS GONE BY, THIS STERN GREEN WOMAN, HOLDING HER TORCH ALOFT, GREETED IMMIGRANTS ARRIVING IN THE UNITED STATES ON SHIPS.

THE STATUE, DESIGNED BY FRÉDÉRIC BARTHOLDI, WAS A GIFT FROM THE FRENCH GOVERNMENT. IT WAS DEDICATED ON OCTOBER 28, 1886.

IN 1890, JACOB RIIS, A DANISH IMMIGRANT AND PHOTOGRAPHER, PUBLISHED A BOOK CALLED **HOW THE OTHER HALF LIVES**. THE WORK DOCUMENTED, IN DRAMATIC FASHION, THE ATROCIOUS LIVING CONDITIONS OF IMPOVERISHED NEW YORKERS.

HEY! I NEVER SIGNED A PHOTO RELEASE.

PHOTOGRAPHY IS A POWERFUL MEDIUM. RIIS BROUGHT AMERICA'S ECONOMIC **INEQUALITY** TO THE ATTENTION OF MILLIONS.

WASN'T THIS SUPPOSED TO BE THE LAND OF **MILK AND HONEY**?

NO WAY! IT WAS SQUALID. THE MILK WAS ALL SPOILED.

DOES A PHOTOGRAPHER HAVE THE RIGHT TO USE PEOPLE TO ADVANCE HIS OWN POLITICAL VIEWS?

ESCAPING POGROMS AS WELL AS RIGID MILITARY AND EDUCATION SYSTEMS, HORDES OF **JEWISH IMMIGRANTS** ARRIVED AT ELLIS ISLAND BETWEEN 1880 AND 1914. THE MAJORITY WERE POOR YIDDISH SPEAKERS FROM SHTETLS IN EASTERN EUROPE'S SO-CALLED "PALE OF SETTLEMENT."

ONE OF MY FAVORITE DEPICTIONS OF JEWISH LIFE IN AMERICA IS HENRY ROTH'S 1934 NOVEL **CALL IT SLEEP**. IT TELLS THE STORY OF A YOUNG BOY COMING OF AGE IN NEW YORK'S LOWER EAST SIDE. THE LANGUAGE IS JOYCEAN. SUPERB!

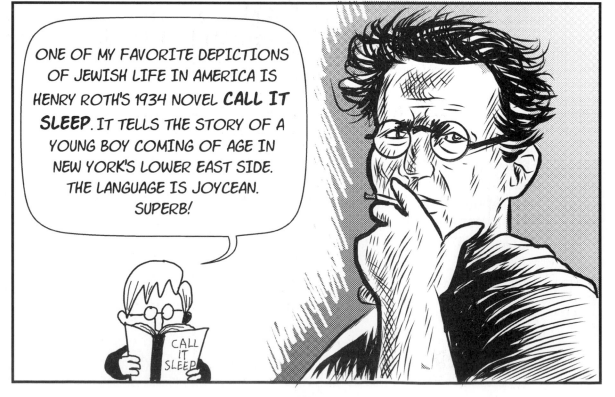

"I PLEDGE ALLEGIANCE TO THE FLAG OF THE UNITED STATES OF AMERICA, AND TO THE REPUBLIC FOR WHICH IT STANDS, ONE NATION UNDER GOD, INDIVISIBLE, WITH LIBERTY AND JUSTICE FOR ALL."

ORIGINALLY COMPOSED IN 1892, THE PLEDGE OF ALLEGIANCE WAS FORMALLY ADOPTED BY CONGRESS IN 1942.

THE FIRST VERSION WAS WRITTEN BY A BAPTIST MINISTER NAMED FRANCIS BELLAMY. IT READ: "I PLEDGE ALLEGIANCE TO **MY FLAG** AND **THE REPUBLIC** FOR WHICH IT STANDS, ONE NATION INDIVISIBLE, WITH LIBERTY AND JUSTICE FOR ALL." LATER, "MY FLAG" WAS CHANGED TO "THE FLAG OF THE UNITED STATES" SO THAT IMMIGRANTS WOULDN'T GET **CONFUSED**.

AND THEN THERE'S THE **"UNDER GOD"** PART. INCORPORATED IN 1954, THIS CONTROVERSIAL LINE IS SEEN BY SOME AS VIOLATING THE **SEPARATION** OF **CHURCH AND STATE**, PROMOTED BY FOUNDING FATHERS SUCH AS BENJAMIN FRANKLIN AND JOHN ADAMS.

EVEN AS IT WAS ABSORBING NEW PEOPLE, AMERICA WAS INTERESTED IN ABSORBING NEW LAND. TOWARD THE END OF THE NINETEENTH CENTURY, THE **CARIBBEAN BASIN** WAS UNDERGOING POLITICAL AGITATION. MANY IN THE UNITED STATES SAW THIS AS AN OPPORTUNITY TO ENLARGE THE NATION'S BORDERS.

JOSÉ MARTÍ, A CUBAN JOURNALIST, ACTIVIST, AND POET, FOUGHT FOR THE INDEPENDENCE OF HIS HOMELAND, EVEN IN EXILE. HE SPENT MUCH OF HIS LIFE IN FLORIDA AND NEW YORK, WHERE HE REPORTED ON THE BUILDING OF THE **BROOKLYN BRIDGE** AND THE UNVEILING OF **THE STATUE OF LIBERTY**.

AT THIS TIME, CUBANS WERE AWAKENING TO A **SPIRIT OF INDEPENDENCE**. MANY SOUGHT TO GAIN FREEDOM FROM **SPANISH RULE**, WHICH DATED BACK TO THE ARRIVAL OF COLUMBUS. THE SPANISH GOVERNMENT DECIDED TO CRUSH THOSE SENTIMENTS, VIOLENTLY. HUNGRY FOR NEW TERRITORY, THE UNITED STATES SOON JOINED THE FIGHT AGAINST SPAIN.

TEDDY ROOSEVELT WAS A VOCAL SUPPORTER OF U.S. INVOLVEMENT IN CUBA. IN 1898, HE WENT THERE IN PERSON AS PART OF THE FIRST UNITED STATES VOLUNTEER CAVALRY, COMMONLY KNOWN AS THE ROUGH RIDERS, HOPING TO **DEFEAT THE SPANISH**. HIS FAMOUS CHARGE UP SAN JUAN HILL MADE HIM A HERO TO CUBANS AND AMERICANS ALIKE. ROOSEVELT WAS ELECTED PRESIDENT IN 1900, TWO YEARS AFTER THE WAR WAS OVER, AND HELD OFFICE UNTIL 1909.

THE **SPANISH-AMERICAN WAR** FORCED SPAIN, BY THEN AN EMPIRE IN DECLINE, TO ABANDON ITS FORMER COLONIES—NOT ONLY CUBA AND PUERTO RICO IN THE CARIBBEAN, BUT ALSO THE PHILIPPINES AND GUAM IN THE PACIFIC. EXCEPT FOR CUBA, ALL OF THESE TERRITORIES WERE THEN ANNEXED BY THE UNITED STATES.

CUBA ACHIEVED INDEPENDENCE IN 1902 BUT REMAINED LARGELY UNDER AMERICAN CONTROL.

PUERTO RICO, MEANWHILE, HAD BECOME A COLONY OF THE UNITED STATES.

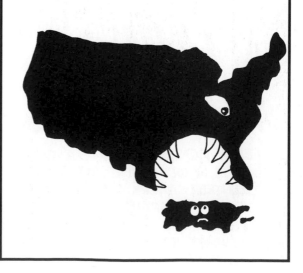

BACK IN THE UNITED STATES, AFRICAN AMERICANS WERE STILL FIGHTING THEIR OWN BATTLE FOR FREEDOM. ONE OF THE MOST IMPORTANT BLACK LEADERS OF THE POST-RECONSTRUCTION ERA WAS **BOOKER T. WASHINGTON**. HE TRIED TO HELP DISENFRANCHISED BLACKS ACHIEVE FULLER PARTICIPATION IN THE AMERICAN PROJECT. HE WAS A SAVVY, PHOTOGENIC FUND-RAISER AND DELIVERED INSPIRING—AND OFTEN MANIPULATIVE—SPEECHES.

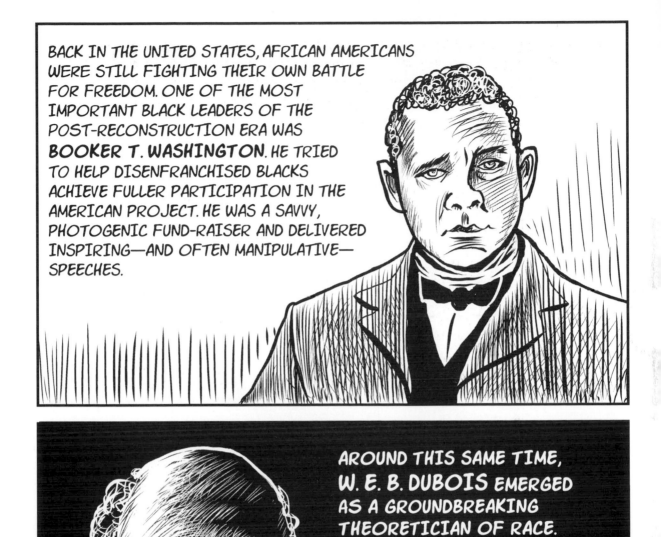

AROUND THIS SAME TIME, **W. E. B. DUBOIS** EMERGED AS A GROUNDBREAKING THEORETICIAN OF RACE.

DUBOIS ONCE SAID, "THE PROBLEM OF THE TWENTIETH CENTURY IS THE PROBLEM OF **THE COLOR LINE**," AND IN MANY WAYS HE WAS RIGHT!

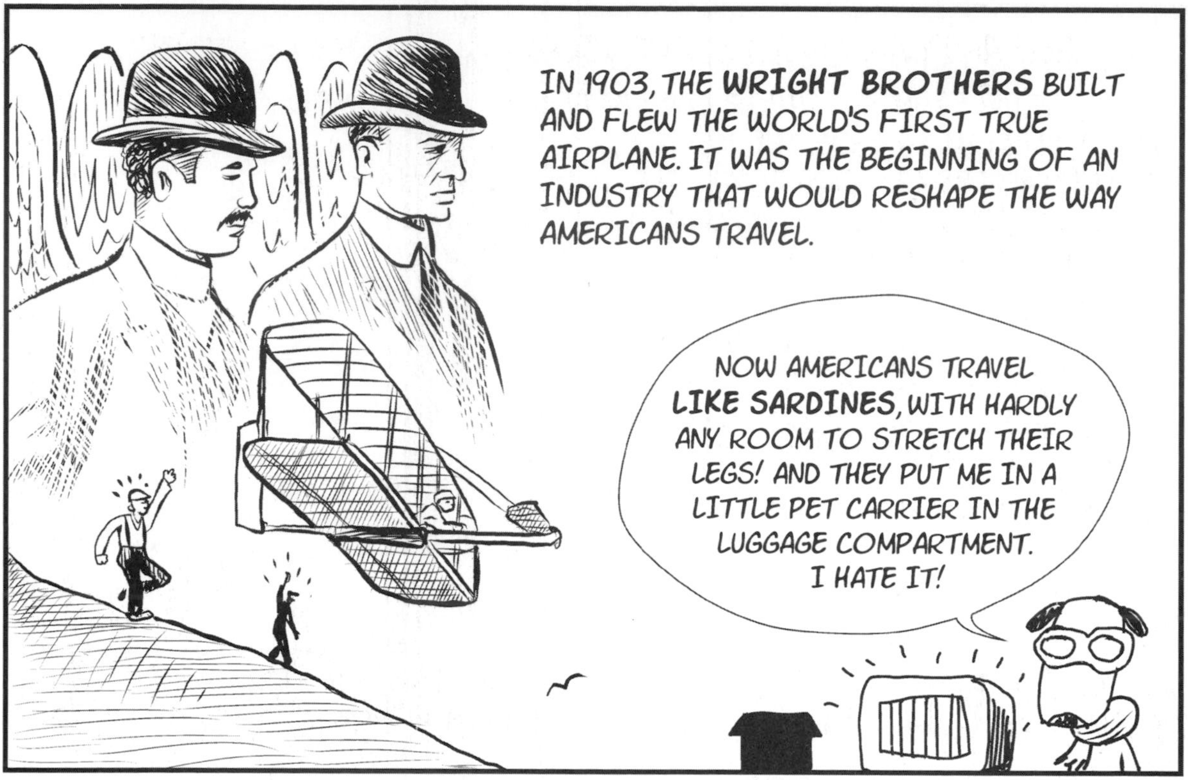
IN 1903, THE **WRIGHT BROTHERS** BUILT AND FLEW THE WORLD'S FIRST TRUE AIRPLANE. IT WAS THE BEGINNING OF AN INDUSTRY THAT WOULD RESHAPE THE WAY AMERICANS TRAVEL.
NOW AMERICANS TRAVEL **LIKE SARDINES**, WITH HARDLY ANY ROOM TO STRETCH THEIR LEGS! AND THEY PUT ME IN A LITTLE PET CARRIER IN THE LUGGAGE COMPARTMENT. I HATE IT!

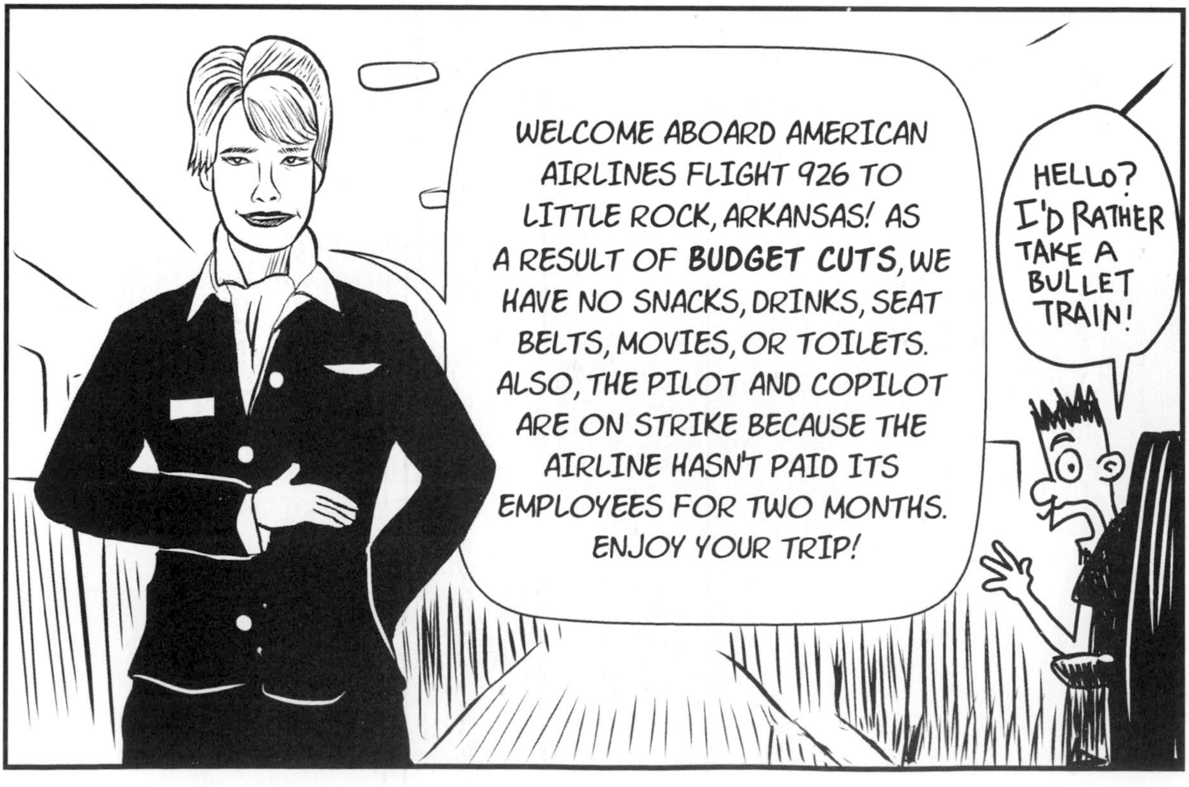
WELCOME ABOARD AMERICAN AIRLINES FLIGHT 926 TO LITTLE ROCK, ARKANSAS! AS A RESULT OF **BUDGET CUTS**, WE HAVE NO SNACKS, DRINKS, SEAT BELTS, MOVIES, OR TOILETS. ALSO, THE PILOT AND COPILOT ARE ON STRIKE BECAUSE THE AIRLINE HASN'T PAID ITS EMPLOYEES FOR TWO MONTHS. ENJOY YOUR TRIP!
HELLO? I'D RATHER TAKE A BULLET TRAIN!

THE AIRPLANE WOULD EVENTUALLY LINK THE COUNTRY TOGETHER, MUCH AS THE TRAIN HAD BEFORE IT.

FOR ME, THIS IDEA OF NATIONAL UNITY RAISES A LOT OF QUESTIONS: WHAT MAKES A NATION ANYWAY? WHY DO MODERN PEOPLE ORGANIZE THEMSELVES INTO COUNTRY-SIZED UNITS? WHAT MAKES US ALL AMERICAN? A SHARED HISTORY?

WELL, YES, BUT THAT HISTORY IS FLUID, SHIFTING, ALWAYS SUBJECT TO REINTERPRETATION.

A COMMON LAND? AN ANTHEM? A CURRENCY?

MY ANSWER: A SHARED MYTHOLOGY.

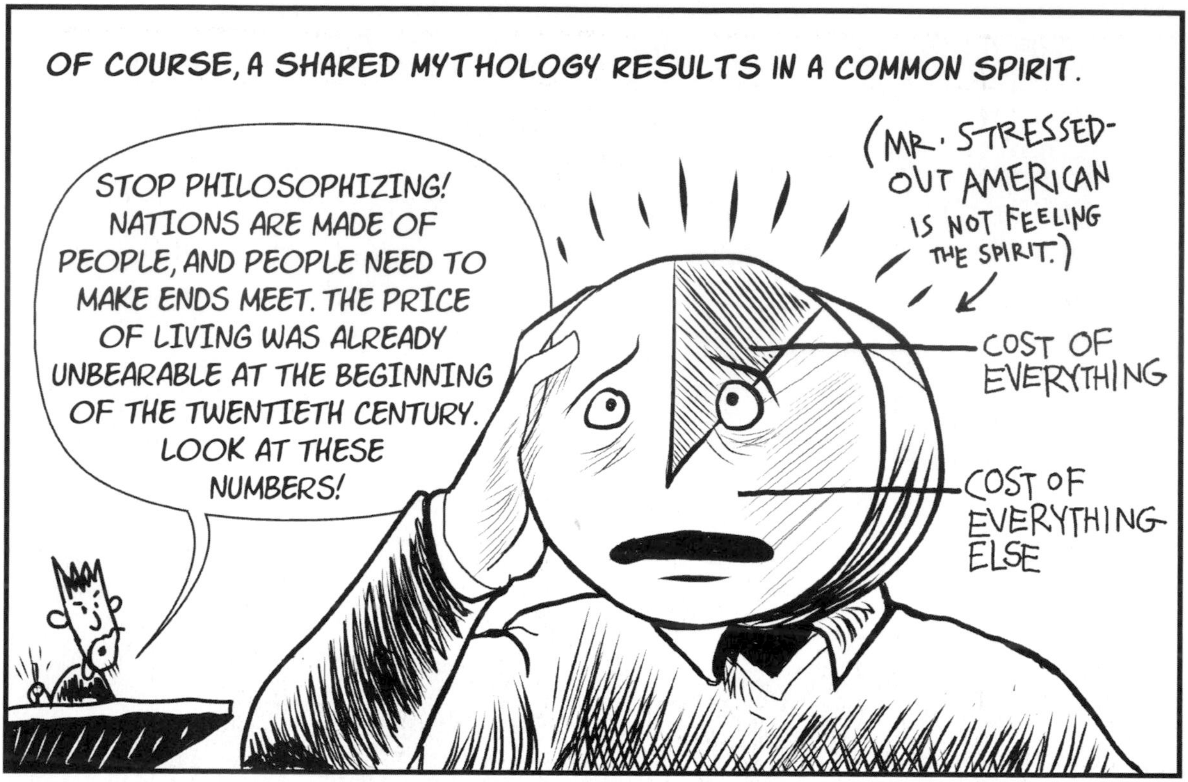
OF COURSE, A SHARED MYTHOLOGY RESULTS IN A COMMON SPIRIT.
STOP PHILOSOPHIZING! NATIONS ARE MADE OF PEOPLE, AND PEOPLE NEED TO MAKE ENDS MEET. THE PRICE OF LIVING WAS ALREADY UNBEARABLE AT THE BEGINNING OF THE TWENTIETH CENTURY. LOOK AT THESE NUMBERS!
(MR. STRESSED-OUT AMERICAN IS NOT FEELING THE SPIRIT.)
COST OF EVERYTHING
COST OF EVERYTHING ELSE

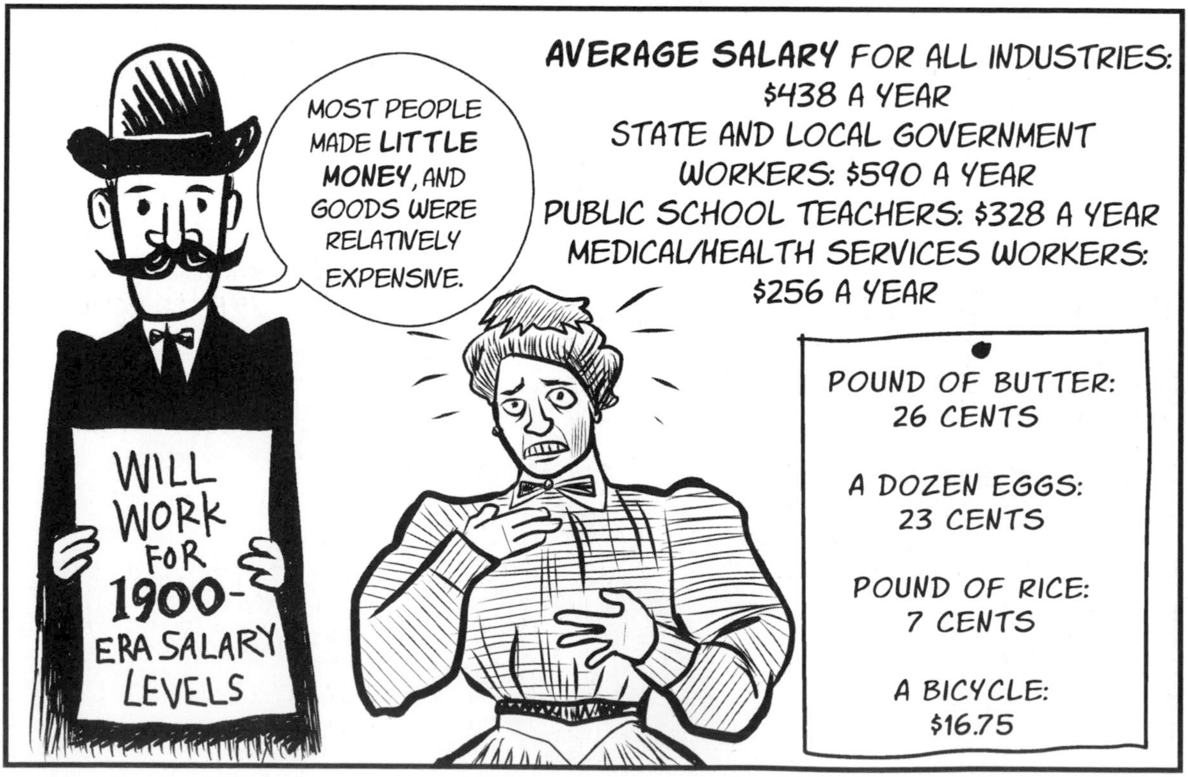
AVERAGE SALARY FOR ALL INDUSTRIES: $438 A YEAR
STATE AND LOCAL GOVERNMENT WORKERS: $590 A YEAR
PUBLIC SCHOOL TEACHERS: $328 A YEAR
MEDICAL/HEALTH SERVICES WORKERS: $256 A YEAR
MOST PEOPLE MADE LITTLE MONEY, AND GOODS WERE RELATIVELY EXPENSIVE.
WILL WORK FOR 1900-ERA SALARY LEVELS
POUND OF BUTTER: 26 CENTS
A DOZEN EGGS: 23 CENTS
POUND OF RICE: 7 CENTS
A BICYCLE: $16.75

AT THIS TIME, PUBLIC ENTERTAINMENT OFTEN TOOK THE FORM OF **ESCAPISM**. PEOPLE YEARNED TO FLEE THE FRANTIC RHYTHM OF LIFE THROUGH SPECTACLES SUCH AS STUNTS, CIRCUS PERFORMANCES, FANTASTIC STORIES, AND THEATRICAL PIROUETTES. THE MOST FAMOUS ENTERTAINER OF THE EARLY TWENTIETH CENTURY WAS **HARRY HOUDINI**, AN ESCAPE ARTIST WHO PERFORMED MIRACULOUS ESCAPES FROM HANDCUFFS AND SEALED CONTAINERS.

AMAZING! I HAVE MAGIC-ALLY FORGOTTEN THAT I AM DIRT POOR!

MEANWHILE, HENRY FORD WAS WORKING HIS OWN FORM OF MAGIC, PUTTING **AUTOMOBILES** WITHIN THE REACH OF MILLIONS OF MIDDLE-CLASS AMERICANS. IN 1908, THE FORD MOTOR COMPANY INTRODUCED THE MODEL T, WHICH WAS LIGHTER, **MORE AFFORDABLE**, AND EASIER TO REPAIR THAN PREVIOUS MODELS. FORD ACCOMPLISHED THIS REVOLUTION THROUGH THE USE OF **ASSEMBLY LINES**, IN WHICH WORKERS ADDED PARTS TO THE CAR IN A FIXED SEQUENCE.

BASEBALL WAS ALSO SURGING IN POPULARITY AROUND THIS TIME, WITH THE FIRST MODERN WORLD SERIES HELD IN 1903. IN THE DECADES TO COME, FIGURES LIKE BABE RUTH, MICKEY MANTLE, JACKIE ROBINSON, AND TONY PÉREZ WOULD BECOME **NATIONAL IDOLS**. IN MANY WAYS, BASEBALL IS A MIRROR OF AMERICAN SOCIETY: RACE, LANGUAGE, AND CLASS ARE ALL REFLECTED IN IT.

SPORTS SHOWCASE AMERICA'S **COMPETITIVE STREAK**. EVERY PITCH DESERVES TO BE ANSWERED WITH A HOME RUN. OTHERWISE, IT'S A WASTE!

DONT FORGET IMMIGRATION, ANOTHER **ESSENTIAL ISSUE**. MANY PLAYERS FROM ASIA AND LATIN AMERICA HAVE ENTERED AMERICA THROUGH THE "BASEBALL DOOR."

AND LET'S NOT FORGET MUSIC— THE EARLY TWENTIETH CENTURY ALSO SAW THE EMERGENCE OF **JAZZ!**

DIZZY GILLESPIE

JAZZ IS AN **AMERICAN INVENTION**, A MUSICAL STYLE INTIMATELY CONNECTED TO BLACK CULTURE. IT ORIGINATED IN THE SOUTH IN THE EARLY 1910S. WITHOUT ACCESS TO FORMAL EDUCATION, **BLACK MUSICIANS**, INFLUENCED BY CHURCH SPIRITUALS, MINSTREL AND SALON MUSIC, AND TRADITIONAL AFRICAN RHYTHMS, CREATED A NEW ARTISTIC FORM THAT INITIALLY THRIVED IN THE MARGINS OF SOCIETY BUT EVENTUALLY BECAME AN AMERICAN STAPLE.

HERBIE HANCOCK

MILES DAVIS

PAQUITO D'RIVERA

RAGTIME

A DIRECT PRECURSOR TO JAZZ, **RAGTIME** WAS A POPULAR MUSIC AND DANCE STYLE AT THE TURN OF THE TWENTIETH CENTURY. IT STARTED IN THE BLACK COMMUNITY BUT QUICKLY CAUGHT ON AMONG THE WHITE POPULATION AS WELL. THERE WERE MANY STYLES OF RAGTIME, INCLUDING FOLK, CLASSIC, AND FOX-TROT. ONE OF THE MOST FAMOUS RAGTIME COMPOSERS WAS SCOTT JOPLIN.

HAVE YOU READ E. L. DOCTOROW'S NOVEL **RAGTIME**?

NO, BUT I'VE SEEN THE MOVIE DIRECTED BY MILOS FORMAN.

IN 1909, **SIGMUND FREUD**, THE FOUNDER OF PSYCHOANALYSIS, VISITED AMERICA. HIS PECULIAR BRAND OF THERAPY WOULD TAKE HOLD IN THE UNITED STATES AND FOREVER CHANGE THE WAY WE THINK ABOUT **OUR OWN MINDS**.

FREUD BELIEVED THAT WE'RE ALL AT THE MERCY OF OUR SEXUAL INSTINCTS, AND THAT WE REPRESS THOSE **INSTINCTS** IN ORDER TO BECOME CIVILIZED. HE ALSO STRESSED THAT THE FAMILY IS THE SOURCE OF **OUR MISERY**.

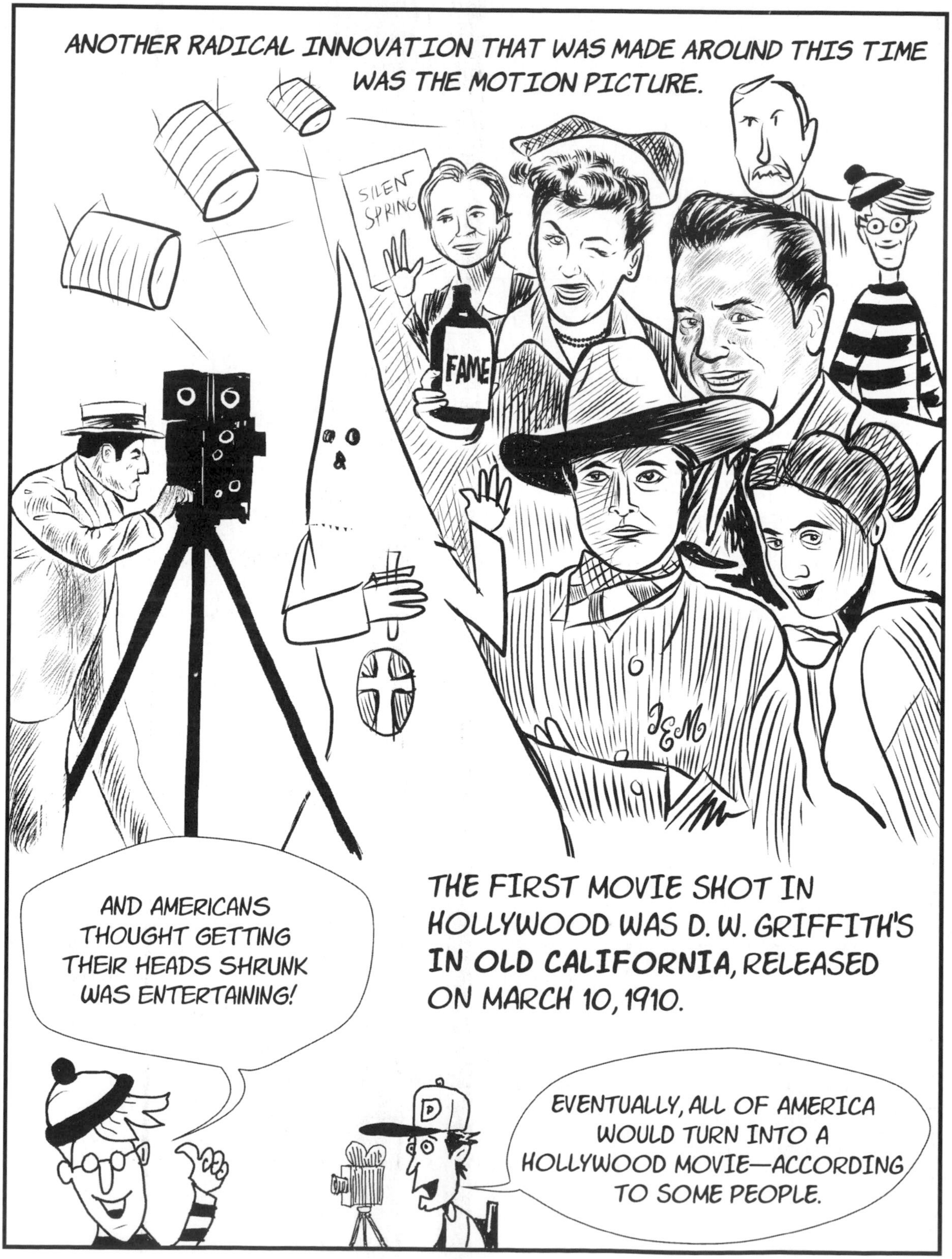
ANOTHER RADICAL INNOVATION THAT WAS MADE AROUND THIS TIME WAS THE MOTION PICTURE.
SILENT SPRING
FAME
J&M
AND AMERICANS THOUGHT GETTING THEIR HEADS SHRUNK WAS ENTERTAINING!
THE FIRST MOVIE SHOT IN HOLLYWOOD WAS D. W. GRIFFITH'S **IN OLD CALIFORNIA**, RELEASED ON MARCH 10, 1910.
EVENTUALLY, ALL OF AMERICA WOULD TURN INTO A HOLLYWOOD MOVIE—ACCORDING TO SOME PEOPLE.

ON MARCH 25, 1911, A **DEADLY FIRE** CONSUMED NEW YORK'S TRIANGLE SHIRTWAIST FACTORY—A DISASTER WHOSE DEVASTATION HAS EVOKED COMPARISONS TO THE TERRORIST ATTACKS OF SEPTEMBER 11. THE FACTORY OCCUPIED THE EIGHTH, NINTH, AND TENTH FLOORS OF THE ASCH BUILDING AT 23-29 WASHINGTON PLACE. BEFORE THE **FIRE**, THE MANAGEMENT HAD LOCKED THE **EXIT DOORS** TO PREVENT THE THEFT OF MERCHANDISE—A COMMON SECURITY MEASURE AT THE TIME—GIVING THE WORKERS NO WAY TO ESCAPE. THE **FIRE DEPARTMENT** HAD NO LADDERS THAT COULD REACH THE TRAPPED WORKERS AND **FALLING BODIES** MADE IT DIFFICULT FOR THE FIREMEN TO DO THEIR JOB. IN THE END, 146 GARMENT WORKERS DIED, MOSTLY JEWISH AND ITALIAN IMMIGRANT WOMEN. THE COMPANY'S OWNERS, MAX BLANCK AND ISAAC HARRIS, WERE INDICTED ON CHARGES OF FIRST- AND SECOND-DEGREE **MANSLAUGHTER** BUT WERE ACQUITTED.

MEANWHILE, ALL THESE IMMIGRANTS WERE HAVING A POWERFUL EFFECT ON AMERICAN CULTURE.

DESPITE REPEATED ATTEMPTS TO ENSHRINE IT AS THE NATION'S OFFICIAL LANGUAGE, THE USE OF ENGLISH IN THE UNITED STATES IS NOT FORMALLY MANDATED BY FEDERAL LAW, THOUGH MANY IMMIGRANTS HAVE CHOSEN TO ADOPT IT. IN ANY CASE, THE FIRST AMENDMENT GUARANTEES AMERICAN CITIZENS THE RIGHT TO FREE SPEECH, AN ESSENTIAL COMPONENT OF OUR DEMOCRACY. **FREEDOM OF SPEECH** MEANS WE HAVE PERMISSION TO **SAY AS MUCH AS WE WANT**—IN ANY LANGUAGE WE WANT—EVEN AGAINST THE NATION'S POLITICAL ELITES.

BILINGUAL EDUCATION IN AMERICA DATES BACK TO THE EIGHTEENTH CENTURY. IN 1961, THE GOVERNMENT BEGAN PROVIDING FEDERAL FUNDS TO SCHOOL DISTRICTS TO ASSIST WITH **BILINGUAL EDUCATION**, LARGELY IN RESPONSE TO HIGH DROPOUT RATES AMONG SPANISH-SPEAKING STUDENTS. TO SOME EXTENT, THE COUNTRY'S RELATIVELY **TOLERANT ATTITUDE** TOWARD OTHER LANGUAGES IS THE RESULT OF THIS NATIONWIDE PROGRAM.

THE FACT THAT THIS IS A COUNTRY OF IMMIGRANTS MEANS THAT PEOPLE COME HERE SPEAKING **A MULTITUDE OF LANGUAGES.** YET, AFTER A GENERATION OR SO, THEIR FAMILIES USUALLY SPEAK ONLY ENGLISH. THIS ASSIMILATION PROCESS IS ACHIEVED PRINCIPALLY THROUGH THE SCHOOL SYSTEM.

← ACTUAL SIGN

RESPECT ARE COUNTRY SPEAK ENGLISH

OF COURSE, SOME PEOPLE THINK IMMIGRANTS AND THEIR FAMILIES DON'T SWITCH LANGUAGES FAST ENOUGH. THUS, OVER THE YEARS, THEY'VE PUSHED FOR **STRICT LAWS CONCERNING ENGLISH.**

SPANGLISH ONLY!

I HAS A RITE TO BIGNURANT

DUH!

SPEAK AMERICAN

SMART

Ynglish
Franglais
Chinglish
Spanglish
Ingrish
Germish
Pidgin

IN FACT, THERE HAVE ALWAYS BEEN **HYBRID WAYS OF SPEAKING** IN THE UNITED STATES. WHEN HE MOVED HERE FROM WARSAW IN 1935, ISAAC BASHEVIS SINGER WAS SHOCKED BY THE WAY JEWISH IMMIGRANTS CONTAMINATED THEIR YIDDISH WITH ENGLISH LOANWORDS.

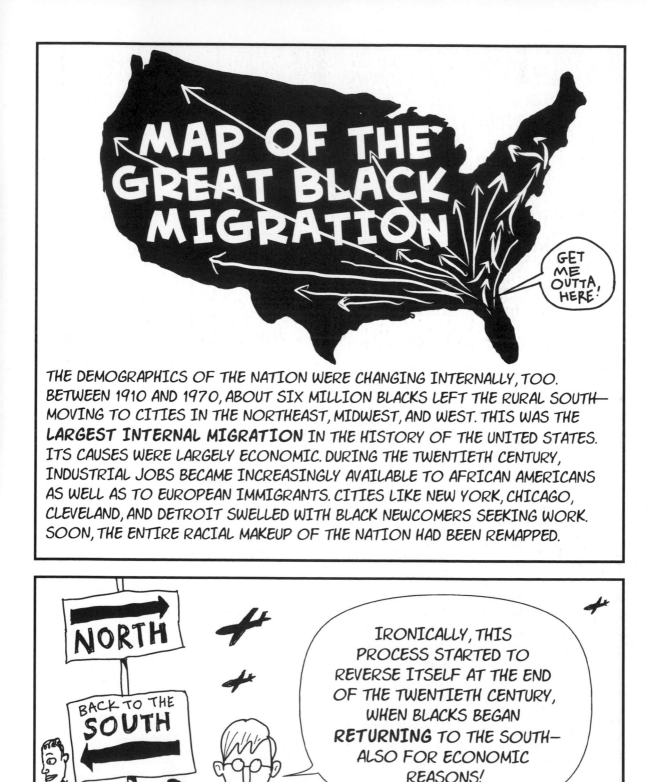

THE DEMOGRAPHICS OF THE NATION WERE CHANGING INTERNALLY, TOO. BETWEEN 1910 AND 1970, ABOUT SIX MILLION BLACKS LEFT THE RURAL SOUTH— MOVING TO CITIES IN THE NORTHEAST, MIDWEST, AND WEST. THIS WAS THE **LARGEST INTERNAL MIGRATION** IN THE HISTORY OF THE UNITED STATES. ITS CAUSES WERE LARGELY ECONOMIC. DURING THE TWENTIETH CENTURY, INDUSTRIAL JOBS BECAME INCREASINGLY AVAILABLE TO AFRICAN AMERICANS AS WELL AS TO EUROPEAN IMMIGRANTS. CITIES LIKE NEW YORK, CHICAGO, CLEVELAND, AND DETROIT SWELLED WITH BLACK NEWCOMERS SEEKING WORK. SOON, THE ENTIRE RACIAL MAKEUP OF THE NATION HAD BEEN REMAPPED.

"POOR Mexico, so far from GOD and so close to the United States."

—Mexican Dictator Porfirio Díaz

MEANWHILE, IN MEXICO, EVENTS WERE UNFOLDING THAT WOULD HAVE A MAJOR IMPACT ON THE UNITED STATES. THE **MEXICAN REVOLUTION**, WHICH STARTED IN 1910, WAS A RESPONSE TO DECADES OF U.S.-BACKED TYRANNY UNDER PRESIDENT PORFIRIO DÍAZ.

HE MAY HAVE BEEN A TYRANT, BUT PORFIRIO DÍAZ HELPED MODERNIZE MEXICO, BUILDING RAILROADS, BRINGING ELECTRICITY TO MAJOR CITIES, AND SO ON.

BUT HE TAXED EVERYTHING! YOU NEEDED TO PAY A TAX IF YOU WANTED TO HAVE A POTTED PLANT ON YOUR BALCONY.

PANCHO VILLA

EMILIANO ZAPATA

¡VIVA MEXICO!

IT'S ESTIMATED THAT BETWEEN 1 AND 2 MILLION PEOPLE DIED IN THE REVOLUTION, WHICH CONCLUDED—MÁS O MENOS—IN 1920. ONE MAJOR CONSEQUENCE OF THE UPHEAVAL WAS INCREASED **MEXICAN IMMIGRATION TO THE UNITED STATES.**

CAUTION

IN MANY WAYS, THE MEXICAN REVOLUTION SERVED AS AMERICA'S DRESS REHEARSAL FOR WORLD WAR I. IN 1916, **GENERAL JOHN J. PERSHING** WAS SENT TO MEXICO WITH 5,000 TROOPS TO CAPTURE THE REVOLUTIONARY LEADER PANCHO VILLA. ALTHOUGH THEY WERE UNSUCCESSFUL, PERSHING'S MEN—AND THE FLEDGLING AMERICAN AIR FORCE—GAINED VALUABLE FIGHTING EXPERIENCE, WHICH THEY WOULD PUT TO GOOD USE ONCE AMERICA JOINED THE GROWING CONFLICT IN EUROPE.

IN THE EARLY STAGES OF WORLD WAR I, AMERICA MAINTAINED A POLICY OF STRICT NEUTRALITY. THIS STARTED TO CHANGE AROUND 1915, WHEN THE GERMANS SANK THE BRITISH OCEAN LINER **RMS LUSITANIA**, KILLING 128 AMERICAN PASSENGERS. PUBLIC OPINION CHANGED DRASTICALLY AFTER THIS, BUT THE UNITED STATES OFFICIALLY STAYED OUT OF THE CONFLICT (DESPITE SUPPORTING BRITAIN) UNTIL 1917, WHEN IT FORMALLY ENTERED THE WAR.

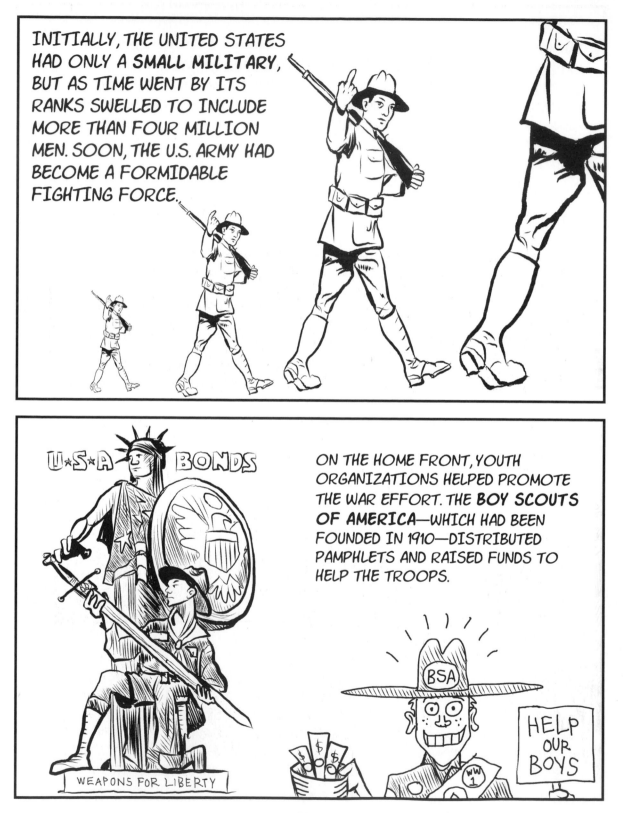

INITIALLY, THE UNITED STATES HAD ONLY A **SMALL MILITARY**, BUT AS TIME WENT BY ITS RANKS SWELLED TO INCLUDE MORE THAN FOUR MILLION MEN. SOON, THE U.S. ARMY HAD BECOME A FORMIDABLE FIGHTING FORCE.

U*S*A BONDS

ON THE HOME FRONT, YOUTH ORGANIZATIONS HELPED PROMOTE THE WAR EFFORT. THE **BOY SCOUTS OF AMERICA**—WHICH HAD BEEN FOUNDED IN 1910—DISTRIBUTED PAMPHLETS AND RAISED FUNDS TO HELP THE TROOPS.

WEAPONS FOR LIBERTY

BSA

WW 1

HELP OUR BOYS

BY THE TIME AN ARMISTICE WAS SIGNED IN NOVEMBER 1918, 116,000 AMERICAN SOLDIERS HAD LOST THEIR LIVES.

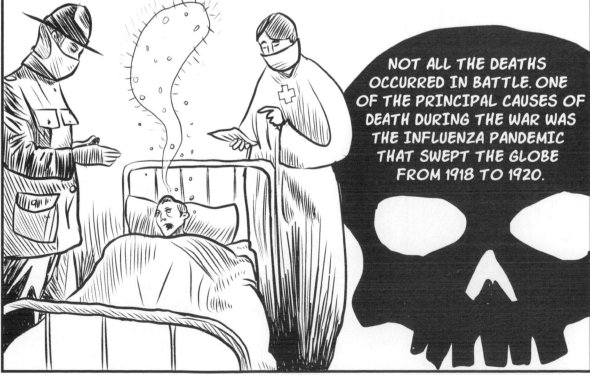

NOT ALL THE DEATHS OCCURRED IN BATTLE. ONE OF THE PRINCIPAL CAUSES OF DEATH DURING THE WAR WAS THE INFLUENZA PANDEMIC THAT SWEPT THE GLOBE FROM 1918 TO 1920.

ON THE PLUS SIDE, AMERICA HAD PURCHASED THE U.S. VIRGIN ISLANDS FROM DENMARK IN 1917, PARTLY OUT OF FEAR THAT THEY WOULD BE SEIZED BY THE GERMANS.

ST. THOMAS

ST. JOHN

WERE THEY REALLY VIRGINS?

NOT AFTER AMERICAN SOLDIERS ARRIVED.

ST. CROIX

THE **TREATY OF VERSAILLES** WAS SIGNED ON JUNE 28, 1919, OFFICIALLY ENDING THE WAR. GERMANY HAD LOST. THE VICTORIOUS ALLIES—INCLUDING BRITAIN, FRANCE, ITALY, AND THE UNITED STATES—IMPOSED HEAVY PENALTIES ON THEIR VANQUISHED FOE.

THAT WILL TEACH YOU, GERMANY!

IN 1916, **LOUIS BRANDEIS** WAS APPOINTED TO THE SUPREME COURT.

HE WAS THE FIRST JEW ON THE COURT! MAYBE THE FIRST MINORITY...

PUERTO RICO

IN 1917, PRESIDENT WOODROW WILSON SIGNED THE JONES-SHAFROTH ACT, COLLECTIVELY TURNING PUERTO RICANS INTO U.S. CITIZENS.

REALLY? I THOUGHT THEY WERE LATIN AMERICANS.

PUERTO RICO, LIKE MASSACHUSETTS AND VIRGINIA, IS A **COMMONWEALTH**—AN OBNOXIOUSLY AMBIGUOUS POLITICAL TERM. DESPITE THE 1917 LAW, PUERTO RICO ISN'T A STATE, AND PUERTO RICANS CAN'T VOTE FOR THE NATION'S PRESIDENT.

MAYBE YOU SHOULD CHANGE THE TEXT TO SAY, "IN 1917, PRESIDENT WOODROW WILSON SIGNED THE JONES-SHAFROTH ACT, COLLECTIVELY TURNING PUERTO RICANS INTO **SECOND-CLASS** U.S. CITIZENS."

THE **PROHIBITION ERA** BEGAN ON JANUARY 17, 1920, WHEN THE EIGHTEENTH AMENDMENT'S BAN ON ALCOHOL WENT INTO EFFECT. THE ERA LASTED UNTIL 1933, WHEN THE TWENTY-FIRST AMENDMENT REPEALED THE EIGHTEENTH.

LEGISLATORS SHOULD HAVE KNOWN BETTER. **BOOZE** IS AN ESSENTIAL COMPONENT OF THE AMERICAN LIFESTYLE.

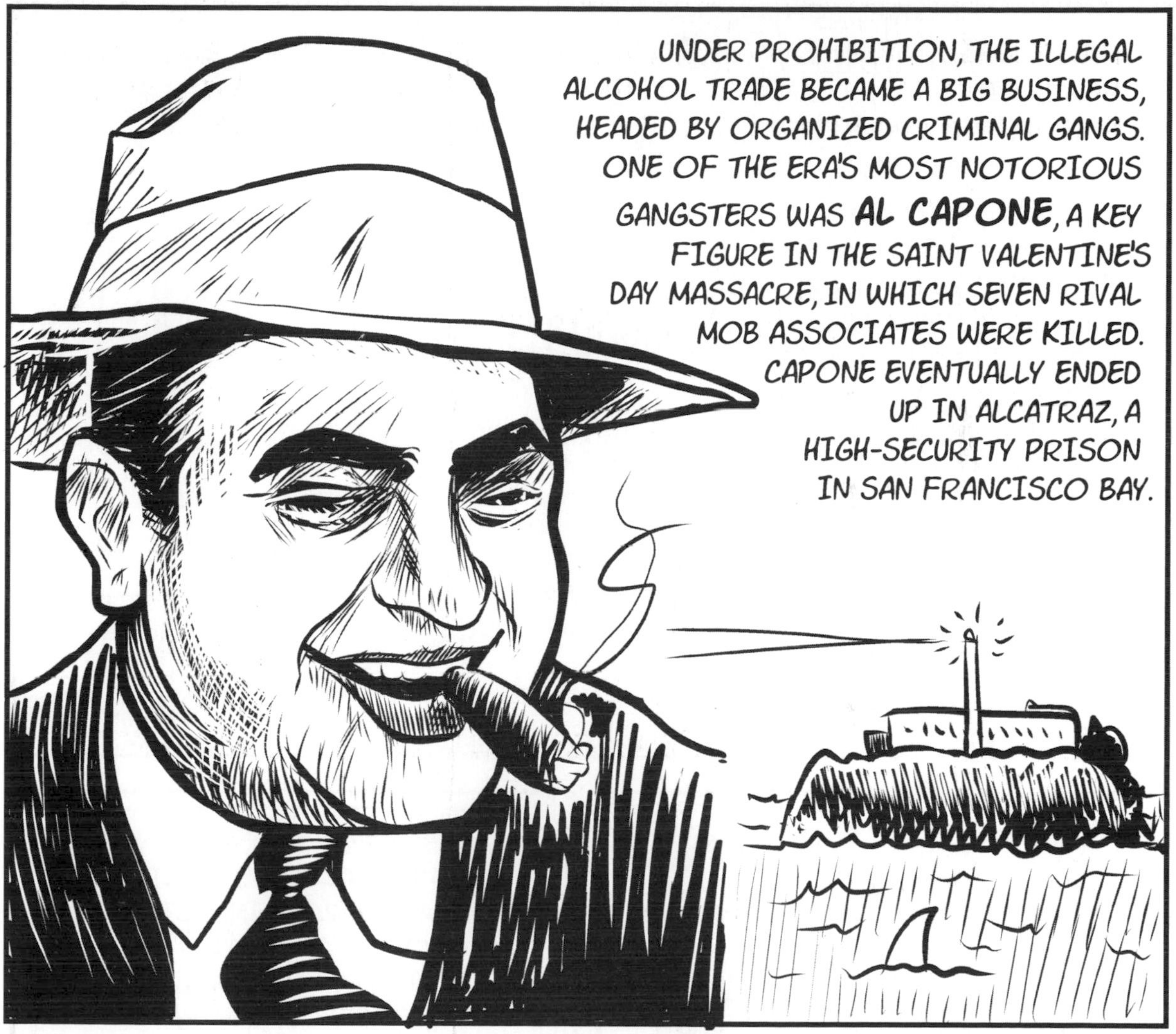
UNDER PROHIBITION, THE ILLEGAL ALCOHOL TRADE BECAME A BIG BUSINESS, HEADED BY ORGANIZED CRIMINAL GANGS. ONE OF THE ERA'S MOST NOTORIOUS GANGSTERS WAS **AL CAPONE**, A KEY FIGURE IN THE SAINT VALENTINE'S DAY MASSACRE, IN WHICH SEVEN RIVAL MOB ASSOCIATES WERE KILLED. CAPONE EVENTUALLY ENDED UP IN ALCATRAZ, A HIGH-SECURITY PRISON IN SAN FRANCISCO BAY.

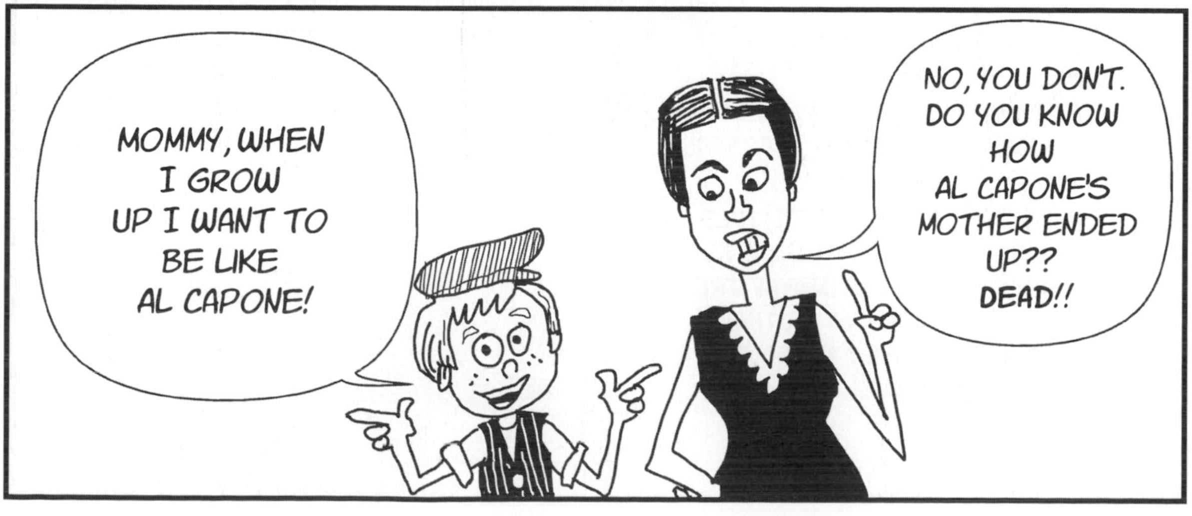
MOMMY, WHEN I GROW UP I WANT TO BE LIKE AL CAPONE!
NO, YOU DON'T. DO YOU KNOW HOW AL CAPONE'S MOTHER ENDED UP?? **DEAD!!**

THE ROARING TWENTIES

WOMEN PLAYED A PROMINENT ROLE IN THE **ANTIALCOHOL MOVEMENT**, AND FEMALE ACTIVISTS ALSO HELPED PASS ANOTHER, MORE ENDURING CONSTITUTIONAL AMENDMENT. RATIFIED IN 1920, THE SAME YEAR PROHIBITION WENT INTO EFFECT, THE NINETEENTH AMENDMENT FINALLY GAVE AMERICAN WOMEN THE RIGHT TO VOTE.

THE FOLLOWING YEAR, AMERICA WAS TRANSFIXED BY A CONTROVERSIAL TRIAL. **NICOLA SACCO** AND **BARTOLOMEO VANZETTI**, TWO LEFT-WING ITALIAN IMMIGRANTS, WERE ACCUSED OF MURDER BY THE STATE OF MASSACHUSETTS. THEY WOULD EVENTUALLY BE TRIED AND SENTENCED TO DEATH.

MANY BELIEVED THAT SACCO AND VANZETTI'S ANARCHIST BELIEFS PLAYED A ROLE IN THEIR CONVICTION. AFTER ALL, THERE'S NOTHING GOVERNMENTS ARE MORE AFRAID OF THAN PEOPLE WHO WANT TO **BRING DOWN** THE GOVERNMENT AND REPLACE IT WITH NOTHING!

ON NOVEMBER 2, 1922, ANOTHER ANARCHIST—THE MEXICAN **RICARDO FLORES MAGÓN**—DIED IN LEAVENWORTH PRISON IN KANSAS. THE U.S. GOVERNMENT HAD ACCUSED HIM OF OBSTRUCTING THE WAR EFFORT.

HIS BIBLE WAS PETER KROPOTKIN'S **THE CONQUEST OF BREAD**, WHICH CLAIMS THAT CAPITALISM CAUSES POVERTY.

JOSÉ VASCONCELOS WAS ANOTHER MEXICAN WHO HAD LIVED TEMPORARILY IN THE UNITED STATES. IN 1925, HE PUBLISHED **THE COSMIC RACE**, WHICH PREDICTED THAT MESTIZOS—LATIN AMERICANS OF MIXED EUROPEAN AND INDIAN ANCESTRY—WOULD COME TO CONQUER THE WORLD. HE SPOKE OF A BRONZE AGE, WHEN HISPANICS WOULD BE ON THE RISE DEMOGRAPHICALLY, POLITICALLY, AND CULTURALLY.

ISN'T THAT WHAT'S HAPPENING IN TWENTY-FIRST CENTURY AMERICA? LATINOS ARE NOW THE LARGEST AND **FASTEST-GROWING MINORITY**, WITH A TOTAL U.S. POPULATION OF APPROXIMATELY 55 MILLION. COMBINED WITH 590 MILLION PEOPLE LIVING THROUGHOUT LATIN AMERICA, THAT CERTAINLY SEEMS TO CONSTITUTE A COSMIC ... SOMETHING.

La Raza Cosmica

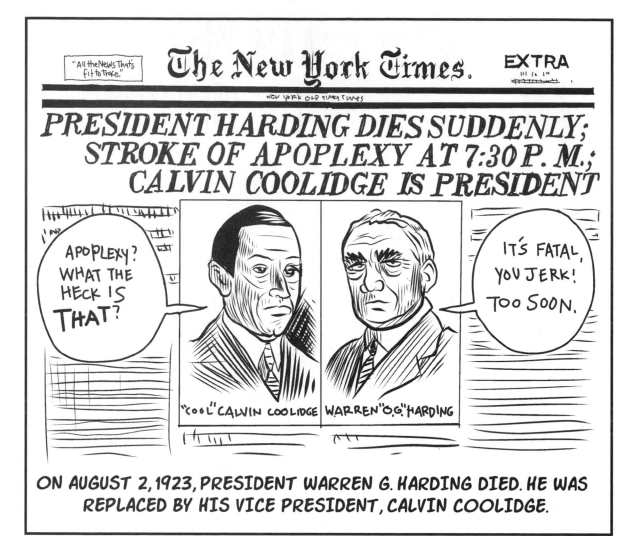

ON AUGUST 2, 1923, PRESIDENT WARREN G. HARDING DIED. HE WAS REPLACED BY HIS VICE PRESIDENT, CALVIN COOLIDGE.

THE NEXT YEAR, COOLIDGE APPOINTED **J. EDGAR HOOVER** TO THE TOP SPOT AT THE BUREAU OF INVESTIGATION, LATER KNOWN AS THE FBI. HOOVER WOULD BE KNOWN FOR HIS **PERSECUTION OF COMMUNISTS** DURING THE RED SCARE OF THE 1950S.

CHAPTER 5
THE PROGRESS MACHINE

THE WORST ECONOMIC DISASTER OF THE TWENTIETH CENTURY SHOOK THE WORLD IN 1929. THE STOCK MARKET CRASHED IN OCTOBER OF THAT YEAR, RESULTING IN A **GLOBAL DEPRESSION** THAT LASTED FOR A DECADE OR MORE. IT AFFECTED NATIONS ALL OVER THE WORLD, FROM FRANCE TO THE NETHERLANDS, JAPAN TO THE SOVIET UNION. IN GERMANY, THE DEPRESSION EVENTUALLY FACILITATED THE RISE OF DICTATOR ADOLF HITLER.

IN MANY WAYS, THE UNITED STATES WAS GROUND ZERO OF THE DEPRESSION. MILLIONS LOST THEIR JOBS. FAMILIES LOST THEIR HOMES AND WERE FORCED TO HIT THE ROAD IN SEARCH OF WORK. JOHN STEINBECK DEPICTED THE JOURNEY OF ONE FAMILY OF TENANT FARMERS FROM OKLAHOMA TO CALIFORNIA IN HIS 1939 NOVEL **THE GRAPES OF WRATH.**

IN 1929, THE UNITED STATES
HAD A TOTAL POPULATION
OF 121,767,000.
ALMOST EVERYONE SUFFERED
IN SOME WAY.

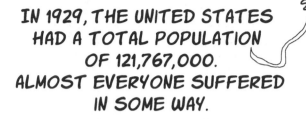

UNEMPLOYMENT RATE:
    1929: 3.2%
    1930: 8.9%
    1931: 16.3%
    1932: 24.1%

1933: 24.9%
1934: 21.7%
1935: 20.1%
1936: 16.9%
1937: 14.3%
1938: 19.0%
1939: 17.2%

DOW JONES INDUSTRIAL AVERAGE
PEAK IN SEPTEMBER 1929: 381.17
TROUGH IN JULY 1932: 41.22

AVERAGE RATE OF
DEATH BY SUICIDE
(PER 100,000 PEOPLE)
1920–1928: 12.1
1929: 18.1
1930–1940: 15.4

THE CAUSES OF THE DEPRESSION WERE MANIFOLD AND INCLUDED **ENORMOUS DEBT, DEFLATION, AND A DECLINE IN PERSONAL INCOME.** MANY AMERICANS FELT THAT BANKS WERE TO BLAME.

BONNIE!

CLYDE!

DIDN'T BONNIE AND CLYDE OPERATE DURING THE DEPRESSION? I SAW A MOVIE ABOUT THEM ONCE!

YES! BY ROBBING BANKS, BONNIE PARKER AND CLYDE BARROW TAPPED INTO THE PUBLIC FRUSTRATION WITH FINANCIAL INSTITUTIONS— THEY BECAME FOLK HEROES! AS FAR AS MOVIES GO, I PREFER BRIAN DE PALMA'S **THE UNTOUCHABLES.**

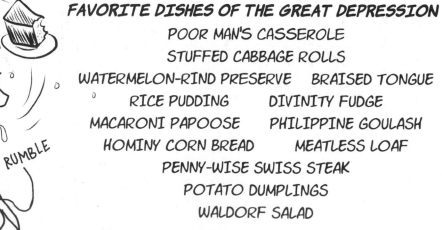

FAVORITE DISHES OF THE GREAT DEPRESSION

POOR MAN'S CASSEROLE

STUFFED CABBAGE ROLLS

WATERMELON-RIND PRESERVE   BRAISED TONGUE

RICE PUDDING   DIVINITY FUDGE

MACARONI PAPOOSE   PHILIPPINE GOULASH

HOMINY CORN BREAD   MEATLESS LOAF

PENNY-WISE SWISS STEAK

POTATO DUMPLINGS

WALDORF SALAD

RUMBLE   RUMBLE

IN THE MIDST OF THE DEPRESSION, A SHOCKING EVENT CAPTURED THE NATION'S ATTENTION. ON MARCH 1, 1932, THE TWENTY-MONTH-OLD SON OF AVIATOR **CHARLES LINDBERGH** WAS ABDUCTED FROM HIS HOME IN EAST AMWELL, NEW JERSEY. LINDBERGH HAD BECOME AN INTERNATIONAL CELEBRITY AFTER FLYING FROM NEW YORK TO PARIS IN A SINGLE-SEAT, SINGLE-ENGINE PLANE CALLED THE **SPIRIT OF ST. LOUIS**. (HE WAS ALSO A PROPONENT OF EUGENICS, AND HAS BEEN ACCUSED OF BEING A NAZI SYMPATHIZER) THE FATE OF THE LINDBERGH BABY, WHOSE BODY WAS ULTIMATELY FOUND MORE THAN TWO MONTHS LATER, NOT FAR FROM HIS HOME, LED TO THE PASSAGE OF THE "LINDBERGH LAW," WHICH MADE IT A FEDERAL CRIME TO TRANSPORT A KIDNAPPING VICTIM ACROSS STATE LINES. RESPONDING TO THE MOOD OF NATIONAL HYSTERIA, H. L. MENCKEN CALLED THE KIDNAPPING **"THE BIGGEST STORY SINCE THE RESURRECTION."**

IN RESPONSE TO THE ONGOING DEPRESSION, PRESIDENT FRANKLIN DELANO ROOSEVELT INTRODUCED THE **NEW DEAL**, A SERIES OF MEASURES DESIGNED TO HELP THE POOR AND PROMOTE ECONOMIC RECOVERY. ROOSEVELT'S OWN STORY WAS MESMERIZING: HE WAS PARALYZED FROM THE WAIST DOWN DUE TO POLIO, WHICH HE'D CONTRACTED WHILE VACATIONING IN 1921. BUT ROOSEVELT WAS AN **INVETERATE OPTIMIST**. ALTHOUGH HE REFUSED TO ACKNOWLEDGE HIS PARALYSIS, HE MANAGED TO ACHIEVE GREAT THINGS IN SPITE OF HIS CONDITION—SPENDING TWELVE YEARS IN OFFICE AND EARNING A REPUTATION AS ONE OF OUR NATION'S GREATEST PRESIDENTS.

IN HIS INAUGURAL ADDRESS, ROOSEVELT FAMOUSLY SAID, "THE ONLY THING WE HAVE TO FEAR IS FEAR ITSELF." NONETHELESS, THE COUNTRY WAS OFTEN PRONE TO PANIC. IN 1938, ORSON WELLES, THE FUTURE DIRECTOR OF **CITIZEN KANE**, CREATED A RADIO DRAMA BASED ON THE H. G. WELLS NOVEL **THE WAR OF THE WORLDS**. THE BROADCAST WAS SO REALISTIC THAT MANY PEOPLE BELIEVED ALIENS HAD LANDED ON EARTH.

IN THAT SAME INAUGURAL ADDRESS, ROOSEVELT TRIED TO ASSUAGE THE FEARS OF NON-AMERICANS AS WELL: "IN THE FIELD OF WORLD POLICY I WOULD DEDICATE THIS NATION TO **THE POLICY OF THE GOOD NEIGHBOR**—THE NEIGHBOR WHO RESOLUTELY RESPECTS HIMSELF AND, BECAUSE HE DOES SO, RESPECTS THE RIGHTS OF OTHERS—THE NEIGHBOR WHO RESPECTS HIS OBLIGATIONS AND RESPECTS THE SANCTITY OF HIS AGREEMENTS IN AND WITH A WORLD OF NEIGHBORS."

BANANA REPUBLIC

MANY YEARS LATER, HUGO CHÁVEZ, THE SOCIALIST LEADER OF VENEZUELA, MOCKED THE "GOOD NEIGHBOR POLICY."

THE UNITED STATES LIKES TO HIDE BEHIND A **FRIENDLY SMILE.** IF WE AREN'T ON GUARD, THEY'LL TAKE CONTROL IN A MATTER OF MINUTES.

147

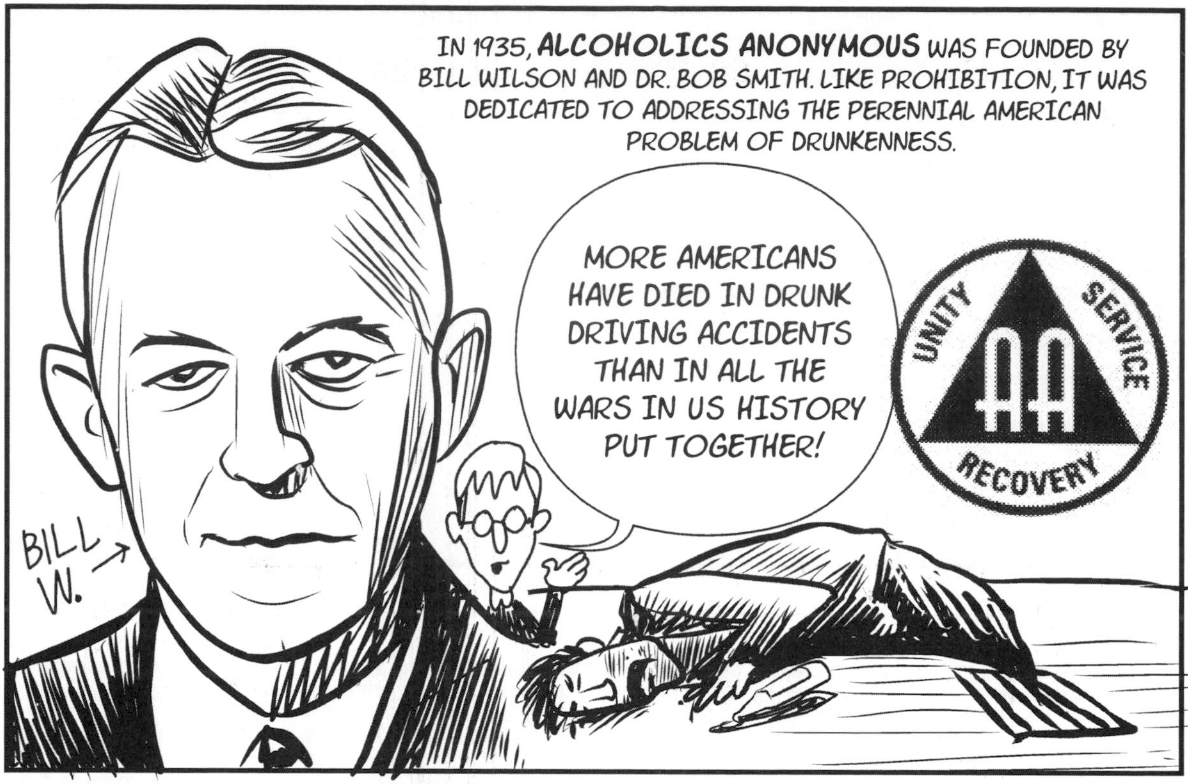
IN 1935, ALCOHOLICS ANONYMOUS WAS FOUNDED BY BILL WILSON AND DR. BOB SMITH. LIKE PROHIBITION, IT WAS DEDICATED TO ADDRESSING THE PERENNIAL AMERICAN PROBLEM OF DRUNKENNESS.
MORE AMERICANS HAVE DIED IN DRUNK DRIVING ACCIDENTS THAN IN ALL THE WARS IN US HISTORY PUT TOGETHER!
UNITY
SERVICE
AA
RECOVERY
BILL W.

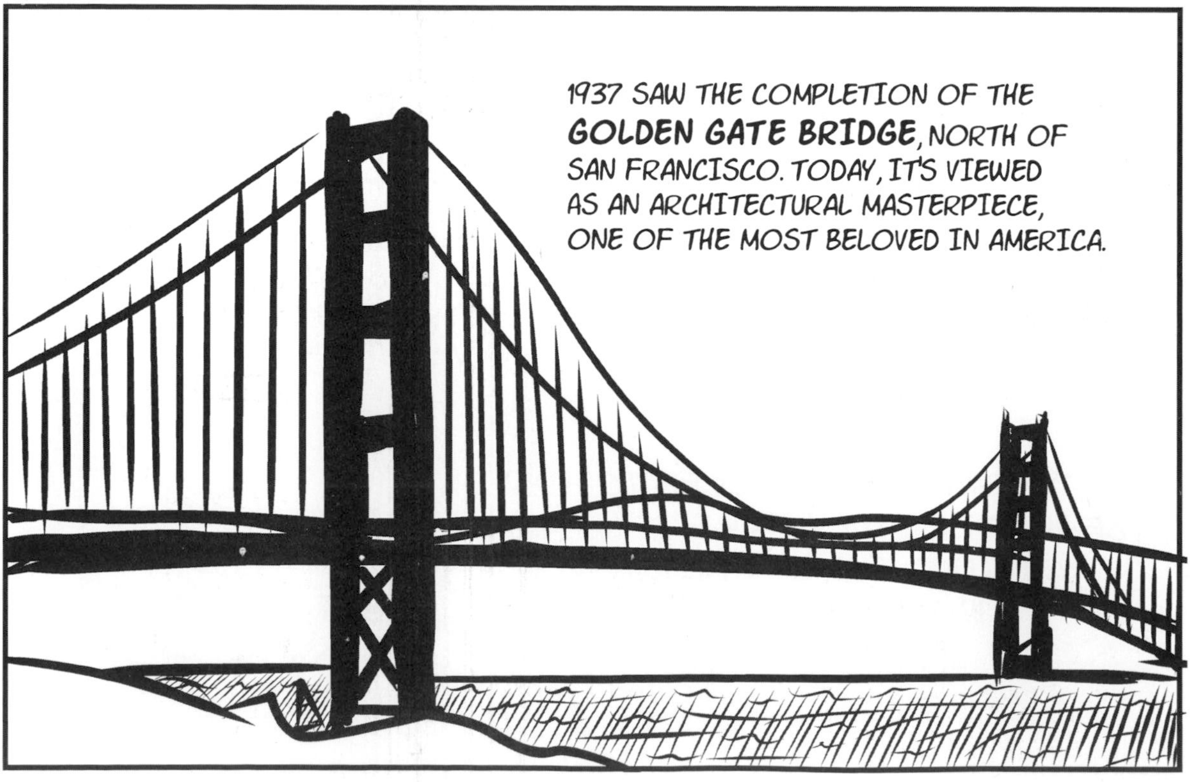
1937 SAW THE COMPLETION OF THE GOLDEN GATE BRIDGE, NORTH OF SAN FRANCISCO. TODAY, IT'S VIEWED AS AN ARCHITECTURAL MASTERPIECE, ONE OF THE MOST BELOVED IN AMERICA.

BELOVED MOVIES WERE ALSO BEING PRODUCED DURING THIS ERA. WITH A RUNNING TIME OF MORE THAN THREE HOURS, 1939'S **GONE WITH THE WIND** WAS AN EPIC CIVIL WAR DRAMA, BASED ON THE NOVEL BY MARGARET MITCHELL. PEOPLE WERE MESMERIZED, AS THEY OFTEN ARE BY NOSTALGIC DEPICTIONS OF TROUBLED PERIODS IN THE PAST.

SOMETIMES, ONE GETS THE IMPRESSION THAT HISTORY HAPPENS SO THAT ARTISTS CAN **APPROPRIATE** IT.

DID YOU KNOW THAT HATTIE MCDANIEL, WHO PLAYED MAMMY, WAS THE **FIRST BLACK ACTOR** TO BE NOMINATED FOR AN OSCAR? AND SHE WON!

MEANWHILE, IN THE REAL WORLD, THE LEGACY OF THE CIVIL WAR HAD CREATED A DEEPLY DIVIDED UNITED STATES. UNDER THE "**SEPARATE BUT EQUAL**" DOCTRINE, BLACKS AND WHITES CONTINUED TO BE SEGREGATED IN THE SOUTH.

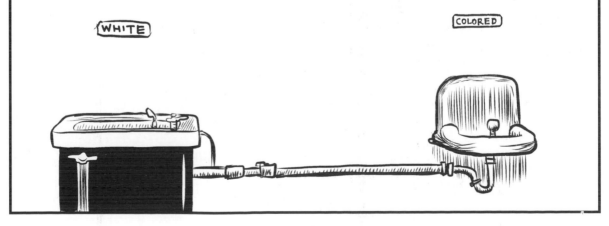

WHITE

COLORED

HAPPY DAYS ARE HERE AGAIN...

IN 1940, ROOSEVELT WAS ELECTED TO AN UNPRECEDENTED THIRD TERM AS PRESIDENT.

OVER THE NEXT SEVERAL YEARS, HE LED THE COUNTRY OUT OF THE DEPRESSION AND SERVED AS A DECISIVE LEADER DURING WORLD WAR II, PARTNERING WITH WINSTON CHURCHILL OF GREAT BRITAIN IN THE FIGHT AGAINST TYRANNY.

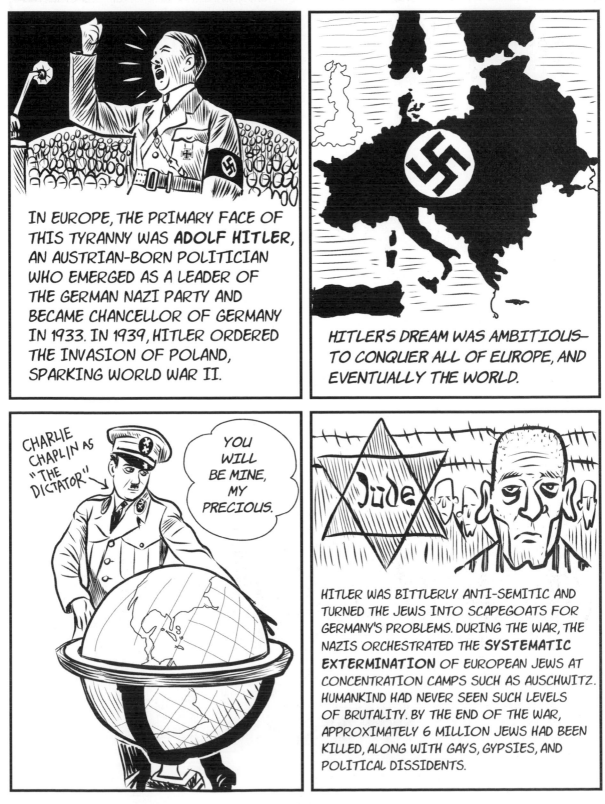

IN EUROPE, THE PRIMARY FACE OF THIS TYRANNY WAS **ADOLF HITLER**, AN AUSTRIAN-BORN POLITICIAN WHO EMERGED AS A LEADER OF THE GERMAN NAZI PARTY AND BECAME CHANCELLOR OF GERMANY IN 1933. IN 1939, HITLER ORDERED THE INVASION OF POLAND, SPARKING WORLD WAR II.

HITLER'S DREAM WAS AMBITIOUS—TO CONQUER ALL OF EUROPE, AND EVENTUALLY THE WORLD.

CHARLIE CHAPLIN AS "THE DICTATOR"

YOU WILL BE MINE, MY PRECIOUS.

HITLER WAS BITTERLY ANTI-SEMITIC AND TURNED THE JEWS INTO SCAPEGOATS FOR GERMANY'S PROBLEMS. DURING THE WAR, THE NAZIS ORCHESTRATED THE **SYSTEMATIC EXTERMINATION** OF EUROPEAN JEWS AT CONCENTRATION CAMPS SUCH AS AUSCHWITZ. HUMANKIND HAD NEVER SEEN SUCH LEVELS OF BRUTALITY. BY THE END OF THE WAR, APPROXIMATELY 6 MILLION JEWS HAD BEEN KILLED, ALONG WITH GAYS, GYPSIES, AND POLITICAL DISSIDENTS.

THE TRAGEDY CAME TO BE KNOWN IN HEBREW AS THE SHOAH AND IN ENGLISH AS THE **HOLOCAUST**. NEWS OF THE ATROCITIES EVENTUALLY REACHED THE UNITED STATES, BUT THE ADEQUACY OF THE AMERICAN RESPONSE IS STILL DEBATED: DID THE GOVERNMENT DO ENOUGH? COULD AMERICAN JEWS HAVE DONE MORE TO STOP THE **DECIMATION OF A CIVILIZATION** IN WHICH THEY HAD THEIR ROOTS?

AND YOU WERE A CRAPPY ARTIST!

AFTER THE WAR, ONE STORY IN PARTICULAR EMERGED FROM THE ASHES: THE TALE OF A YOUNG JEWISH GIRL NAMED **ANNE FRANK**. IN HER DIARY, SHE DESCRIBED THE ARRIVAL OF NAZI FORCES IN AMSTERDAM AND THE SECRET ROOM WHERE SHE HID WITH HER FAMILY. IN THE END, ANNE FRANK WAS CAPTURED BY THE NAZIS AND DIED AT A CONCENTRATION CAMP.

DIARY OF ANNE FRANK

AFTER ITS PUBLICATION IN 1952, ANNE'S DIARY BECAME A BEST SELLER AND WAS LATER MADE INTO A BROADWAY PLAY. IRONICALLY, THE PLAY CLEANSED ANNE'S STORY OF ITS JEWISH REFERENCES TO MAKE THE STORY MORE UNIVERSAL. THE AMERICAN NOVELIST MEYER LEVIN ATTACKED ANNE'S FATHER, OTTO, FOR COMPLYING WITH THIS APPROACH.

HOW EMBARRASSING!

I STILL BELIEVE PEOPLE REALLY ARE GOOD AT HEART.

ALTHOUGH THE HOLOCAUST DIDN'T HAPPEN ON AMERICAN SOIL, IT'S STILL AN IMPORTANT PART OF THE AMERICAN STORY. CITIZENS OF THE UNITED STATES HAVE CREATED MANY NOVELS, PLAYS, MOVIES, AND SCHOLARLY WORKS ABOUT THE TRAGEDY. THE **HOLOCAUST MEMORIAL MUSEUM IN WASHINGTON, DC**, OPENED TO THE PUBLIC IN 1993.

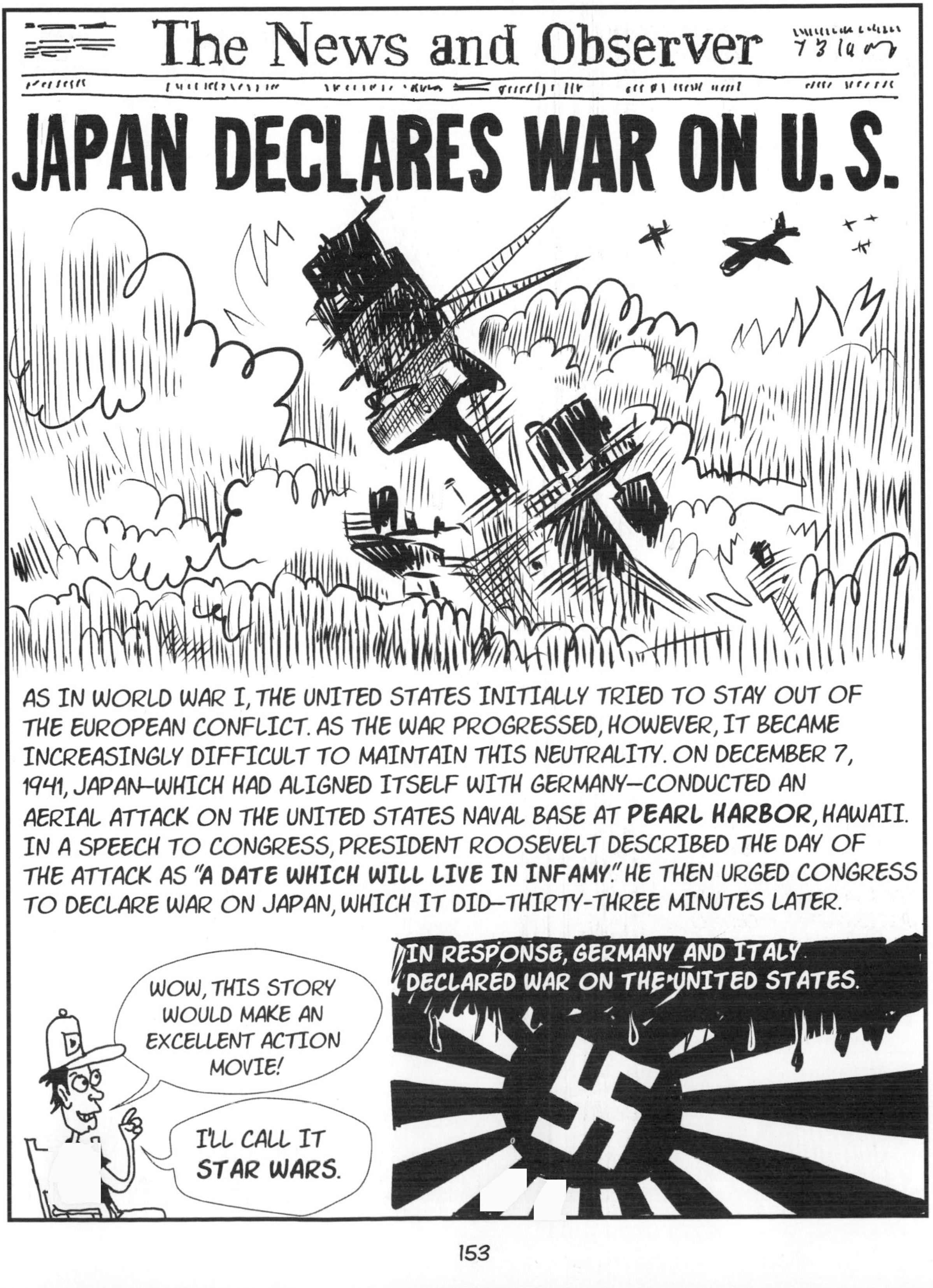
The News and Observer
JAPAN DECLARES WAR ON U.S.
AS IN WORLD WAR I, THE UNITED STATES INITIALLY TRIED TO STAY OUT OF THE EUROPEAN CONFLICT. AS THE WAR PROGRESSED, HOWEVER, IT BECAME INCREASINGLY DIFFICULT TO MAINTAIN THIS NEUTRALITY. ON DECEMBER 7, 1941, JAPAN—WHICH HAD ALIGNED ITSELF WITH GERMANY—CONDUCTED AN AERIAL ATTACK ON THE UNITED STATES NAVAL BASE AT **PEARL HARBOR**, HAWAII. IN A SPEECH TO CONGRESS, PRESIDENT ROOSEVELT DESCRIBED THE DAY OF THE ATTACK AS "**A DATE WHICH WILL LIVE IN INFAMY.**" HE THEN URGED CONGRESS TO DECLARE WAR ON JAPAN, WHICH IT DID—THIRTY-THREE MINUTES LATER.
WOW, THIS STORY WOULD MAKE AN EXCELLENT ACTION MOVIE!
I'LL CALL IT **STAR WARS.**
IN RESPONSE, GERMANY AND ITALY DECLARED WAR ON THE UNITED STATES.

ONE OF THE GREATEST MOVIES FROM THE WAR PERIOD WAS **CASABLANCA**, RELEASED IN 1942. SET IN VICHY-CONTROLLED MOROCCO, IT COMBINES A CLASSIC LOVE STORY WITH THE STORY OF THE STRUGGLE AGAINST THE NAZIS.

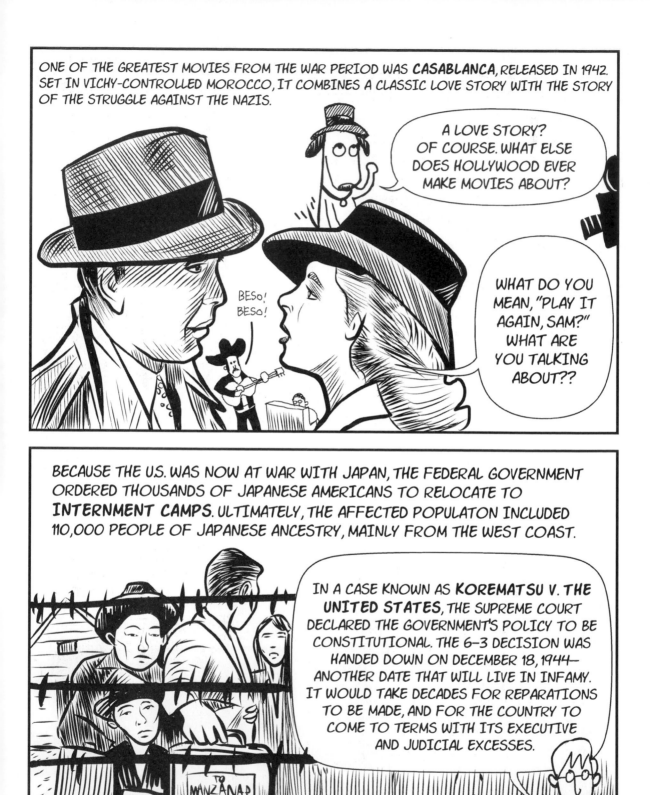

A LOVE STORY? OF COURSE. WHAT ELSE DOES HOLLYWOOD EVER MAKE MOVIES ABOUT?

BESO! BESO!

WHAT DO YOU MEAN, "PLAY IT AGAIN, SAM?" WHAT ARE YOU TALKING ABOUT??

BECAUSE THE U.S. WAS NOW AT WAR WITH JAPAN, THE FEDERAL GOVERNMENT ORDERED THOUSANDS OF JAPANESE AMERICANS TO RELOCATE TO **INTERNMENT CAMPS**. ULTIMATELY, THE AFFECTED POPULATON INCLUDED 110,000 PEOPLE OF JAPANESE ANCESTRY, MAINLY FROM THE WEST COAST.

IN A CASE KNOWN AS **KOREMATSU V. THE UNITED STATES**, THE SUPREME COURT DECLARED THE GOVERNMENT'S POLICY TO BE CONSTITUTIONAL. THE 6–3 DECISION WAS HANDED DOWN ON DECEMBER 18, 1944— ANOTHER DATE THAT WILL LIVE IN INFAMY. IT WOULD TAKE DECADES FOR REPARATIONS TO BE MADE, AND FOR THE COUNTRY TO COME TO TERMS WITH ITS EXECUTIVE AND JUDICIAL EXCESSES.

TO MANZANAR

JAPANESE AMERICANS WEREN'T THE ONLY VICTIMS OF XENOPHOBIA DURING THE WAR YEARS. ON AUGUST 2, 1942, THE BODY OF **JOSÉ DÍAZ** WAS FOUND NEAR A SWIMMING HOLE ON THE WILLIAMS RANCH IN SOUTHEAST LOS ANGELES. THE MEDIA USED THE INCIDENT TO PERPETUATE THE IDEA THAT MEXICANS WERE CRIMINALS, UNDERSCORING **THE XENOPHOBIC MINDSET OF AMERICANS** AT THE TIME. THE MURDER LED TO THE CONVICTION OF 17 MEXICAN AMERICAN YOUTHS, BUT THE CONVICTION WAS REVERSED IN 1944 ON THE GROUNDS THAT THEY HADN'T RECEIVED A FAIR TRIAL. IT'S CALLED **THE SLEEPY LAGOON MURDER.**

★@X!

★@X!

AS THE WAR PROGRESSED, **THE CRISIS IN EUROPE** FORCED THOUSANDS OF REFUGEES TO SEEK ASYLUM IN THE UNITED STATES. THOSE WHO ARRIVED HERE CAME FROM MANY DIFFERENT WALKS OF LIFE AND INCLUDED WRITERS SUCH AS HANNAH ARENDT, BERTOLT BRECHT, THEODORE ADORNO, AND THOMAS MANN.

UNHAPPY THE LAND WHERE HEROES ARE NEEDED.

MEN, NOT MAN, LIVE ON THE EARTH AND INHABIT THE WORLD. IT IS TIME FOR PHILOSOPHERS TO STOP THINKING IN THE ABSTRACT.

THEODORE ADORNO

THOMAS MANN

BERTOLT BRECHT

HANNAH ARENDT

BRECHT

THE FACT THAT SO MANY YOUNG MEN WERE FIGHTING OVERSEAS LED TO A DEPLETION OF AMERICA'S LABOR FORCE. IN RESPONSE, THE GOVERNMENT INITIATED THE **MEXICAN FARM LABOR PROGRAM** (ALSO KNOWN AS THE BRACERO PROGRAM.) LASTING FROM 1942 TO 1964, THE PROGRAM ALLOWED MEXICANS TO COME TO THE UNITED STATES LEGALLY AS GUEST WORKERS. IT EVENTUALLY SPONSORED AROUND 4.5 MILLION BORDER CROSSINGS.

MEANWHILE, THE FEDERAL GOVERNMENT SOUGHT TO STRENGTHEN TIES WITH LATIN AMERICA, TO COUNTERACT THE INFLUENCE OF NAZI GERMANY IN THE REGION. THIS LED TO THE PRODUCTION OF TWO DISNEY FILMS SHOWCASING THE WONDERS OF LATIN AMERICA: **SALUDOS AMIGOS** (1941) AND THE **THREE CABALLEROS** (1944).

156

THE ALLIED INVASION OF NORMANDY COMMENCED ON JUNE 6, 1944—ALSO KNOWN AS **D-DAY**.

THE SUPREME COMMANDER OF THE ALLIED FORCES WAS AMERICAN **GENERAL DWIGHT D. EISENHOWER**—THE UNITED STATES HAD ENTERED THE WAR WITH A VENGEANCE!

ALLIED FORCES

THIS IS AN INSTANCE WHERE THE **HISTORY OF THE UNITED STATES** AND **THE HISTORY OF THE WORLD** GO HAND IN HAND. OTHER COUNTRIES INVOLVED IN THE INVASION INCLUDED FRANCE, ENGLAND, CANADA, POLAND, NEW ZEALAND, AUSTRALIA, AND NORWAY.

THEN WE DON'T NEED TO DO A HISTORY OF THE WORLD. JUST TRANSLATE THIS BOOK TO OTHR TONGUES. HA, HA!

(STUNNINGLY HANDSOME AND BRILLIANT EDITOR)

WHAT ABOUT THE INNER LIVES OF THE SOLDIERS? FOR THE MOST PART, THEY BELIEVED THEY WERE FIGHTING FOR A **GOOD CAUSE.** STILL, ALL OF THEM HAD LIVES BACK HOME THEY WERE EAGER TO GET BACK TO ...

IS WAR EVER **JUSTIFIED?**

ONLY WHEN EVIL NEEDS TO BE STOPPED IN ITS TRACKS.

APOLOGIES TO BILL MAULDIN!

ONE OF THE MOST PROMINENT FIGURES TO EMERGE FROM THE WAR WAS **GENERAL DOUGLAS MACARTHUR.** HE LED TWO CAMPAIGNS AGAINST THE JAPANESE IN THE PHILIPPINES, AND AFTER THE WAR BECAME THE LEADER OF THE ALLIED OCCUPATION OF JAPAN—A POSITION HE HELD UNTIL 1951.

IN A COUNTRY FULL OF HEROES, MACARTHUR STANDS TALLER THAN MOST.

THAT'S BECAUSE THE AVERAGE SOLDIER WAS DOWN IN THE TRENCHES! I'M TIRED OF ALL THIS **HERO WORSHIP.**

158

AFTER A TECHNOLOGICAL RACE AGAINST THE GERMANS, THE UNITED STATES CREATED THE WORLD'S FIRST **NUCLEAR WEAPONS.** ON AUGUST 6 AND 9, 1945, AMERICAN PLANES DROPPED ATOMIC BOMBS ON THE JAPANESE CITIES OF HIROSHIMA AND NAGASAKI. BETWEEN 90,000 AND 166,000 PEOPLE DIED IN HIROSHIMA, AND BETWEEN 60,000 AND 80,000 IN NAGASAKI.

TODAY, OF COURSE, THE UNITED STATES IS CONSTANTLY SEEKING TO STOP THE PROLIFERATION OF THE NUCLEAR ARSENAL. ISN'T THAT IRONIC?

IN MY OPINION, NO ONE SHOULD HAVE THE **BOMB**— NOT EVEN AMERICANS!

MANY STILL PERCEIVE THESE ACTIONS AS MORALLY JUSTIFIED, GIVEN JAPAN'S INVOLVEMENT IN THE WAR, BUT HOW CAN THEY BE? YES, **JAPANESE AGGRESSION** HAD LED TO THE DEATHS OF MILLIONS OF PEOPLE, BUT DID THAT GIVE AMERICA THE RIGHT TO KILL HUNDREDS OF THOUSANDS OF INNOCENT CIVILIANS?

BY THE TIME THE BOMBS WERE DROPPED ON HIROSHIMA AND NAGASAKI, THE WAR IN EUROPE WAS ALREADY OVER. ON APRIL 30, 1945, WITH THE ALLIES CLOSING IN ON BERLIN, ADOLF HITLER—WHO HAD SINGLE-HANDEDLY CAUSED MORE DESTRUCTION THAN ANYONE ELSE IN HISTORY— COMMITTED **SUICIDE** IN HIS UNDERGROUND BUNKER.

WAR IS OVER

THE WAR IN EUROPE **ENDED** ON MAY 8, 1945, AND JAPAN FORMALLY SURRENDERED ON SEPTEMBER 2.

IN 1947, PARTLY IN RESPONSE TO THE HORRORS OF THE HOLOCAUST, THE UNITED NATIONS ENDORSED THE ESTABLISHMENT OF A JEWISH STATE IN PALESTINE.

"FRIENDS FOREVER"

THE NEW **STATE OF ISRAEL** HAD A POPULATION MADE UP OF LOCAL ARABS, SEPHARDIC JEWS, AND ASHKENAZI JEWS FROM EASTERN EUROPE. AT FIRST, THE JEWISH STATE HAD SOCIALIST ASPIRATIONS. IT APPEARED THAT IT MIGHT ALIGN ITSELF WITH THE SOVIET UNION.

OY GEVALT! WHAT WE HAVE AHEAD OF US ... **AN UNENDING TIDE OF BLOODSHED.** FROM THE VERY BEGINNING, ISRAEL'S ARAB NEIGHBORS—AND ARAB CITIZENS— WERE HOSTILE TOWARD ITS VERY EXISTENCE. IN 1948, IMMEDIATELY AFTER ISRAEL WAS FOUNDED, IT WAS INVADED BY A COALITION OF ARAB FORCES. IN THE ENSUING DECADES, THE THREAT FROM THE ARAB WORLD HAS BEEN UNRELENTING ...

IN 1947, AN UNIDENTIFIED OBJECT CRASHED OUTSIDE OF ROSWELL, NEW MEXICO. TO THIS DAY, UFO ENTHUSIASTS BELIEVE THAT THE OBJECT WAS AN **ALIEN VEHICLE**, AND THAT THE TRUE NATURE OF THE CRASH HAS BEEN COVERED UP BY THE U.S. GOVERNMENT. THE INCIDENT HAS BEEN THE SUBJECT OF COUNTLESS BOOKS, MOVIES, COMICS, AND TV SHOWS, UNDERSCORING THE **AMERICAN OBSESSION WITH ALIEN LIFE.** WE LOVE ASKING QUESTIONS LIKE: IS THERE INTELLIGENT LIFE ELSEWHERE IN THE UNIVERSE, OR ARE WE THE ONLY FOLKS IN TOWN? WILL ALIENS EVER VISIT US? AND IF THEY DO, WILL THEY POSE FOR OUR PHOTOS?

IF THEY POSE, WE'LL BE READY FOR THEM! **POLAROID** RELEASED THE WORLD'S FIRST INSTANT CAMERA TO THE PUBLIC IN 1948.

EVERYONE BECAME A PHOTOGRAPHER.

TOO BAD! IT NEEDS A SPECIAL EYE TO SEE THROUGH THE LENS.

PHOTOGRAPHS CHANGE THE WAY WE SEE THE WORLD. THEY FREEZE REALITY. THEY MAKE US **REMEMBER** EVENTS IN SPECIFIC— AND SOMETIMES INACCURATE—WAYS.

WITH THE ADVENT OF **PHOTOGRAPHY,** FAMILIES STARTED CREATING PHOTO ALBUMS, WHICH OFTEN SERVED AS REPLACEMENTS FOR ACTUAL MEMORIES.

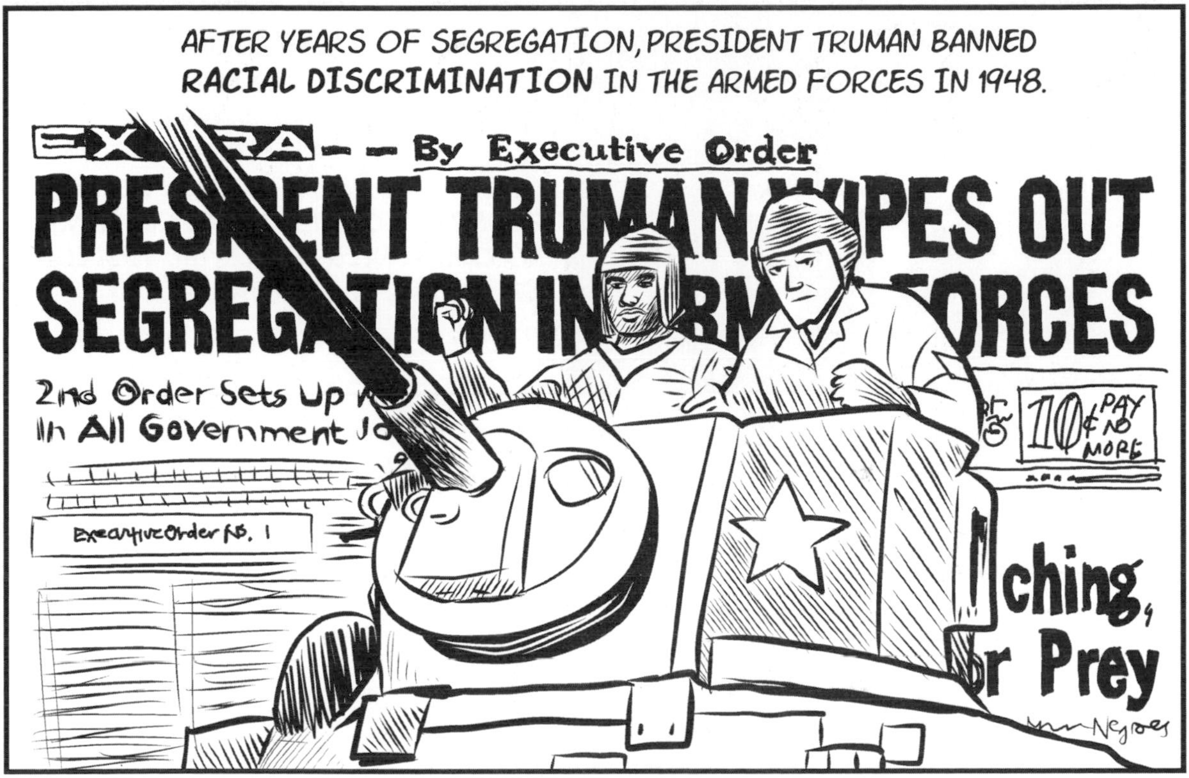
AFTER YEARS OF SEGREGATION, PRESIDENT TRUMAN BANNED RACIAL DISCRIMINATION IN THE ARMED FORCES IN 1948.
By Executive Order
2nd Order Sets Up
In All Government
Executive Order No. 1
ching,
r Prey
10¢ PAY NO MORE
Negroes

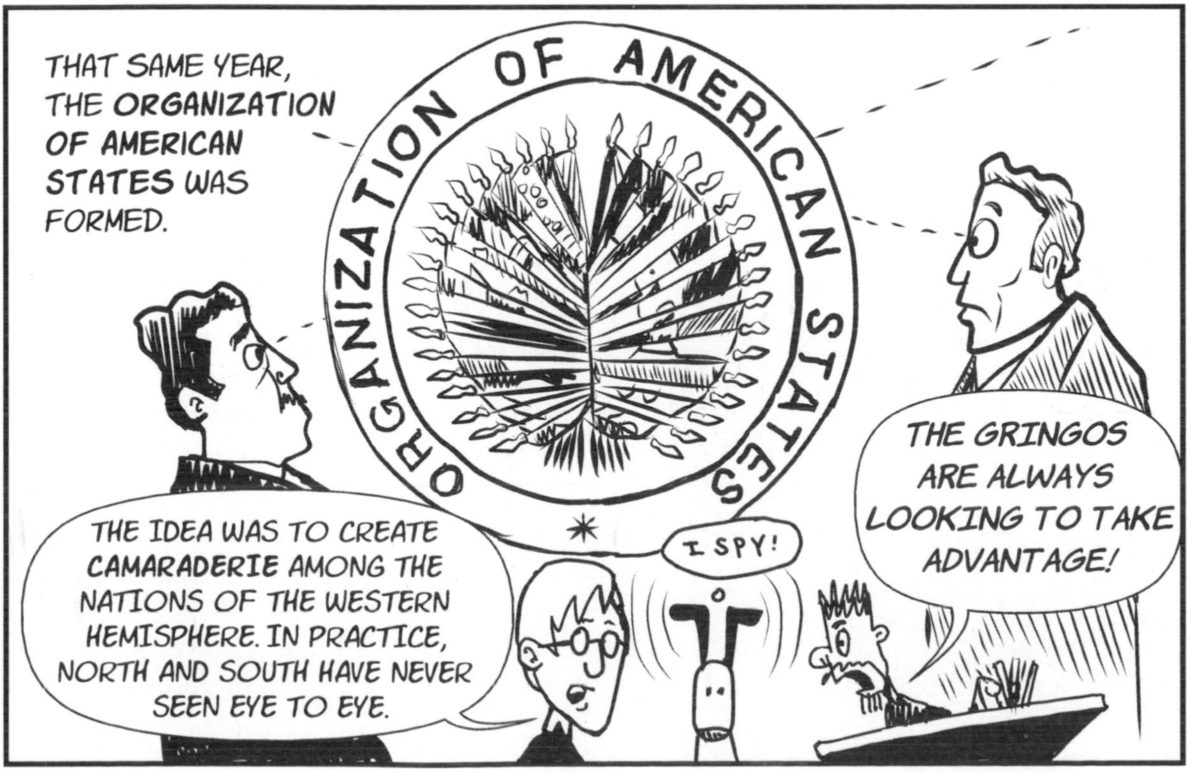
THAT SAME YEAR, THE ORGANIZATION OF AMERICAN STATES WAS FORMED.
ORGANIZATION OF AMERICAN STATES
THE IDEA WAS TO CREATE CAMARADERIE AMONG THE NATIONS OF THE WESTERN HEMISPHERE. IN PRACTICE, NORTH AND SOUTH HAVE NEVER SEEN EYE TO EYE.
I SPY!
THE GRINGOS ARE ALWAYS LOOKING TO TAKE ADVANTAGE!

IN 1949, THE **NORTH ATLANTIC TREATY ORGANIZATION** (NATO) WAS FORMED. ITS MISSION WAS DEFENSIVE: AGGRESSION AGAINST ANY ONE OF ITS MEMBER STATES WOULD PROMPT AN ORCHESTRATED RESPONSE. NO ONE WANTED TO SEE THE VIOLENCE OF THE WAR YEARS RETURN.

AT THE SAME TIME, **TENSION** WAS MOUNTING BETWEEN **THE WEST** (THE UNITED STATES AND ITS EUROPEAN PARTNERS) AND **THE EAST** (THE SOVIET UNION AND ITS ALLIES). THIS CULMINATED IN THE DIVISION OF GERMANY INTO TWO SEPARATE STATES, ONE ALLIED WITH EACH SIDE.

MEANWHILE, SOME FORMER GERMAN LEADERS WERE NOW DEAD OR BEHIND BARS. THE **NUREMBERG TRIALS** OF 1945–1946 HAD SOUGHT TO PUNISH THOSE RESPONSIBLE FOR THE NAZI ATROCITIES.

HOW DO NATIONS GRAPPLE WITH CRIMES COMMITTED IN THEIR NAME? TO BRING **CHARGES AGAINST THE PERPETRATORS,** TO HOLD A PUBLIC TRIAL, TO USE THE LEGAL SYSTEM TO PUNISH THEM—ALL THIS CONSTITUTES A VALUABLE ATTEMPT AT CLOSURE. YET THE WOUNDS STILL RUN DEEP. IT OFTEN TAKES A GENERATION TO OVERCOME THEM.

WE MUST FORGIVE BUT NEVER FORGET.

THE **KOREAN WAR** TOOK PLACE BETWEEN 1950 AND 1953. AFTER WORLD WAR II, THE ALLIES HAD DIVIDED THE KOREAN PENINSULA IN TWO, THE SOUTH BEING ALIGNED WITH THE UNITED STATES, AND THE NORTH WITH THE SOVIET UNION. WHEN THE NORTH INVADED THE SOUTH, THE UNITED STATES SENT IN TROOPS, AND SOON IT WAS INVOLVED IN ANOTHER FULL-SCALE CONFLICT.

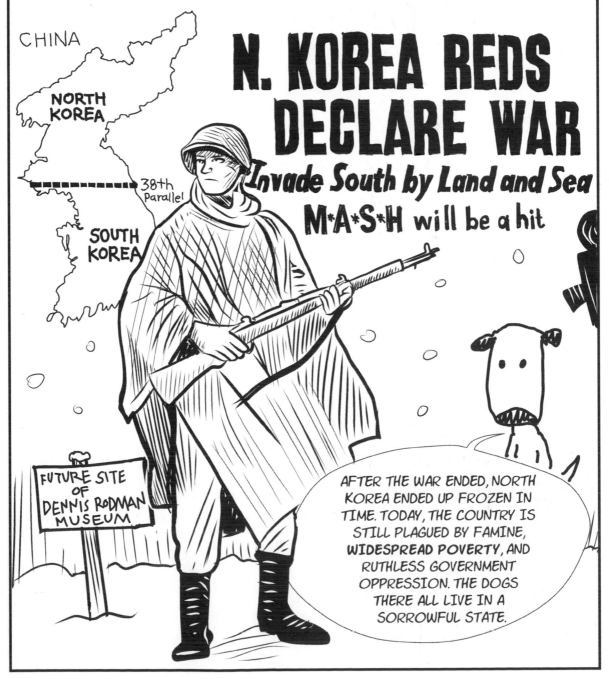

CHINA

NORTH KOREA

38th Parallel

SOUTH KOREA

N. KOREA REDS DECLARE WAR
Invade South by Land and Sea
M*A*S*H will be a hit

FUTURE SITE OF DENNIS RODMAN MUSEUM

AFTER THE WAR ENDED, NORTH KOREA ENDED UP FROZEN IN TIME. TODAY, THE COUNTRY IS STILL PLAGUED BY FAMINE, WIDESPREAD POVERTY, AND RUTHLESS GOVERNMENT OPPRESSION. THE DOGS THERE ALL LIVE IN A SORROWFUL STATE.

CHAPTER 6
BEAT THE SOVIETS

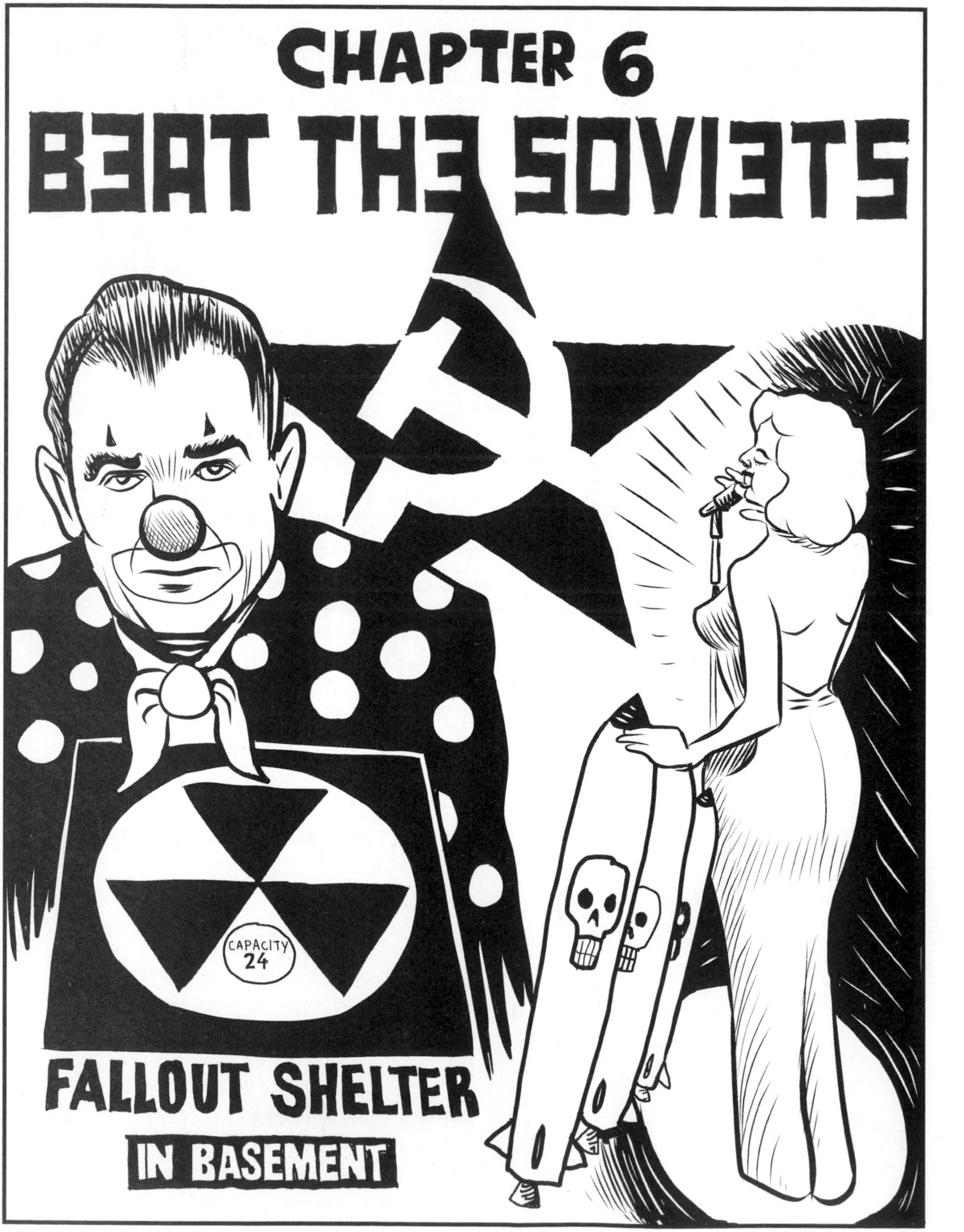
CAPACITY
24
FALLOUT SHELTER
IN BASEMENT

IN THE WAKE OF WORLD WAR II, THE TENSION BETWEEN THE UNITED STATES AND THE SOVIET UNION SOON ESCALATED INTO A SIMMERNG CONFLICT KNOWN AS **THE COLD WAR**. IN AMERICA, ITS **SIGNATURE BOGEYMAN** WAS THE COMMUNIST SPY, READY TO SELL THE NATION'S SECRETS TO THE ENEMY. DUE TO THE ANTICOMMUNIST HYSTERIA, CITIZENS WITH LEFT-WING POLITICAL VIEWS WERE OFTEN ACCUSED OF BETRAYAL. AMONG THE MOST FAMOUS WERE **JULIUS AND ETHEL ROSENBERG**, A SECULAR JEWISH COUPLE CHARGED WITH COMMITTING ESPIONAGE BY PASSING INFORMATION ABOUT THE ATOMIC BOMB TO THE SOVIETS. THEY WERE EXECUTED ON JUNE 19, 1953—THE FIRST TIME IN THE NATION'S HISTORY THAT CIVILIANS HAD PAID SUCH A PRICE FOR **ESPIONAGE**.

IMPERFECT UNION? WHAT, ME WORRY?

EVER SEEN **DR. STRANGELOVE**? IT'S ONE OF MY FAVORITES! STANLEY KUBRICK SATIRIZES THE NUCLEAR ARMS RACE WITH **HILARIOUS ACCURACY**.

AT THE HEIGHT OF THE COLD WAR, A SERIES OF COMMUNIST WITCH HUNTS TOOK PLACE, SPEARHEADED BY **SENATOR JOSEPH MCCARTHY** AND THE MEMBERS OF THE HOUSE UN-AMERICAN ACTIVITIES COMMITTEE. THEIR GOAL WAS TO ACCUSE, AND ULTIMATELY OSTRACIZE, INDIVIDUALS SUSPECTED OF HARBORING COMMUNIST SYMPATHIES. MANY OF THE CITIZENS TARGETED BY MCCARTHY AND HIS COHORT WORKED IN THE ENTERTAINMENT INDUSTRY.

BETWEEN 1950 AND 1954, MCCARTHY RUINED MANY PEOPLE'S LIVES. HIS TACTICS ARE NOW KNOWN AS **MCCARTHYISM!**

AN ENTIRE GENERATION LIVED IN FEAR OF BEING **BLACKLISTED**. AMONG THOSE ACCUSED WERE NELSON ALGREN, CHARLIE CHAPLIN, ARTHUR MILLER, LANGSTON HUGHES, DOROTHY PARKER, AARON COPLAND, AND DASHIELL HAMMETT.

I BELIEVE THAT ALL GOVERNMENT IS EVIL, AND THAT TRYING TO IMPROVE IT IS LARGELY A WASTE OF TIME.

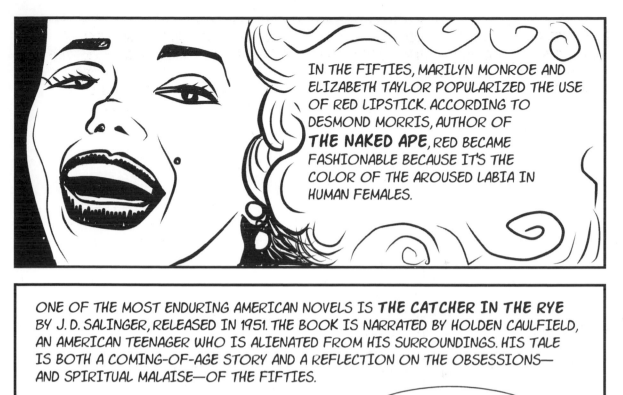

IN THE FIFTIES, MARILYN MONROE AND ELIZABETH TAYLOR POPULARIZED THE USE OF RED LIPSTICK. ACCORDING TO DESMOND MORRIS, AUTHOR OF **THE NAKED APE,** RED BECAME FASHIONABLE BECAUSE IT'S THE COLOR OF THE AROUSED LABIA IN HUMAN FEMALES.

ONE OF THE MOST ENDURING AMERICAN NOVELS IS **THE CATCHER IN THE RYE** BY J. D. SALINGER, RELEASED IN 1951. THE BOOK IS NARRATED BY HOLDEN CAULFIELD, AN AMERICAN TEENAGER WHO IS ALIENATED FROM HIS SURROUNDINGS. HIS TALE IS BOTH A COMING-OF-AGE STORY AND A REFLECTION ON THE OBSESSIONS— AND SPIRITUAL MALAISE—OF THE FIFTIES.

IRONICALLY, SALINGER DIDN'T SHARE AMERICA'S OBSESSION WITH FAME. HE DIDN'T WANT TO BE SEEN, PHOTOGRAPHED, OR EVEN TALKED TO ...

WHY DO READERS IDENTIFY WITH A YOUNG MAN ON THE FRINGE? IS IT BECAUSE WE ALL FEEL ALIENATED FROM SOCIETY ON SOME LEVEL?

FAME IS A BITCH! IT LOVES YOU WHEN YOU HAVE POWER AND MONEY, BUT WHEN YOU DON'T...

J.D. was not here

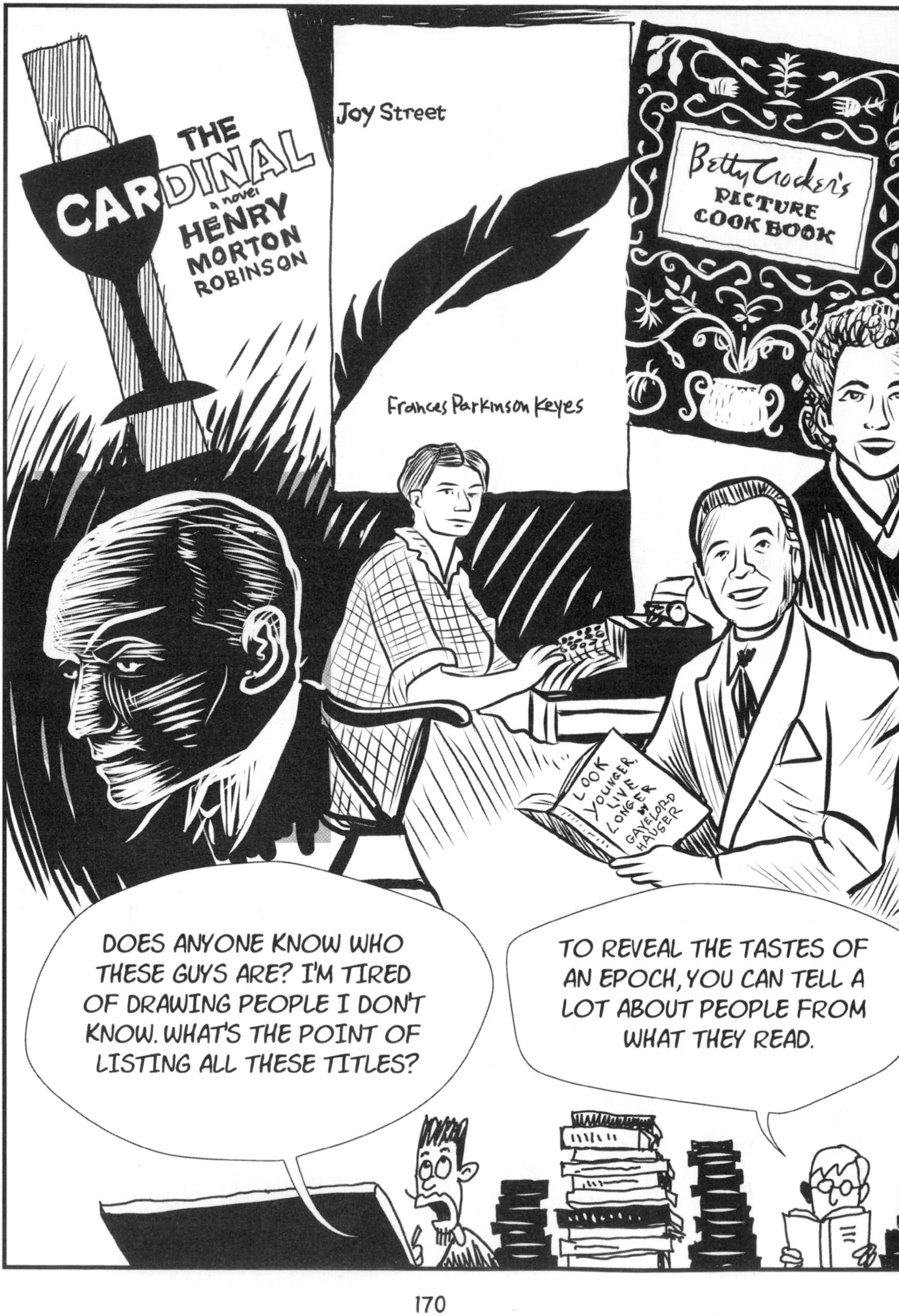
THE CARDINAL a novel HENRY MORTON ROBINSON
Joy Street
Frances Parkinson Keyes
Betty Crocker's PICTURE COOK BOOK
LOOK YOUNGER, LIVE LONGER BY GAYELORD HAUSER
DOES ANYONE KNOW WHO THESE GUYS ARE? I'M TIRED OF DRAWING PEOPLE I DON'T KNOW. WHAT'S THE POINT OF LISTING ALL THESE TITLES?
TO REVEAL THE TASTES OF AN EPOCH, YOU CAN TELL A LOT ABOUT PEOPLE FROM WHAT THEY READ.

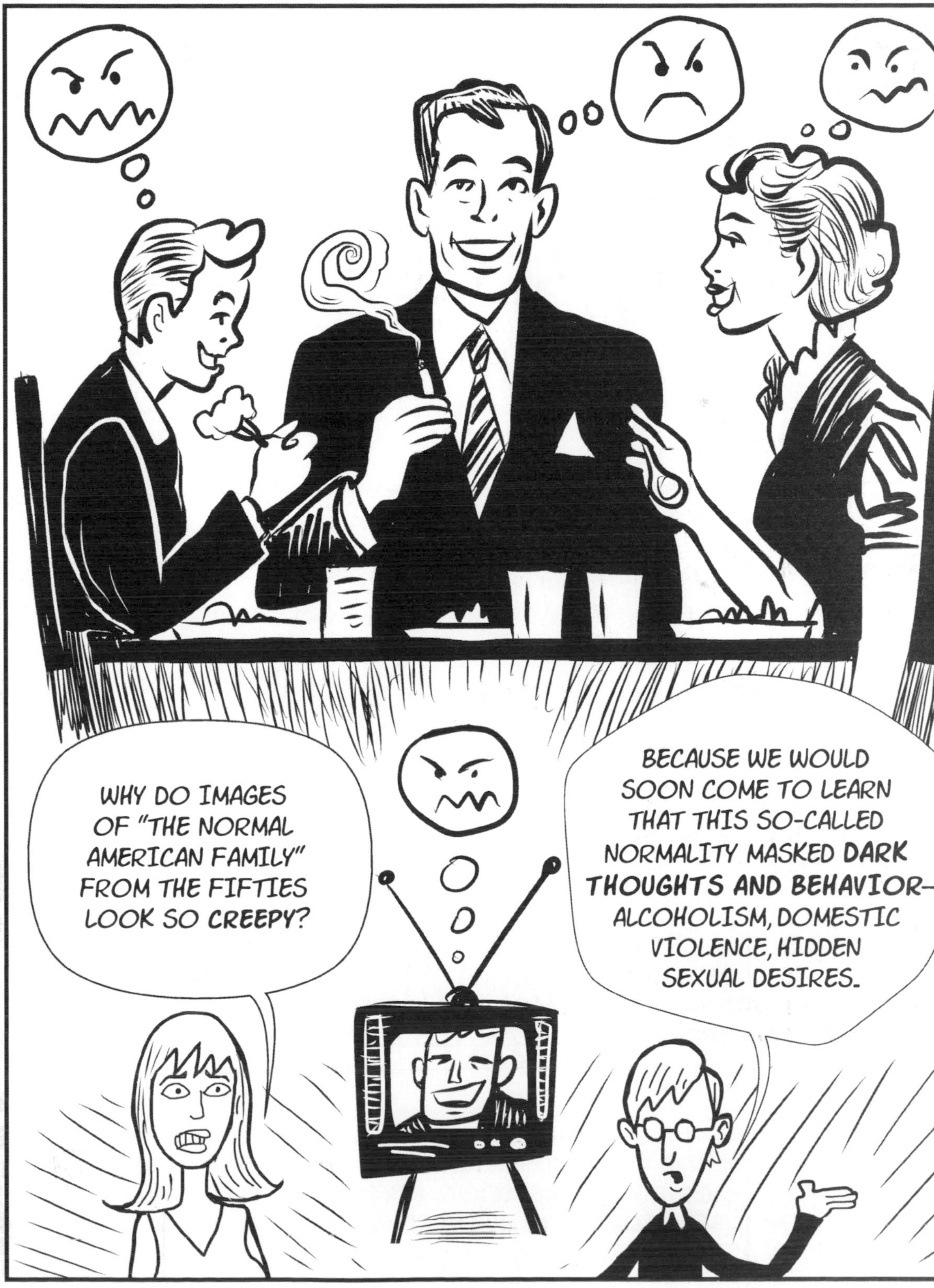
WHY DO IMAGES OF "THE NORMAL AMERICAN FAMILY" FROM THE FIFTIES LOOK SO **CREEPY**?
BECAUSE WE WOULD SOON COME TO LEARN THAT THIS SO-CALLED NORMALITY MASKED **DARK THOUGHTS AND BEHAVIOR**—ALCOHOLISM, DOMESTIC VIOLENCE, HIDDEN SEXUAL DESIRES.

AS AMERICA WAS MOVING INTO THE CLEAN-CUT ERA OF PRESIDENT DWIGHT D. EISENHOWER, DR. ALFRED KINSEY, ALONG WITH HIS COLLEAGUES AT INDIANA UNIVERSITY, PUBLISHED TWO BOOKS: **SEXUAL BEHAVIOR IN THE HUMAN MALE** (1948) AND **SEXUAL BEHAVIOR IN THE HUMAN FEMALE** (1953). TOGETHER, THESE BECAME KNOWN AS THE KINSEY REPORTS.

KINSEY INTERVIEWED THOUSANDS OF MEN AND WOMEN ABOUT THEIR SEXUAL BEHAVIOR. HE CONCLUDED THAT MEN WERE MORE **SEXUALLY ACTIVE** THAN WOMEN IN THE UNITED STATES, BUT THAT WOMEN WERE MORE ACTIVE THAN WAS COMMONLY BELIEVED. HE ALSO ARGUED THAT HUMAN MATING PATTERNS WERE FAR LESS MONOGAMOUS THAN SOCIETY WAS WILLING TO ACCEPT.

DID WE REALLY NEED A DOCTOR TO TELL US HOW MANY **AFFAIRS** AMERICANS HAVE?

AND THAT WAS BEFORE THE ERA OF "FREE LOVE" AND THE SEXUAL REVOLUTION OF THE **SIXTIES**.

THAT'S WHEN THE COUNTRY'S SEXUALITY WENT ON **OVERDRIVE** ...

BY THE MID-TWENTIETH CENTURY, NEW YORK CITY WAS HOME TO THE MAINLAND'S **LARGEST CONCENTRATION OF PUERTO RICANS.** MANY HAD LEFT THEIR NATIVE LAND IN SEARCH OF BETTER JOB OPPORTUNITIES AND STANDARDS OF LIVING AFTER EFFORTS TO **MODERNIZE** THE ISLAND STALLED OUT. FORTUNATELY, PUERTO RICANS FACED FAR FEWER BARRIERS TO IMMIGRATION THAN PEOPLE FROM OTHER REGIONS BECAUSE THEY WERE ALREADY AMERICAN CITIZENS!

WHY IS IT THAT, IN A COUNTRY WHERE **ASSIMILATION** IS THE NORM, PUERTO RICANS STILL ALIGN THEMSELVES ACROSS ETHNIC LINES WHEN IT COMES TO HOLIDAYS AND CELEBRATIONS?

NY PUERTO RICAN DAY PARADE

HAPPY CINCO de MAYO

ONE OF THE TWENTIETH CENTURY'S MOST PROMINENT PUERTO RICANS WAS THE POET AND ACTIVIST **JULIA DE BURGOS.** BORN IN CAROLINA, PUERTO RICO, IN 1914, SHE ROSE FROM POVERTY TO GRADUATE FROM THE UNIVERSITY OF PUERTO RICO WITH A DEGREE IN TEACHING. SHE THEN JOINED THE WOMEN'S BRANCH OF THE PUERTO RICAN NATIONALIST PARTY, WHICH, UNDER THE LEADERSHIP OF PEDRO ABIZU CAMPOS, FOUGHT FOR THE INDEPENDENCE OF THE ISLAND FROM THE UNITED STATES. UNFORTUNATELY, BURGOS FOUND THAT HER NATIONALIST VIEWS ESTRANGED HER FROM HER HUSBAND, AND THEY DIVORCED IN 1937. SHE LATER SETTLED IN NEW YORK, WHERE SHE WROTE MOST OF HER POETRY, INCLUDING THE SOMBER **"FAREWELL IN WELFARE ISLAND."** IN 1953, BURGOS COLLAPSED ON A SIDEWALK IN SPANISH HARLEM AND DIED SHORTLY AFTERWARD.

SINCE HER BODY WASN'T IDENTIFIED, SHE WAS BURIED IN A **POTTER'S FIELD.** EVENTUALLY, HER REMAINS WERE CLAIMED AND REBURIED ON HER NATIVE ISLAND.

MEANWHILE, THE TENDENCY TOWARD **CONFORMITY** WAS BECOMING STRONGER IN THE UNITED STATES.

EVEN DOGS HAD TO CONFORM! SIT UP! STAY!

HAPPY FAMILIES ARE ALIKE!

AND, AS TOLSTOY TAUGHT, ALL UNHAPPY FAMILIES ARE UNHAPPY IN THEIR OWN WAY.

STORE!

A MAJOR ASPECT OF THIS CONFORMITY WAS **CONSPICUOUS CONSUMPTION—** THE ACQUISITION OF MORE AND BETTER MATERIAL GOODS.

OVER THE COURSE OF THE FIFTIES, MANY AMERICANS WERE MOVING FROM CITIES TO THE **SUBURBS**. METROPOLITAN CENTERS DEVELOPED SATELLITE COMMUNITIES, WHICH, AS TIME WENT BY, BECAME AUTONOMOUS AND SELF-SUFFICIENT. SOON, A NEW WAY OF LIFE WAS EVOLVING FOR THE AMERICAN MIDDLE-CLASS—BASED ON A NEW PHYSICAL LANDSCAPE, IN WHICH HOUSES WERE SPREAD OUT, AND COMMERCE WAS CONDUCTED AT **SHOPPING CENTERS** AND **MALLS**. **SUBURBIA** WAS THE SITE OF A **NEW AMERICAN AESTHETIC**.

STILL, THIS NEW SUBURBAN FACADE OFTEN MASKED LONELINESS AND DESPERATION. ARTHUR MILLER'S 1949 PLAY **DEATH OF A SALESMAN** IS A WRENCHING PORTRAIT OF WILLY LOMAN'S STRUGGLE TO KEEP HIMSELF AND HIS FAMILY AFLOAT AS HIS MENTAL STATE DETERIORATES.

THE ROLE OF A LIFETIME!

WE'RE ALL WILLY LOMAN.... HE REPRESENTS THE LOST DREAMS OF THE AMERICAN MIDDLE CLASS.

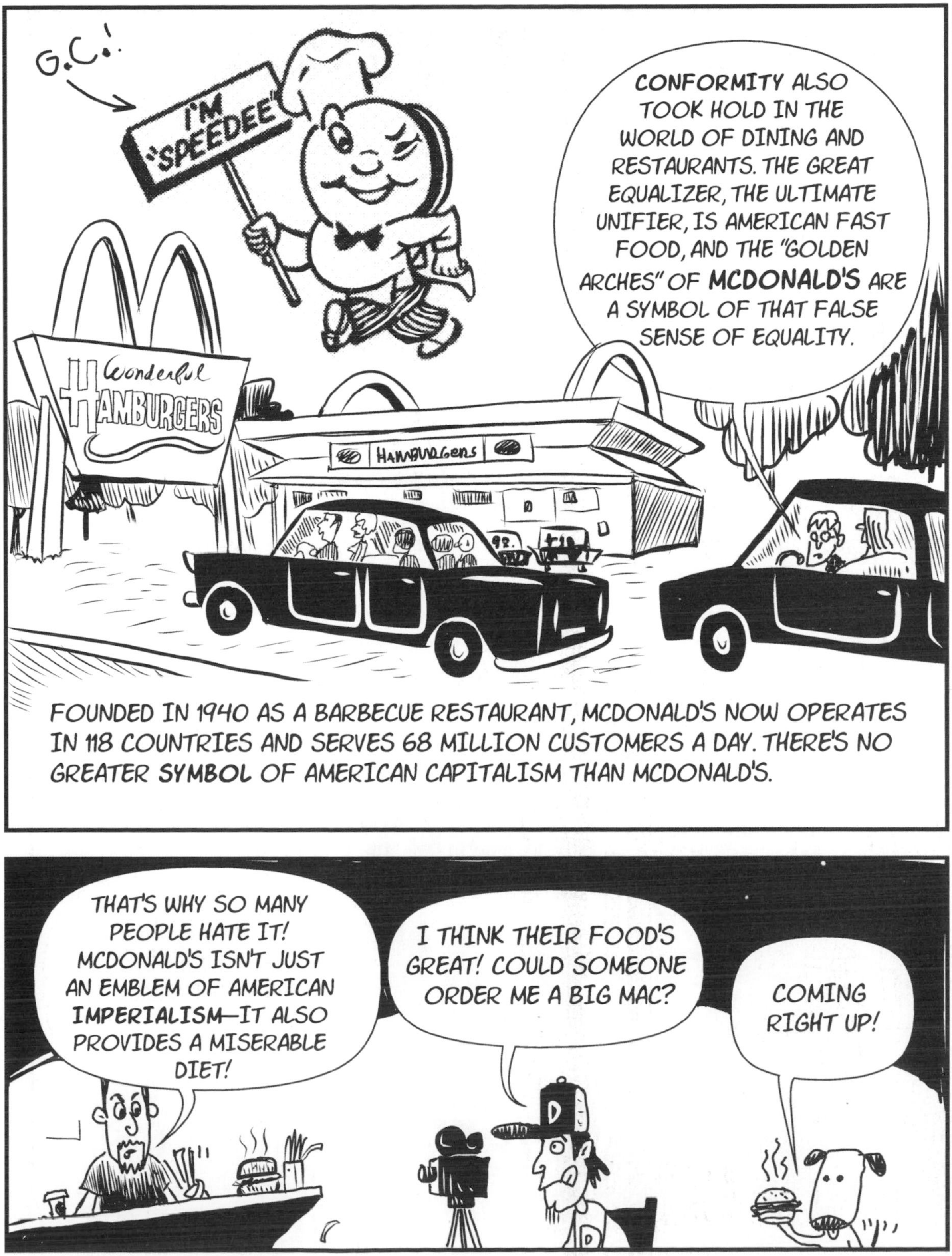
G.C.!
I'M "SPEEDEE"
CONFORMITY ALSO TOOK HOLD IN THE WORLD OF DINING AND RESTAURANTS. THE GREAT EQUALIZER, THE ULTIMATE UNIFIER, IS AMERICAN FAST FOOD, AND THE "GOLDEN ARCHES" OF MCDONALD'S ARE A SYMBOL OF THAT FALSE SENSE OF EQUALITY.
Wonderful HAMBURGERS
HAMBURGERS
FOUNDED IN 1940 AS A BARBECUE RESTAURANT, MCDONALD'S NOW OPERATES IN 118 COUNTRIES AND SERVES 68 MILLION CUSTOMERS A DAY. THERE'S NO GREATER SYMBOL OF AMERICAN CAPITALISM THAN MCDONALD'S.
THAT'S WHY SO MANY PEOPLE HATE IT! MCDONALD'S ISN'T JUST AN EMBLEM OF AMERICAN IMPERIALISM—IT ALSO PROVIDES A MISERABLE DIET!
I THINK THEIR FOOD'S GREAT! COULD SOMEONE ORDER ME A BIG MAC?
COMING RIGHT UP!

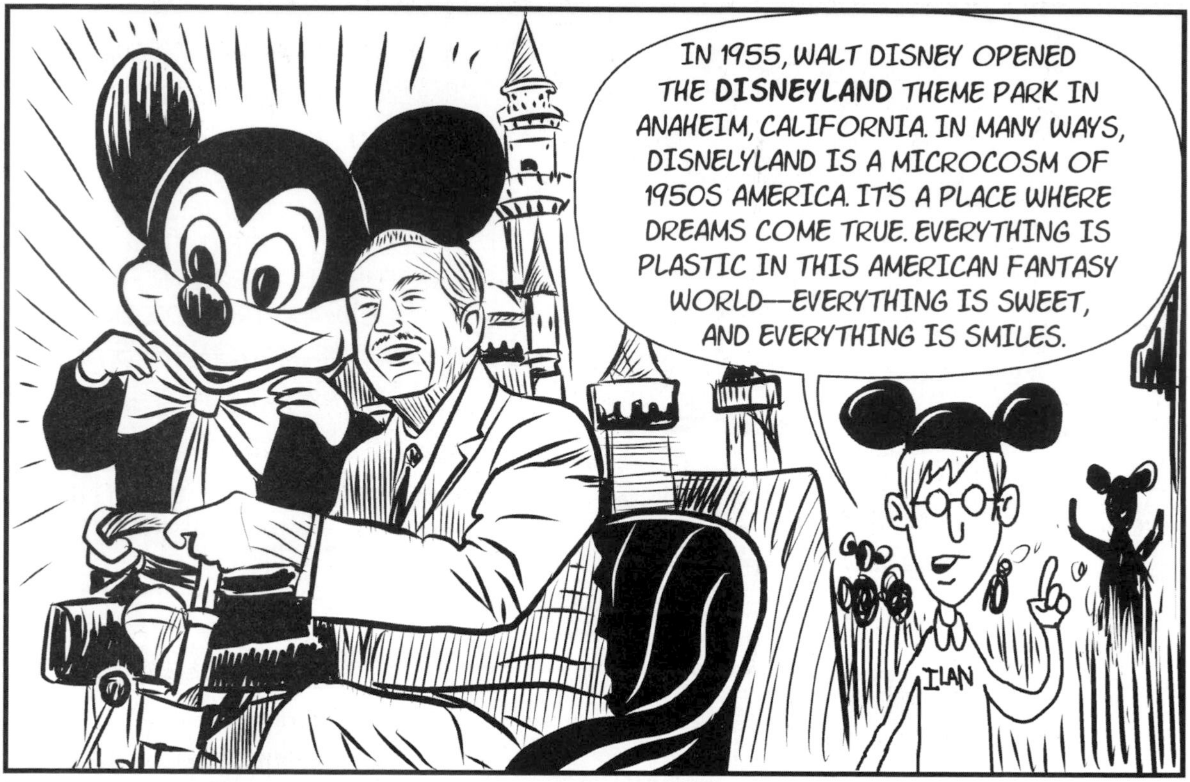
IN 1955, WALT DISNEY OPENED THE **DISNEYLAND** THEME PARK IN ANAHEIM, CALIFORNIA. IN MANY WAYS, DISNELYLAND IS A MICROCOSM OF 1950S AMERICA. IT'S A PLACE WHERE DREAMS COME TRUE. EVERYTHING IS PLASTIC IN THIS AMERICAN FANTASY WORLD—EVERYTHING IS SWEET, AND EVERYTHING IS SMILES.
ILAN

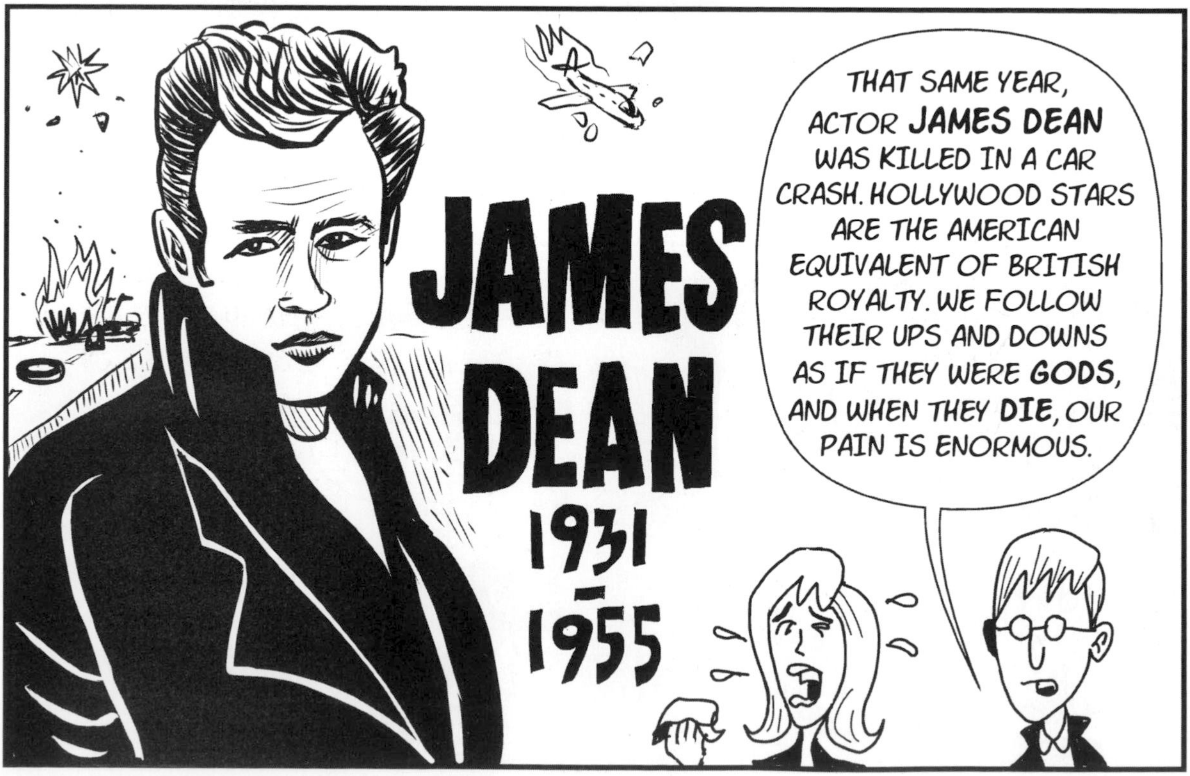
JAMES DEAN
1931 – 1955
THAT SAME YEAR, ACTOR **JAMES DEAN** WAS KILLED IN A CAR CRASH. HOLLYWOOD STARS ARE THE AMERICAN EQUIVALENT OF BRITISH ROYALTY. WE FOLLOW THEIR UPS AND DOWNS AS IF THEY WERE **GODS**, AND WHEN THEY **DIE**, OUR PAIN IS ENORMOUS.

DID YOU KNOW MY FULL NAME IS BARBARA MILLICENT ROBERTS?

Barbie™

DURING A TRIP TO EUROPE IN 1956, RUTH HANDLER BOUGHT THREE GERMAN DOLLS—ONE FOR HER DAUGHTER, BARBARA, AND TWO FOR HER HUSBAND, ELLIOT, THE COFOUNDER OF THE MATTELL TOY COMPANY. RUTH ADMIRED THE GERMAN DOLL'S **ADULT BODY**, **SVELTE PHYSIQUE**, AND **FASHIONABLE WARDROBE**, AND ENCOURAGED ELLIOT TO CREATE AN AMERICAN DOLL WITH THE SAME AESTHETIC. NAMED AFTER RUTH'S DAUGHTER, **BARBIE DOLLS** MADE THEIR FIRST APPEARANCE IN MARCH 1959 AND WENT ON TO ACHIEVE GREAT SUCCESS. THEY NOT ONLY REDEFINED THE NATURE OF DOLLS, BUT ALSO HELPED SHAPE THE NATION'S STANDARDS OF BEAUTY AND THE WAY AMERICAN GIRLS LOOK AT THEIR BODIES. UNLUCKILY FOR THEM, THE BARBIE DOLL IS NOT PROPORTIONAL TO ANY REAL-LIVE WOMAN'S BODY.

MCDONALD'S, BARBIE ... THESE ARE SUCH ICONIC BRANDS NOW. WE SEE ADS FOR THEM EVERYWHERE. SHOULDN'T THERE BE SOMETHING IN THIS BOOK ABOUT **ADVERTISING**?

STOP RUSHING ME! I'M GETTING THERE. WITH THE POPULARIZATION OF TELEVISION IN THE MID-TWENTIETH CENTURY, THE AMERICAN ADVERTISING INDUSTRY WENT INTO OVERDRIVE. **BRANDS** BECAME ALL-IMPORTANT, AND COMPANIES SPENT MILLIONS TO PROMOTE THEM. TODAY, BRANDS ARE EVERYWHERE— ON OUR T-SHIRTS, IN THE NAMES OF SPORTS STADIUMS. WHEREVER WE REST OUR EYES IN THE MODERN WORLD, SOMETHING IS BEING SOLD TO US.

THIS BARRAGE OF ADVERTISING AND CORPORATE LOGOS HAS BECOME AN ILLNESS IN AMERICAN SOCIETY—A SYMBOL OF CONSUMERISM RUN AMOK. I, RALPH NADER, THUS INVITE YOU TO PARTICIPATE IN AN **ANTIADVERTISING CAMPAIGN**. LOOK OUTSIDE THIS PAGE AT THE ENVIRONMENT AROUND YOU. WHAT DO YOU SEE? YOU'RE PROBABLY SURROUNDED BY ADS TRYING TO CONVINCE YOU TO BUY THINGS. DON'T BELIEVE THE HYPE! LEARN TO VIEW ADS WITH SKEPTICISM. DON'T BECOME **A CONSUMERIST ROBOT**.

AMERICANS HAVE TO WORK SO HARD TO AFFORD EVERY THING WE WANT TO BUY. THERE'S A HIGHER COST...

LIFE IS GOOD IN THE FIFTIES, BUT WE STILL WORRY ABOUT MONEY. RITZ CRACKERS ARE THIRTY-TWO CENTS. A **PORTABLE** SEWING MACHINE IS $19.90. FROZEN FRENCH FRIES ARE CHEAP AND EASY TO MAKE: JUST STICK THEM IN THE OVEN. I'D LIKE TO SEE FRANK SINATRA ON THURSDAY, BUT I DON'T THINK WE CAN AFFORD THE TICKETS.

THE **AVERAGE** YEARLY INCOME IN 1950 IS $3,210. A GALLON OF GAS COSTS EIGHTEEN CENTS. A DIAMOND RING IS $399. A NEW CAR WILL SET ME BACK ABOUT TWO THOUSAND DOLLARS—A BIG CHUNK OF MY INCOME. THE FIRST MODERN CREDIT CARD WON'T BE INVENTED UNTIL 1958, SO I GUESS I'LL HAVE TO TAKE OUT A LOAN.

THE FIFTIES WERE ALSO A TIME OF **TECHNOLOGICAL INNOVATION.** IN 1951, MEXICAN CHEMIST LUIS E. MIRAMONTES FIRST SYNTHESIZED A KEY INGREDIENT IN **ORAL CONTRACEPTIVES,** WHICH WOULD LATER REVOLUTIONIZE AMERICAN SOCIETY. IN 1958, JACK KILBY INVENTED THE MIRCOCHIP!

DADS SEEM LIKE THEY'RE ALWAYS AT WORK THESE DAYS. IS THAT BECAUSE THEY'RE BUSY **INVENTING** THINGS?

ON MAY 17, 1954, THE SUPREME COURT ISSUED A DECISION IN THE LANDMARK CASE **BROWN V. BOARD OF EDUCATION.** IN A UNANIMOUS VOTE, THE COURT DECLARED THAT RACIAL SEGREGATION IN PUBLIC SCHOOLS WAS UNCONSTITUTIONAL, STRIKING DOWN THE DOCTRINE OF *"SEPARATE BUT EQUAL."*

WHITES ONLY CLASSROOM

TODAY'S LESSON!
WHY WE'RE BETTER

IT'S ABOUT TIME! THE OUTRAGEOUS SEPARATION OF WHITE AND BLACK STUDENTS IS FINALLY COMING TO AN END.

ARE WE ONE NATION OR TWO?

CIVIL RIGHTS AND WRONGS

THE PLAINTIFFS' CASE HAD BEEN ARGUED BY **THURGOOD MARSHALL,** THE CHIEF COUNSEL FOR THE NAACP. IN THIS ROLE, MARSHALL WOULD EVENTUALLY ARGUE A TOTAL OF THIRTY-TWO CASES BEFORE THE **SUPREME COURT,** AND WIN ALL BUT THREE OF THEM. IN 1967, HE BECAME THE FIRST AFRICAN AMERICAN SUPREME COURT JUSTICE— AS WELL AS A **FOLK HERO,** SYMBOLIZING THE NEW, MULTIRACIAL AMERICA.

THE **BROWN** DECISION INAUGURATED A NEW ERA IN THE AMERICAN CIVIL RIGHTS MOVEMENT—THE ONGOING STRUGGLE TO END DISCRIMINATION AGAINST BLACKS. UNFORTUNATELY, THERE WAS MUCH WORK LEFT TO DO. IN AUGUST 1955, A BLACK TEENAGER NAMED **EMMETT TILL** WAS BRUTALLY BEATEN AND KILLED IN MISSISSIPPI, FOR THE CRIME OF ALLEGEDLY WHISTLING AT A WHITE WOMAN.

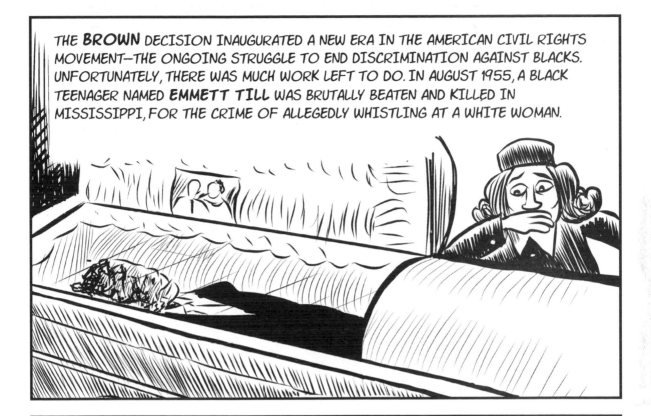

ROY BRYANT AND J. W. MILAM WERE ARRESTED FOR THE MURDER, BUT WERE ACQUITTED BY THE **ALL-WHITE** JURY. LATER, THEY ADMITTED TO THE CRIME. THE TRAVESTY OF JUSTICE SURROUNDING THE DEATH OF EMMETT TILL ENERGIZED CIVIL RIGHTS ACTIVISTS OF THE ERA.

SADLY, TILL'S MURDER WAS NOT AN ISOLATED INCIDENT—
TALES OF RACIALLY MOTIVATED VIOLENCE CONTINUED
TO INFLAME THE NATION OVER THE COURSE OF
THE FIFTIES AND SIXTIES. MEDGAR EVARS, THE MOST
PROMINENT BLACK LEADER IN MISSISSIPPI, WAS
ASSASSINATED IN 1963. THE FOLLOWING YEAR, THREE
CIVIL RIGHTS WORKERS WERE MURDERED IN THE STATE
BY MEMBERS OF THE **KU KLUX KLAN**, WHO
HAD ALSO BURNED DOWN AN AFRICAN
AMERICAN CHURCH. OFFICIALS
IN MISSISSIPPI REFUSED TO
PROSECUTE THE **SUSPECTS**,
WHICH WAS HARDLY
SURPRISING, GIVEN
THAT **LOCAL POLICE**
HAD BEEN INVOLVED
IN THE **MURDERS**.
EVENTUALLY,
PRESIDENT
LYNDON JOHNSON
ORCHESTRATED A
FEDERAL RESPONSE.
IN 1967, THE
CONSPIRATORS
WERE FOUND
GUILTY AND SENT
TO PRISON.

I SAW IT FROM ABOVE! TWO OF THE CONSPIRATORS WERE BADLY BEATEN BY BLACK INMATES IN THE FEDERAL PRISON AT TEXARKANA.

HERP DERP.

IN THEIR OWN WAY, THE NATION'S WRITERS AND ARTISTS WERE ALSO ADDRESSING THE PROBLEM OF RACISM. IN 1960, HARPER LEE PUBLISHED THE CLASSIC NOVEL **TO KILL A MOCKINGBIRD**, THE STORY OF A GIRL LIVING IN A SMALL SOUTHERN TOWN, WHOSE FATHER DEFENDS A BLACK MAN AGAINST A WHITE WOMAN'S **ACCUSATIONS OF RAPE**.

TROUBLE AT HOME MIRRORED TROUBLE ABROAD. AFRAID THE RED MENACE WAS TAKING OVER SOUTHEAST ASIA, THE UNITED STATES BECAME SLOWLY ENTANGLED IN WHAT CAME TO BE KNOWN AS THE **VIETNAM WAR,** A LONG AND TREACHEROUS CONFLICT THAT LASTED FROM 1955 TO 1975 AND EVENTUALLY EXPANDED TO CAMBODIA AND LAOS.

AS THE VIOLENCE ESCALATED, THE WAR BECAME INCREASINGLY UNPOPULAR, LEADING TO ANTIWAR DEMONSTRATIONS AND MARCHES.

THE DEER HUNTER

LATER, MANY GREAT FILMMAKERS WOULD EXPLORE THOSE PAINFUL YEARS.

UPON RETURNING FROM VIETNAM, MANY AMERICAN SOLDIERS FELT THEIR **SACRIFICE** WASN'T APPRECIATED. TODAY, A MEMORIAL NEAR THE WASHINGTON MALL HONORS THOSE WHO SERVED.

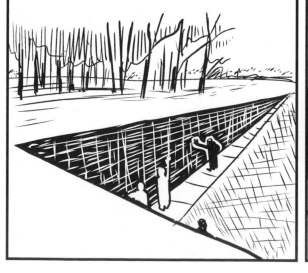

BACK HOME, NASA WAS FOUNDED IN 1958.

ANOTHER MANIFESTATION OF COLD WAR PARANOIA: THE SPACE RACE WAS LARGELY DRIVEN BY A DESIRE TO OUTSHINE THE RUSSIANS.

IN 1960, CUBAN LEADER **FIDEL CASTRO** BEGAN TO ALIGN HIS REGIME WITH THE SOVIET UNION. THE UNITED STATES COULDN'T TOLERATE HAVING A COMMUNIST COUNTRY JUST NINETY MILES AWAY, AND IN APRIL 1961, LESS THAN THREE MONTHS INTO HIS FIRST TERM, PRESIDENT JOHN F. KENNEDY SECRETLY ENDORSED AN INVASION OF CUBA BY CIA-TRAINED CUBAN EXILES. NOW KNOWN AS THE **BAY OF PIGS INVASION**, THE MISSION WAS A MONUMENTAL DISASTER, AND ONE WHICH INCREASED THE TENSION BETWEEN THE U.S. AND THE SOVIETS. THIS TENSION ONCE AGAIN CAME TO THE FORE IN 1962, WHEN RUSSIAN PREMIER NIKITA KRUSHCHEV DEPLOYED NUCLEAR MISSILES TO CUBA. AFTER DISCOVERING THE MISSILES, THE U.S. ENFORCED A NAVAL BLOCKADE OF THE ISLAND. THIS RESULTED IN A FOURTEEN-DAY STANDOFF THAT TOOK THE WORLD TO THE **BRINK OF NUCLEAR WAR**.

NOT USA

DID YOU KNOW THAT FIDEL CASTRO WAS EXCOMMUNICATED BY POPE JOHN XXIII?

WHY IS IT THAT WHEN A PERSON THREATENS VIOLENCE, WE CALL HIM A **LUNATIC**, BUT WHEN A POLITICIAN DOES IT, WE CALL HIM A **LEADER**?

DR. ILAN STAVANS
DOCTOR OF LITERATURE AND
PROCTO...

THE CUBAN MISSILE CRISIS UNDERSCORED THE DANGER OF NUCLEAR TECHNOLOGY, BUT SCIENCE WAS ALSO BEING USED FOR GOOD. ONE OF THE MOST FASCINATING STORIES IN MEDICAL HISTORY IS THAT OF **HENRIETTA LACKS**. A WORKING-CLASS BLACK WOMAN WITH NO SCIENTIFIC EXPERTISE, LACKS IS ONE OF THE **UNACKNOWLEDGED HEROES** OF MODERN MEDICINE. HER TALE RAISES MANY QUESTIONS ABOUT AMERICAN RESEARCH PRACTICES AND **ECONOMIC INEQUALITY**.

IN 1951, DR. GEORGE OTTO GEY, HEAD OF TISSUE-CULTURE RESARCH AT JOHNS HOPKINS UNIVERSITY, DEVELOPED A TECHNIQUE FOR GROWING CELLS FROM **HUMAN CANCER TISSUES IN** THE LAB. AS PART OF HIS RESEARCH, HE USED CELLS EXTRACTED FROM A POOR **BLACK WOMAN** NAMED HENRIETTA LACKS, WHO WAS SUFFERING FROM A SEVERE CASE OF CERVICAL CANCER. THESE CELLS—KNOWN BY THE NAME **HELA**, A SHORTENED FORM OF LACKS'S NAME—WOULD BECOME AMONG THE MOST USED IN THE WORLD, AND WERE INSTRUMENTAL IN **VACCINE DEVELOPMENT**, **GENE MAPPING**, **CLONING**, AND OTHER AREAS OF SCIENTIFIC RESEARCH. DESPITE THE GREAT BENEFIT PROVIDED BY HER CELLS, NEITHER LACKS NOR HER FAMILY EVER BENEFITTED FROM THIS RESEARCH ECONOMICALLY.

IN 2010, REBECCA SKLOOT FOCUSED NATIONAL ATTENTION ON THIS STORY WITH HER BOOK **THE IMMORTAL LIFE OF HENRIETTA LACKS**.

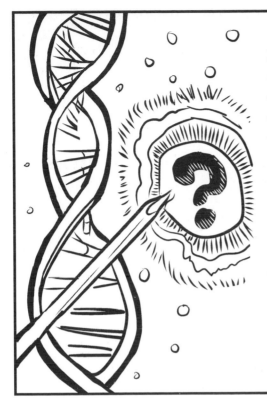

IN 1953, JAMES D. WATSON AND FRANCIS CRICK MADE A CRITICAL SCIENTIFIC DISCOVERY: THEY FOUND THAT DNA—THE CHEMICAL THAT CONTAINS ALL OUR GENETIC INFORMATION—HAS THE SHAPE OF A **DOUBLE HELIX**, MADE UP OF TWO INTERTWINING STRANDS. ALONG WITH MAURICE WILKINS, WATSON AND CRICK WON A NOBEL PRIZE FOR THEIR WORK IN 1962, BUT THERE WERE OTHER IMPORTANT SCIENTISTS WHO MADE CONTRIBUTIONS TO THEIR WORK. ROSALIND PARKER, IN PARTICULAR, PLAYED AN IMPORTANT ROLE, THOUGH SHE DIED IN 1958 AND WAS THUS INELIGIBLE FOR THE NOBEL PRIZE. WATSON LATER WROTE A CONTROVERSIAL ACCOUNT OF THE **DISCOVERY OF DNA**, IN WHICH HE MADE MANY DISPARAGING, SEXIST COMMENTS ABOUT PARKER.

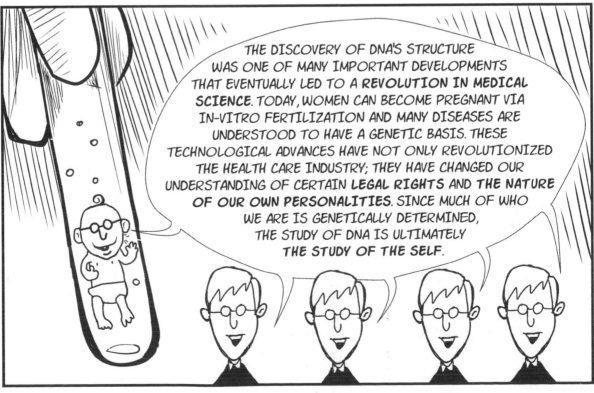

THE DISCOVERY OF DNA'S STRUCTURE WAS ONE OF MANY IMPORTANT DEVELOPMENTS THAT EVENTUALLY LED TO A **REVOLUTION IN MEDICAL SCIENCE**. TODAY, WOMEN CAN BECOME PREGNANT VIA IN-VITRO FERTILIZATION AND MANY DISEASES ARE UNDERSTOOD TO HAVE A GENETIC BASIS. THESE TECHNOLOGICAL ADVANCES HAVE NOT ONLY REVOLUTIONIZED THE HEALTH CARE INDUSTRY; THEY HAVE CHANGED OUR UNDERSTANDING OF CERTAIN **LEGAL RIGHTS** AND **THE NATURE OF OUR OWN PERSONALITIES**. SINCE MUCH OF WHO WE ARE IS GENETICALLY DETERMINED, THE STUDY OF DNA IS ULTIMATELY **THE STUDY OF THE SELF**.

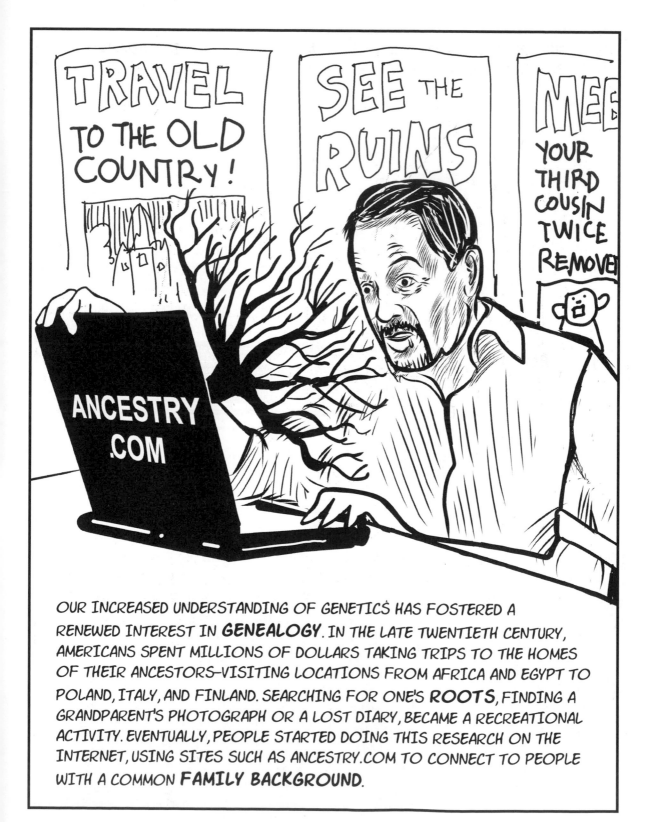

OUR INCREASED UNDERSTANDING OF GENETICS HAS FOSTERED A RENEWED INTEREST IN **GENEALOGY**. IN THE LATE TWENTIETH CENTURY, AMERICANS SPENT MILLIONS OF DOLLARS TAKING TRIPS TO THE HOMES OF THEIR ANCESTORS—VISITING LOCATIONS FROM AFRICA AND EGYPT TO POLAND, ITALY, AND FINLAND. SEARCHING FOR ONE'S **ROOTS**, FINDING A GRANDPARENT'S PHOTOGRAPH OR A LOST DIARY, BECAME A RECREATIONAL ACTIVITY. EVENTUALLY, PEOPLE STARTED DOING THIS RESEARCH ON THE INTERNET, USING SITES SUCH AS ANCESTRY.COM TO CONNECT TO PEOPLE WITH A COMMON **FAMILY BACKGROUND**.

ON AUGUST 28, 1963, **MARTIN LUTHER KING JR.**—THE MOST INFLUENTIAL CIVIL RIGHTS LEADER OF HIS ERA—DELIVERED HIS "I HAVE A DREAM" SPEECH ON THE STEPS OF THE LINCOLN MEMORIAL. IN THIS SPEECH, HE ENVISIONED A FUTURE IN WHICH THE NATION WAS NO LONGER DIVIDED ALONG THE COLOR LINE. HE RECEIVED THE NOBEL PEACE PRIZE IN 1964.

"I HAVE A DREAM THAT MY FOUR LITTLE CHILDREN WILL ONE DAY LIVE IN A NATION WHERE THEY WILL NOT BE JUDGED BY THE COLOR OF THEIR SKIN BUT BY THE CONTENT OF THEIR CHARACTER."

THREE MONTHS LATER, ON NOVEMBER 22, 1963, **PRESIDENT JOHN F. KENNEDY** WAS SHOT AND KILLED WHILE RIDING IN A PARADE IN DOWNTOWN DALLAS. **CONSPIRACY THEORIES** RELATING TO THE ASSASSINATION ABOUND TO THIS DAY.

IN 1968, MARTIN LUTHER KING JR. WOULD BE ASSASSINATED, TOO!

THE SIXTIES WERE A TIME OF UPHEAVAL FOR EVERYONE. IN 1963, BETTY FRIEDAN PUBLISHED **THE FEMININE MYSTIQUE**, WHICH DISCUSSED THE CHRONIC UNHAPPINESS OF **AMERICAN HOUSEWIVES**. SHE CALLED FOR A CHANGE IN THE NATION'S GENDER RELATIONS, DEMANDING THAT WOMEN BE TREATED AS **EQUAL TO MEN**.

THIS BOOK "PULLED THE TRIGGER OF HISTORY."

ALVIN TOFFLER

THAT SAME YEAR, BOB DYLAN MADE A SPLASH WITH HIS ALBUM **THE FREEWHEELIN' BOB DYLAN**.

LATER, IN A NEW YORK HOTEL ROOM, DYLAN WOULD INTRODUCE A RISING BRITISH POP GROUP TO **MARIJUANA**.

THAT POP GROUP WAS **THE BEATLES—** THE BEST-SELLING ROCK BAND OF ALL TIME. THEY CAME TO TOWN IN 1964 TO MAKE THEIR HISTORIC APPEARANCE ON **THE ED SULLIVAN SHOW**.

THE CHANGING MORES OF THE SIXTIES EVENTUALLY BLOSSOMED INTO THE **HIPPIE** MOVEMENT. ANTIESTABLISHMENT FEELINGS WERE IN THE AIR— A DESIRE TO DEFY AUTHORITY AND USHER IN A FREER, MORE OPEN SOCIETY. THE HIPPIES EXPERIMENTED WITH DRUGS SUCH AS LSD AND MARIJUANA, AS WELL AS "**FREE LOVE**" AND **CASUAL SEX**. THE THIN LINE SEPARATING NORMALITY FROM MENTAL ILLNESS BECAME EPHEMERAL.

AS TIME WENT BY, MANY FORMER HIPPIES ASSUMED POSITIONS OF POWER, EMBODYING THE VERY PRINCIPLES THEY HAD SOUGHT TO BRING DOWN.

Steve Jobs

I AM A MAN

CIV RIG HTS

IN 1964, CONGRESS PASSED A **LANDMARK CIVIL RIGHTS ACT**, PROHIBITING SEGREGATION AND MOST FORMS OF DISCRIMINATION BASED ON RACE OR GENDER. NOT SINCE THE THIRTEENTH AMENDMENT HAD THE NATION UNDERGONE SUCH A SWEEPING SOCIAL RECONFIGURATION.

A GIFT FROM HEAVEN!

MEDICAID AND MEDICARE WERE ESTABLISHED IN 1965 TO HELP GIVE POOR AND ELDERLY AMERICANS ACCESS TO HEALTH CARE.

RADICALISM WAS IN THE AIR.

ONE OF THE MOST VISIBLE EXPONENTS OF THIS RADICALISM WAS **MALCOLM X**, A MILITANT CIVIL RIGHTS ACTIVIST. ON FEBRUARY 21, 1965, AS HE PREPARED TO ADDRESS THE ORGANIZATION OF AFRO-AMERICAN UNITY IN MANHATTAN'S AUDUBON BALLROOM, HE WAS SHOT AND KILLED BY THREE ASSAILANTS. FOR A WHILE, IT FELT LIKE AMERICA WAS KILLING ITS MOST IMPORTANT VOICES.

BURN BABY BURN

THE SIXTIES ALSO SAW THE EMERGENCE OF THE **WOMEN'S LIBERATION MOVEMENT**. CONTRARY TO POPULAR MYTH, FEMINISTS OF THE TIME DIDN'T BURN BRAS—THIS STORY SEEMS TO HAVE ITS ORIGIN IN A 1968 PROTEST OF THE MISS AMERICA PAGEANT, DURING WHICH A FEW BRAS MAY HAVE BEEN DUMPED IN THE TRASH.

I AM WOMAN, HEAR ME FIST-ROAR!

GLORIA STEINEM WENT UNDER-COVER AS A PLAYBOY BUNNY!

AT THE HEAD OF THE MOVEMENT WERE FIGURES SUCH AS **GLORIA STEINEM**, AUTHOR OF A SEMINAL 1969 ARTICLE ENTITLED "AFTER BLACK POWER, WOMEN'S LIBERATION" AND COFOUNDER OF **MS. MAGAZINE**. ALONG WITH OTHER FEMINIST LUMINARIES, INCLUDING BETTY FRIEDAN, STEINEM BUILT ON THE SUFFRAGISTS' REVOLUTION OF AN EARLIER GENERATION AND MADE WOMEN CONSCIOUS OF HOW FAR THEY HAD TO GO IN ACHIEVING **TRUE EQUALITY**.

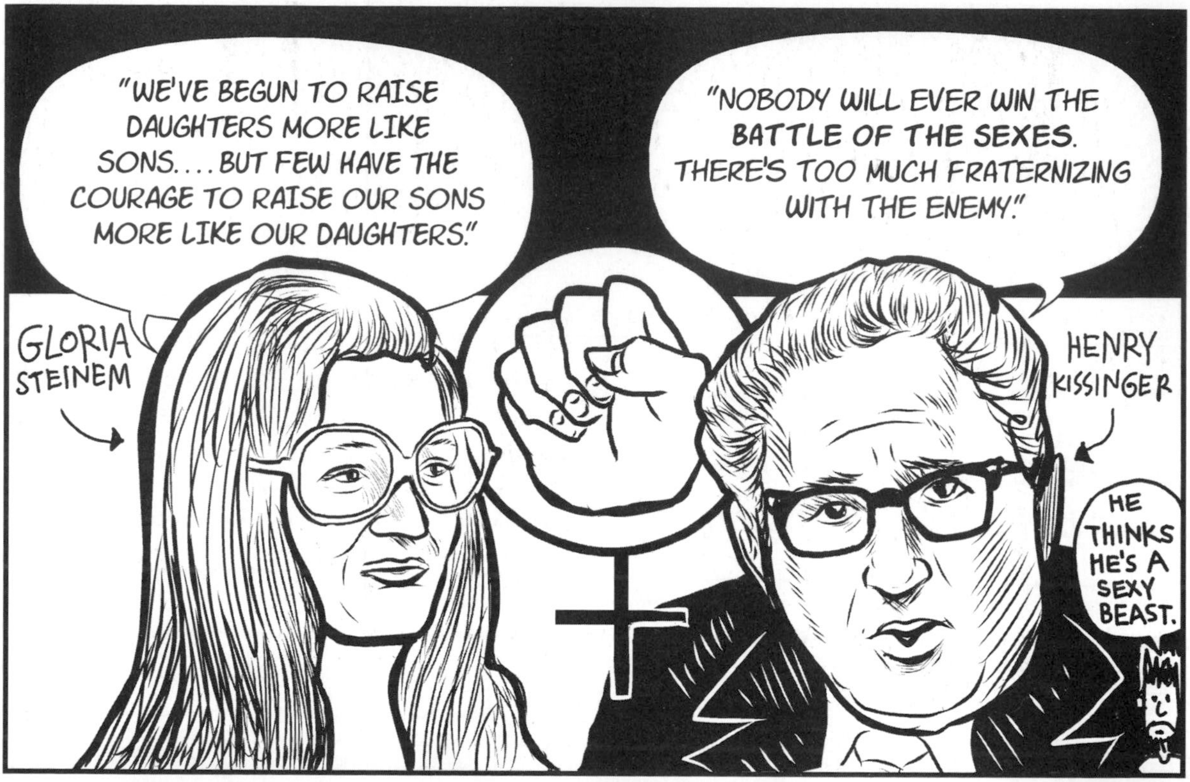
"WE'VE BEGUN TO RAISE DAUGHTERS MORE LIKE SONS.... BUT FEW HAVE THE COURAGE TO RAISE OUR SONS MORE LIKE OUR DAUGHTERS."
GLORIA STEINEM
"NOBODY WILL EVER WIN THE BATTLE OF THE SEXES. THERE'S TOO MUCH FRATERNIZING WITH THE ENEMY."
HENRY KISSINGER
HE THINKS HE'S A SEXY BEAST.

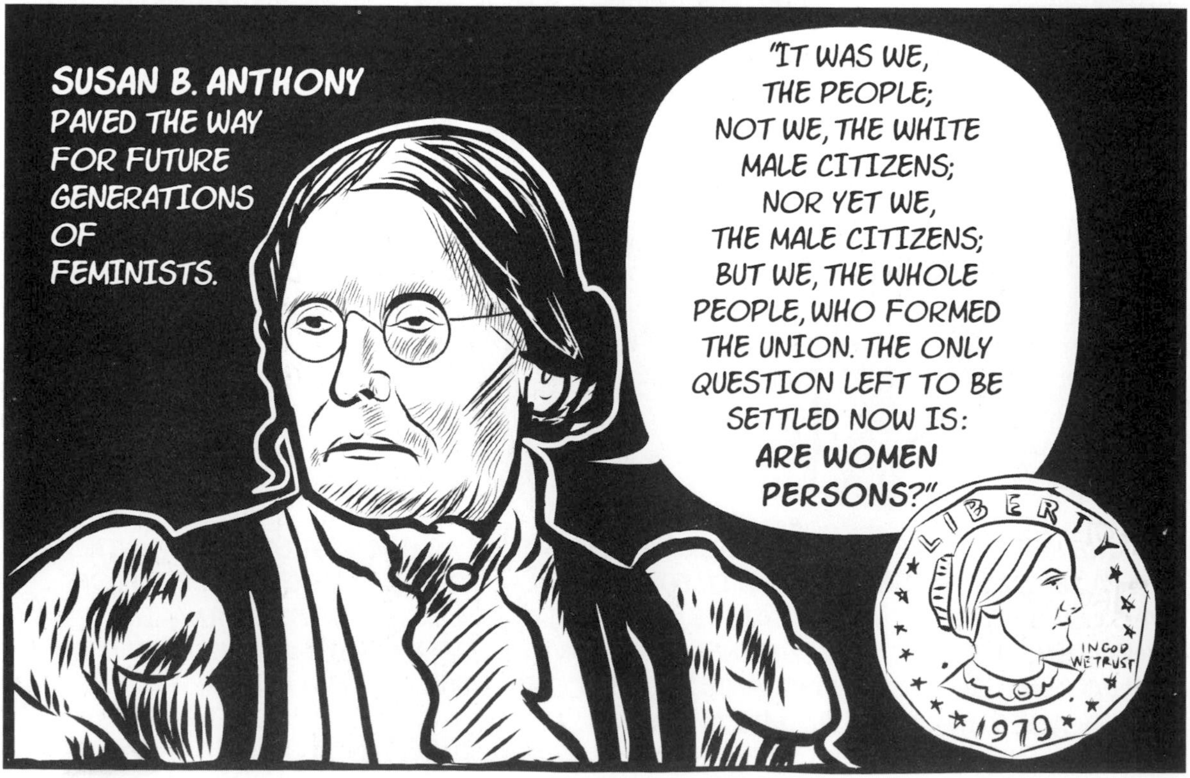
SUSAN B. ANTHONY PAVED THE WAY FOR FUTURE GENERATIONS OF FEMINISTS.
"IT WAS WE, THE PEOPLE; NOT WE, THE WHITE MALE CITIZENS; NOR YET WE, THE MALE CITIZENS; BUT WE, THE WHOLE PEOPLE, WHO FORMED THE UNION. THE ONLY QUESTION LEFT TO BE SETTLED NOW IS: ARE WOMEN PERSONS?"
LIBERTY
IN GOD WE TRUST
1979

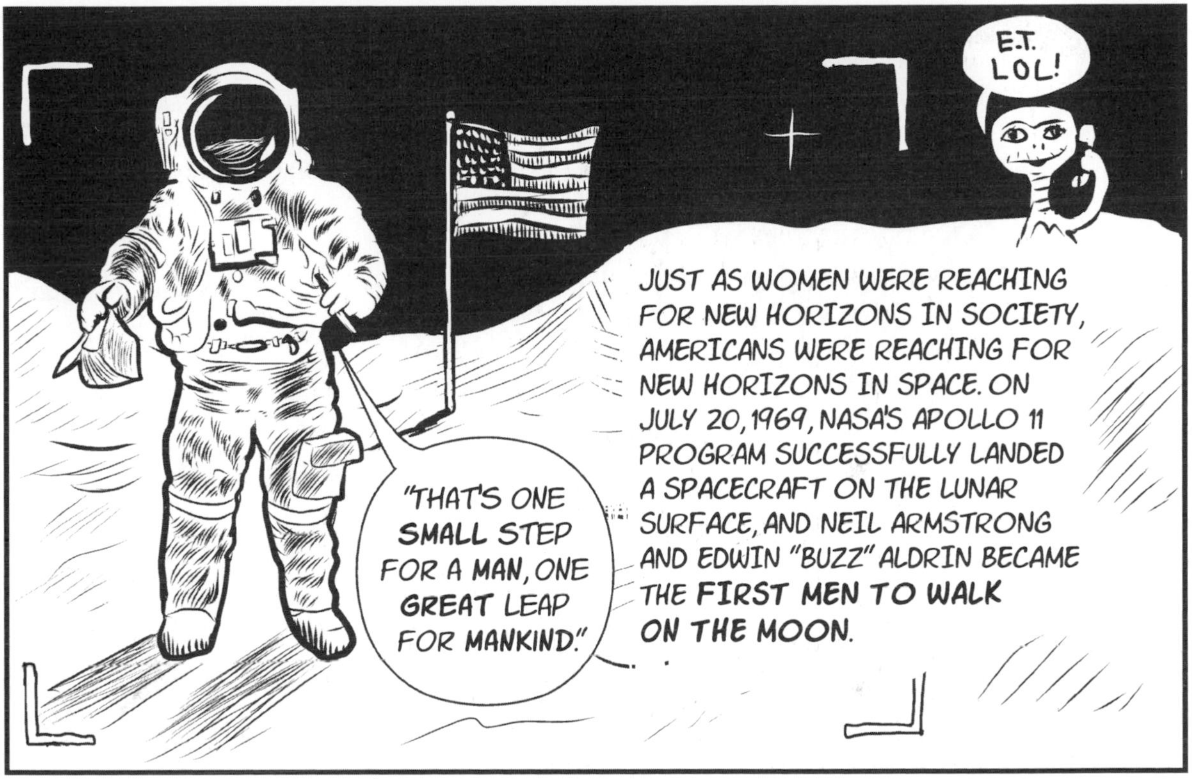
E.T. LOL!
JUST AS WOMEN WERE REACHING FOR NEW HORIZONS IN SOCIETY, AMERICANS WERE REACHING FOR NEW HORIZONS IN SPACE. ON JULY 20, 1969, NASA'S APOLLO 11 PROGRAM SUCCESSFULLY LANDED A SPACECRAFT ON THE LUNAR SURFACE, AND NEIL ARMSTRONG AND EDWIN "BUZZ" ALDRIN BECAME THE FIRST MEN TO WALK ON THE MOON.
"THAT'S ONE SMALL STEP FOR A MAN, ONE GREAT LEAP FOR MANKIND."

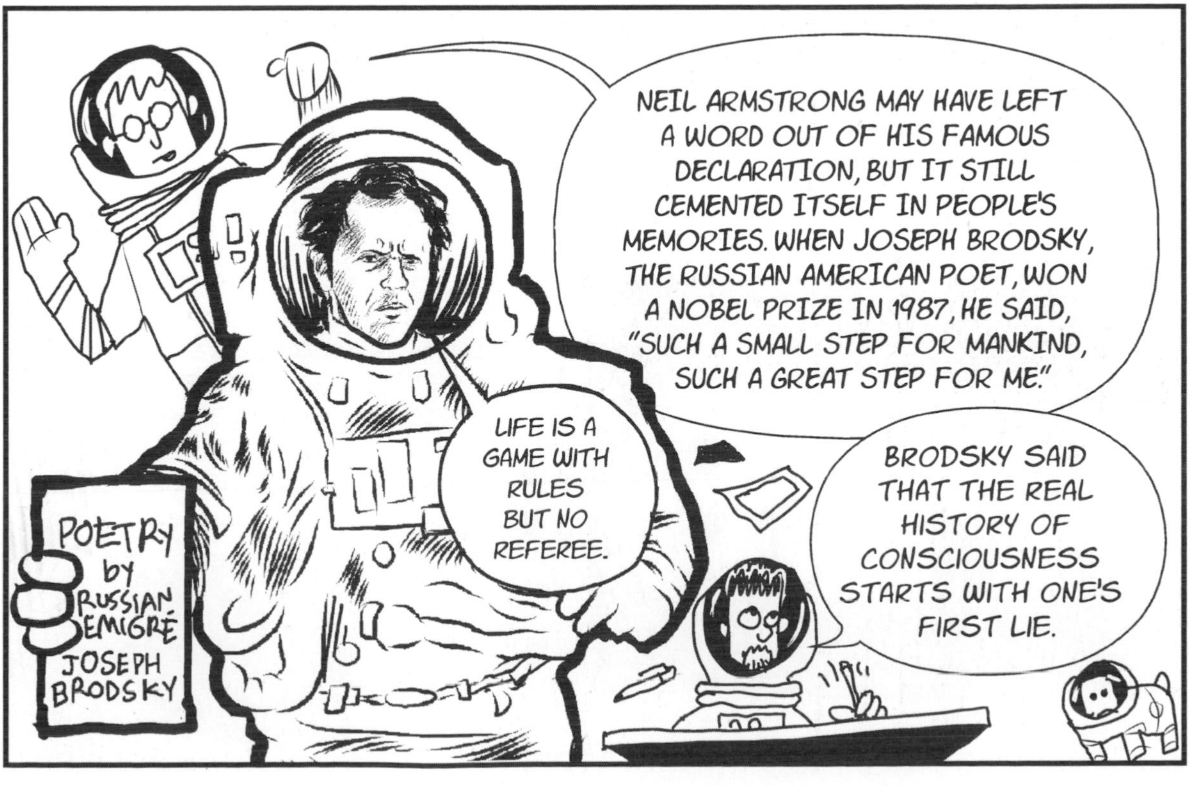
NEIL ARMSTRONG MAY HAVE LEFT A WORD OUT OF HIS FAMOUS DECLARATION, BUT IT STILL CEMENTED ITSELF IN PEOPLE'S MEMORIES. WHEN JOSEPH BRODSKY, THE RUSSIAN AMERICAN POET, WON A NOBEL PRIZE IN 1987, HE SAID, "SUCH A SMALL STEP FOR MANKIND, SUCH A GREAT STEP FOR ME."
LIFE IS A GAME WITH RULES BUT NO REFEREE.
BRODSKY SAID THAT THE REAL HISTORY OF CONSCIOUSNESS STARTS WITH ONE'S FIRST LIE.
POETRY by RUSSIAN EMIGRÉ JOSEPH BRODSKY

IN 1969, THE **WOODSTOCK FESTIVAL** WAS HELD IN UPSTATE NEW YORK. BILLED AS "THREE DAYS OF PEACE AND MUSIC," THE EVENT WAS A DEFINING MOMENT FOR A **GENERATION**.

THAT SAME YEAR, A SERIES OF RIOTS OCCURRED IN RESPONSE TO A POLICE RAID OF THE STONEWALL INN, A GAY BAR IN MANHATTAN. MANY SEE THIS EVENT AS THE BEGINNING OF THE **GAY RIGHTS** MOVEMENT.

IN 1970, THE **PUBLIC BROADCASTING SERVICE**—BETTER KNOWN AS PBS—WAS CREATED AS A SUCCESSOR TO THE EXISTING NATIONAL EDUCATIONAL TELEVISION (NET) NETWORK. THE FOUNDERS OF PBS SAW IT AS A NETWORK THAT WOULDN'T BE HOSTAGE TO CORPORATE MONEY, AND THAT WOULD BROADCAST PROGRAMS REPRESENTATIVE OF THE NATION'S POPULATION.

OF COURSE, IT HASN'T ALWAYS LIVED UP TO ITS OWN EXPECTATIONS! MOST PBS SHOWS ARE TARGETED TO A WHITE **VIEWERSHIP** CAPABLE OF SENDING THE NETWORK A **CHECK** AFTER WATCHING REPORTS OF GUERILLA FIGHTERS IN LATIN AMERICA AND HUNGRY CHILDREN IN AFRICA.

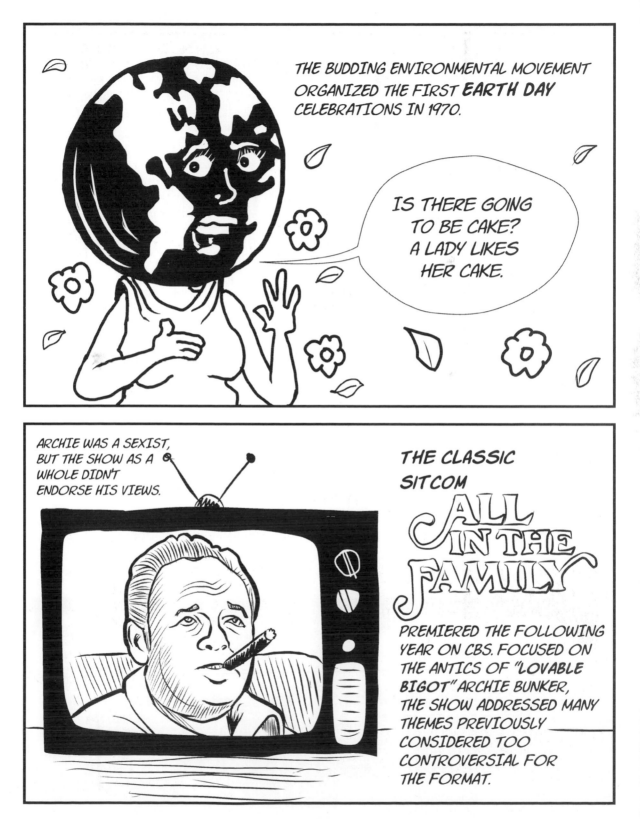

THE BUDDING ENVIRONMENTAL MOVEMENT ORGANIZED THE FIRST **EARTH DAY** CELEBRATIONS IN 1970.

IS THERE GOING TO BE CAKE? A LADY LIKES HER CAKE.

ARCHIE WAS A SEXIST, BUT THE SHOW AS A WHOLE DIDN'T ENDORSE HIS VIEWS.

THE CLASSIC SITCOM

ALL IN THE FAMILY

PREMIERED THE FOLLOWING YEAR ON CBS. FOCUSED ON THE ANTICS OF "LOVABLE BIGOT" ARCHIE BUNKER, THE SHOW ADDRESSED MANY THEMES PREVIOUSLY CONSIDERED TOO CONTROVERSIAL FOR THE FORMAT.

AS IF ALL THE CULTURAL TURMOIL WASN'T DESTABILIZING ENOUGH, AMERICAN POLITICS WENT DOWN THE TUBES IN THE EARLY SEVENTIES. ONE MIGHT CALL IT THE WATERGATE FLUSH. IN JUNE 1972—IN THE MIDST OF PRESIDENT RICHARD NIXON'S CAMPAIGN TO DEFEAT HIS **DEMOCRATIC RIVAL**, GEORGE MCGOVERN—A **BREAK-IN** OCCURRED AT THE HEADQUARTERS OF THE DEMOCRATIC NATIONAL COMMITTEE, IN THE WATERGATE OFFICE COMPLEX IN WASHINGTON, DC. THE INVESTIGATION OF THE BREAK-IN AND SUBSEQUENT COVER-UP ULTIMATELY LED TO **NIXON** HIMSELF, WHO SUFFERED FROM SYMPTOMS OF **PARANOIA**. IN ONE OF THE SCANDAL'S MOST DRAMATIC EPISODES, IT WAS REVEALED THAT **SECRET WHITE HOUSE TAPES** EXISTED THAT WERE POTENTIALLY DAMAGING TO NIXON. NIXON REFUSED TO RELEASE THE **RECORDINGS**, AND A LENGTHY BATTLE ENSUED—FINALLY, NIXON WAS UNANIMOUSLY ORDERED TO HAND OVER THE TAPES BY THE SUPREME COURT. IN THE END, FACING POSSIBLE IMPEACHMENT IN THE HOUSE OF REPRESENTATIVES, NIXON **RESIGNED** IN DISGRACE.

I WAS THERE RIGHT BEFORE HE TOOK OFF IN HIS HELICOPTER FROM THE WHITE HOUSE LAWN. I WAS THIRTEEN YEARS OLD, VISITING THE CAPITAL WITH MY AUNT BONNIE AND MY COUSIN RICHIE. MY FACE EVEN APPEARED IN THE **WASHINGTON POST**!

YOU'RE A WITNESS TO HISTORY!

NAH, I WAS JUST A MEXICAN **TOURIST** SPENDING MY **BAR MITZVAH** MONEY. MOST AMERICANS THINK OF THAT DAY WITH SHAME.

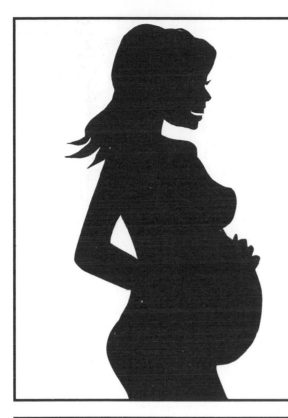

IN 1973, THE SUPREME COURT ISSUED ITS LANDMARK **ROE V. WADE** DECISION, DECLARING THAT WOMEN HAD THE CONSTITUTIONAL RIGHT TO AN **ABORTION.** SUPPORTERS OF THE DECISION FEEL THAT IT SIMPLY GAVE WOMEN CONTROL OVER THEIR OWN BODIES, BUT THE DECISION CONTINUES TO BE THE SUBJECT OF A POLARIZED DEBATE.

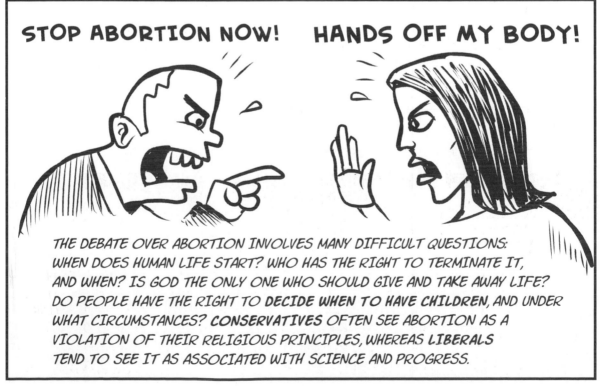

STOP ABORTION NOW! HANDS OFF MY BODY!

THE DEBATE OVER ABORTION INVOLVES MANY DIFFICULT QUESTIONS: WHEN DOES HUMAN LIFE START? WHO HAS THE RIGHT TO TERMINATE IT, AND WHEN? IS GOD THE ONLY ONE WHO SHOULD GIVE AND TAKE AWAY LIFE? DO PEOPLE HAVE THE RIGHT TO **DECIDE WHEN TO HAVE CHILDREN**, AND UNDER WHAT CIRCUMSTANCES? **CONSERVATIVES** OFTEN SEE ABORTION AS A VIOLATION OF THEIR RELIGIOUS PRINCIPLES, WHEREAS **LIBERALS** TEND TO SEE IT AS ASSOCIATED WITH SCIENCE AND PROGRESS.

ALTHOUGH THE FIGHT FOR BLACK CIVIL RIGHTS RECEIVED MORE NATIONAL ATTENTION, LATINO ACTIVISM WAS ALSO INCREASING DURING THE SIXTIES AND SEVENTIES. THE MOST IMPORTANT MEXICAN AMERICAN ACTIVIST OF THIS TIME WAS **CESAR CHAVEZ**. A MIGRANT WORKER WITH LIMITED EDUCATION, CHAVEZ EMERGED AS A PROMINENT LABOR ORGANIZER, COFOUNDING THE NATIONAL FARM WORKERS ASSOCIATION (LATER KNOWN AS **UNITED FARM WORKERS**) AND PARTICIPATING IN ACTIONS SUCH AS THE DELANO GRAPE STRIKE OF 1965. INSPIRED BY THE EXAMPLES OF GANDHI AND MARTIN LUTHER KING, CHAVEZ BELIEVED IN NONVIOLENT RESISTANCE, AND USED TOOLS SUCH AS LABOR STRIKES, HUNGER STRIKES, AND MARCHES TO BRING ATTENTION TO THE **DEPLORABLE LIVING AND WORKING CONDITIONS** OF THOUSANDS OF MIGRANT WORKERS IN THE SOUTHWEST. CHAVEZ WAS ONE OF THE ESSENTIAL VOICES IN WHAT HAS COME TO BE KNOWN AS THE CHICANO MOVEMENT. TO THIS DAY, HIS UFW COFOUNDER DOLORES HUERTA REMAINS AN ICONIC FIGHTER FOR **WORKERS' RIGHTS** AND **ECONOMIC JUSTICE**.

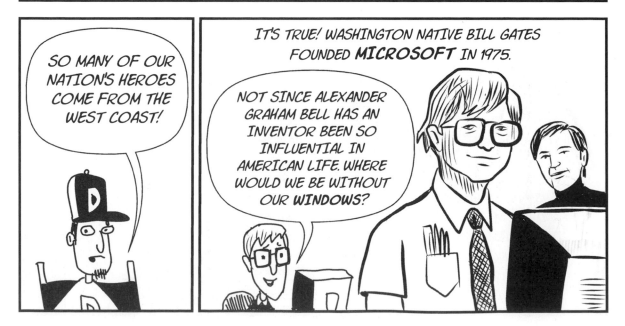

SO MANY OF OUR NATION'S HEROES COME FROM THE WEST COAST!

IT'S TRUE! WASHINGTON NATIVE BILL GATES FOUNDED **MICROSOFT** IN 1975.

NOT SINCE ALEXANDER GRAHAM BELL HAS AN INVENTOR BEEN SO INFLUENTIAL IN AMERICAN LIFE. WHERE WOULD WE BE WITHOUT OUR **WINDOWS**?

HARVEY MILK—ANOTHER WEST COAST ACTIVIST—WAS ASSASSINATED ON NOVEMBER 27, 1978. MILK WAS AN **OUTSPOKEN ADVOCATE** OF GAY RIGHTS, AND HIS DEATH HELPED PROPEL THE MOVEMENT TO NATIONAL PROMINENCE.

MEANWHILE, AMERICA WAS EVOLVING INTO AN INCREASINGLY **PLURALISTIC SOCIETY**, AS **MULTICULTURALISM** BECAME A PERMANENT FIXTURE OF THE NATION'S SOUL. WE'RE NOW A NATION OF KOREANS, CHINESE, INDIANS, RUSSIANS, CAPE VERDEANS, PALESTINIANS, HONDURANS, ETHIOPIANS, SYRIANS, PORTUGUESE, SCANDINAVIANS, FRENCH, BRITONS, VENEZUELANS, NIGERIANS, LEBANESE, NEW ZEALANDERS, ARGENTINES, MOROCCANS, SENEGALESE, DOMINICANS . . .

STARTING IN THE SEVENTIES, SOCIOLOGISTS STOPPED USING THE TERM **MELTING POT** TO DESCRIBE THE IMMIGRANT EXPERIENCE BECAUSE NOTHING REALLY MELTS ANYMORE. THE **FUSING PROCESS** . . . WELL, NO LONGER FUSES. INSTEAD, SEPARATE CULTURAL IDENTITIES ARE SEEN AS BEING JUXTAPOSED. THE PREFERRED TERM TO DESCRIBE THE AMERICAN SOCIAL EXPERIMENT IS NOW **SALAD BOWL** OR **MOSAIC**. TAKE YOUR PICK!

IN THE CULTURAL SALAD BOWL OF 1970S AMERICA, **AFFIRMATIVE ACTION** WAS OFTEN THE SUBJECT OF DEBATE.

APPLICATION
☑ WHITE
☑ MALE

OUR SOCIETY WAS FOUNDED BY EUROPEANS BUT IS CONSTANTLY BEING REDEFINED BY PEOPLE FROM OTHER NATIONS—AND THE TENSION BETWEEN THE VARIOUS ETHNIC GROUPS INEVITABLY CREATES CHALLENGES. IN 1978, **ALLAN BAKKE**, A THIRTY-TWO-YEAR-OLD WHITE MAN, APPLIED TO THE MEDICAL SCHOOL AT THE UNIVERSITY OF CALIFORNIA, DAVIS. BAKKE WAS REJECTED, BUT APPLICANTS FROM **DISADVANTAGED MINORITY** GROUPS WHO HAD LOWER TEST SCORES WERE ADMITTED. BAKKE FILED A LAWSUIT CLAIMING **REVERSE DISCRIMINATION**, AND THE CASE WAS ULTIMATELY BROUGHT BEFORE THE SUPREME COURT.

WHAT IS REVERSE DISCRIMINATION EXACTLY? IS IT WHEN YOU OFFEND OTHERS BY SAYING THINGS **BACKWARDS**?

JUSTICE LEWIS F. POWELL JR. WROTE THE OPINION FOR THE COURT, SUGGESTING THAT **THE IMPORTANCE OF DIVERSITY IN THE CLASSROOM** JUSTIFIES THE PRACTICE OF CONSIDERING RACE AS ONE OF THE FACTORS IN ADMITTING A CANDIDATE TO A SCHOOL.
JUSTICE POWELL
JUSTICE BLACKMUN
JUSTICE BRENNAN
JUSTICE WHITE
JUSTICE MARSHALL
MT. JUDGEMORE
WHY SHOULD MINORITIES GET SPECIAL TREATMENT? SHOULD WE REALLY BE ADMITTING PEOPLE BASED ON THE **COLOR OF THEIR SKIN**? WHO CARES IF WE HAVE DIVERSITY IN THE CLASSROOM?
NO AA
I DO, FOR ONE! AFTER SOME THIRTY YEARS OF TEACHING, I CAN SAY, WITHOUT RESERVATIONS, THAT A MULTICULTURAL CLASSROOM IS FAR **RICHER** AND **MORE CONDUCIVE** TO LEARNING THAN A MONOCHROMATIC ONE.

CHAPTER 7 NEW WORLD DISORDER

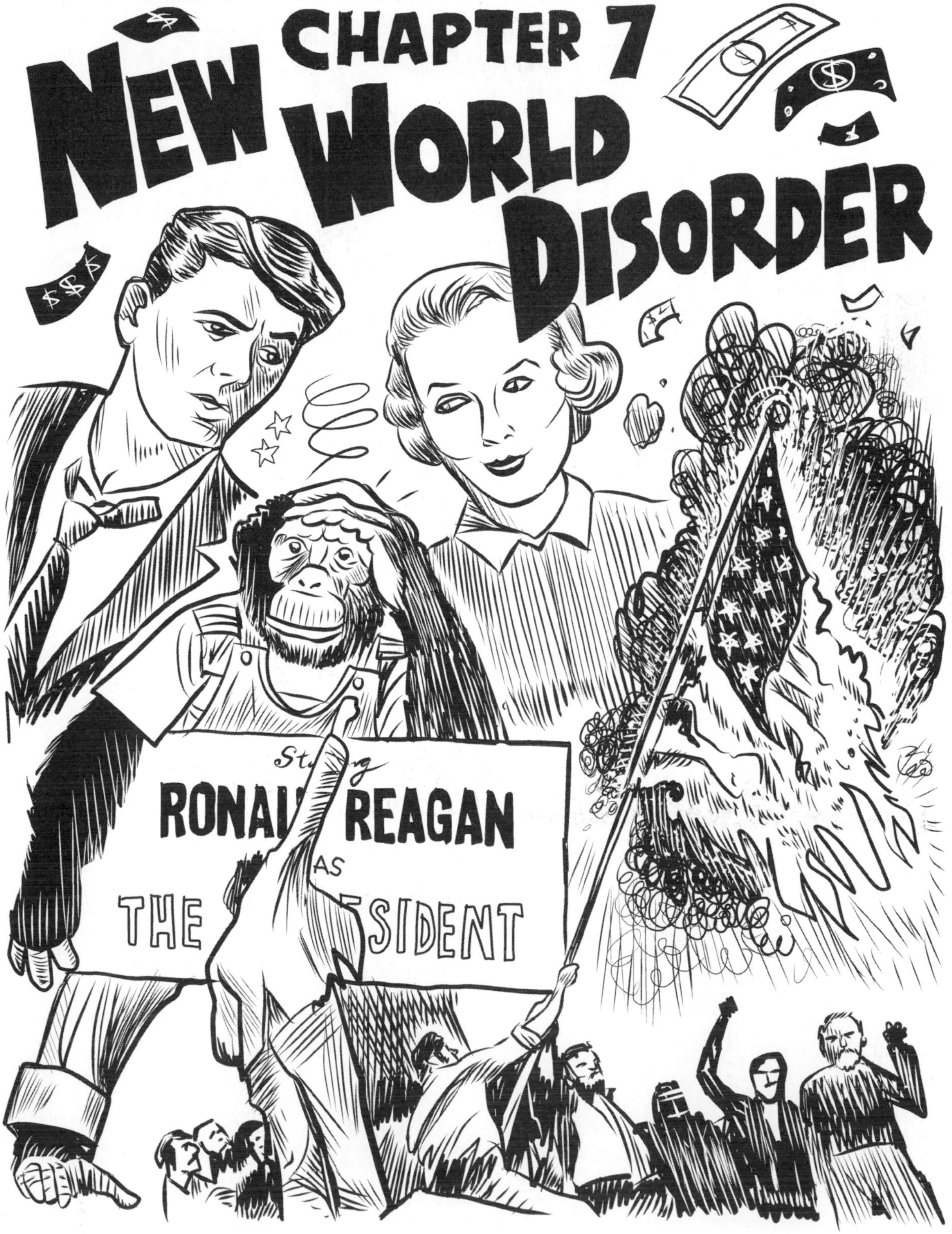
RONAL
REAGAN
AS
THE
SIDENT

ON NOVEMBER 4, 1979, A GROUP OF **ISLAMIC STUDENTS** AND MILITANTS INVADED THE AMERICAN EMBASSY IN TEHRAN, IRAN, AND TOOK FIFTY-TWO AMERICANS **HOSTAGE**. THE ENSUING CRISIS HELD THE WORLD'S ATTENTION FOR 444 DAYS, UNTIL THE HOSTAGES WERE FINALLY RELEASED ON JANUARY 20, 1981. IN MANY WAYS, THIS INCIDENT WAS THE BEGINNING OF WHAT HISTORIAN SAMUEL HUNTINGTON CALLS "THE CLASH OF CIVILIZATIONS"—A MOUNTING CONFLICT THAT PITS THE UNITED STATES AND ITS WESTERN ALLIES AGAINST SOME OF THE MOST **FUNDAMENTALIST FACTIONS IN THE ARAB WORLD.**

FOR DECADES, IRAN HAD BEEN RULED BY THE US-BACKED SHAH MOHAMMAD REZA PAHLAVI. IN FEBRUARY 1979, THE SHAH WAS OVERTHROWN IN A RELIGIOUS UPRISING AND REPLACED BY THE **AYATOLLAH RUHOLLAH KHOMEINI**, AN ISLAMIC LEADER WHO HAD BEEN EXILED BY THE SHAH FOR FIFTEEN YEARS. KHOMEINI REFERRED TO THE UNITED STATES AS "THE GREAT SATAN,"

UNDERSCORING AMERICA'S HABIT OF ACTING AS THE WORLD'S POLICEMAN AND BACKING POLITICAL REGIMES THAT WERE FRIENDLY TO AMERICAN INTERESTS BUT WHOSE RECORDS OF HUMAN RIGHTS VIOLATIONS WERE OFTEN DISGRACEFUL. THE LEADERS OF **THE IRANIAN REVOLUTION** TOOK EXISTING ANTI-AMERICAN SENTIMENT AND INTENSIFIED IT GREATLY, PORTRAYING WESTERN CIVILIZATION AS **ESSENTIALLY IMMORAL.**

THE NAME **SATAN** COMES FROM A HEBREW WORD MEANING "THE ADVERSARY." WITH THE EXCEPTION OF GOD, NO FIGURE IS MORE FREQUENTLY INVOKED IN MODERN POLITICS.

IN 1989, KHOMEINI ISSUED A FATWA AGAINST BRITISH AUTHOR SALMAN RUSHDIE, CLAIMING THAT HIS NOVEL **THE SATANIC VERSES** DEFAMED ISLAM AND THE KORAN. IN 2006, THE ISLAMIC WORLD HAD A SIMILAR REACTION TO A COLLECTION OF DANISH CARTOONS THAT DEPICTED **THE PROPHET MUHAMMAD.**

ALTHOUGH HE REFUSED TO NEGOTIATE WITH A TERRORIST STATE, **PRESIDENT JIMMY CARTER** WORKED AROUND THE CLOCK TO BRING THE HOSTAGE CRISIS TO AN END. NEVERTHELESS, HIS **FAILURE TO SECURE** THE RELEASE OF THE HOSTAGES CONTRIBUTED TO THE PUBLIC PERCEPTION OF CARTER AS A WEAK PRESIDENT, A PERCEPTION THAT HELPED PROPEL FORMER ACTOR **RONALD REAGAN** TO THE **WHITE HOUSE**. IN AN ENDING WORTHY OF HOLLYWOOD, THE HOSTAGES WERE RELEASED ON THE EXACT DAY THAT REAGAN WAS INAUGURATED AS PRESIDENT.

VOTE E.T.

INDEED, REAGAN COULD BE SEEN AS A BRIDGE BETWEEN POLITICS AND ENTERTAINMENT. WAS HIS PRESIDENCY A KIND OF PERFORMANCE? SHOULD HIS MOVIES BE SEEN AS **POLITICAL METAPHORS**? IN ANY CASE, THE AMERICAN FILM INDUSTRY WAS COMMITTED TO PRODUCING BLOCKBUSTERS—**E.T.**, ONE OF THE MOST BELOVED MOVIE CHARACTERS OF ALL TIME, LANDED ON EARTH IN 1982.

THAT SAME YEAR, MICHAEL JACKSON, FORMERLY OF THE JACKSON FIVE, RELEASED HIS ALBUM **THRILLER**, WHICH BECAME THE BEST-SELLING ALBUM OF ALL TIME. AS TIME WENT ON, JACKSON BECAME A **CONTROVERSIAL FIGURE**—HE WAS ACCUSED OF PEDOPHILIA, AND WAS KNOWN FOR HIS EXTENSIVE PLASTIC SURGERY AND THE VISIBLE WHITENING OF HIS SKIN.

JACKSON DIED OF A DRUG OVERDOSE ON JUNE 25, 2009. THE CONTROVERSY SURROUNDING HIS **CHANGING APPEARANCE** HIGHLIGHTED THE COMPLEXITY OF RACIAL ISSUES IN AMERICA.

SIGNS OF A MACHO

AGE LINES

TAN

STRONG CHIN

DENIM

HAT

NO GAY ZONE

REAGAN WAS A B-LIST ACTOR WITH A-LIST POLITICAL ASPIRATIONS.

WELL, IF I'D BEEN A BETTER ACTOR, I WOULDN'T HAVE BECOME PRESIDENT.

HE OFTEN HAD A SELECTIVE MEMORY. FOR EXAMPLE, HE CLAIMED TO HAVE FORGOTTEN KEY DETAILS OF THE IRAN-CONTRA AFFAIR, IN WHICH THE U.S. SOLD ARMS TO IRAN AND USED THE MONEY TO FUND THE REBEL CONTRAS IN NICARAGUA. REAGAN REMEMBERED WHAT HE WANTED, WHEN HE WANTED.

TO CONGRESS

IRAN-CONTRA SCANDAL

SHREDOMATIC

THE TEN COMMANDMENTS OF REAGANOMICS

1. THE MOST IMPORTANT CONCERN IN LIFE IS CONCERN FOR YOURSELF.
2. IF YOU'RE NOT FOR YOURSELF, WHO WILL BE FOR YOU?
3. IF YOU'RE ONLY FOR YOURSELF, YOU'RE A TRUE AMERICAN.
4. GOVERNMENT STINKS.
5. THE FOURTH COMMANDMENT IS RIGHT.
6. POOR PEOPLE ARE POOR BECAUSE THEY DON'T WANT TO BE RICH.
7. EGOTISM IS ADMIRABLE.
8. THE DUTY OF A FIRST-RATE POLITICIAN IS TO CONVINCE THE ELECTORATE THAT COMMUNISM STINKS.
9. DID WE ALREADY MENTION THAT EGOTISM RULES? IF SO, REPLACE EGOTISM WITH PATRIOTISM IN THIS COMMANDMENT.
10. DON'T FORGET TO PUT A FLAG OR TWO ON YOUR LAWN!

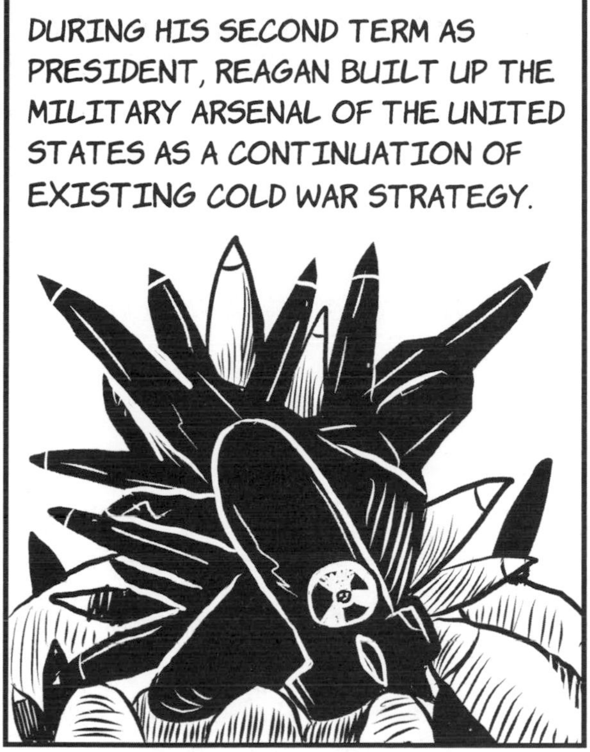
DURING HIS SECOND TERM AS PRESIDENT, REAGAN BUILT UP THE MILITARY ARSENAL OF THE UNITED STATES AS A CONTINUATION OF EXISTING COLD WAR STRATEGY.

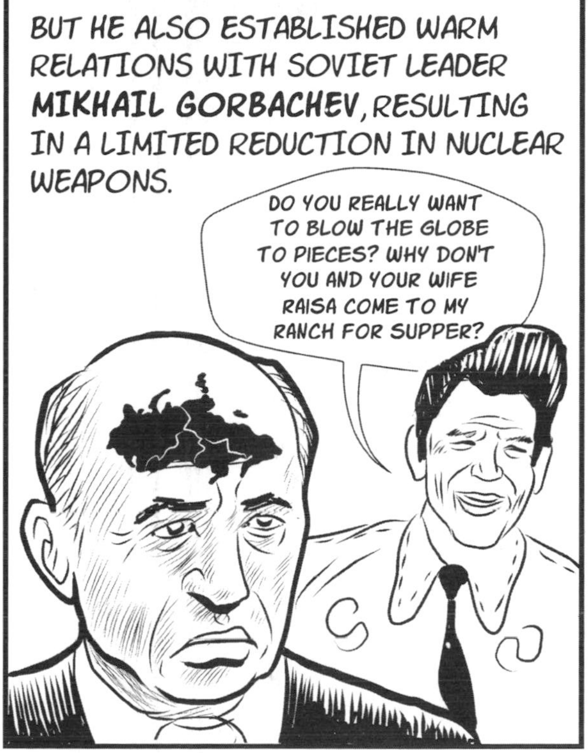
BUT HE ALSO ESTABLISHED WARM RELATIONS WITH SOVIET LEADER **MIKHAIL GORBACHEV**, RESULTING IN A LIMITED REDUCTION IN NUCLEAR WEAPONS.
DO YOU REALLY WANT TO BLOW THE GLOBE TO PIECES? WHY DON'T YOU AND YOUR WIFE RAISA COME TO MY RANCH FOR SUPPER?

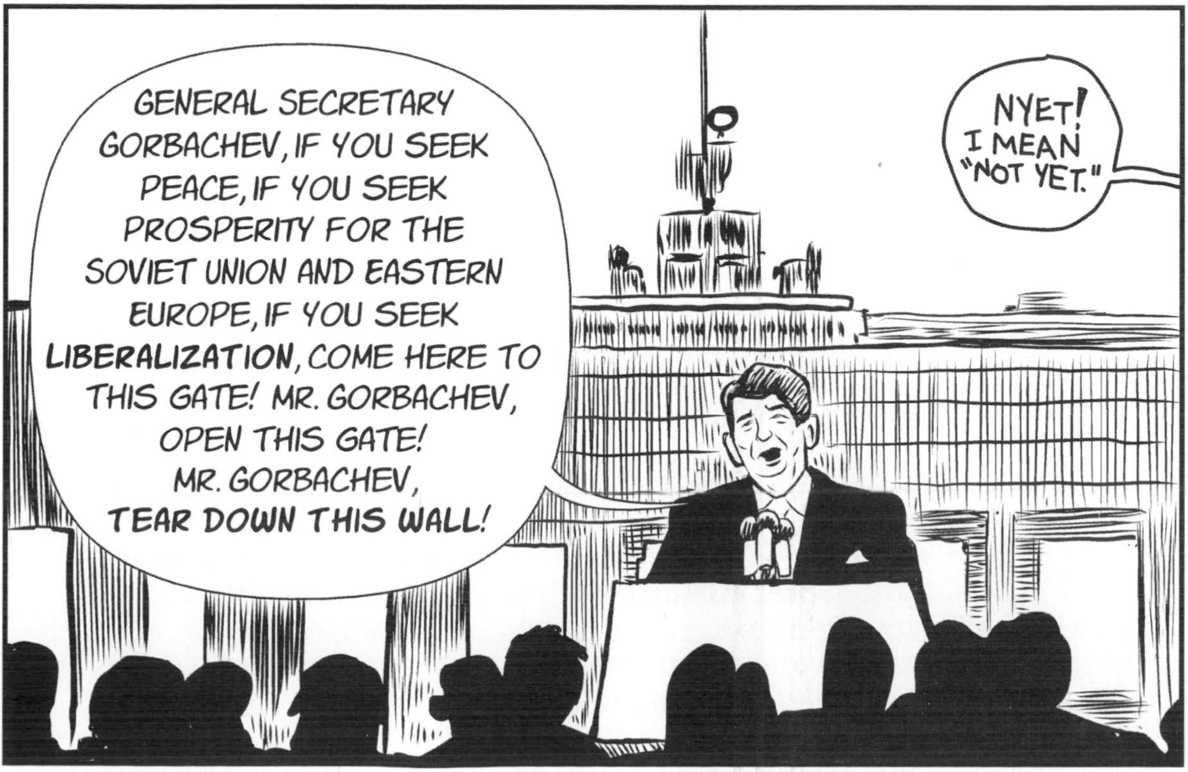
GENERAL SECRETARY GORBACHEV, IF YOU SEEK PEACE, IF YOU SEEK PROSPERITY FOR THE SOVIET UNION AND EASTERN EUROPE, IF YOU SEEK **LIBERALIZATION**, COME HERE TO THIS GATE! MR. GORBACHEV, OPEN THIS GATE! MR. GORBACHEV, **TEAR DOWN THIS WALL!**
NYET! I MEAN "NOT YET."

AS AMERICA WAS MAKING PEACE WITH ITS BIGGEST EXTERNAL ENEMY, A NEW
ENEMY WAS EMERGING FROM WITHIN. STARTING IN THE EARLY EIGHTIES, THE
UNITED STATES WAS SWEPT BY A MYSTERIOUS VIRUS THAT NEUTRALIZED THE
HUMAN IMMUNE SYSTEM. INITIALLY CALLED "GAY CANCER" DUE TO ITS PREVALENCE
IN THE GAY COMMUNITY, IT HAD KILLED 121 AMERICANS BY THE END OF 1981. SOON,
SCIENTIFIC TERMINOLOGY WAS ESTABLISHED: THE VIRUS WAS CALLED THE **HUMAN
IMMUNODEFICIENCY VIRUS (HIV),** AND THE RESULTING DISEASE WAS CALLED
ACQUIRED IMMUNODEFICIENCY SYNDROME (AIDS). THE VIRUS IS TRANSMITTED
THROUGH UNPROTECTED SEX AS WELL AS CONTAMINATED BLOOD TRANSFUSIONS
AND INTRAVENOUS DRUG USE.

IGNORANCE = FEAR

SILENCE = DEATH

FIGHT AIDS
ACT UP

AIDS

OVER THE NEXT SEVERAL YEARS, THE PROBLEM TURNED INTO A MAJOR PANDEMIC.
IN 1993, THE ANNUAL DEATH RATE APPROACHED 45,000 IN THE UNITED STATES, AND
THE IMPACT ON THE GAY COMMUNITY WAS ENORMOUS. BY 2008, 490,696 PEOPLE
IN THE UNITED STATES WERE LIVING WITH HIV: 42.6 PERCENT OF THEM WERE
BLACK, 21.4 PERCENT WERE LATINOS, AND 33.3 PERCENT WERE WHITE. TODAY, NEW
ANTIRETROVIRAL DRUGS HAVE GREATLY PROLONGED THE LIFE EXPECTANCY OF
THOSE WITH HIV, BUT SCIENTISTS HAVE NOT YET FOUND A CURE.

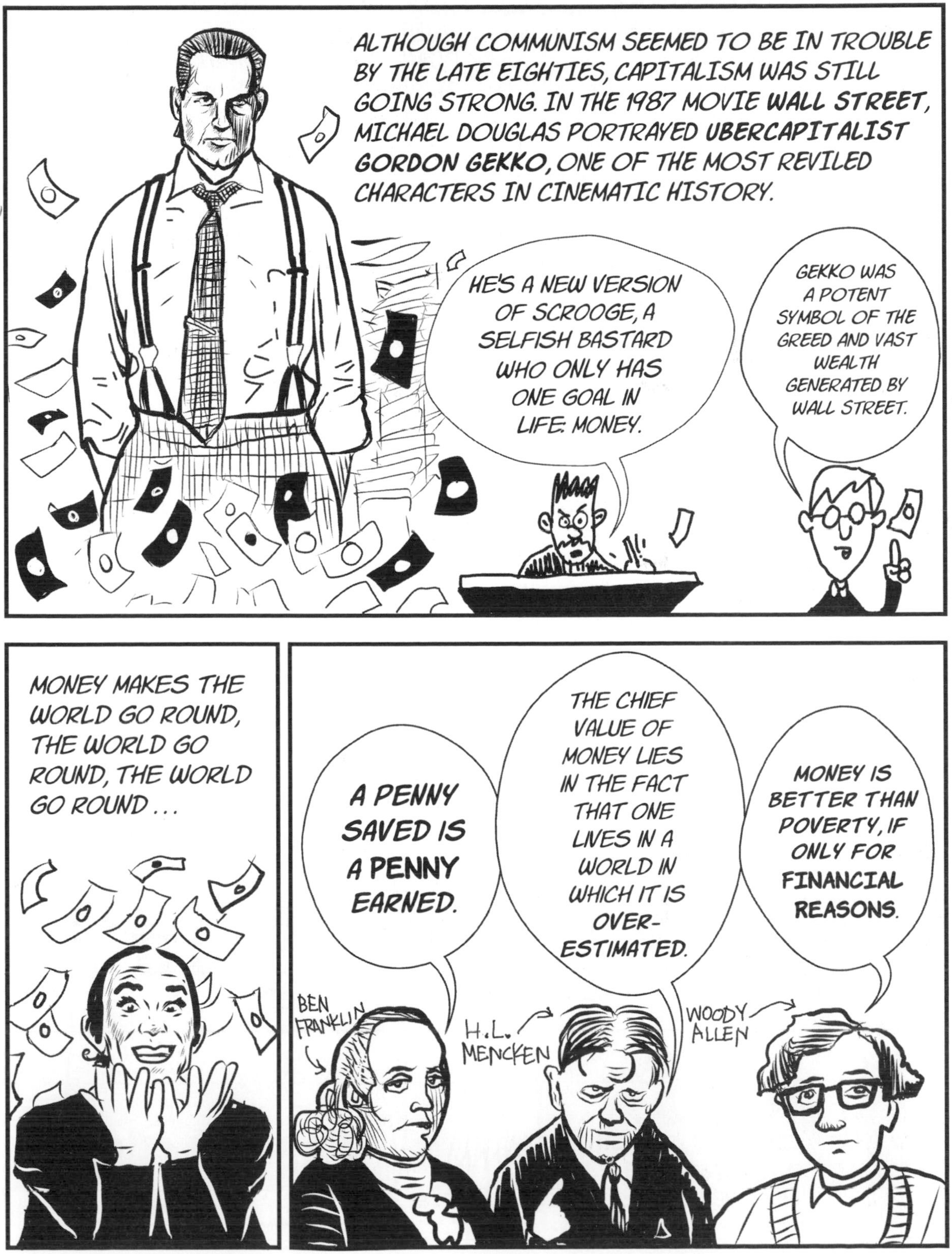
ALTHOUGH COMMUNISM SEEMED TO BE IN TROUBLE BY THE LATE EIGHTIES, CAPITALISM WAS STILL GOING STRONG. IN THE 1987 MOVIE **WALL STREET**, MICHAEL DOUGLAS PORTRAYED **UBERCAPITALIST GORDON GEKKO**, ONE OF THE MOST REVILED CHARACTERS IN CINEMATIC HISTORY.
HE'S A NEW VERSION OF SCROOGE, A SELFISH BASTARD WHO ONLY HAS ONE GOAL IN LIFE: MONEY.
GEKKO WAS A POTENT SYMBOL OF THE GREED AND VAST WEALTH GENERATED BY WALL STREET.
MONEY MAKES THE WORLD GO ROUND, THE WORLD GO ROUND, THE WORLD GO ROUND . . .
BEN FRANKLIN
A PENNY SAVED IS A PENNY EARNED.
H.L. MENCKEN
THE CHIEF VALUE OF MONEY LIES IN THE FACT THAT ONE LIVES IN A WORLD IN WHICH IT IS **OVER-ESTIMATED**.
WOODY ALLEN
MONEY IS BETTER THAN POVERTY, IF ONLY FOR FINANCIAL REASONS.

AY, THE CAULDRON OF HISTORY! HOW MUCH HUMANITY HAS BEEN FOOLISHLY SACRIFICED AT THE ALTAR OF THE HAMMER AND SICKLE?

GORBY

AT THE END OF THE EIGHTIES, THE COLD WAR CAME TO AN END, AS RELATIONS THAWED BETWEEN THE UNITED STATES AND THE SOVIET UNION. EVER SINCE WORLD WAR II, THE TWO SUPERPOWERS HAD BEEN ENGAGED IN **CONSTANT CONFRONTATION**, DRIVEN BY THE IDEOLOGICAL DIVIDE BETWEEN THE INDIVIDUALISTIC CAPITALISM OF THE WEST AND THE COLLECTIVIST COMMUNISM OF THE EAST. SUPPOSEDLY, THE TWO SIDES HAD BEEN ENEMIES TO THE CORE—YET IN AMERICA THERE HAD ALWAYS BEEN DEEP-SEATED EMPATHY FOR THE RUSSIAN PEOPLE, WHO WERE BEING FORCED TO LIVE UNDER TYRANNY. WHEN GORBACHEV CAME INTO POWER IN 1985, HE BEGAN TRANSFORMING THE SOVIET UNION INTO A MORE OPEN SOCIETY—THE POLICY OF **GLASNOST** INCREASED TRANSPARENCY IN OFFICIAL INSTITUTIONS, WHEREAS **PERESTROIKA** ALLOWED FOR THE RESTRUCTURING OF THE GOVERNMENT.

MEANWHILE, CHINA WAS ALSO MOVING IN A CAPITALIST DIRECTION.

CHAIRMAN MAO'S

SAME GREAT TASTE

SAME EVERY-THING

SAME FOR EVERYONE

IN 1979, **DENG XIAOPING** BEGAN ENACTING A SERIES OF ECONOMIC REFORMS THAT INSTILLED HIS COUNTRY WITH THE MODERN SPIRIT OF FREE ENTERPRISE.

Delicious Capitalist Deng Dongs

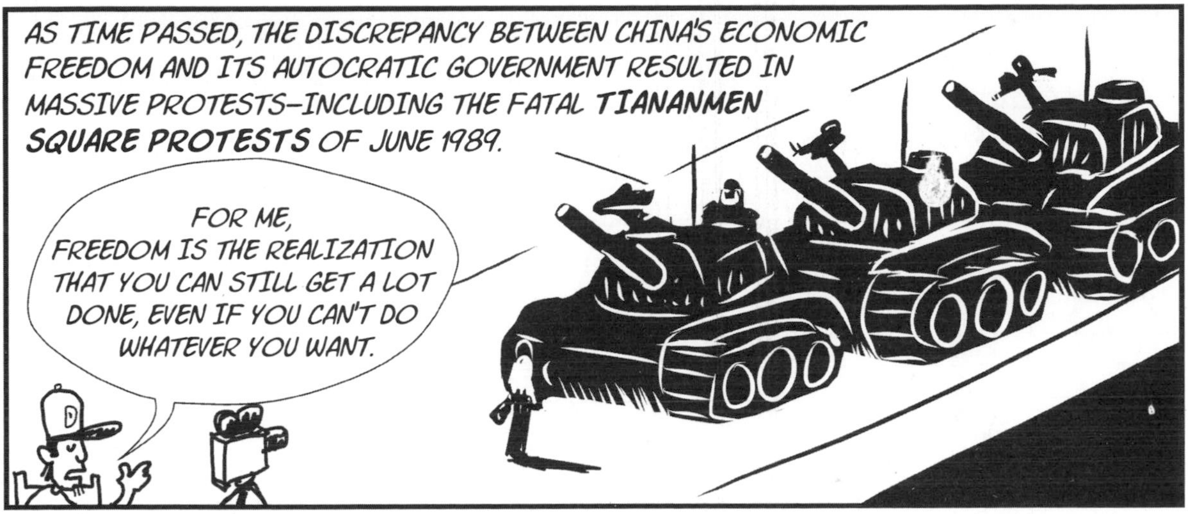
AS TIME PASSED, THE DISCREPANCY BETWEEN CHINA'S ECONOMIC FREEDOM AND ITS AUTOCRATIC GOVERNMENT RESULTED IN MASSIVE PROTESTS—INCLUDING THE FATAL **TIANANMEN SQUARE PROTESTS** OF JUNE 1989.
FOR ME, FREEDOM IS THE REALIZATION THAT YOU CAN STILL GET A LOT DONE, EVEN IF YOU CAN'T DO WHATEVER YOU WANT.

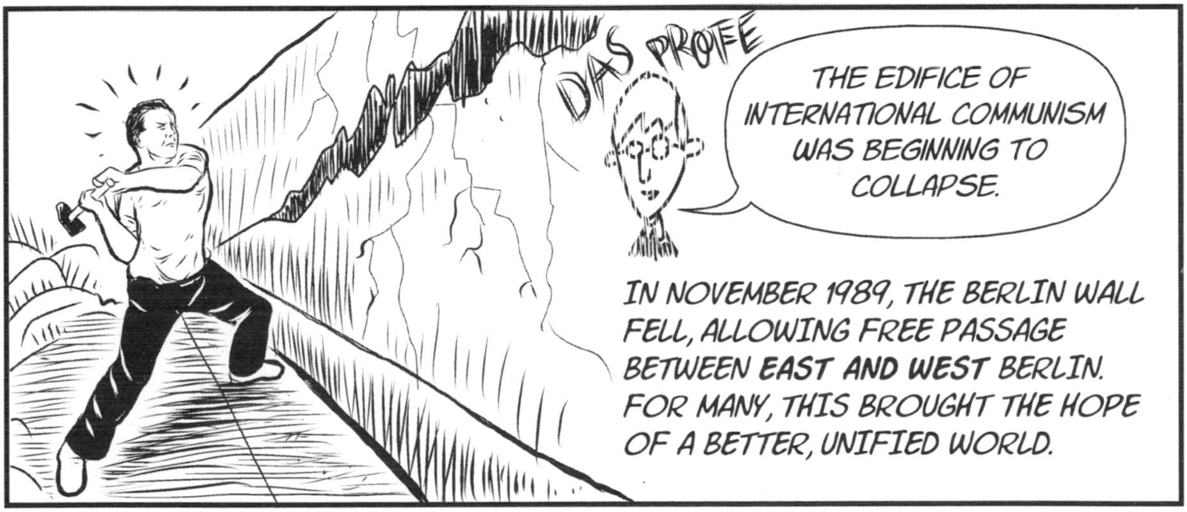
DAS PROFE
THE EDIFICE OF INTERNATIONAL COMMUNISM WAS BEGINNING TO COLLAPSE.
IN NOVEMBER 1989, THE BERLIN WALL FELL, ALLOWING FREE PASSAGE BETWEEN **EAST AND WEST** BERLIN. FOR MANY, THIS BROUGHT THE HOPE OF A BETTER, UNIFIED WORLD.

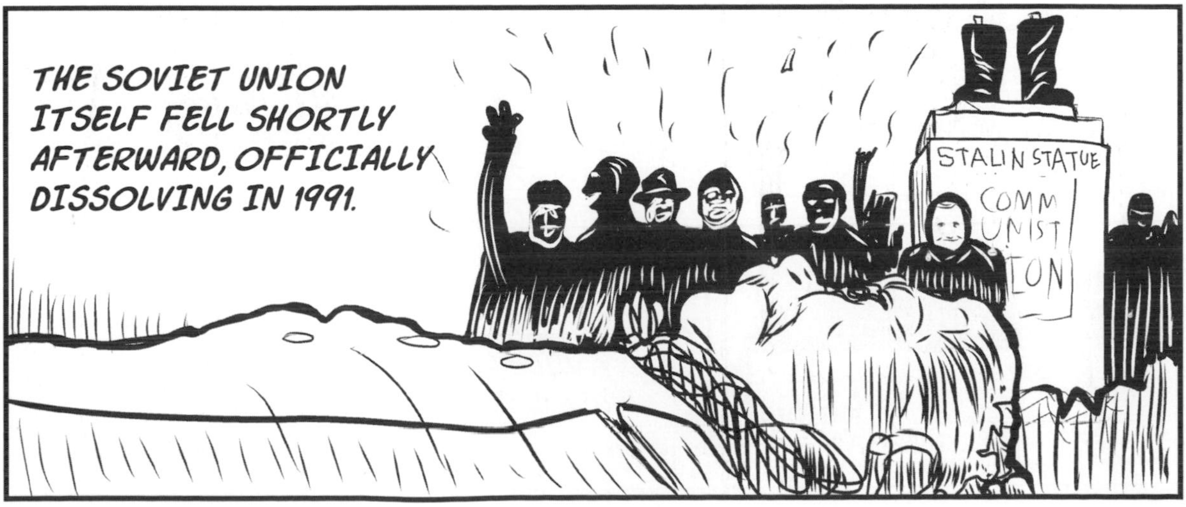
THE SOVIET UNION ITSELF FELL SHORTLY AFTERWARD, OFFICIALLY DISSOLVING IN 1991.
STALIN STATUE

CNN, FOUNDED IN 1980, SET THE **PARADIGM** FOR ITS RIVALS: IT BROADCAST TWENTY-FOUR HOURS A DAY, AND SHOWCASED NEWS FROM AROUND THE WORLD. WITH CABLE NEWS, VIEWERS COULD WATCH EVENTS UNFOLD MINUTE-BY-MINUTE—FROM THE FALL OF THE BERLIN WALL AND THE COLLAPSE OF THE SOVIET UNION TO THE TRIAL OF FORMER FOOTBALL STAR **O. J. SIMPSON**, WHO WAS ACCUSED OF MURDERING HIS EX-WIFE IN 1994. BY THE 1990s, THE LINE BETWEEN **JOURNALISM AND ENTERTAINMENT** WAS GROWING INCREASINGLY BLURRY, AND THE **TWENTY-FOUR-HOUR CABLE NEWS** CYCLE WAS AFFECTING POLITICAL STRATEGIES AND CHANGING THE VERY FABRIC OF THE SOCIETY IT PURPORTED TO COVER.

TODAY, THE NEWS IS STAGE-MANAGED TO MAXIMIZE AUDIENCE ENJOYMENT.

WHAT COUNTS AS NEWS ANYWAY? IF SOMETHING'S ON A TV SCREEN, DOES THAT MAKE IT TRUE? IN MANY WAYS, TELEVISION IS A **THERAPEUTIC MEDIUM**. WHENEVER A DISASTER OCCURS, PEOPLE RUSH TO THE TV IN AN ATTEMPT TO MAKE SENSE OF THINGS. AS THEY WATCH THE **TELEVISED IMAGES**, THEY EXPERIENCE A WIDE RANGE OF EMOTIONS, FROM DESPAIR TO EXHILARATION.

THE LATE TWENTIETH CENTURY ALSO SAW THE RISE OF **GRAFFITI** AS PART OF THE URBAN LANDSCAPE. WHAT'S AN AMERICAN CITY WITHOUT GRAFFITI?

A BORING PLACE.

GRAFFITI IS TRASH.

NO, NO, NO ... GRAFFITI IS ART: SPONTANEOUS, EPHEMERAL, AND DEMOCRATIC.

STARTING IN THE NINETIES THE **DOT-COM INDUSTRY**, BASED IN CALIFORNIA'S SILICON VALLEY, PLACED THE INTERNET AT THE CENTER OF AMERICAN LIFE. EVERYTHING—FROM SHOPPING TO READING, FROM POLITICS TO SEX—NOW TAKES PLACE ONLINE. LIKE GRAFFITI, THE INTERNET IS SPONTANEOUS, EPHEMERAL, AND DEMOCRATIC. IT'S ALSO REDEFINED OUR SOCIAL INTERACTIONS—AS WELL AS THE **NATION'S MORAL COMPASS!**

EVERYONE NOW HAS TWO LIVES: THE REAL AND **THE VIRTUAL.** THE COUNTRY HAS BECOME DISSOCIATED, LIKE **DR. JEKYLL AND MR. HYDE.**

HAVE WE ALREADY TALKED ABOUT HOW AMERICA HAS BECOME MORE RELIGIOUS OVER THE YEARS? IT COULD BE ARGUED THAT NO NATION ON THE PLANET IS MORE **GOD-FEARING** THAN THE UNITED STATES— NOT EVEN MEXICO, IRAN, OR ISRAEL.

THE LIST OF AMERICAN-MADE RELIGIONS AND SUB-DIVISIONS WITHIN THOSE RELGIONS IS EVER-EXPANDING:
- PENTECOSTALISM
- SCIENTOLOGY
- CHRISTIAN SCIENCE
- RECONSTRUCTIONIST JUDAISM
- NATION OF ISLAM
- CHURCH OF CHRIST
- ADVENTISM
- JEHOVAH'S WITNESSES
- CHURCH OF JESUS CHRIST OF LATTER-DAY SAINTS (AKA MORMONS)

WHY DON'T YOU START YOUR OWN RELIGION— **STAVANSISM?**

NO, THANK YOU! I'M AN ATHEIST, THANK GOD.

RELIGIOUS CULTS ARE AN ESSENTIAL COMPONENT OF AMERICA'S SPIRITUAL LANDSCAPE. OFTEN, THEY INVOLVE AN **EXPLOSIVE MIX OF FAITH AND POLITICS.** ONE FAMOUS EXAMPLE WAS THE BRANCH DAVIDIAN SECT, LED BY HOUSTON NATIVE **DAVID KORESH** (BORN VERNON WAYNE HOWELL IN 1959). IN 1993, FEDERAL AGENTS LAID SIEGE TO THE BRANCH DAVIDIANS' COMPOUND IN WACO, TEXAS, BASED ON ALLEGATIONS THAT THE GROUP POSSESSED ILLEGAL FIREARMS. THE **SIEGE** CAME TO A TRAGIC END WHEN A RAID ON THE COMPOUND RESULTED IN A FIRE, KILLING SEVENTY-SIX PEOPLE, INCLUDING KORESH, TWO PREGNANT WOMEN, AND TWENTY CHILDREN.

DAVID KORESH? SOUNDS LIKE A PHILIP ROTH CHARACTER!

THE CULT MEMBERS HAD BEEN **INDOCTRINATED** TO BELIEVE THAT **MASS SUICIDE** WAS THE PREFERRED FORM OF SALVATION, AND SALVATION HAS ALWAYS BEEN THE CORE OF THE AMERICAN RELIGIOUS ENTERPRISE.

WASN'T THE NATION ITSELF STARTED BY A **CULT?** THE RENEGADE PURITANS WERE SEEKING A NEW PARADISE!

THE WACO SIEGE WAS ONLY ONE OF MANY SCANDALS INVOLVING THE FEDERAL GOVERNMENT THAT EMERGED IN THE NINETIES. IN 1998, PRESIDENT BILL **CLINTON'S ZIPPER** BECAME A NATIONAL OBSESSION WHEN IT WAS REVEALED THAT HE'D ENGAGED IN ORAL SEX WITH WHITE HOUSE INTERN **MONICA LEWINSKY.**

THE VILLAIN OF THE STORY WAS **LINDA TRIPP**, A DEFENSE DEPARTMENT EMPLOYEE WHO SECRETLY TAPED LEWINSKY'S CONFESSIONS. MEANWHILE, FIRST LADY HILLARY CLINTON STOOD STOICALLY BY HER HUSBAND'S SIDE.

ON DECEMBER 19, 1998, PRESIDENT CLINTON WAS **IMPEACHED** ON CHARGES OF PERJURY AND OBSTRUCTION OF JUSTICE, BUT MOST OF THE COUNTRY SAW THE IMPEACHMENT AS A POLITICAL CHARADE.

IMPEACHED

FOR GOD'S SAKE, WHO CARES ABOUT THE PRIVATE LIVES OF POLITICIANS? JFK'S INDISCRETIONS WERE **COMMON KNOWLEDGE,** AND THEY MADE HIM MORE APPEALING TO THE PUBLIC!

WE CARTOONISTS OUGHT TO BE THANKFUL: CLINTON AND HIS SUCCESSOR, GEORGE W. BUSH, SEEM TO HAVE BEEN BORN TO BE LAMPOONED.

ULTIMATELY, CLINTON REMAINED IN OFFICE, BUT ANOTHER PRESIDENTIAL CONTROVERSY WOULD ROCK THE NATION AT THE DAWN OF THE NEW MILLENNIUM. IN THE 2000 ELECTION, CLINTON'S VICE PRESIDENT, AL GORE, RAN AGAINST TEXAS GOVERNOR **GEORGE W. BUSH** ...

IS OUR CHILDREN LEARNING?

HOW IS THIS GUY BEATING ME?!?

ACTUALLY, THE (FALSE) RUMOR WAS THAT BUSH'S IQ WAS 91 ...

HE COULDN'T EVEN SPEAK IN **GRAMMATICALLY CORRECT** SENTENCES!

THE RACE BETWEEN BUSH AND GORE WAS **INCREDIBLY TIGHT.** IN FLORIDA, THEY HAD TO PAINSTAKINGLY RECOUNT THE BALLOTS.

WHY DO THE NATION'S PROBLEMS SO OFTEN ORIGINATE IN FLORIDA?

THINGS WERE SO MUCH BETTER WHEN WE RAN THE JOINT.

THE TASK OF DETERMINING THE WINNER OF THE ELECTION ULTIMATELY FELL TO THE SUPREME COURT. THE WILL OF THE PEOPLE WAS NOW BEING INTERPRETED BY A GANG OF **POMPOUS ELITES**—SOMETHING THAT HADN'T HAPPENED SINCE 1824, WHEN THE RACE BETWEEN JOHN QUINCY ADAMS AND ANDREW JACKSON WAS DECIDED BY THE HOUSE OF REPRESENTATIVES. IN THE END, THE COURT'S CONSERVATIVE MAJORITY ENDORSED BUSH, THE REPUBLICAN, AS THE WINNER.

WAS THE BUSH/GORE DEBACLE AN ELECTION OR A COUP D'ÉTAT?

I THOUGHT THIS WAS A DEMOCRACY. AREN'T WE IN CHARGE OF DECIDING WHO LEADS US?

IN THE YEAR 2000, MEXICO WAS MORE DEMOCRATIC THAN THE UNITED STATES WAS! AFTER MORE THAN SEVENTY YEARS OF **ONE-PARTY RULE,** THE MEXICAN PEOPLE ELECTED OPPOSITION CANDIDATE VICENTE FOX.

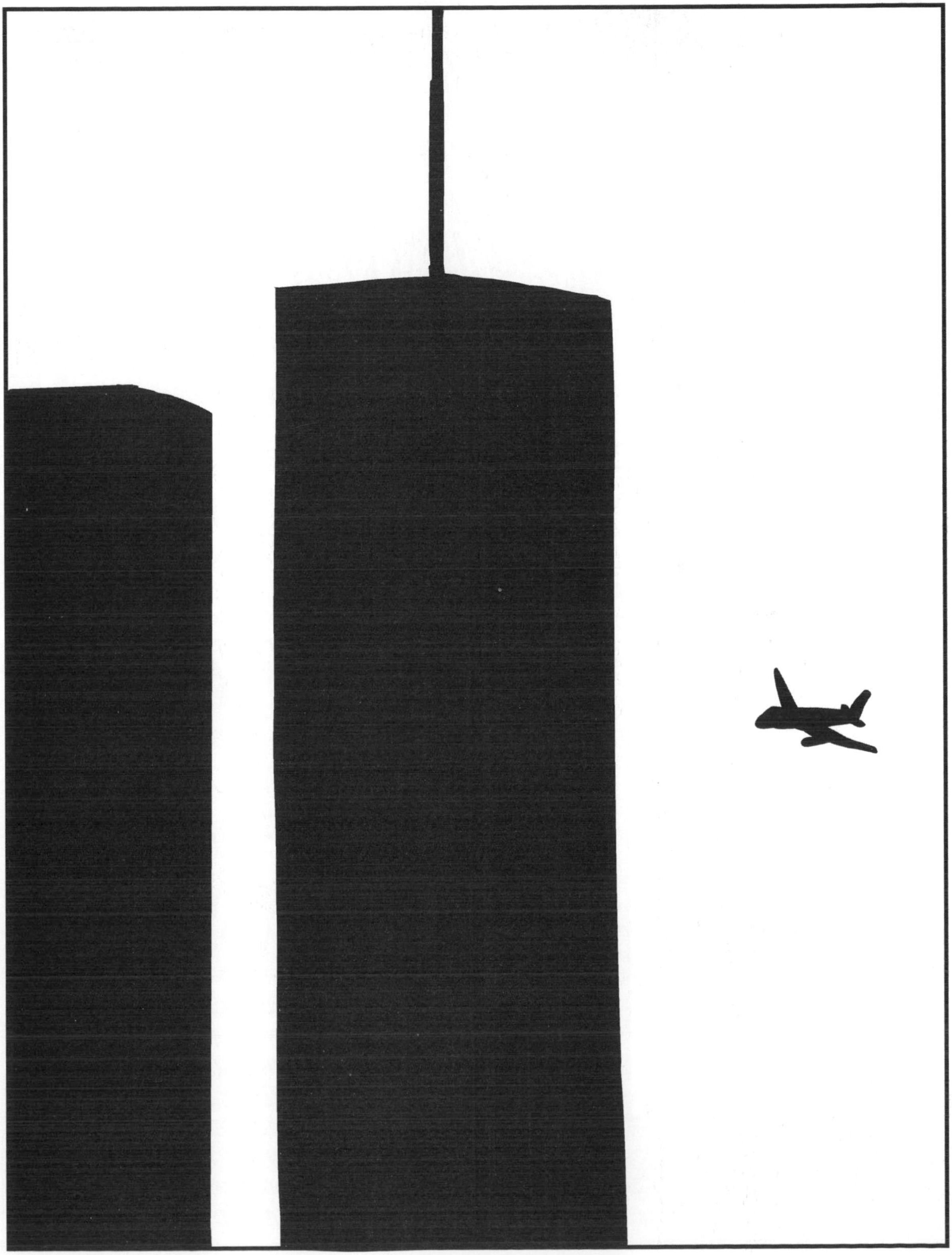

ON SEPTEMBER 11, 2001, AL-QAEDA, A FUNDAMENTALIST ISLAMIC ORGANIZATION LED BY OSAMA BIN LADEN, LAUNCHED AN UNPRECEDENTED **ATTACK AGAINST THE UNITED STATES**. TERRORISTS CRASHED CIVILIAN AIRPLANES INTO THE WORLD TRADE CENTER IN MANHATTAN, AS WELL AS THE PENTAGON. ANOTHER PLANE WENT DOWN BEFORE IT COULD REACH THE U.S. CAPITOL. THE COUNTRY WAS STUNNED.

NEARLY 3,000 PEOPLE DIED.

THE IMMEDIATE RESPONSE WAS ONE OF EMPATHY. PEOPLE ACROSS THE GLOBE MOURNED THE VICTIMS.

BUSH'S SUBSEQUENT ACTIONS, HOWEVER, SQUANDERED THIS GLOBAL GOODWILL. AFTER LAUNCHING A WAR AGAINST AFGHANISTAN, WHICH HAD HARBORED AL-QAEDA LEADERS, BUSH TRAINED HIS SIGHTS ON **IRAQ**, WHICH HAD NO CONNECTION TO THE SEPTEMBER 11 ATTACKS. BUSH JUSTIFIED HIS INVASION OF THE COUNTRY BY CLAIMING THAT DICTATOR SADDAM HUSSEIN WAS HARBORING **WEAPONS OF MASS DESTRUCTION**.

NO SUCH WEAPONS EXISTED, THOUGH.

WMD LOCKER MOTEL
VACANCY

BRING OUR TrOOPS HOME!

STOP the WAR NOW IMPEACH BUSH!

DROP BUSH NOT BOMBS

ALTHOUGH MANY AMERICANS SUPPORTED THE WAR, OTHERS WERE INFURIATED BY THEIR PRESIDENT'S LIES AND ABUSE OF POWER.

ON SEPTEMBER 11, 2011, THE NATIONAL SEPTEMBER 11 MEMORIAL AND MUSEUM WAS UNVEILED. THE NAMES OF ALL THE VICTIMS ARE RECORDED ON PLAQUES WITHIN THE MONUMENT.

DID YOU KNOW THERE ARE SEVERAL UNDOCUMENTED MEXICANS WHOSE NAMES AREN'T INCLUDED?

AH, THE ILLEGITIMACY OF MEMORY!

I DON'T LIKE MEMORIALS! WHAT'S THE POINT OF THEM? THEY TURN MEMORY INTO STONE.

MEMORY

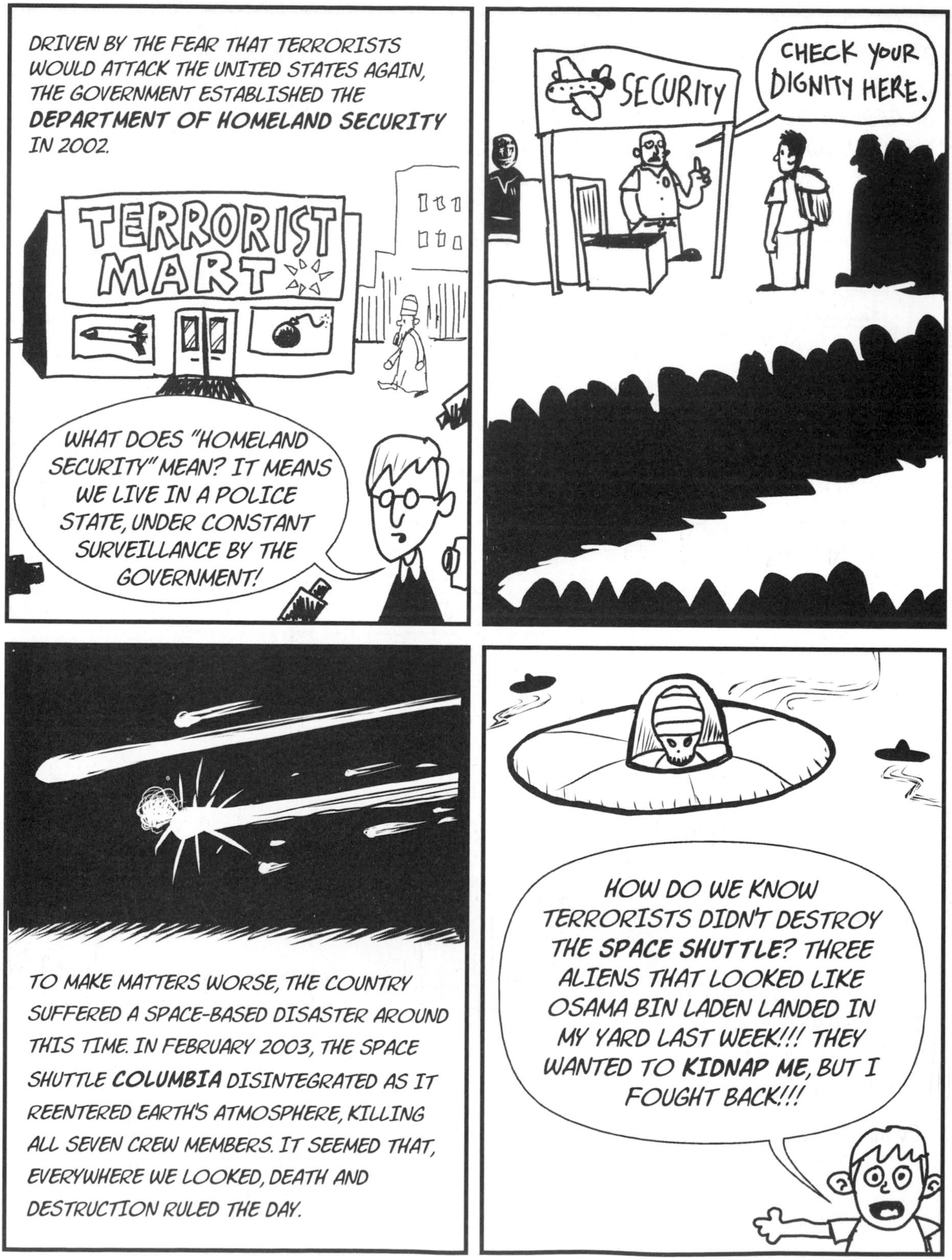

DRIVEN BY THE FEAR THAT TERRORISTS WOULD ATTACK THE UNITED STATES AGAIN, THE GOVERNMENT ESTABLISHED THE **DEPARTMENT OF HOMELAND SECURITY** IN 2002.
TERRORIST MART
WHAT DOES "HOMELAND SECURITY" MEAN? IT MEANS WE LIVE IN A POLICE STATE, UNDER CONSTANT SURVEILLANCE BY THE GOVERNMENT!
SECURITY
CHECK YOUR DIGNITY HERE.
TO MAKE MATTERS WORSE, THE COUNTRY SUFFERED A SPACE-BASED DISASTER AROUND THIS TIME. IN FEBRUARY 2003, THE SPACE SHUTTLE **COLUMBIA** DISINTEGRATED AS IT REENTERED EARTH'S ATMOSPHERE, KILLING ALL SEVEN CREW MEMBERS. IT SEEMED THAT, EVERYWHERE WE LOOKED, DEATH AND DESTRUCTION RULED THE DAY.
HOW DO WE KNOW TERRORISTS DIDN'T DESTROY THE **SPACE SHUTTLE**? THREE ALIENS THAT LOOKED LIKE OSAMA BIN LADEN LANDED IN MY YARD LAST WEEK!!! THEY WANTED TO **KIDNAP ME**, BUT I FOUGHT BACK!!!

IN THE POST-9/11 ERA, THE BUSH ADMINISTRATION CULTIVATED AN ATMOSPHERE OF **FEAR, XENOPHOBIA, AND MISTRUST.** THIS LED TO DISGRACEFUL EXCESSES, SUCH AS THE MISTREATMENT OF INMATES AT IRAQ'S ABU GHRAIB PRISON, WHERE AMERICAN SOLDIERS WERE IMPLICATED IN RAPE, TORTURE, SODOMY, AND EVEN DEATH.

POWER CORRUPTS, AND EXCESSIVE POWER CORRUPTS EXCESSIVELY.

IN MANY WAYS, THE NATION HAD LOST ITS MORAL COMPASS. THE ALTRUISTIC IMPULSES THAT HAD GUIDED OUR ENTRY INTO WORLD WAR II HAD BEEN TURNED ON THEIR HEAD. AMERICA HAD BEEN TRANSFORMED FROM A GLOBAL POLICEMAN INTO **A GLOBAL CLOWN.**

THE SOLDIERS AT ABU GHRAIB DOCUMENTED THEIR ABUSE BY TAKING PICTURES WITH THEIR CELL PHONES—A FORM OF TECHNOLOGY THAT HAS NOW BECOME UBIQUITOUS, AND WHICH I SEE AS AN EMBLEM OF SLAVERY.

WHY SLAVERY?

PEOPLE DO EVERYTHING ON THEIR CELL PHONES! THEY TALK TO EACH OTHER, THEY LISTEN TO MUSIC, THEY WATCH MOVIES, THEY SHOP, THEY CHECK THE STOCK MARKET, THEY HAVE SEX. THAT, TO ME, IS A **RETURN TO SLAVERY!** SLAVERY TO TECHNOLOGY!

CAN WE TALK ABOUT PIZZA HERE? YOU CAN'T WRITE ALL THIS CRAP AND NOT TALK ABOUT PEPPERONI PIZZA.

INVENTED IN NAPLES, PIZZA WAS BROUGHT HERE BY ITALIAN IMMIGRANTS IN THE NINETEENTH CENTURY.

MAMMA MIA!

STEREO-TYPICALLY DELICIOUS!

TONY'S PIZZERIA

WHY IS PIZZA SO POPULAR? WHAT DO AMERICANS LIKE SO MUCH ABOUT IT? IT'S JUST BREAD, TOMATO, AND CHEESE.

HAVE YOU TRIED PORK-CHOP PIZZA WITH PESTO AND BIG CHUNKS OF GARLIC?

THE RISE OF NEW DIGITAL TECHNOLOGIES HAS COINCIDED WITH A SPEEDING-UP OF AMERICANS' DAILY LIVES. NOW, WE—LIKE OUR DEVICES—ARE EXPECTED TO ALWAYS BE **ON**. WORKING, ORGANIZING, STAYING LATE AT THE OFFICE, AMERICANS ARE ALWAYS ON THE GO, PARTLY BECAUSE THIS IS A COUNTRY WHERE **SUCCESS IS MEASURED IN TERMS OF PRODUCTIVITY**.

NATURALLY, THIS ACCELERATED SCHEDULE HAS AFFECTED AMERICAN SLEEPING HABITS.

WHAT SLEEPING HABITS? I'VE BEEN WORKING ON THIS BOOK THIRTY-SIX HOURS A DAY.

LACK OF SLEEP MAKES YOU GRUMPY.

I'M OVERWORKED, TOO! TO MAKE ENDS MEET, I WORK FOUR JOBS: I FLIP HAMBURGERS AT WENDY'S, REPAIR EQUIPMENT AT A **NANOTECHNOLOGY** STARTUP, WRITE SPEECHES FOR THREE REPUBLICAN CONGRESSMEN, AND WATCH MY FIVE-MONTH-OLD BABY WHILE MY WIFE IS AT SCHOOL. I'LL SLEEP WHEN I'M DEAD.

THE RECOMMENDED SLEEPING TIME FOR MOST ADULTS IS BETWEEN SEVEN AND NINE HOURS PER NIGHT. A STUDY CONDUCTED BY RESEARCHERS AT NORTHWESTERN UNIVERSITY FOUND THAT WHITES TEND TO SLEEP LONGER THAN OTHER ETHNIC GROUPS, ASIANS ARE MORE LIKELY TO SUFFER FROM DAYTIME **SLEEPINESS**, AND BLACKS GENERALLY EXPERIENCE THE LOWEST QUALITY OF SLEEP.

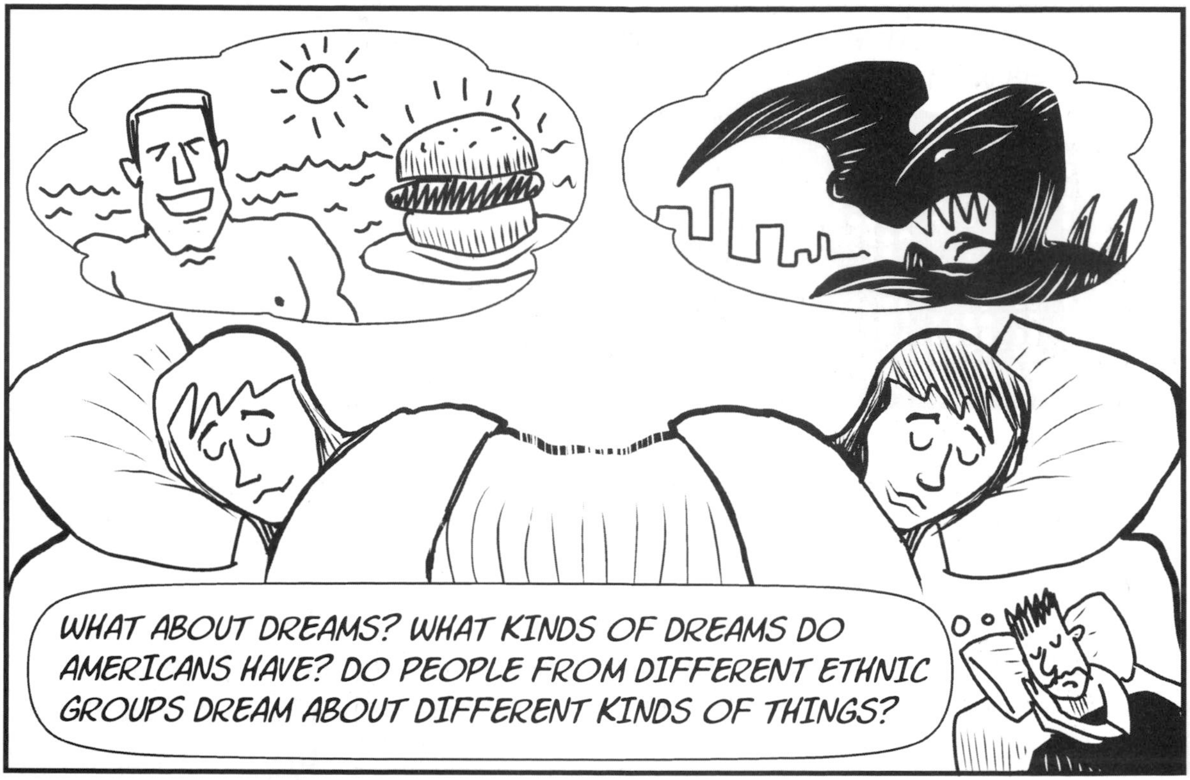
WHAT ABOUT DREAMS? WHAT KINDS OF DREAMS DO AMERICANS HAVE? DO PEOPLE FROM DIFFERENT ETHNIC GROUPS DREAM ABOUT DIFFERENT KINDS OF THINGS?

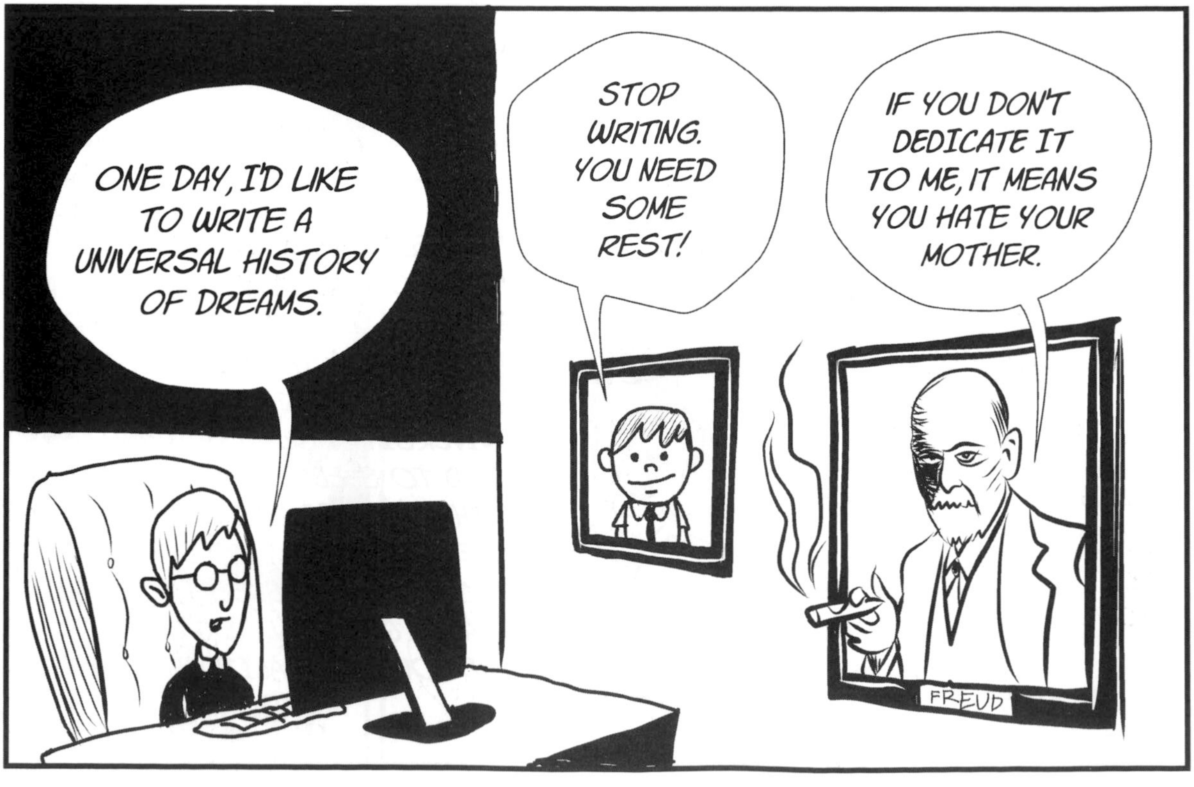
ONE DAY, I'D LIKE TO WRITE A UNIVERSAL HISTORY OF DREAMS.
STOP WRITING. YOU NEED SOME REST!
IF YOU DON'T DEDICATE IT TO ME, IT MEANS YOU HATE YOUR MOTHER.
FREUD

BACK IN THE TECHNOLOGY WORLD, THE ADVENT OF **E-MAIL** HAS INAUGURATED NEW STANDARDS OF CORRESPONDENCE. OUR MESSAGES ARE NOW QUICKLY COMPOSED, GRAMMATICALLY CARELESS, OFTEN ADDRESSED TO MULTIPLE RECIPIENTS, AND, MOST IMPORTANTLY, INSTANTANEOUS.

THIS ENTIRE BOOK WAS COMPOSED VIA E-MAILS I SENT MYSELF FROM DIFFERENT PARTS OF THE WORLD.

IN 2004, MARK ZUCKERBERG, AN UNDERGRADUATE AT HARVARD UNIVERSITY, LAUNCHED A SOCIAL NETWORK CALLED **FACEBOOK**. ITS MISSION WAS TO LINK TOGETHER PEOPLE WHO SHARED FRIENDS AND COMMON INTERESTS. AT FIRST, MEMBERSHIP ON THE NETWORK WAS RESTRICTED EXCLUSIVELY TO HARVARD STUDENTS, BUT IT SOON EXPANDED TO THE POPULATION AT LARGE. TODAY, FACEBOOK IS A MAJOR FORCE AROUND THE GLOBE, WITH THE CAPACITY TO FURTHER POLITICAL CAUSES AND EVEN HELP BRING DOWN NATIONAL GOVERNMENTS. IN CONJUNCTION WITH OTHER SOCIAL NETWORKING SITES, SUCH AS **MYSPACE** AND **GOOGLE PLUS**, FACEBOOK HAS HELPED TO DEMOCRATIZE THE TRANSMISSION OF INFORMATION.

Panel 1:

MY FAVORITE SOCIAL NETWORK IS **TWITTER**. IN 2013, THERE WERE OVER 230 MILLION ACTIVE USERS. THE COUNTRIES WITH THE MOST ACTIVITY WERE CHINA, INDIA, AND THE UNITED STATES. AROUND 500 MILLION TWEETS ARE SENT EVERY DAY. MY ACCOUNT IS @ILANSTAVANS.

@laloalcaraz

MUCH FUNNIER

Ilan Stavans @IlanStavans
Mediocrity: The will to be as extraordinary as everyone else.

Ilan Stavans @IlanStavans
Academic freedom is wasted on academics.

Ilan Stavans @IlanStavans
Twitter turns us all into Fortune Cookie thinkers.

Ilan Stavans @IlanStavans
A fatalist hopes ours is the best possible universe. An optimist knows it is.

Panel 2:

NOW THAT PEOPLE ARE CONNECTED THE WORLD OVER, IS THE CONCEPT OF "NATION" STILL RELEVANT? THESE DAYS, YOU DON'T EVEN NEED TO BE IN THE SAME PLACE TO BE PART OF A COMMUNITY.

SOME ACADEMICS CALL ONLINE GROUPS "IMAGINED COMMUNITIES." I THINK ALL COMMUNITIES ARE IMAGINED, DON'T YOU?

IN AUGUST 2005, **HURRICANE KATRINA** DEVASTATED THE COASTAL REGIONS OF LOUISIANA, MISSISSIPPI, AND ALABAMA. FOR A COUNTRY OBSESSED WITH ACHIEVING MASTERY OVER NATURE, THIS WAS A DEMORALIZING SHOCK. THE ENVIRONMENTAL, ECONOMIC, SOCIAL, AND POLITICAL CONSEQUENCES WERE LONG-LASTING, ESPECIALLY IN THE CITY OF NEW ORLEANS.

LOOK AT THOSE *SPECIAL EFFECTS!* THIS IS MORE EPIC THAN ANY HOLLYWOOD BLOCKBUSTER.

AND MORE TRAGIC!

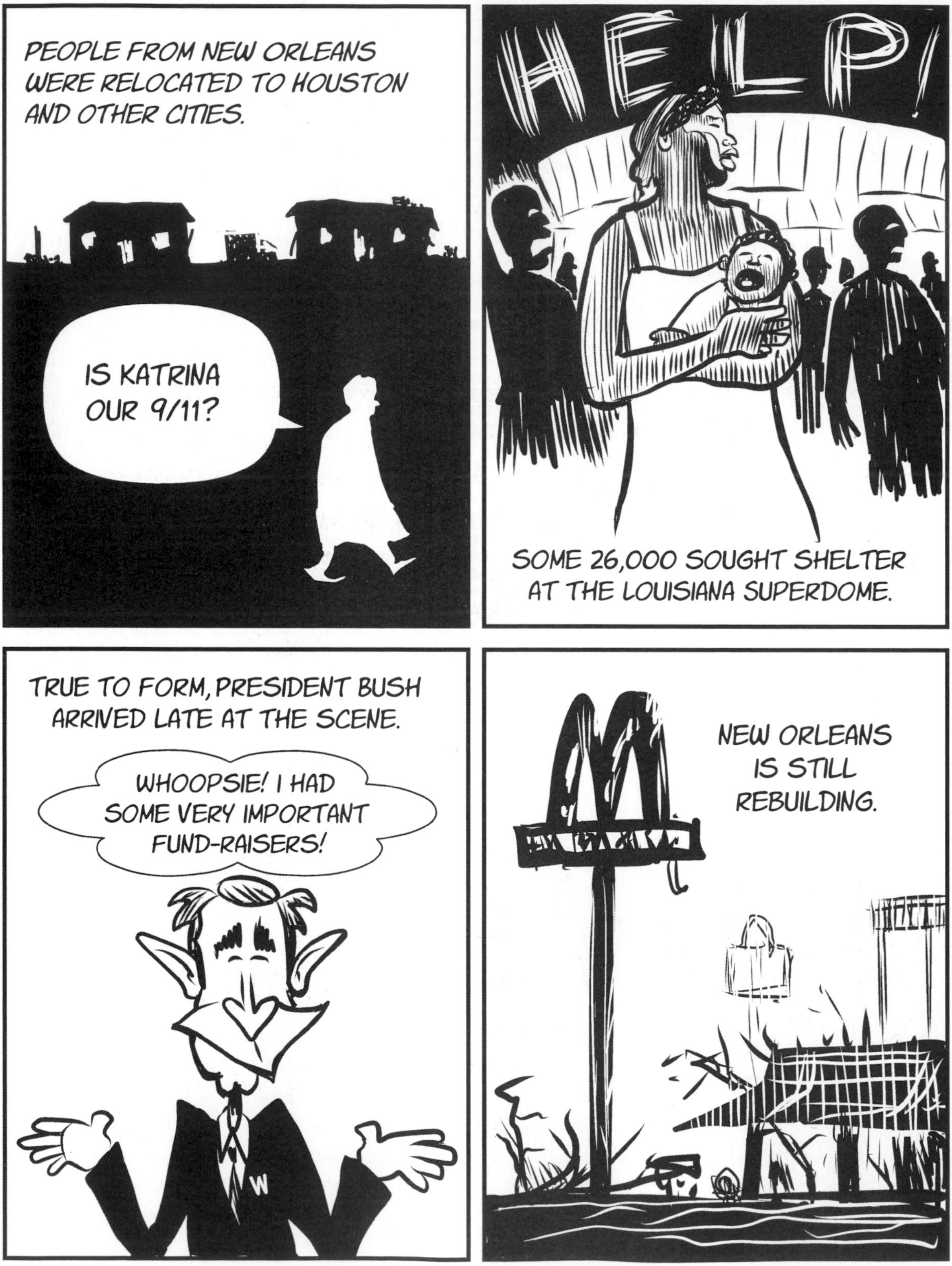
PEOPLE FROM NEW ORLEANS WERE RELOCATED TO HOUSTON AND OTHER CITIES.
IS KATRINA OUR 9/11?
HELP!
SOME 26,000 SOUGHT SHELTER AT THE LOUISIANA SUPERDOME.
TRUE TO FORM, PRESIDENT BUSH ARRIVED LATE AT THE SCENE.
WHOOPSIE! I HAD SOME VERY IMPORTANT FUND-RAISERS!
W
NEW ORLEANS IS STILL REBUILDING.

IN 2008, AFTER A HISTORIC CAMPAIGN, **BARACK OBAMA** WON ELECTION TO THE NATION'S HIGHEST OFFICE, BECOMING BOTH THE FORTY-FOURTH PRESIDENT OF THE UNITED STATES AND THE FIRST NONWHITE PRESIDENT IN AMERICAN HISTORY. OBAMA PROMISED TO END THE INCOMPETENCE AND CRONYISM THAT HAD PREVAILED DURING THE BUSH YEARS, USHERING IN AN ERA OF HOPE AND CHANGE.

WHY DO YOU CALL HIM "NONWHITE"? OBAMA ISN'T A NONWHITE PRSIDENT— HE'S A BLACK PRESIDENT.

REV. AL SHARPTON

OBAMA HAS NEVER IDENTIFIED HIMSELF EXPLICITLY AS A BLACK PRESIDENT, AND THE DEBATE OVER HIS **RACIAL LOYALTIES** HAS PERSISTED THROUGHOUT HIS ADMINISTRATION.

I VOTED FOR HIM THINKING HE WOULD REPRESENT THE NONWHITE POPULATION, BUT IN REALITY HE NEVER DID. I DON'T THINK HE GETS WHAT IT MEANS TO MOVE BEYOND THE **BLACK-AND-WHITE** PARADIGM.

LATINA VOTER

RACE WASN'T THE ONLY ISSUE IN THE DEMOCRATIC PRIMARY LEADING UP TO THE ELECTION.

MAY THE BEST **MAN** WIN!

AND MAY THE BEST MAN BE A **WOMAN!**

2008

OBAMA'S CHIEF RIVAL IN THE DEMOCRATIC PRIMARIES WAS **HILLARY RODHAM CLINTON,** WIFE OF FORMER PRESIDENT BILL CLINTON. A LAWYER BY TRAINING AND A TRUE FORCE OF NATURE, CLINTON HAS SERVED ADMIRABLY AS FIRST LADY AS WELL AS A U.S. SENATOR. OBAMA WAS SO IMPRESSED BY HIS FORMER RIVAL THAT, AFTER ASSUMING THE PRESIDENCY, HE APPOINTED CLINTON TO HIS CABINET, WHERE SHE SERVED FOR FOUR YEARS AS A FIRST-RATE SECRETARY OF STATE. TODAY, CLINTON IS ADORED AND DETESTED IN EQUAL MEASURE AND SPECULATION ABOUNDS THAT SHE MAY RUN FOR THE PRESIDENCY AGAIN IN 2016.

IN 2007, THE COUNTRY WAS HIT BY A **MAJOR FINANCIAL CRISIS**, WHICH SOON SPREAD ACROSS THE GLOBE. STALWART FINANCIAL INSTITUTIONS SUCH AS LEHMAN BROTHERS, WASHINGTON MUTUAL, AIG, FANNIE MAE, AND FREDDIE MAC EITHER **COLLAPSED** OR WERE BAILED OUT BY THE GOVERNMENT AT **TAXPAYER EXPENSE**. ULTIMATELY, THE ENSUING **CRISIS** WAS THE WORST SINCE THE GREAT DEPRESSION, RAISING THE QUESTION: ARE THERE CERTAIN BANKS THAT ARE TOO BIG TO FAIL?

WALL STREET 3

TOO FAT TO FAIL

BANK

OUT TO LUNCH: I'M HAVING A FINANCIAL MELTDOWN!

THE COLLECTIVE FEELING OF FRUSTRATION WAS ENORMOUS, BUT EVEN BIGGER WAS THE ANGER TOWARD THE SO-CALLED **1 PERCENT**, THE RICHEST FRACTION OF PEOPLE IN THE COUNTRY, WHOSE WELL-BEING WAS LARGELY UNAFFECTED BY THE CRISIS. IN FACT, IN MANY CASES THE RICHEST 1 PERCENT HAD BECOME RICHER, WHILE THE REMAINING 99 PERCENT FACED FINANCIAL RUIN.

AT WHAT POINT DO PEOPLE GET FED UP WITH THEIR POLITICIANS AND FIRE THEM FOR DOING A LOUSY JOB?

THAT DEPENDS ON YOUR DEFINITION OF **LOUSY**. AMERICAN POLITICIANS HAVE ALWAYS DONE WHAT'S **IN THE BEST INTEREST OF THEMSELVES** AND THEIR RICHEST DONORS. ACTUALLY, THE CRISIS SHOWED JUST HOW GOOD A JOB THEY'D BEEN DOING . . .

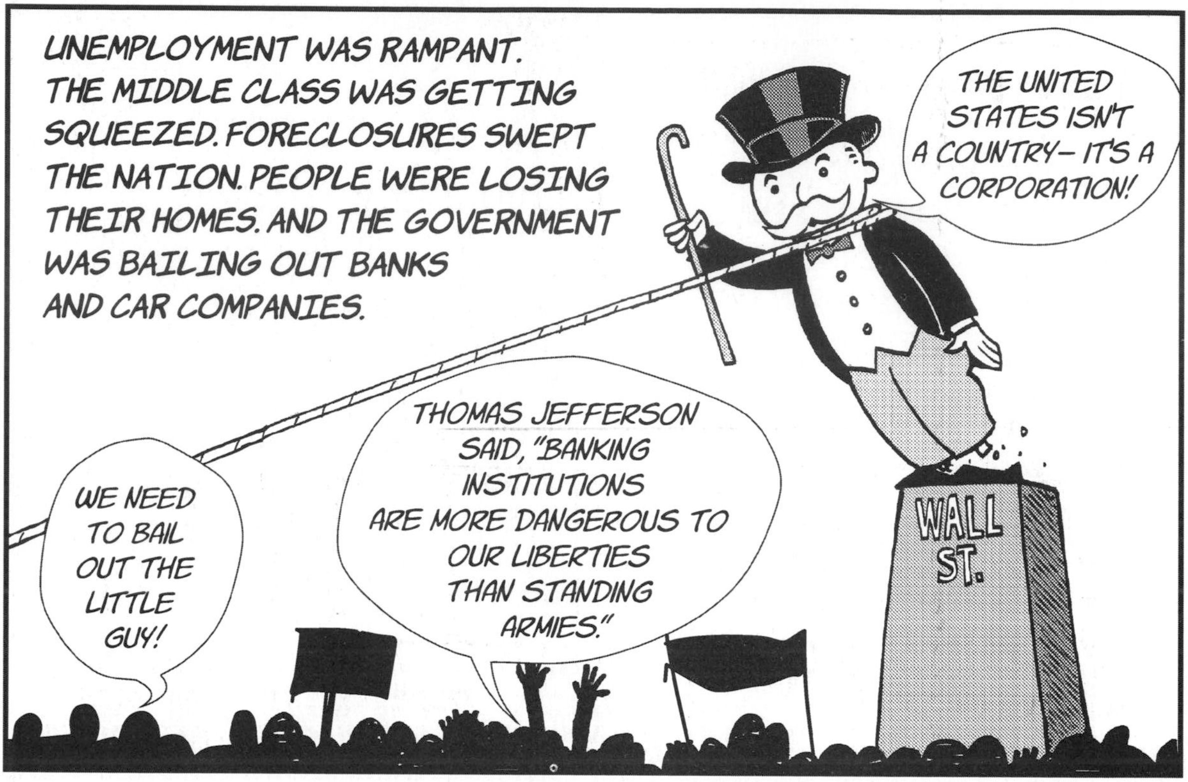
UNEMPLOYMENT WAS RAMPANT. THE MIDDLE CLASS WAS GETTING SQUEEZED. FORECLOSURES SWEPT THE NATION. PEOPLE WERE LOSING THEIR HOMES. AND THE GOVERNMENT WAS BAILING OUT BANKS AND CAR COMPANIES.
THE UNITED STATES ISN'T A COUNTRY– IT'S A CORPORATION!
WE NEED TO BAIL OUT THE LITTLE GUY!
THOMAS JEFFERSON SAID, "BANKING INSTITUTIONS ARE MORE DANGEROUS TO OUR LIBERTIES THAN STANDING ARMIES."
WALL ST.

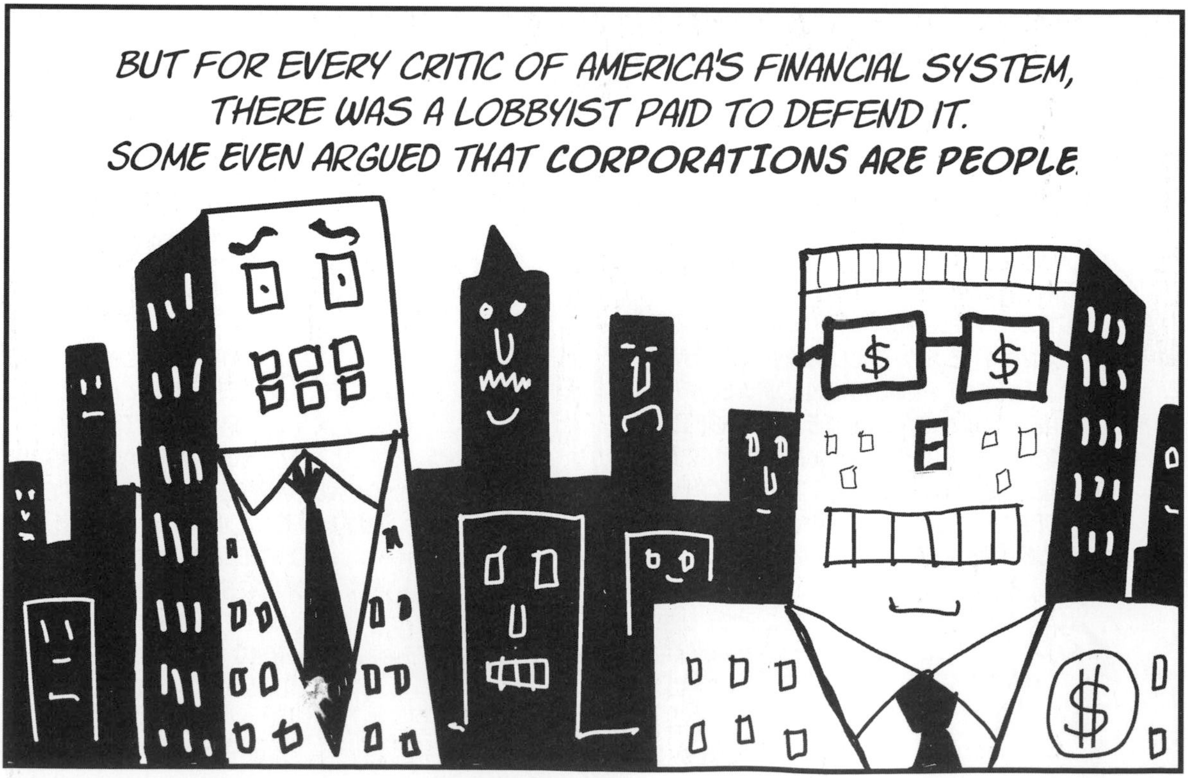
BUT FOR EVERY CRITIC OF AMERICA'S FINANCIAL SYSTEM, THERE WAS A LOBBYIST PAID TO DEFEND IT. SOME EVEN ARGUED THAT **CORPORATIONS ARE PEOPLE**.

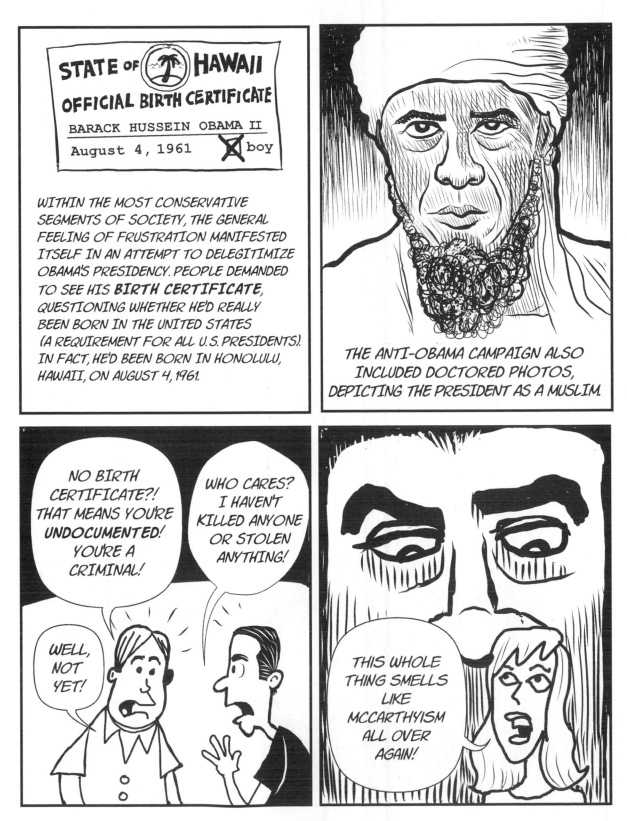

STATE OF HAWAII
OFFICIAL BIRTH CERTIFICATE
BARACK HUSSEIN OBAMA II
August 4, 1961 ☒ boy

WITHIN THE MOST CONSERVATIVE SEGMENTS OF SOCIETY, THE GENERAL FEELING OF FRUSTRATION MANIFESTED ITSELF IN AN ATTEMPT TO DELEGITIMIZE OBAMA'S PRESIDENCY. PEOPLE DEMANDED TO SEE HIS **BIRTH CERTIFICATE**, QUESTIONING WHETHER HE'D REALLY BEEN BORN IN THE UNITED STATES (A REQUIREMENT FOR ALL U.S. PRESIDENTS). IN FACT, HE'D BEEN BORN IN HONOLULU, HAWAII, ON AUGUST 4, 1961.

THE ANTI-OBAMA CAMPAIGN ALSO INCLUDED DOCTORED PHOTOS, DEPICTING THE PRESIDENT AS A MUSLIM.

NO BIRTH CERTIFICATE?! THAT MEANS YOU'RE **UNDOCUMENTED**! YOU'RE A CRIMINAL!

WHO CARES? I HAVEN'T KILLED ANYONE OR STOLEN ANYTHING!

WELL, NOT YET!

THIS WHOLE THING SMELLS LIKE MCCARTHYISM ALL OVER AGAIN!

THOSE WHO FELT DISENFRANCHISED WITH THE GOVERNMENT—AND WITH PRESIDENT OBAMA IN PARTICULAR—ORGANIZED MARCHES AND VIGILS, CALLING FOR LOWER TAXES, STRICTER ADHERENCE TO THE CONSTITUTION, AND, BECAUSE GOVERNMENT SPENDING HAD SKYROCKETED IN RECENT YEARS, **TIGHTER CONTROLS ON THE BUDGET.**

THIS POLITICAL MOVEMENT CAME TO BE KNOWN AS THE **TEA PARTY.** IT WAS INSPIRED BY THE BOSTON TEA PARTY OF 1773, WHEN ACTIVISTS DUMPED TEA INTO BOSTON HARBOR TO PROTEST THE BRITISH POLICY OF TAXATION WITHOUT REPRESENTATION, AND THE MONOPOLY OF THE EAST INDIA COMPANY ON THE TEA TRADE.

AN ANTI-CORPORATE MOVEMENT ALSO TOOK SHAPE AT THE SAME TIME. PEOPLE DESCENDED ON WALL STREET IN NEW YORK, OCCUPYING ITS STREETS AND PARKS WITH TENTS. A SYMBOL OF THE EVENTS WERE THE PICTURES FROM ZUCCOTTI PARK ON NOVEMBER 15, 2011, IN WHICH THE OCCUPIERS WERE FORCED OUT BY THE AUTHORITIES. IN PART, THE OCCUPIERS' PRESENCE WAS A REACTION TO THE LARGE BONUS CHECKS WALL STREET EXECUTIVES CONTINUED TO RECEIVE WHILE THE NATION'S ECONOMY UNDERPERFORMED.

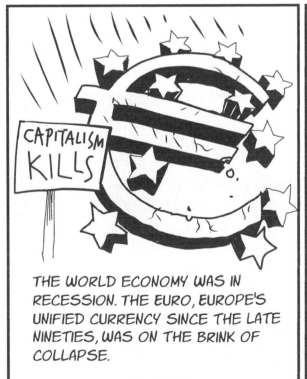

THE WORLD ECONOMY WAS IN RECESSION. THE EURO, EUROPE'S UNIFIED CURRENCY SINCE THE LATE NINETIES, WAS ON THE BRINK OF COLLAPSE.

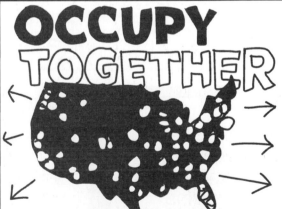

THE PROTEST MOVEMENT CAME TO BE KNOWN AS **OCCUPY WALL STREET**. IT WASN'T LIMITED TO NEW YORK'S FINANCIAL CENTER. THE OCCUPY MOVEMENT POPPED UP IN OTHER URBAN CENTERS IN THE UNITED STATES AND IN CLOSE TO 100 CITIES IN 85 COUNTRIES.

ON FEBRUARY 26, 2012, A PART WHITE LATINO, PART JEWISH, 28-YEAR-OLD WATCHMAN IN SANFORD, FLORIDA, BY THE NAME OF GEORGE ZIMMERMAN KILLED A 17-YEAR-OLD BLACK KID CALLED TRAYVON MARTIN. THE SHOOTING CAUSED A NATIONAL UPROAR.

MURDERER!

THUG!

ONCE AGAIN, WE'RE ON THE BLACK-AND-WHITE DIVIDE.

ISSUES OF RACE WILL NEVER DISAPPEAR. BUT CAN WE TALK ABOUT THEM IN CIVIL FASHION? OR DO WE NEED TO SCREAM AT EACH OTHER? DEMOCRACY, BY DEFINITION, IS MESSY. AND A **MULTIETHNIC DEMOCRACY** IS MESSY IN COLORFUL WAYS.

RACE

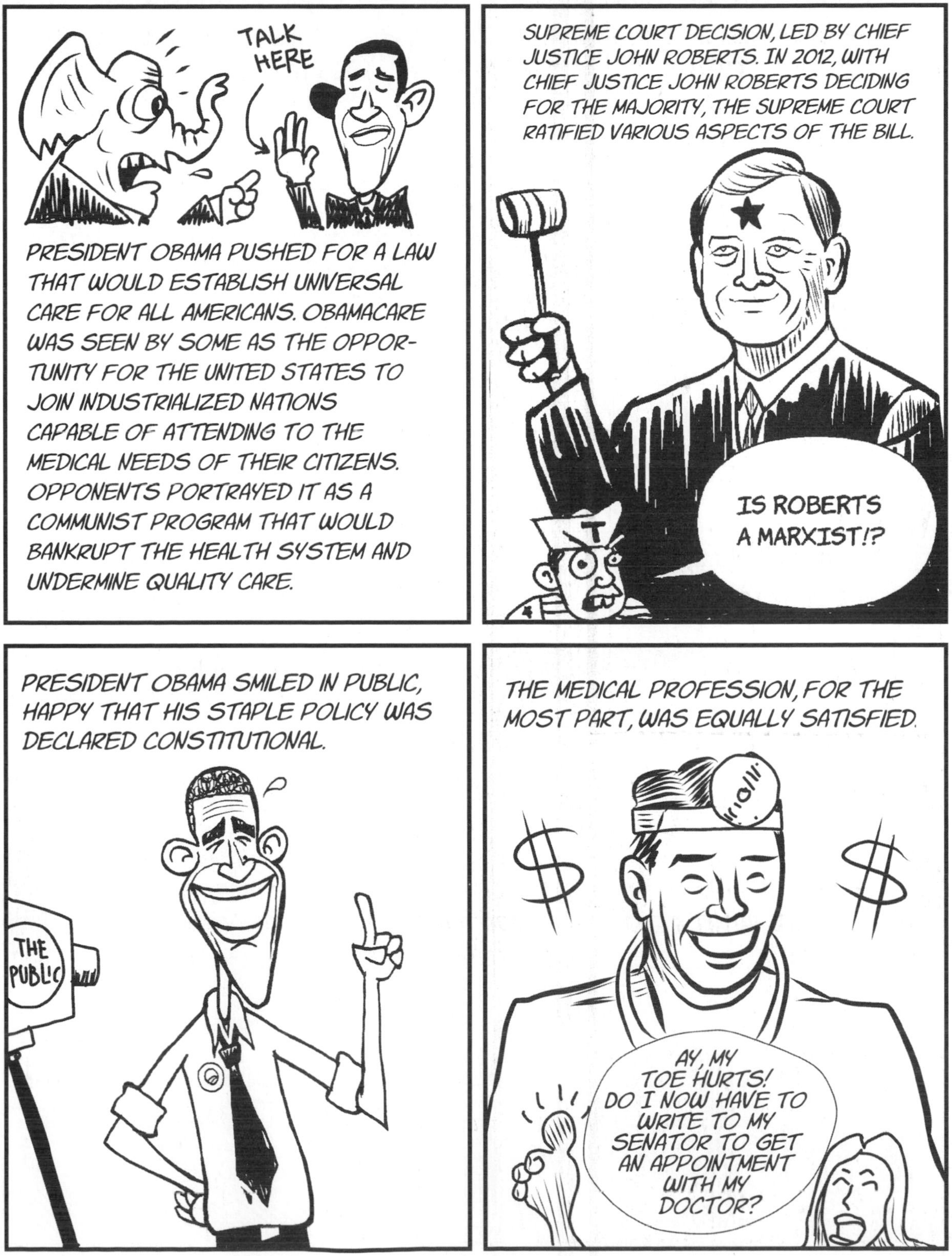
TALK HERE
PRESIDENT OBAMA PUSHED FOR A LAW THAT WOULD ESTABLISH UNIVERSAL CARE FOR ALL AMERICANS. OBAMACARE WAS SEEN BY SOME AS THE OPPORTUNITY FOR THE UNITED STATES TO JOIN INDUSTRIALIZED NATIONS CAPABLE OF ATTENDING TO THE MEDICAL NEEDS OF THEIR CITIZENS. OPPONENTS PORTRAYED IT AS A COMMUNIST PROGRAM THAT WOULD BANKRUPT THE HEALTH SYSTEM AND UNDERMINE QUALITY CARE.
SUPREME COURT DECISION, LED BY CHIEF JUSTICE JOHN ROBERTS. IN 2012, WITH CHIEF JUSTICE JOHN ROBERTS DECIDING FOR THE MAJORITY, THE SUPREME COURT RATIFIED VARIOUS ASPECTS OF THE BILL.
IS ROBERTS A MARXIST!?
PRESIDENT OBAMA SMILED IN PUBLIC, HAPPY THAT HIS STAPLE POLICY WAS DECLARED CONSTITUTIONAL.
THE PUBLIC
THE MEDICAL PROFESSION, FOR THE MOST PART, WAS EQUALLY SATISFIED.
AY, MY TOE HURTS! DO I NOW HAVE TO WRITE TO MY SENATOR TO GET AN APPOINTMENT WITH MY DOCTOR?

WHAT OTHER BIG ISSUES FACED THE NATION AT THE DAWN OF THE THIRD MILLENNIUM? DEBATES CONTINUED TO RAGE ABOUT THE ROLE OF GOVERNMENT, THE DISTRIBUTION OF WEALTH, AND THE NATURE OF THE FREE-MARKET SYSTEM. SOME ARGUED THAT WE HAD **TOO MUCH** INDIVIDUALISM! FOREIGN POLICY, TOO, WAS THE SUBJECT OF CONTROVERSY. MANY FELT AMERICA HAD BECOME TOO ATTACHED TO ITS **SELF-PROCLAIMED STATUS AS EXCEPTIONAL AMONG THE NATIONS** OF THE WORLD.

MEANWHILE, CHINA WAS IN THE MIDST OF AN **ECONOMIC BONANZA**, BUT THE SURPLUS OF UNSOLD GOODS WAS ACCUMULATING. THE CONSTRUCTION INDUSTRY HAD BUILT COUNTLESS BUILDINGS THAT REMAINED EMPTY.

IN MANY PLACES ON THE PLANET, PEOPLE DON'T HAVE ROOFS—LIKE HAITI AFTER ITS DEVASTATING 2010 EARTHQUAKE. BUT THERE'S SO MUCH CONSTRUCTION GOING ON IN CHINA THAT THE ROOFS DON'T HAVE PEOPLE!

SO MUCH TROUBLE IN THE WORLD! THAT'S WHY THE ONLY PART OF THE NEWSPAPER I READ IS THE SPORTS SECTION. SPORTS ARE ABOUT HEROICS, WHEREAS EVERYTHING ELSE IS ABOUT **DOOM**.

AGAIN, I WANT THE AUTHOR OF THIS BOOK FIRED!

HERE'S SOMETHING POSITIVE! IN 2012, THE ROBOTIC NASA ROVER **CURIOSITY** LANDED ON MARS. ITS OBJECTIVE WAS TO EXPLORE THE RED PLANET.

WHO KNOWS WHAT THEY'LL FIND!

EPILOGUE
ARE WE THERE YET??!!
WE PRETEND TO BE **ONE NATION**, SPEAKING WITH A SINGLE VOICE, BUT IN FACT WE'RE ALWAYS UNDECIDED, PUSHING IN MANY DIRECTIONS AT ONCE. WE CLAIM TO BE DEDICATED TO LIBERTY, EQUALITY, AND THE PURSUIT OF HAPPINESS, BUT LARGE PORTIONS OF THE AMERICAN POPULATION GET **LEFT BEHIND** AND NEVER HAVE THE OPPORTUNITY TO ENJOY THESE PRIVILEGES. AT THE SAME TIME, OUR **VORACIOUS QUEST** FOR WEALTH AND DOMINANCE OFTEN LEAVES OTHER NATIONS EMPTY-HANDED. UNFORTUNATELY, WE AMERICANS ARE OFTEN DEFINED BY **ARROGANCE**, **RAPACIOUSNESS**, AND THE **PURSUIT OF POWER**!

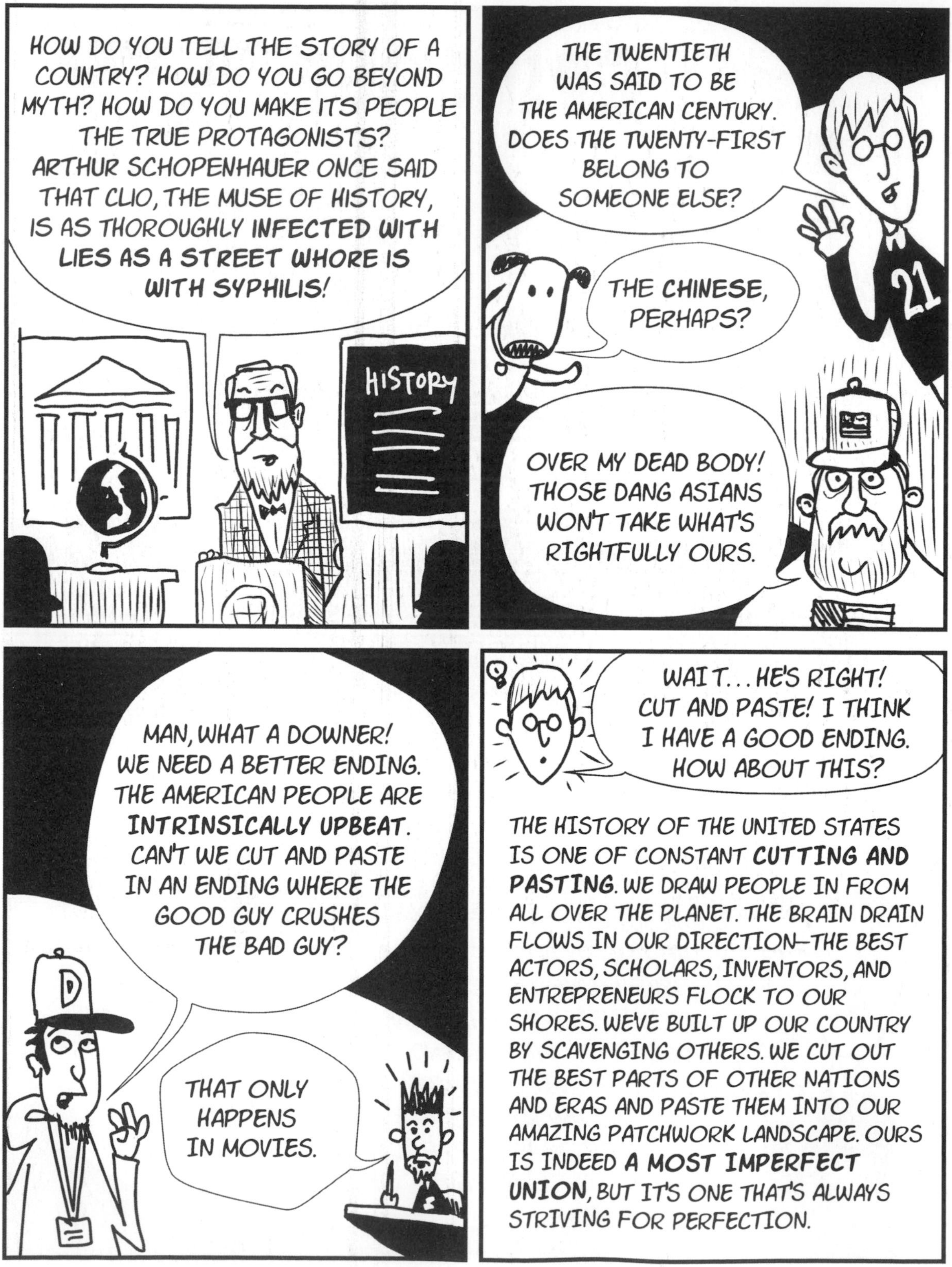
HOW DO YOU TELL THE STORY OF A COUNTRY? HOW DO YOU GO BEYOND MYTH? HOW DO YOU MAKE ITS PEOPLE THE TRUE PROTAGONISTS? ARTHUR SCHOPENHAUER ONCE SAID THAT CLIO, THE MUSE OF HISTORY, IS AS THOROUGHLY INFECTED WITH LIES AS A STREET WHORE IS WITH SYPHILIS!
HISTORY
THE TWENTIETH WAS SAID TO BE THE AMERICAN CENTURY. DOES THE TWENTY-FIRST BELONG TO SOMEONE ELSE?
21
THE CHINESE, PERHAPS?
OVER MY DEAD BODY! THOSE DANG ASIANS WON'T TAKE WHAT'S RIGHTFULLY OURS.
MAN, WHAT A DOWNER! WE NEED A BETTER ENDING. THE AMERICAN PEOPLE ARE INTRINSICALLY UPBEAT. CAN'T WE CUT AND PASTE IN AN ENDING WHERE THE GOOD GUY CRUSHES THE BAD GUY?
D
THAT ONLY HAPPENS IN MOVIES.
WAIT... HE'S RIGHT! CUT AND PASTE! I THINK I HAVE A GOOD ENDING. HOW ABOUT THIS?
THE HISTORY OF THE UNITED STATES IS ONE OF CONSTANT CUTTING AND PASTING. WE DRAW PEOPLE IN FROM ALL OVER THE PLANET. THE BRAIN DRAIN FLOWS IN OUR DIRECTION—THE BEST ACTORS, SCHOLARS, INVENTORS, AND ENTREPRENEURS FLOCK TO OUR SHORES. WE'VE BUILT UP OUR COUNTRY BY SCAVENGING OTHERS. WE CUT OUT THE BEST PARTS OF OTHER NATIONS AND ERAS AND PASTE THEM INTO OUR AMAZING PATCHWORK LANDSCAPE. OURS IS INDEED A MOST IMPERFECT UNION, BUT IT'S ONE THAT'S ALWAYS STRIVING FOR PERFECTION.

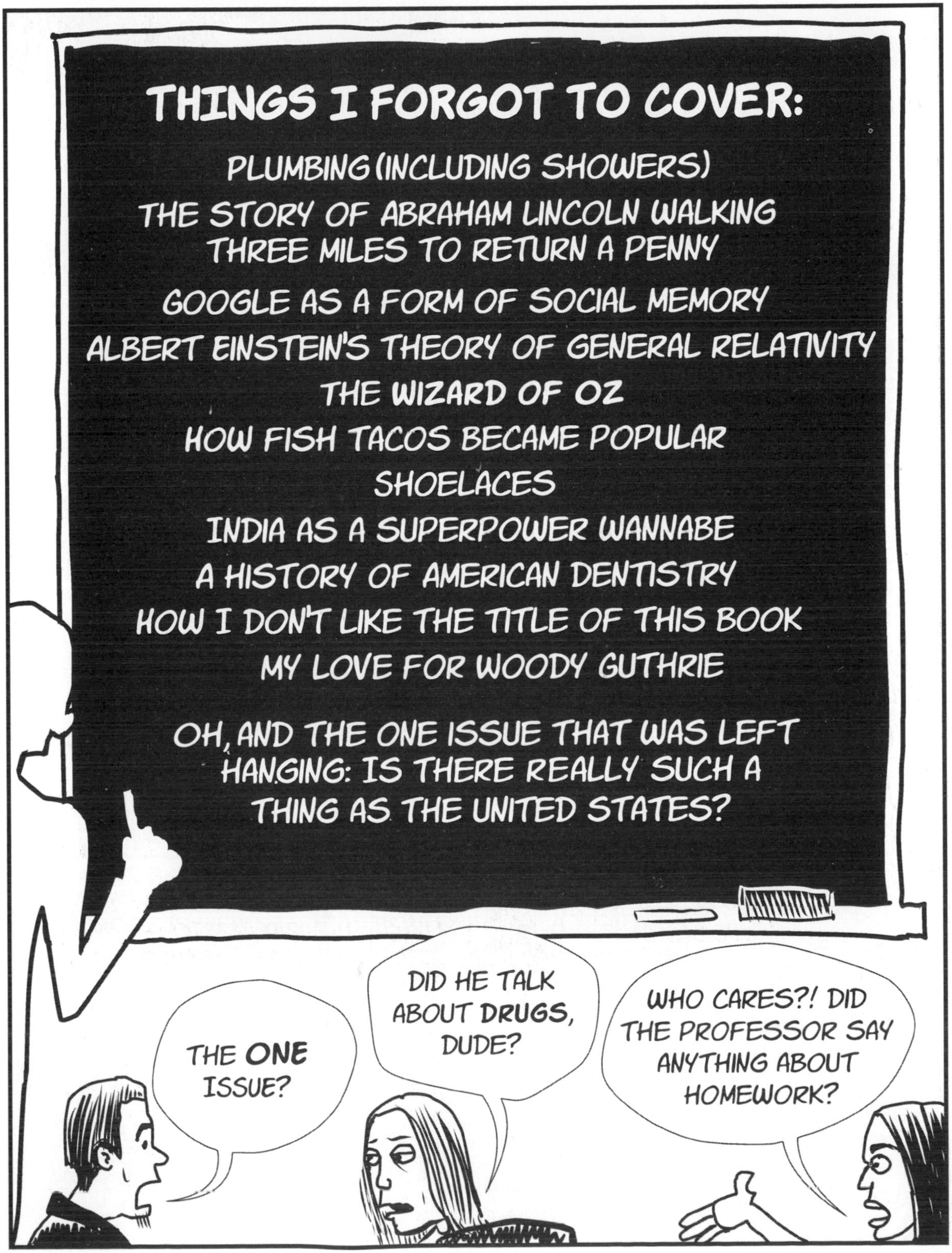
THINGS I FORGOT TO COVER:
PLUMBING (INCLUDING SHOWERS)
THE STORY OF ABRAHAM LINCOLN WALKING THREE MILES TO RETURN A PENNY
GOOGLE AS A FORM OF SOCIAL MEMORY
ALBERT EINSTEIN'S THEORY OF GENERAL RELATIVITY
THE WIZARD OF OZ
HOW FISH TACOS BECAME POPULAR
SHOELACES
INDIA AS A SUPERPOWER WANNABE
A HISTORY OF AMERICAN DENTISTRY
HOW I DON'T LIKE THE TITLE OF THIS BOOK
MY LOVE FOR WOODY GUTHRIE
OH, AND THE ONE ISSUE THAT WAS LEFT HANGING: IS THERE REALLY SUCH A THING AS THE UNITED STATES?
THE **ONE** ISSUE?
DID HE TALK ABOUT **DRUGS**, DUDE?
WHO CARES?! DID THE PROFESSOR SAY ANYTHING ABOUT HOMEWORK?

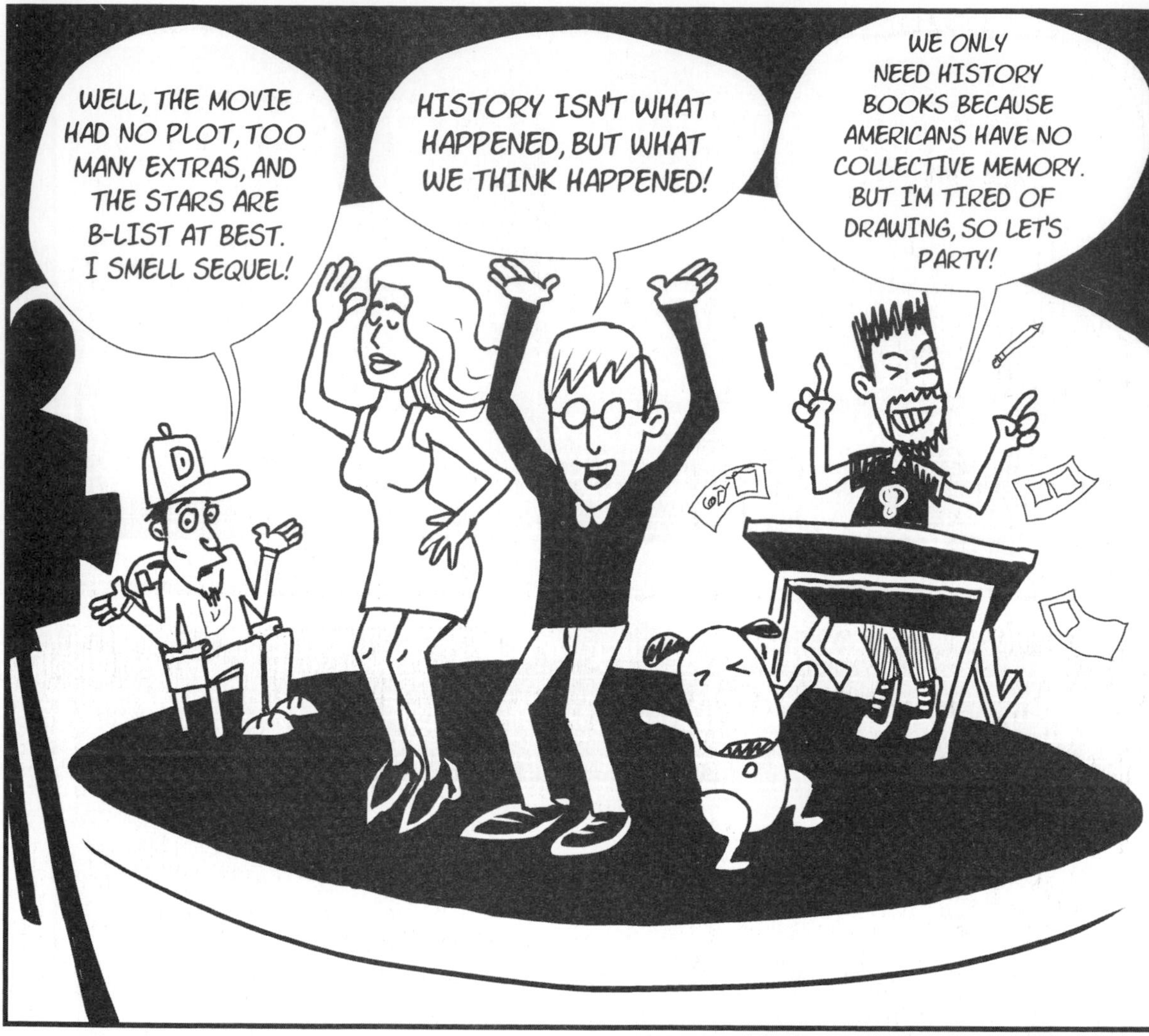
WELL, THE MOVIE HAD NO PLOT, TOO MANY EXTRAS, AND THE STARS ARE B-LIST AT BEST. I SMELL SEQUEL!
HISTORY ISN'T WHAT HAPPENED, BUT WHAT WE THINK HAPPENED!
WE ONLY NEED HISTORY BOOKS BECAUSE AMERICANS HAVE NO COLLECTIVE MEMORY. BUT I'M TIRED OF DRAWING, SO LET'S PARTY!
D

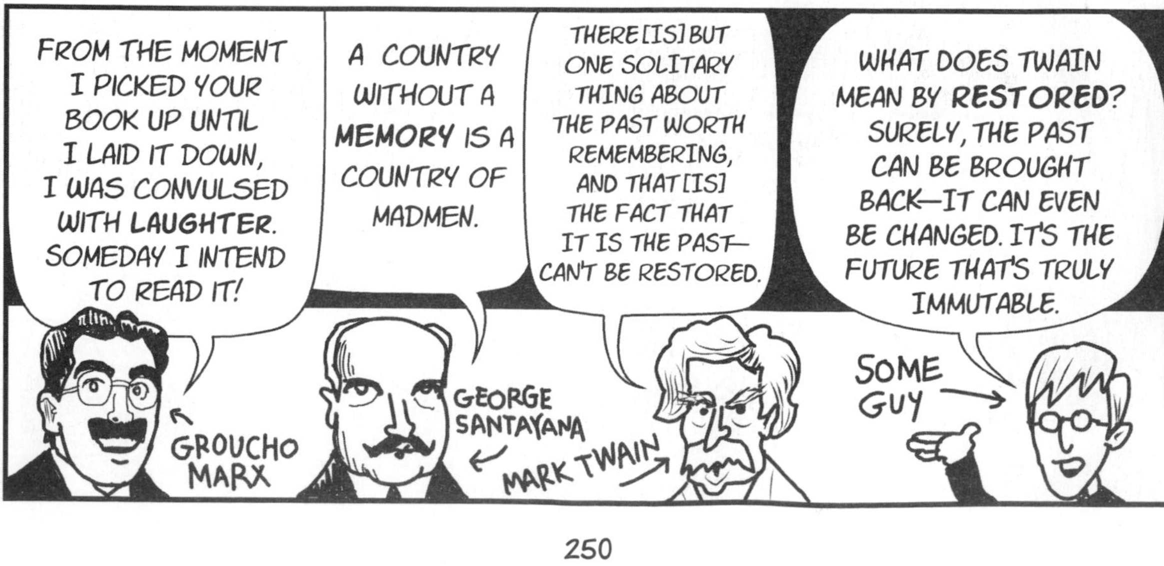
FROM THE MOMENT I PICKED YOUR BOOK UP UNTIL I LAID IT DOWN, I WAS CONVULSED WITH **LAUGHTER**. SOMEDAY I INTEND TO READ IT!
A COUNTRY WITHOUT A **MEMORY** IS A COUNTRY OF MADMEN.
THERE [IS] BUT ONE SOLITARY THING ABOUT THE PAST WORTH REMEMBERING, AND THAT [IS] THE FACT THAT IT IS THE PAST— CAN'T BE RESTORED.
WHAT DOES TWAIN MEAN BY **RESTORED**? SURELY, THE PAST CAN BE BROUGHT BACK—IT CAN EVEN BE CHANGED. IT'S THE FUTURE THAT'S TRULY IMMUTABLE.
GROUCHO MARX
GEORGE SANTAYANA
MARK TWAIN
SOME GUY

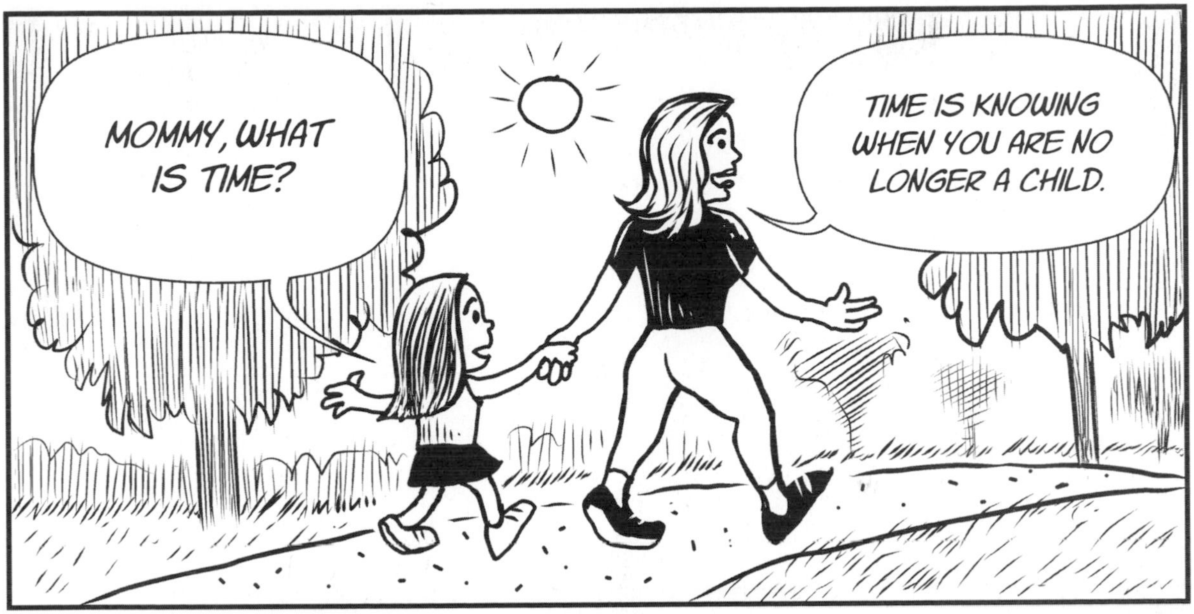
MOMMY, WHAT IS TIME?
TIME IS KNOWING WHEN YOU ARE NO LONGER A CHILD.

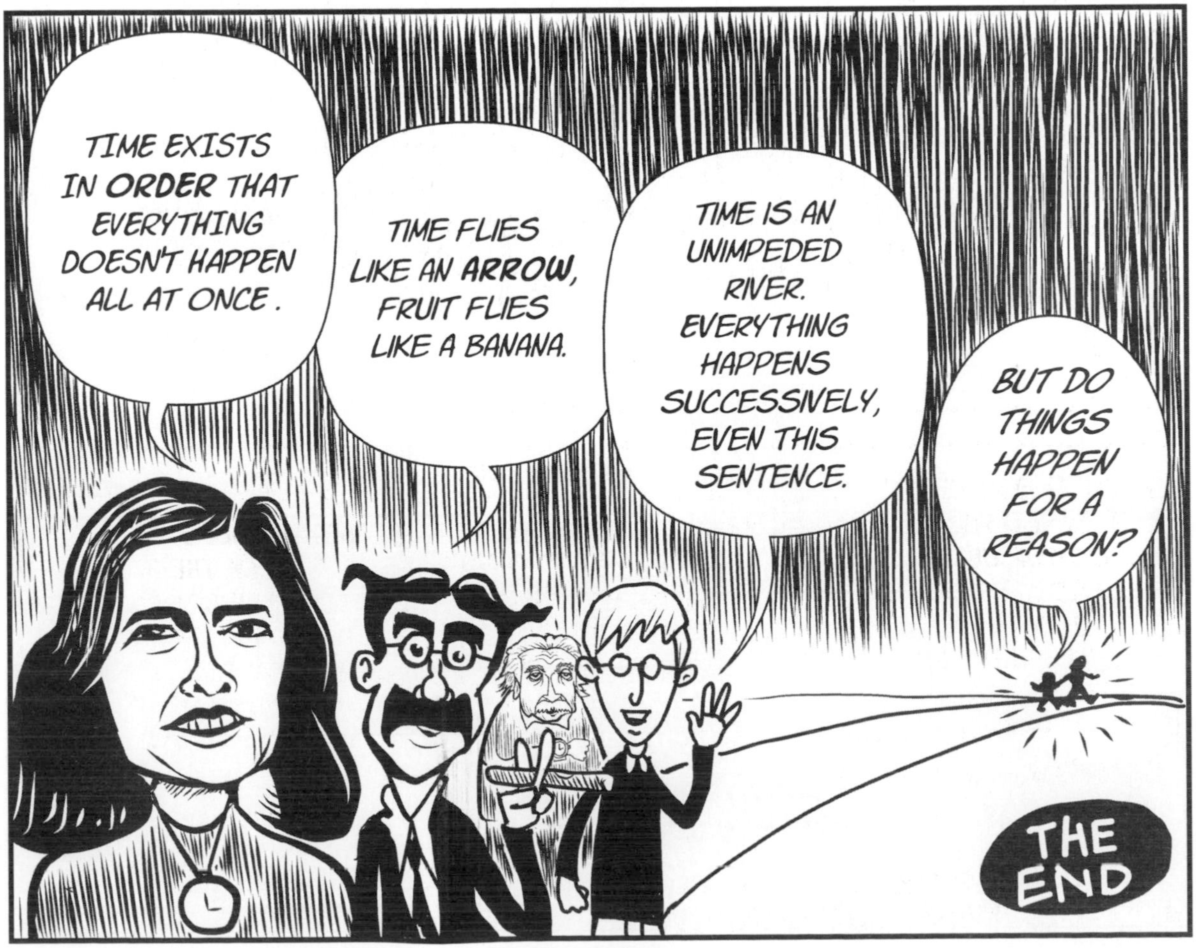
TIME EXISTS IN ORDER THAT EVERYTHING DOESN'T HAPPEN ALL AT ONCE.
TIME FLIES LIKE AN ARROW, FRUIT FLIES LIKE A BANANA.
TIME IS AN UNIMPEDED RIVER. EVERYTHING HAPPENS SUCCESSIVELY, EVEN THIS SENTENCE.
BUT DO THINGS HAPPEN FOR A REASON?
THE END

"A MOST IMPERFECT UNION
A CONTRARIAN HISTORY OF THE UNITED STATES"

A STUPENDOUS STAVANS PICTURES PRODUCTION
IN CONJUNCTION WITH CUCARACHA STUDIOS

DIRECTOR
THE DIRECTOR

WRITER
ILAN STAVANS

PRODUCER/ART DIRECTOR
LALO ALCARAZ

EDITOR
ALEX LITTLEFIELD

CAST
HISTORICAL ACTORS
THE AUTHOR
THE CARTOONIST
THE ACTRESS
THE DOG

MUSIC
WHATEVER YOU PLAYED
WHILE YOU READ THIS, DUH

NO HISTORICAL FIGURES WERE HARMED DURING
THE PRODUCTION OF THIS BOOK, THOUGH A FEW
MISCONCEPTIONS MAY HAVE BEEN KNOCKED DOWN.

ACKNOWLEDGMENTS

This book has been in the making for longer than you might think—ever since I crossed the border from Mexico to the United States in 1985. I am indebted to countless people, a complete list of whom it would be impossible to reduce to a couple of pages. However, some acknowledgments are essential: John Sherer at Basic Books suggested the idea, and Lara Heimert endorsed it; my friend Philip Lief, our commander on *Latino USA*, shaped its contours and made it persuasive; Alex Littlefield, our magnificent editor, devoted himself to the project beyond the call of duty. *Gracias* also to Melissa Veronesi and Rachel King, who shepherded the book through its production; to John Searcy, who did a superb copyediting job; to Kaitlyn Zafonte, who made things happen from the get-go; and to Cynthia Young for the design.

My wife, Alison Sparks, and my two boys, Joshua and Isaiah Stavchansky, cheered me up during the development process. My student assistants Derek García and Daniel Carrizales helped with logistics. The staff of Restless Books, especially executive editor Joshua Ellison and my assistant Jackson Saul, have served as anchors in stormy times. The bright, engaged students of my Amherst College course "Hispanic Humor" helped refine some ideas. My gratitude also goes out to my friends and colleagues Paula Abate, Frederick Luis Aldama, Ruth Behar, Chris Benfey, David W. Blight, Uri Cohen, Javier Corrales, Henry Louis Gates Jr., Jorge J. E. Gracia, Steven G. Kellman, John Sayles, Steve Sheinkin, Alejandro Springall, Peter Temes, Helen Vendler, David Ward, and James E. Young.

My love for history comes from the movies, and *A Most Imperfect Union* pays tribute to the cinematic quality of the nation's past. Of course, what is on screen is never true, because truth, no matter what form it comes in, is never easily packaged.

A list of essential American films about the past will always be incomplete because we are constantly upending that past on the screen. If I were to design a year-long regimen of historical films and TV series, here are the ones I would recommend in approximate chronological order: *John Adams* (2008), *Amistad* (1997), *Dances with Wolves* (1990), *Cold Mountain* (2003), *Glory* (1989), *Lincoln* (2012), *True Grit* (2010), *Washington Square* (1997), *The Age of Innocence* (1993), *East of Eden* (1955), *The Music Man* (1962), *Ragtime* (1981), *Johnny Got His Gun* (1971), *The Great Gatsby* (1974), *The Grapes of Wrath* (1940), *Mr. Smith Goes to Washington* (1939), *To Kill a Mockingbird* (1962), *Saving Private Ryan* (1998), *Flags of Our Fathers* (2006), *Good Night and Good Luck* (2005), *The Manchurian Candidate* (1962), *Dr. Strangelove or: How I Learned to Stop Worrying and Love the Bomb* (1964), *Malcolm X* (1992), *Hair* (1979), *Apocalypse Now* (1979), *Born on the Fourth of July* (1989), *Frost/Nixon* (2008), *The People vs. Larry Flynt* (1996), *Wall Street* (1987), *Black Hawk Down* (2001), *United 93* (2006), *The Social Network* (2010), *Zero Dark Thirty* (2012), and _____. (Did I miss one? ¡Carajo!)

I have used countless print sources. For general information, I looked at Howard Zinn's *A People's History of the United States* (2003), which left a deep impression on me when I first read it, although my attempts at revisiting it have been met with disappointment. Valuable also is Paul Johnson's *A History of the American People* (1998), even though it was published before the events of September 11, 2001, making it seem antiquated. The arrival of immigrants to the United States and the multi-ethnic nature of the nation has been told by Ronald Takaki in *A Different Mirror: A History of Multicultural America* (1993).

About the colonial period, see David E. Stannard's *American Holocaust: The Conquest of the New World* (1992). Three useful resources are *1491: New Revelations of the Americas before Columbus* (2005) by Charles C. Mann, *1492: The Year the World Began* (2009) by Felipe Fernández-Armesto, and *1493: Uncovering the New World Columbus Created* (2011), also by Charles C. Mann. I also resorted to consulting my own *Imagining Columbus: The Literary Voyage* (1992).

For the period of independence, Robert Middlekauff offers a valuable map of drives in *The Glorious Cause: The American Revolution, 1763–1789* (2005). My obsession with the Founding Fathers denotes a thirst for biblical foundations—the work of my colleague Joseph J. Ellis has been a source of inspiration in this regard. I enjoyed his *Revolutionary Summer: The Birth of American Independence* (2013), as well as *His Excellency, George Washington* (2004), *Founding Brothers: The Revolutionary Generation* (2002), and *American Sphinx: The Character of Thomas Jefferson* (1997).

Doris Kearns Goodwin's work on Abraham Lincoln in *Team of Rivals: The Political Genius of Abraham Lincoln* (2005) is superb. See also Ronald C. White Jr.'s *A. Lincoln: A Biography* (2009). A wonderful depiction of the Civil War can be found in James M. McPherson's *Battle Cry of Freedom: The Civil War Era* (1998). And Gary Wills's memorable book *Lincoln at Gettysburg: The Words That Remade America* (1992) is a deft analysis of the most famous speech in American history.

On World War II, Doris Kearns Goodwin's book *No Ordinary Time: Franklin and Eleanor Roosevelt: The Home Front in World War II* (1994) is an inspiring read. Regarding the tepid fight of the United States against the Nazis, I also consulted David S. Wyman's *The Abandonment of the Jews: America and the Holocaust, 1941–1945* (1984).

Susan L. Mizruchi makes a deft analysis of multiethnic nuance in *The Rise of Multicultural America* (2008). I also perused my own *Becoming Americans: Four Centuries of Immigrant Writing* (2009). For those who are interested, I describe my own personal immigrant journey in *On Borrowed Words: A Memoir of Language* (2001).

My own *Latino USA: A Cartoon History* (2000) served as the backbone for the sections on Hispanic culture. I also used material from *The Norton Anthology of Latino Literature* (2010). Simon Winchester's *The Men Who United the States: America's Explorers, Inventors, Eccentrics, and Mavericks, and the Creation of One Nation, Indivisible* (2013) is an excellent survey of American trailblazers. Finally, George Packer delivers a powerful portrait of the United States at the turn of the twenty-first century in *The Unwinding: An Inner History of the New America* (2013).

To learn from the past, it isn't enough to study it; it is crucial to reimagine it. And in the modern world there is no better way to do that than by making good use of Photoshop—or else by creating a cartoon history with Lalo Alcaraz.

—I.S.

* * *

From this end, boy, did this project live up to half of its title: IMPERFECT. Wow! Not the easiest mountain I've ever climbed. But the effort was not only mine, nor Ilan's. There are so many people to thank, but above all, I've got to single out my family. During the very long process for this book, I still had to draw my daily comic strip, La Cucaracha, and teach at Otis College of Art & Design, and manage speaking gigs and freelance illustration work and my new TV writing gig on the animated Fox show "Bordertown," plus be a work-at-home papi. It got a little hairy. My family put up with Daddy being chained to the drawing table for a very long time. They learned to sometimes just avoid the unshaven grumpy man in the studio. Thank you to my wife Victoria and my three wild kids, Aya, Chago and Lomis.

This project was sooo huge, that I had to take some revolutionary steps (for me). . . . First, I went digital. (This is a big deal for old school cave wall artist me.) However, I'm not going to acknowledge my Cintiq tablet, as I don't believe that corporations are people, nor that drawing tools are human. But my new tablet is a very helpful and productive weapon in my arsenal, and it made *Imperfect Union* possible. The second huge move I made was to get an actual drawing assistant for this project, and thankfully, one of my amazing former Editorial Illustration students from Otis stepped up to the challenge. He made it possible for us to get through several sections of *Imperfect Union* without me collapsing from sleep deprivation or terminal carpal tunnel. So, special thanks to Eduardo Herrera (the other Lalo) for his assistance in sketching and ideation.

I also could not have gotten through the project without the patience of my comics editor Shena Wolf at my syndicate, Universal Uclick. Shena and all the folks over there have always had my back while I was chronically overloaded with other side projects. Particularly when I upload the wrong file because I am too sleepy at the hours between 1 a.m. and 5 a.m. Special shout out to retiring Universal Uclick president Lee Salem, for always being supportive of whatever I did to further my comics career.

Thanks to our man in the East, Philip Lief, who still believes in the rambunctious odd couple that is the Stavans/Alcaraz team, and to our endlessly patient IU editor Alex Littlefield, who held it together, and kept things calm and measured, which is saying a lot where I am involved.

Claro, I'd like to thank my project partner Ilan for not reaching through the phone and wrapping his fingers around my neck on many an occasion. And in the home stretch, all the folks at Basic Books for helping us pull it all together.

But the product is the pretty damn good book you hold in your hands, so any friction, long nights, deadline stress was all worth it. Thus, I must acknowledge you, nerdy reader, who just got through devouring the acknowledgements because that's what you do. Thanks for reading *Imperfect Union*!

—L.A.

INDEX

A

Abolition, 39, 67, 97

Abortion, 201

Abu Ghraib prison, abuses at, 229, 230

Acquired Immunodeficiency Virus Syndrome (AIDS), death rate from, 214

Adams, Abigail, 58, 59

Adams, John, 42, 58, 59, 70, 111

Adams, John Quincy, 58, 73, 224

Adams, Sam, 57

Adorno, Theodore, 155

Adventures of Huck Finn, The (Twain), slavery and, 94

Advertising, 180

Affirmative action, 205

Afghanistan War, 226

"After Black Power, Women's Liberation" (Steinem), 195

Ahab, Captain, 90

Airplanes, 116, 117

Al-Qaeda, 226

Alcohol
ban on, 136, 138
illegal trade in, 137

Alcoholics Anonymous, founding of, 148

Alcoholism, 171

Alcott, Louisa May, 89

Aldrin, Edwin "Buzz," 197

Algren, Nelson, 168

Alien life, obsession with, 162

All in the Family, 199

Allen, Woody, 215

Allerton, John, 19

American culture, 87
immigrants and, 126

American Dream, 7, 178

American Language, The (Mencken), 71

American Mercury, 71

American Revolution, 38, 43, 44, 50, 51

Anarchism, 138, 139

Ancestry.com, 190

Anthony, Susan B., 85, 196

Anti-Semitism, 151

Anticommunist hysteria, 167, 168

Apollo 11: 197
Arendt, Hannah, 155
Armstrong, Neil, 197
Assimilation, 75, 127, 174
Automobiles, first, 119
Aztecs, 16, 63

B

Bakke, Allan: lawsuit by, 205
Banks, criticism of, 56, 239
Barbie Dolls, 179, 180
Barrow, Clyde, 144
Bartholdi, Frédéric, 108
Baseball, 102, 120
Battle of the Alamo, 78
Bay of Pigs Invasion, 187
Beatles, The, 192
Bell, Alexander Graham, 104, 202
Bellamy, Francis: Pledge of Allegiance
    and, 111
Berlin Wall, fall of, 217, 218
Betty Crocker's Picture Cookbook, 170
Bill of Rights, 42
Bin Laden, Osama, 226, 228
Blacklisting, 168
Blackmun, Harry, 206
Blanck, Max: charges against, 125
Bluett, Thomas, 28–29
Booth, John Wilkes, 101
Boston Tea Party, 38, 242
Bourbon dynasty, 36
Boy Scouts of America, war effort and,
    132
Bracero Program, 156
Branch Davidians, 221
Brandeis, Louis: appointment of, 135
Brecht, Bertolt, 155

Brennan, William, 206
Brodsky, Joseph, 197
Brooklyn Bridge, 112
Brown v. Board of Education (1954), 182,
    183
Bryant, Roy: Till murder and, 183
Bunker, Archie, 199
Burgos, Julia de, 174
Burnet, David G., 80
Bush, George W., 223, 224, 237
    Katrina and, 236
    September 11th and, 226

C

Cabeza de Vaca, Álvar Núñez, 18
Cabot, John: arrival of, 16
California Gold Rush, 83, 84
Call It Sleep (Roth), 110
Cameras, 162
Campos, Pedro Abizu, 174
Capitalism, 139, 156, 177, 215, 216
Capone, Al, 137
Cardinal, The (Robinson), 170
Carter, Jimmy: Iranian hostage crisis
    and, 210
Carter, Robert, 19
Casablanca (movie), 154
Castro, Fidel, 187
Catcher in the Rye, The (Salinger), 169
Catholic Church, 12, 24, 32
Caulfield, Holden, 169
Cayuga, 16
Cervantes, 94
Chaplin, Charlie, 83, 151, 168
Chavez, Cesar, 3, 202
Chávez, Hugo: *Good Neighbor Policy*
    and, 147

Cherokee, 43

Chewing gum, 63

Chicano movement, 82, 202

Chickamauga, 47

China, economic boom in, 246, 248

Chronicle of the Narváez Expedition
     (Cabeza de Vaca), 18

Church-state separation, 111

Churchill, Winston: Roosevelt and, 150

Citizen Kane (Welles), 146

Civil Rights Act (1964), 194

Civil rights movement, 182, 183, 184, 191,
     194, 202

Civil War, 95, 98
     casualties during, 102
     impact of, 96, 97, 103, 149

Clark, William, 69

Clay, Henry: Whig Party and, 72

Clinton, Bill, 222, 223

Clinton, Hillary Rodham, 222, 238

CNN, founding of, 218

Coke, formula for, 62

Cold War, 167, 168, 186, 213, 216

Colonists, 21, 26, 32, 37
     Indian ideas and, 25
     protests by, 38

Color line, 115

Columbia (shuttle), disintegration of,
     228

Columbus, Christopher, 11, 12

Communism, 215, 216, 217

Communists, persecution of, 140

Conformity, 175, 177

Conquest of Bread, The (Kropotkin), 139

Conquistadors, 12

Constitution, 48, 49, 56, 60

Consumerism, 175, 180

Continental Congress, 53, 58

Contraceptives, 181

Contras, aid for, 212

Coolidge, Calvin, 140

Copland, Aaron, 168

Cosmic Race, The (Vasconcelos), 139

Cotton gin, 68

Credit cards, 181

Crèvecoeur, Hector St. John de, 51, 52

Crick, Francis, 189

Crucible, The (Miller), 35

Cuban Missile Crisis, 188

Curiosity (Mars rover), 246

D

Davis, Miles, 121

De Narváez, Pánfilo, 18

De Oñate, Juan, 32

De Palma, Brian, 144

De Soto, Hernan, 14

Dead, communicating with, 102

Dean, James, 178

Death of a Salesman (Miller), 176

Declaration of Independence, 9, 39,
     45, 53

Deer Hunter, The (movie), 186

"Defense of Fort McHenry" (poem), 74

Deganwidah, 16

Democracy, 24
     multiethnic, 244

Democratic Party, 72, 238

Democratic-Republican Party, 60, 65

Deng Xiaoping, economic reform by, 216

Department of Homeland Security, 228

Diallo, Ayuba Suleiman (Job Ben
     Solomon), 28–29, 30

Diary of Anne Frank (Frank), as
     Broadway play, 152

Díaz, José, 155
Díaz, Porfirio: modernization and, 129
Dickinson, Emily: style/syntax of, 91
Dictator, The (movie), 151
Discrimination, 163, 183, 194
    reverse, 205
Disney, Walt, 178
Disneyland, 178
Divine providence, 73
DNA, study of, 189
Dr. Strangelove (movie), 167
Doctorow, E. L., 122
Dot-com industry, 219
Douglas, Michael, 215
Douglas, Stephen A.: Lincoln and, 92
Douglass, Frederick, 61, 67
Dreams, ethnic groups and, 232
D'Rivera, Paquito, 121
Drunk driving, deaths from, 148
DuBois, W. E. B.: on color line, 115
Dylan, Bob, 192

E

Earth Day, first, 199
East India Company, 242
Economic inequality, 109, 188, 202
Ed Sullivan Show, The: Beatles on, 192
Education, 34, 105, 106, 110, 121, 127
    bilingual, 126
Eighteenth Amendment, 136
Einstein, Albert, 249, 251
Eisenhower, Dwight D., 157, 172
El Iluminado, 32
Ellis Island, 110
Emancipation Proclamation (1863), 97

Emerson, Ralph Waldo, 89
English language, 8, 31, 71, 82
    immigrants and, 126, 127
    protecting, 70
Enlightenment, 105
Entertainment, 119, 218
Environmental movement, 96, 199
Erik the Red, 13
Esquiano, Olaudah, 61
E.T. (movie), 211
Ethnic groups, 205
    dreams and, 232
    sleep habits of, 231
Evars, Medgar: assassination of, 184

F

Facebook, 233
Family, normal American, 171
Fannie Mae, 239
"Farewell in Welfare Island" (Burgos), 174
Federal Bureau of Investigation (FBI), 140
Federalist Papers, The, 49, 70
Federalist Party, establishment of, 60
Feltman, Charles: frankfurters and, 82
Feminine Mystique, The (Friedan), 192
Feminists, 195, 196
Financial crisis, 239
Finn, Huck, 94
Flag, treatment of, 74, 82
Ford, Henry, 119
Ford Motor Company, 119
Forman, Milos, 122
Founding Fathers, 41, 61
Fox, Vicente, 224
Frank, Anne, 152

Frank, Otto, 152
Franklin, Benjamin, 41, 111, 215
Freddie Mac, 239
Free love, 173, 193
Free market, 246
Freedman's Bureau, 103
Freedom, 27, 28, 50, 67, 217
Freedom of speech, 126
Freewheelin' Bob Dylan, The (Dylan), 192
French and Indian War, 51
French Revolution (1789), 50
Freud, Sigmund, 123, 232
Friedan, Betty, 192, 195
Frost, Robert: poem by, 13
Fuller, Margaret, 89
Fundamentalists, 208, 226

G

Gandhi, 5, 101
Gates, Bill: Microsoft and, 202
Gay community, AIDS and, 214
Gay rights movement, 198, 203
Gekko, Gordon, 215
Gender equality, 192, 195
Genealogy, interest in, 190
Genetics, understanding, 190
Genocide, 15
Gettysburg, casualties of, 98
Gettysburg Address, text at, 99
Gey, George Otto, 188
"Gift Outright, The" (Frost), 13
Gillespie, Dizzy, 121
Gold, discovery of, 83
Gold Rush, The (movie), Chaplin and, 83
Golden Gate Bridge, completion of, 148

Gone with the Wind (Mitchell), 149
Good Neighbor Policy, criticism of, 147
Google, 233, 249
Gorbachev, Mikhail, 213, 216
Gorbachev, Raisa, 213
Gore, Al, 223, 224
Gosling, Ryan, 93
Graffiti, 219
Grapes of Wrath, The (Steinbeck), 142
Great Depression, 142, 146, 150, 239
    favorite dishes of, 144
    unemployment during, 143
Grey, Joel, 215
Griffith, D. W., 124
Guest workers, Mexicans as, 156
Guthrie, Woody, 249

H

Haiti, earthquake in, 246
Hamilton, Alexander, 42, 49, 60
Hammett, Dashiell, 168
Hancock, Herbie, 121
Handler, Elliott, 179
Handler, Ruth, 179
Happiness, pursuit of, 9, 247
Harding, Warren G.: death of, 140
Harris, Isaac: charges against, 125
Harvard University, founding of, 24
Hauser, Gayelord, 170
Hawthorne, Nathaniel, 89
Hemings, Sally, 42
Hiawatha, 16
Hippie movement, 193
Hiroshima, 159, 160
History, 20, 117, 248, 250
    formation of, 1, 3, 5
    US/world, 157

Hitler, Adolf, 142, 151, 160
Hobbes, Thomas: social contract and, 6
Holocaust, 151, 152, 161
Holocaust Memorial Museum, 152
"Home on the Range," 75
Homosexuality, 64
Hoover, J. Edgar: appointment of, 140
Hot dogs, 82
Houdini, Harry, 119
House Un-American Activities
    Committee, 168
Houston, Sam, 80
How the Other Half Lives (Riis), 109
Hudson, Henry, 26
Huerta, Dolores, 202
Hughes, Langston, 168
Huguenots, 19
Human Immunodeficiency Virus (HIV),
    214
Human rights, violations of, 209
Huntington, Samuel: clash of
    civilizations and, 208
Hurricane Katrina: New Orleans and,
    235, 236
Hussein, Saddam, 226

I
"I Have a Dream" speech (King), 191
Ice cream, 61, 62
Immigrants, 7, 8, 108, 125
    English language and, 126, 127
Immigration, 8, 120, 130, 174
Immortal Life of Henrietta Lacks, The
    (Skloot), 188
In Old California (movie), 124
Incas, 16, 62
Income, average annual, 118, 181

Independence, 36, 39, 112
Individualism, 6, 91, 246
Industrial revolution, 76, 90, 96
Influenza pandemic, impact of, 133
Inquisition, 32
Internet, 190, 219, 233
Internment camps, relocation to, 154
Iran-Contra affair, 212
Iranian hostage crisis, 208, 210
Iranian Revolution, 209
Iraq War, 226
Irish Famine, deaths during, 106
Iroquois, 16, 47
Israel, establishment of, 161

J
Jackson, Andrew, 72, 106, 224
Jackson, Michael: controversy for, 211
Jamestown Massacre, 22, 23
Japanese Americans, relocation of,
    154
Jay, John, 42, 49
Jazz, 120, 121
Jefferson, Thomas, 42, 53, 59, 60
    banks and, 56, 240
    Declaration of Independence of, 67
    Lewis and Clark and, 69
    slavery and, 42
Jews, 32, 80, 110, 125, 161
    extermination of, 156
Jobs, Steve, 193
John XXIII, Pope: Castro and, 187
Johnson, Andrew, 101
Johnson, Lyndon, 184
Johnson, Samuel, 70
Jones-Shafroth Act (1917), 135
Journalism, entertainment and, 218

Joy Street (Keyes), 170
Julius Caesar, 101

K

Kennedy, John F., 106, 222
    assassination of, 191
    Bay of Pigs and, 187
Keyes, Frances Parkinson, 170
Khomeini, Ayatollah Ruhollah, 209
Khrushchev, Nikita, 187
Kilby, Jack: microchip and, 181
King, Martin Luther, Jr., 202
    assassination of, 191
Kinsey, Alfred, 172, 173
Kinsey Reports, 172, 173
Kissinger, Henry, 196
Klondike Gold Rush, 83
Koch, Ed, 219
Korean War, 165
Korematsu v. The United States (1944),
    154
Koresh, David, 221
Kropotkin, Peter, 139
Ku Klux Klan, 184
Kubrick, Stanley, 167

L

La Relación (Cabeza de Vaca), 18
Lacks, Henrietta, 188
Last of the Mohicans (movie), 23
Latin Americans, 135, 139, 156, 202, 237
Lazarus, Emma, 108
Leaves of Grass (Whitman), 88
Lee, Harper, 185
Lehman Brothers, 239
Letters from an American Farmer
    (Crèvecoeur), 51, 52

Leutze, Emanuel Gottlieb, 46
Levin, Meyer, 152
Lewinsky, Monica, 222
Lewis, Meriwether, 69
Lincoln, Abraham, 249
    assassination of, 101
    election of, 93, 95
    Emancipation Proclamation and, 97
    Gettysburg Address and, 99
    New York City riots and, 98
    slavery and, 3, 92
    as vampire slayer, 100
Lindbergh, Charles, 45
Lindbergh baby, kidnapping of, 145
Lindbergh Law, 145
Locke, John: classical republicanism and,
    6
Loman, Willy, 176
Look Younger, Live Longer (Hauser), 170
Louisiana Purchase, 68
LSD, 193

M

M*A*S*H, 165
MacArthur, Douglas, 158
Madison, Dolly: ice cream and, 61
Madison, James, 42, 60, 61
    Federalist and, 49
    Jefferson and, 56
Magón, Ricardo Flores, 139
Malcolm X, 194
Manifest Destiny, 73, 81
Mann, Thomas, 155
Mantle, Mickey, 120
Mao Zedong, 216
Marijuana, 192, 193
Mars landing, 246

Marshall, John: nomination of, 57
Marshall, Thurgood, 182, 206
Martí, José: independence and, 112
Martin, Trayvon: death of, 244
Marx, Groucho, 250, 251
Mattell Toy Company, 179
Mayflower, 13, 19
McCarthy, Joseph, 35, 168
McCarthyism, 35, 168, 241
McDaniel, Hattie, 149
McDonalds, 177, 180
McGovern, George, 200
Medicaid/Medicare, 194
Medicine, 105, 189, 245
Mediums, 102
Melville, Herman, 90
Mencken, H. L., 71, 145, 215
Mestizos, 139
Mexican-American War (1846–1848), 81
Mexican Farm Labor Program, 156
Mexican Revolution, 129, 130, 131
Mexicans, as guest workers, 156
Microchips, 181
Microsoft, founding of, 202
Middle class, 176, 240
Middle Passage, 27
Migration, internal, 128
Milam, J. W.: Till murder and, 183
Military, growth of, 132, 213
Milk, Harvey: assassination of, 203
Miller, Arthur, 35, 168, 176
Minorities, special treatment for, 205,
    206
Minter, Desire, 19
Miramontes, Luis E., 181
Mississippi River, 14, 94
Mitchell, Margaret, 149
Moby-Dick (Melville), 90, 94

Mohammad Reza Pahlavi, Shah, 209
Mohawks, 16, 17, 43
Money, 37, 55
    attitude toward, 9, 181
Monroe, Marilyn, 169
Moon landing, 197
Moore, Michael, 23
Morris, Desmond, 169
Movies, first, 124
Ms. Magazine, 195
Muhammad, Prophet, 209
Multiculturalism, 204, 206
Music, 120, 122, 123
Muslims, 241
MySpace, 233
Myths, 2, 3, 7, 195, 248
    origin, 19
    shared, 117, 118

N

NAACP, 182
Nader, Ralph, 180
Nagasaki, 159, 160
Naked Ape, The (Morris), 169
NASA, 186, 197, 246
Nation, concept of, 234
National anthem, 74
National Bank, 42, 72
National Educational Television (NET),
    198
National Farm Workers Association, 202
National unity, idea of, 117
National Women's Rights Convention,
    85
Native peoples, 13, 24
    depopulation of, 15
Nazi Party, 151, 154

Neutrality, 131, 153

Neville, John, 65

"New Colossus, The" (Lazarus), text of, 108

New Deal, 146

New England, development of, 33

New Netherland, 20, 26, 31

New Orleans, Katrina and, 235, 236

New York City, 26
poverty in, 109
riots in, 98
slavery in, 26

New York Fire Department, 125

News, cable, 218

Nineteenth Amendment, 86, 138

Nixon, Richard M.: resignation of, 200

Nonviolence, 38, 202

North Atlantic Treaty Organization (NATO), formation of, 164

Nuclear weapons, 159, 167, 187

Nuremberg Trials, 164

O

Obama, Barack, 106, 238, 242
birth certificate of, 241
election of, 237
health care and, 245

Obamacare, opposition to/support for, 245

Oil industry, Civil War and, 96

"On Being Brought from Africa to America" (Wheatley), text of, 30

1 Percent, anger toward, 239

Oneida, 16

Onondaga, 16

Organization of Afro-American Unity, 194

Organization of American States, formation of, 163

Organized crime, 137

P

Parker, Bonnie, 144

Parker, Dorothy, 168

Parker, Rosalind, 189

Party system, 60, 72

Past, 1, 250
present and, 2, 20

Pearl Harbor, 153

Pérez, Tony, 120

Pershing, John J.: Villa and, 131

Photography, 109, 162

Pieter, Pedro, 4

Pilgrims, arrival of, 19

Pizza, 230

Pledge of Allegiance, text of, 111

Poems on Various Subjects Religious and Moral (Wheatley), 30

Pogroms, 110

Politicians, 187, 239

Politics, 60, 72, 92, 106, 112
women and, 41, 51, 58, 85, 138

Population
during Great Depression, 143
pre-European, 15

Poverty, 66, 109, 139

Powell, Lewis F., Jr., 206

Power
abuse of, 227
pursuit of, 247

Powhatans, 22, 23

Present, past and, 2, 20

Progress, 4, 76, 85, 105
Prohibition, 136, 137, 138, 148
Property ownership, 9, 77
Psychoanalysis, 123
Public Broadcasting Service (PBS),
    creation of, 198
Pudeator, Ann: witchcraft and, 35
Pueblo Indians, revolt by, 32
Puerto Rican Nationalist Party,
    174
Puerto Ricans, 174
    as second-class citizens, 135
Puerto Rico
    as commonwealth, 135
    independence for, 114
Puritans, 13, 19, 35, 221

Q

Quixote, Don, 94

R

Race, talking about, 244
Racial loyalties, 128, 237
Racism, addressing, 185
Radicalism, 194
Ragtime, 122
Ragtime (Doctorow), 122
Railroads, 117
    progress and, 76
Reagan, Ronald, 27, 106, 211, 212
    Iranian hostage crisis and,
        210
    military and, 213
Reaganomics, ten commandments
    of, 212
Reconstruction, 103

Red Scare, 140
Refugees, asylum for, 155
Religion, 14, 19, 33, 106, 221
    American-made, 220
    disentangling from, 105
Republicans, 60
Resistance movements, 38, 202
Revolution, The (journal), 85
Riis, Jacob, 109
RMS Lusitania, sinking of, 131
Roberts, Barbara Millicent, 179
Roberts, John: Obamacare and,
    245
Robinson, Henry Morton, 170
Robinson, Jackie, 120
Roe v. Wade (1973), 201
Roosevelt, Franklin Delano
    Churchill and, 150
    inaugural addresses of, 146, 147
    New Deal and, 146
Roosevelt, Teddy: Rough Riders and, 113
Rosenberg, Ethel and Julius, 167
Roth, Henry, 110
Roth, Philip, 221
Rough Riders, 113
Rushdie, Salman: fatwa against, 209
Ruth, Babe, 120

S

Sacagawea, 69
Sacco, Nicola: trial of, 138
Saint Valentine's Day Massacre, 137
Salem witch trials, 35, 36
Salinger, J. D., 169
Saludos Amigos (movie), 156
San Francisco, growth of, 84
Santa Anna, Antonio López de, 78, 79

Santayana, George, 250
Satan, 209
Satanic Verses, The (Rushdie), 209
Schopenhauer, Arthur: history and, 248
Séance sessions, 102
Security, increase in, 228
Segregation, 149, 182, 194
Self, group and, 5
Self-determination, 37
Self-government, 92
Seneca, 16, 43
"Separate but Equal" doctrine, 149, 182
September 11 Memorial and Museum, 227
September 11th, 225, 226, 227, 229, 236
Seven Years' War, 36
Seward, William H., 101
Sexual Behavior in the Human Female
    (Kinsey), 172, 173
Sexual Behavior in the Human Male
    (Kinsey), 172, 173
Sexual practices, 64, 123, 171, 172, 173, 193
Sharpton, Al, 237
Shawnee, 47
Sherman, William Tecumseh, 61
Simpson, O. J., 218
Sinatra, Frank, 181
Singer, Isaac Bashevis, 127
Six Nations, 16
Skloot, Rebecca, 188
Slave Abolition Act (1833), 97
Slavery, 28, 29, 42, 54, 88
    abolishing, 27, 39, 67, 92, 94, 97, 101,
       103
    in New York City, 26
    opposition to, 95
    spread of, 68, 92
    support for, 72
    technology and, 230

Slaves, 34, 67, 94, 103
    arrival of, 27, 32
    freedom for, 3, 39, 97
    population of, 31, 54
Sleeping habits, changes in, 231
Smith, Bob: AA and, 148
Smith, John: Jamestown Massacre and,
    22
Social contract, 6
Social memory, 249
Social networking, 233
Social state, natural state and, 6
Soldiers, lives of, 158
Some Memoirs of the Life of Job . . .
    (Bluett), 29
Soviet Union, 161
    fall of, 217, 218
    tension with, 164, 165, 167, 187
Space race, Cold War and, 186
Spanish-American War, 112, 113, 114
Spanish Empire, Columbus and, 12
Spanish language, speaking, 126
Spirit of St. Louis (airplane), 145
Sports, 120, 246
Springsteen, Bruce, 46
"Star-Spangled Banner, The" (song),
    75
    text of, 74
Star Wars, 153
Statue of Liberty, 108, 112
Steinbeck, John, 142
Steinem, Gloria, 195, 196
Stone, Lucy, 85
Stonewall Inn, riots at, 198
Stowe, Harriet Beecher, 61, 67, 87
Strikes, 202
Stuyvestant, Peter, 26
Suburbs, moving to, 176

Suicide, death by, 143
Supreme Court, 57, 135

T

Tacos, 82, 249
Taxes, 37, 65, 66, 129, 242
Taylor, Elizabeth, 169
Tea Party, founding of, 242
Technology, 104, 105, 181, 233
   digital, 231
   nuclear, 188
   slavery to, 230
Telephone, invention of, 104
Television, popularization of, 180, 218
Terrorism, 225–228
Texas
   annexation of, 79, 80, 81
   independence of, 78, 79, 80
Theory of General Relativity, 249
Thirteenth Amendment, 97, 194
Thoreau, Henry David, 89
Three Caballeros, The (movie), 156
Thriller (Jackson), 211
Tiananmen Square protests, 217
Till, Emmett: death of, 183, 184
To Kill a Mockingbird (Lee), 185
Tobacco, early use of, 17
Tocqueville, Alexis de: writing of, 77
Toffler, Alvin, 192
Tolstoy, Leo, 175
Transcendentalism, 89
Treaty of Breda (1667), 31
Treaty of Guadalupe Hidalgo (1848),
   81
Treaty of Paris (1783), 47
Treaty of Versailles (1919), 134
Triangle Shirtwaist Factory, fire at, 125
Tripp, Linda, 222

Truman, Harry S.: racial discrimination
   and, 163
Tuscarora, 17
Twain, Mark, 94, 250
Twenty-first Amendment, 136
Twitter, 234

U

UFOs, 162
Uncle Tom's Cabin (Stowe), influence of,
   87
Unemployment, 143, 240
United Farm Workers, 202
Universal Health Care, Obama and, 245
Untouchables, The (movie), 144

V

Vanzetti, Bartolomeo: trial of, 138
Vasconcelos, José, 139
Vespucci, Amerigo, 13
Vietnam Memorial, 186
Vietnam War, 186
Vikings, arrival of, 13
Villa, Pancho, 129, 130, 131
Village green, described, 34
Violence, 38, 56, 187
   domestic, 171
   racially motivated, 184
Virgin Islands, purchase of, 134

W

Wall Street (movie), 215, 239
War of the Worlds, The (Wells), 146
Washington, Booker T.: speeches by, 15
Washington, D.C.: poverty in, 66

Washington, George, 42, 46, 65
   dollar bill and, 55
   slaves and, 54
   Wheatley and, 30
Washington, Martha, 54
Washington Mutual, 239
Washington Post, 200
Watergate, 200
Watson, James D.: DNA and, 189
Watson, Thomas A.: telephone and, 104
Weapons of mass destruction, 226, 227
Webster, Noah: dictionary and, 70
Welles, Orson, 146
Wheateley, John, 30
Wheatley, Phillis, 30
Whig Party, 60, 72
Whiskey tax, repeal of, 65
White, Byron, 206
White House tapes, 200
Whitman, Walt, 88, 91
Whitney, Eli: cotton gin and, 68
Whittier, John Greenleaf, 67
Wiesel, Elie, 164
Wilkins, Maurice, 189
Wilson, Bill: AA and, 148
Wilson, Woodrow: Puerto Ricans and, 135

Windows, 202
Wizard of Oz, The (movie), 249
Women
   antialcohol movement and, 138
   politics and, 41, 51, 58, 85, 138
Women's liberation movement, 195
Women's suffrage, 85, 138
Woodstock Festival, 198
World Trade Center, attack on, 226
World War I, 131, 133, 153
World War II, 150, 151, 153, 157, 158, 160, 165, 167, 216, 229
Wright Brothers, 116

X

Xenophobia, 155, 229

Y

Yiddish Policeman's Union, The (novel), 80

Z

Zapata, Emiliano, 130
Zimmerman, George, 244
Zuckerberg, Mark, 233